POVERTY AND RURAL
DEVELOPMENT

Other Titles Authored by Dr. K. Puttaswamaiah

POVERTY AND RURAL DEVELOPMENT

Planners, Peasants and Poverty

Editor
K. PUTTASWAMAIAH

Foreword by Michael Lipton

Practical
ACTION
PUBLISHING

INTERMEDIATE TECHNOLOGY
PUBLICATIONS
1990

Practical Action Publishing Ltd
25 Albert Street, Rugby, CV21 2SD, Warwickshire, UK
www.practicalactionpublishing.com

© Intermediate Technology Publications 1990

First published 1990\Digitised 2013

ISBN 10: 1 85339 058 5
ISBN 13: 9781853390586
ISBN Library Ebook: 9781780443003
Book DOI: http://dx.doi.org/10.3362/9781780443003

A catalogue record for this book is available from the British Library.

The authors, contributors and/or editors have asserted their rights under
the Copyright Designs and Patents Act 1988 to be identified as authors of
their respective contributions.

Since 1974, Practical Action Publishing has published and disseminated
books and information in support of international development work
throughout the world. Practical Action Publishing is a trading name
of Practical Action Publishing Ltd (Company Reg. No. 1159018), the
wholly owned publishing company of Practical Action. Practical Action
Publishing trades only in support of its parent charity objectives and any
profits are covenanted back to Practical Action (Charity Reg. No. 247257,
Group VAT Registration No. 880 9924 76).

Dedicated to the loving memory of my
beloved son **P. Nagendra**

Contents

Foreword

The Study Seminars of the Institute of Development Studies, at the semi-rural campus of Sussex University in England, typically bring together thirty or so administrators and scholars, mostly from developing countries, for six weeks to exchange knowledge and experience on a particular theme: structural adjustment, or land reform, or statistical policy. The role of the Seminar Director is to set a framework, a structure, into which the participants can set their experience for analysis—and to provide them with lectures and other means to impart new expertise or techniques. The goal is to improve both analysis and policy design. A Senior Director needs to have a clear idea of structure and content, but to be flexible and modest in face of participants who often have much more locally applied experience.

In our 106th Study Seminar, Dr. Puttaswamaiah was an outstanding participant—even more so than his earlier work had led us to hope. We at IDS are delighted at his efforts in preparing this symposium of papers, based on some of the contributions to the Seminar.

This seminar had a title and a subtitle. Was it about "planners, peasants and poverty", or about "rural-urban and farm-nonfarm relations in economic development"? My work leads me to believe that in most developing countries, most of the time, these are very nearly the same question. In other words, the evils of peasant poverty that planners seek to reduce—being due to low agricultural growth, and to bad intra-agricultural and rural-urban resource distribution—are primarily the result of decisions centred in, and made in the interests of, cities and urban groups. Such decisions tend to produce inefficient and inequitable outcomes *within* the rural sector—not just between rural and urban sectors.

For example, tractorisation, the steering of credit to large farms, and "extractive" pricing of farm inputs and outputs, all often have these sorts of causation. Where urban-based development depends on the flow of surpluses—marketed food; savings—from country to town, it is a natural urban reaction to put such resources as the rural sector does get at the disposal of larger farmers, who will use them to generate surpluses of that sort.

However, though I tried to bring the seminar back to this issue at times (for example, on the question of whether markets and/or States provide necessary proportions of imports and of investment to agriculture, if given quantitative targets are to be met), participants were free to consider other, purely rural, issues affecting "planners, peasants and poverty". In view of enormous range of experience and knowledge, participants were *not* constrained to set such issues into the context of rural-urban relations, if they deemed it inappropriate.

Some of the planning issues affecting "poverty and peasants" are in fact issues of describing and measuring. Where and who are those with little purchasing power? Where and why is food production potential low? Some of these issues are more credibly presented as intra-rural than as rural-urban. And in a few cases rural poverty would not be greatly affected by inputs of resources, whether limitations upon those inputs are due to urban bias or to an unpromising physical and institutional environment; it is sometimes more plausible to assign rural problems to international factors affecting trade, or to national project-cycles (especially for small countries and small projects respectively).

However, I believe that the central model stands. This is the model in which urban power is the major explanation of inefficient and inequitable distribution of resources (a) between town and country, and (b) between the rural rich (generating surpluses) and the rural poor.

The historical introduction to this seminar (not reprinted here) presented three very different policy experiences. However, Britain, China and Russia (introduced respectively by Drs. Mingay and Nove) all showed considerable agricultural development—institutional and technical—prior to the extraction of a surplus from agriculture. All fed the heifer before they milked the cow. In *Britain*, enclosures made available formerly common land for intensive farming (albeit with severe harm to some of the displaced workers); technical change took the form of rotations including turnips, marling ("mining" of manure), horse-ploughing, etc. Only later did savings or food marketings (or labour) move on a large scale from the rural areas. In *Russia*, emancipation of the serfs, together with new techniques on the black-earth soils, preceded two attempts to squeeze agriculture in order to fuel urban development—two attempts (under Vyshnegradaskii and Witte before the Revolution, and under Stalin after it) which did not succeed in extracting significant surpluses or in developing the urban economy on the basis of them, precisely because prior agricultural growth had been insufficient. In *China*, the pre-revolutionary gentry squeezed agriculture for their urban interests only via the price system, and did not significantly use the squeeze to support capital-intensive industrialisation; after the revolution, urban-rural income disparities were kept to about 2.5:1, but the post-1953 effective ban on migration from villages to towns constituted a very powerful means of maintaining low relative rural incomes.

One general historical point worth bearing in mind is this. In all the nine or ten now-developed countries for which we have reliable figures, the disparity in income-per-head between non-agricultural and agricultural activities was about 1.1-2.3 to 1. In almost all developing countries for which figures are available now, the disparity is 3 to 1 or more—in Africa closer to 5 or 6 to 1. Furthermore, there is little or no historical precedent for the situation prevailing today in typical developing countries, where 70% of people engaged in agriculture and allied activities, typically, are receiving about 20% of investible resources, although those investible resources are usually associated with significantly more output than in the rest of economy.

This collection concentrates on presenting papers by seminar participants. However, in unpublished lectures by IDS and outside contributors, a few key topics also emerged. First, rural disadvantage in health and education is *professionalized*, by preferences of providers (teachers and doctors), in a way that does not have any clearly applicable analogies in the field of rural investment allocations. One result appeared in an unpublished data set from one of our participants, Mrs. K. Dandekar; extremely low body size was linked to higher death-rates in rural, but not in urban, Maharashtra. Ashok Mitra's book *Indian Population: Aspects of Quality and Control*, makes clear that marked rural mortality-rate disadvantages exist at all ages, especially for women, throughout India.

Second, the physical-investment disadvantage of agriculture persists, despite widespread evidence on the relative returns to physical investment in agriculture and elsewhere (and indeed in small vis-à-vis large industry), and on the impact of agricultural failures on the non-farm sector. In India there has been some increase in the share of investment going to agriculture—the 70% of workers there are supported by 22-24% of investment, instead of 18-21% as was the case in the early 1960s. For most of the Third World, the share of investment in agriculture has not been increasing in the last twenty years—despite "Green Revolutions" that raise returns in agriculture, and oil price explosions that reduce returns in transport, infrastructure and industry. Formerly compensating donor allocations of aid have dwindled since their peak in the late 1970s; the World Bank/IDA group (source of over a third of all official foreign flows to Third World agriculture) provided 30 per cent of its total disbursements to that sector's projects in 1977-9 but only 17 per cent in 1986-8, corresponding to a 23 per cent *fall* in real dollar value from the peak.

Third, some modification of the agriculture-"industry", or even rural-urban, dichotomy may be needed. Construction, transport and infrastructural activity (in each case with "standards" set and maintained by an urban and indeed professional elite), rather than "industry", may constitute the set of economic activities which harmfully rival agriculture in competition for resources. The rural-urban debate in questions such as infrastructure tends to be sidelined; for example, people seeking to improve resource allocation in road construction concentrate substantially upon labour-intensive construction of rural roads, when 80-95% of the roads budget is being spent on large metalled interurban highways. The diversion to "rural roads", of people whose main concern is with poverty reduction, prevents them from getting to grips with resources that go to activities with gigantic scale, overstated or dubious returns, and poor equity outcomes.

Fourth, on the rural content of non-farm activity, several points were made: (a) The enemy of the really small-scale rural artisan activity is often not the large urban activity but the subsidised intermediate one, sometimes termed "small industry". (b) South-south transfer of technology might possibly be the key to the efficient development of the very small-scale rural sector, which had been largely neglected by big-scale research (even in the crop research institutes—see for example the labour-displacing "IRRI rice transplanter"). (c) Appropriate and economic micro-technology might in turn be the key to reducing the food deficit in much of Africa, e.g. animal-drawn, village-made row transplanters in Maharashtra are relevant in several semi-arid areas of East Africa, especially where millet is mixed with another seeded crop.

A fifth key topic was that there had not been as much urbanisation as many people believed. Certainly, permanent migration from village to city is insufficient to enable large proportions of poor people to redress the disadvantages of life in rural areas. Indeed, such migration as does happen may increase these disadvantages for those who do *not* migrate. In particular, the flows of remittances and technology from migrants to rural hinterland, which are much discussed, are counterbalanced and sometimes outweighed by flows in the reverse direction, especially when migrants are seeking urban jobs or receiving urban education. Since urbanisation tends to favour the better-off rural groups (partly because they have better information about opportunities, partly because they are better able to afford to wait while seeking *good* urban jobs), such migration—while it certainly benefits the migrants themselves and probably the economy of which they are a part—usually does not reduce rural poverty, intra-rural inequality, rural-urban inequality, or urban bias.

Sixth, land allocation and land use, in the geographer's or town and country planner's sense, emerged as a neglected and important dimension of rural-urban and farm-nonfarm relationships. In their different ways, Dr. Farmer's lectures and the presentation of Chinese experience by Dr. Brecher made this point.

Seventh, following on the point about South-south transfers, technical and research change—as embodied in land and capital and affecting factor efficiency—were seen as a key to the relative rates of growth of rural and urban incomes, partly along the lines presented in Dr. Mathur's paper. The way in which mechanisation of agriculture might enrich, not large or small farmers, but contractors or tractor-owners, was cited as an example. So was the fact that high-yielding varieties of cereals are inherently pro-poor (labour-using, producing cheap food, risk-reducing), yet *at first*—before the cost-price squeeze cuts into profits!—go mainly, alongside fertilizers and credit, to the better-off farmers who provide surplus food for the towns. It was suggested, in a talk by Martin Greeley of IDS, that innovation, and derived research, in rural energy and post-harvest technology were very far from pro poor, and were again orientated towards farmers providing the surplus, and towards urban and foreign suppliers of "sophisticated" but not always locally efficient bits of capital. Food processing and post-harvest sectors, indeed, were spotlit as an area where very substantial and effective propaganda, both private and public, had been misdirected towards the adoption of methods not economically tested under local conditions, and in fact not benefiting rural people.

Participants' papers pointed to five areas related to urban-rural relations, and affecting the impact of planners on peasants and poverty. They are: the adequacy of investment and resource allocation; pricing; the role of institutions, institutional stability, and institutional bias towards big surplus sub-sectors; types of state action; and the structure of research and innovation.

As indicated, investment and resource allocation appear as major disproportions, as between rural and urban sectors, when we compare them with the workforce and GNP shares in these sectors. This was shown for agriculture in Guinea, Nigeria, the Yemen (despite verbal "top priority"), and elsewhere by participants' papers. On tha other hand, high ratios of agricultural to total investment were identified in Fiji (by Mr. Naidu) and Malawi (by Dr. Sriramappa), and have cut the rural-urban disparities, possibly reversing them in Fiji. However, unsupported by other policies, investment reallocations alone lead to disappointing output growth in the rural sector; for example, Mr. Godding pointed out that in Rwanda the "small is beautiful" approach to projects has been shown to carry a risk of a very high ratio of "rip-off" to total investment! In general, partial (incomplete) redressals of urban bias can lead to odd results: for instance, on education in Kenya, Mrs. Mawiyoo suggested (see her paper below) that, if it is not seriously proposed to increase substantially the returns to educated persons in rural areas, it would be much better to scrap the idea of vocational training, which claims to train people for rural rewards that in fact do not exist. Similarly, for Nigeria, better rural education could well lead to more brain-drain unless other things are done to improve chances in the rural sector for people who have been educated, as Mr. Kiyawa's paper (reprinted here) showed.

Our discussion of price policy pointed to the polar opposites of Guinea (see the paper by Mr. Shotton) and Malawi, with Malawi's agricultural performance far better, yet with one lesson in common: that quite high inputs of investment and current resources to agriculture, in default of carefully thought-out price policies, do not produce incentives for efficient growth. In a system with a big state sector, as in Guinea or the Yemen (Mr. Saeed), correct price signals have to be set for parastatals, as otherwise there is not clear guidance about the proportion of inputs which any parastatal should allocate to one, rather than to another, possible activity. Discussion of Tanzania, Guinea, Nigeria, Uganda and Malawi indicated that where borders are open (and very few countries can control them) the State, by setting prices that are very far out of line with relative prices on world markets, tends to lose control of the "parallel economy" and thus of its own tax base, and even to lose political control. (Paradoxically, a greater degree of effective State control and action may therefore require more, rather than less, willingness to allow prices to return towards market levels.) However, the motion that price corrections—especially without corrections of the under allocations of *real* resources to rural people—can produce major increases in total farm output is very seldom correct. One particular problem was that of *pan-territorial price structures*, which were discussed in the context of both Tanzania (Dr. Ngasongwa) and Malawi; they induce further distortions, are not clearly equitable (the more distant farmers are not necessarily poorer), and even if equitable are a very inefficient means of helping the poor (Tanzania's recent well-thought-out reversal of the pan-territorial price policy was cited and discussed in this regard). *Monopoly procurement*, if at prices below those reflecting cost of production plus normal profits for many farmers, had been shown by a brief Indian experiment to carry enormous risks of perverse incentives, and did not seem to most of the participants to be sensible. It was stressed that such a conclusion did not imply an attack on "the State" (which is here to stay anyway, and will probably get bigger in most developing countries relatively as well as absolutely), but suggested that there are principles of efficient resource allocation that apply to the public sector and the private sector alike, and which are particularly important when the public sector is being enlarged.

Despite all this, we all had our reservations about the extreme forms of "getting the prices right" sometimes advocated for agricultural planning by some advisers—seldom at the "sharp end"—within some international organisations, and in 1980-86 (but less so since) too often hypostatized into conditions for international lending. First, we felt that better prices, while often necessary to redress the rural-urban balance and improve equity and efficiency within the rural sector, were seldom sufficient to do so; for instance the experience of Rwanda, with very little price squeeze but also rather little strategy for agricultural invest-ment, has poor prospects as land exhaustion approaches. Second, conflicts between producers and consumers, created by "better prices" under circumstances where major food subsidies were either too costly or largely urban in their influence (Bangladesh, Egypt, Thailand), were real.   Third, "higher producer prices" for export crops in price-inelastic demand were highly question-able for large producer countries in a particular crop—and for the Third World as a whole, if advice was given independently, however innocently, to large numbers of individual small pro-ducers who acting together provided price incentives to suppliers who then glutted the market. Mr. Mayaki's comments on cocoa in Nigeria were especially relevant here. And if several dozen countries with the role in world sugar production of, say, Fiji, were to undertake the very sensible policy set—looking at Fiji in isolation—that Mr. Naidu advocated there (see his paper below), the effects on world sugar prices, and thus on the South as a whole, could be damaging. Fourth, the apparently neat prescription of "higher, i.e. more realistic, prices of both inputs and outputs in the agricultural sector" had equity consequences that may be undesirable, as in the analysis presented by Mrs. Kabeer of Kumarpur village, Bangladesh, where just these changes in price policy have induced the smallest farmers to share-crop their land out to larger tenants and to become labourers (and hence more vulnerable). Finally (and we shall return to this) it was stressed that better price incentives—if there is neither a lot of land to expand agriculture into, nor available and economic research for farmers to adopt—are rather like "pushing on a piece of string".

On institutional policy, the distinction between what is appropriate in big countries and in small countries seems crucial, combined with the need to embody an institutional policy in a *stable* commitment. India, Bangladesh or Nigeria—all large—can perhaps gain from lots of distinct experiments in distinct areas; in small countries like Rwanda or Fiji, such an approach to the rural sector would constitute—perhaps has constituted—a lack of strategy. Participants heavily criticised self-contained experimental schemes with their own, usually foreign, funds and experts and with no proper liaison or integration with the machinery of agricultural and rural administration that must continue when they depart. Such projects easily degenerate into islands or showpieces, not replicable and often not even continuable. Just as universities sometimes freeze course-structures and examinations to allow time to see whether things work, perhaps some developing countries should consider freezing experiments in rural institutional change, to give what has been tried a chance to settle down and work?

Even if this is admitted, some fascinating examples of institutional innovation were presented. In each case we must ask if they involved a thrust to independence or dependence, by rural people, on (inevitably, the world being what it is, ultimately self-interested) urban involvement, extraction and control. First, it was interesting in this context to contrast the experiences of the Employment Guarantee Scheme in Maharashtra, originated in the city but certainly providing very substantial and at present wholly rural and localised jobs, and Proshika in Bangladesh, which certainly seems a splendid idea to allow rural poor people to control their own assets, but which appears to depend heavily upon urban initiatives and leaders; interesting accounts were given by Professor Dandekar and Dr. Wood respectively. Second, we heard from Dr. Bailur of the evolution in India of the Small Farmers' Development Association and the Marginal Farmers and Landless Labourers programme into the structurally distinct Rural Development Agency, and discussed possible organisational problems arising from conflicts between concentration on the poor and the old community development ethos—and also between local integration of services and departmental responsibilities (see Dr. Puttaswamaiah's paper in this collection). Third, following on Mr. Jayewardene's contribution, (Paper No. 6 reproduced below), we discussed the implications of interventions to favour the "tailenders" in irrigation schemes by issuing water first to their small turnout groups in Mahaweli, Sri Lanka. Fourth, for Malawi, Mr. Sriramappa (in his paper for this collection) examines the possibility of institutionalising the development of field-orientated research and extension. Fifth, Mr. Godding's paper (below) allows us to examine carefully the contributions of non-governmental organisations in Rwanda.

Towards the close of the seminar, two visitors from the FAO gave us, in effect, two sides of the coin—or two different coins?—in regard to the role of inputs and institutions. Certainly there are no bricks without straw, but also no bricks without organisation. Oddly, we still seem to have a model of inputs as being what produces outputs, and institutions as being what produces equity (or the reverse); but bad institutions harm both output and equity, and are particularly liable to do so if they are (a) unstable and constantly being changed, or (b) used by the urban rich either to deprive the rural sector of resources (this is nothing wicked, just a natural use of power) or to allocate rural resources towards those people who provide the surplus for the towns.

On institutional forms, we do have some evidence that for many activities, inside and outside farming, small, labour-intensive and efficient go together in many developing countries. However, in respect of Indonesia, Dr. Saragih presented interesting evidence that some forms of plantation processing did require large scale—and that it was possible to use this to support and help small farmers' profitably, without extraction of surplus.

Conversely, Dr. Speller indicated the regional distortions induced by migration to N Brazil—even with generous land entitlement—by South Brazilian farmers displaced by multinational "corporate farming", where neither old nor new lands were farmed in labour-intensive ways. Here as elsewhere, it is not a question of efficiency versus equity, but of the power structure that often militates against both. Since Dr. Speller wrote, serious environmental threats to stable production in the NW have also emerged from this sequence.

Should the State, then, have a high or a low profile, if the inefficiencies and inequities likely to be associated with the rural urban power balance are to be minimised? "Left" and "Right" appear to converge on an analysis in which the bureaucrats are cast as villains, creaming off the surplus. Yet we all came to the view—not only the bureaucrats among us!—that this was naive. Bashing the engineers, professionals, academics, middlemen, or bureaucrats are all pretty useless forms of scapegoating. All these animals are necessary (abolishing middlemen would be crazy even if feasible), and are here to stay (having power positions of their own). The very low policy profiles vis-à-vis the rural and agricultural sectors adopted by Rwanda and Nigeria do not appear to be any more conducive to rural development than biased interventionism by an urban State, such as characterises several other developing countries. This leads to the question: "How can an active State be induced to respond to the needs of the rural poor?" The easy answer of "participation" is too localised, too decentralised, while the major area of non-response and of bias is macro and central. One very hopeful possibility is that many of the organisations represented at this very seminar are, as it were, parts of government in which the career structure itself "rewards" activities designed to improve the well-being of the rural poor. Even if a State or government as a whole has an inevitable urban bias (being where it is, comprising whom it does), there will inevitably be many bits and pieces of the State machinery, centrally and locally, pulling in the other direction. States are not monoliths. Career structures such as that of the Indian Rural Development Agency can favour the rural poor. Even more important is the development of institutions of "civil society" through which the poor can review, expose, and engage with the powerful; a journal like Bombay's *Economic and Political Weekly*; a smallholders' association like Zimbabwe's, or a diverse and technically skilled agricultural economics division at a freely functioning university, is worth any number of "policy planning units" and other gimmicks in improving and democratizing rural planning.

Invention, innovation, and the diffusion of innovation—institutional as well as material—may hold the long-term key to the structure of development processes and gains as between urban and rural, agriculture and non-agriculture, rich and poor. The key problem is the "Singer effect": the tendency, at international level, for most research to be done into activities and products and processes, and for scales of production and levels of capital-intensity, that suit the great bulk of demand, of surplus, and of pressures. As a result of this, research brings down—for example—the average cost of using tractors much faster (due to innovation), than the average cost of using animal traction; this brushes off even onto developing countries. This works, too, *within* a national economy, as between rural and urban, agriculture and non-agriculture, etc., unless it is explicitly controlled (by whom?) or counteracted. Thus the growth of urban demand and of large-farmer power, will generate research that systematically increases the relative advantage of those who generate surplus from the rural sector for urban use. At present, the mechanics of intermediate-technology development and South-south transfer are seriously inadequate; there is much talk, but not all that much happening for particular technologies. For instance, how much has sub-Saharan Africa learned from ecologically comparable areas in Latin America, West India, and North Africa about such matters as low-lift irrigation and row-planter construction at village level? (Of course there are plenty of lessons the other way too.) The point is that the *existing* structures and imbalances of supply and demand create patterns of research which in turn reinforce those imbalances, and cause relative costs to move in perverse ways. The first three papers in this book examine some of the ways in which *international* impacts can strengthen or weaken such effects. I hope we did not go away too gloomy. South Asia has grown faster in the past thirty years than in the previous three hundred—possibly three thousand.

There has been real modernisation—and, more important, real improvement in life-indicators such as infant mortality, literacy, safety against famine. Even the worst period for Africa, 1970-86 saw continued growth of real output per head for several countries (though for few in agriculture, or in the group of seventeen least-developed countries). The trouble—in both Africa and Asia—is that the proportions in poverty in most countries remain as high in the late 1980s as in the early 1960s, and are especially high in rural areas. The developing countries that have seriously attacked urban bias, I contend, while politically a very mixed bag, form striking exceptions, and have generally got some benefits through to the poor.

Whether or not we agreed with this, we did learn from each other something about which lines of attack upon these problems are relatively promising, and which have, and have not, worked elsewhere under similar conditions. It is our hope that this book may convey some of these lessons more widely.

International Food Policy   MICHAEL LIPTON.
Research Institute, Washington D.C., U.S.A.
30th June 1989

Preface

Mass poverty in the developing and developed world is still baffling in spite of the efforts put in by the concerned nations. The World Bank itself, having realized that poverty should be mitigated through rural development programmes has pursued the rural development strategy in different nations for 15 years, based on experiences of the previous 25 years. In spite of these efforts the poverty and hunger of the masses in several nations— under-developed and developing—have not touched the fringe of the problem. Secondly, there has been a drift from the agricultural to non-agricultural activities and in India alone, it is estimated that 27.7 per cent of the urban population is living below the poverty line. India is now on the threshold of the Eight Five Year Plan and innovative schemes, in addition to modifying the existing schemes like IRDP, RLEGP and the like (Integrated Rural Development Programme and National Rural Employment Programme), the nations should come out of the employment riddle and try to correct urban-rural imbalance.

Keeping these factors in view, the Institute of Development Studies, under the direction of Prof. Michael Lipton, conducted a seminar under the title "planners, peasants and poverty" in which about 35 participants from different parts of the globe participated. Each participant had to present a paper in the seminar. Some papers were too short with only points and some spoke without writeups. Therefore, I could find 19 papers relating to 19 participants. The countries to which these participants relate are Brazil, Tanzania, Nigeria, Kenya, Rwanda, Republic of Guinea, Malawi, Fiji, Jakarta, Indonesia, Sri Lanka, Bangladesh and India. These papers are brought together in this volume duly updated and edited. At the outset, I am grateful to Prof.

Michael Lipton and the Institute of Development Studies for their kind permission for me to bring together the editable papers and have them published. I am more particularly grateful to Prof. Lipton for having encouraged me to do this work and for his kind foreword which he has written in the midst of his busy schedule. I am again grateful for his kind words used in the foreword.

As part of the seminar, an International Conference was organised and these papers are also included. I am grateful to Prof. Michael Lipton for his suggestion to include these papers and to the Institute of Development Studies for their kind permission to reproduce these three papers. These papers contain "on rural-urban relations in the development process. Michael Lipton, in a paper entitled 'Aid to agriculture and rural development', examines the changing scale of aid to agriculture, and the need for corresponding changes in the project cycle if such aid is to produce the expected rates of return. Jean-Pierre Godding, in 'Foreign aid as an obstacle to development: the case of Rwanda's rural development project', contributes a first-hand field report on the problems facing rural aid projects in Rwanda. Finally, Martin Godfrey, in 'International migration and rural-urban balance', outlines the scale, pattern and prospects of international migration, reviews the costs and benefits of exporting workers from the point of view of a low-income, labour-surplus economy and, in the light of a Sri Lankan survey, assesses the likely impact on rural-urban balance within such an economy."[1]

I fully acknowledge with gratitude the permission to reproduce these already published papers in DP 197 of IDS and, in particular, my thanks are due to Ann Segrave, Editorial Assistant, IDS. Further, Prof. Lipton in his lengthy foreword has given the summary of the seminar which had made my task easy as it avoided my summarising the papers in this 'Preface.' My grateful thanks to him in this regard.

Coming to the participants, I am glad that each one of them whose papers are included have shown interest. In particular,

1. Michael Lipton, Jean-Pierre Godding and Martin Godfray, '*International Perspectives on Rural Development—Discussion paper,*' IDS, Sussex, DP 197 Nov. 1984.

I shall be failing in my duty if I do not mention the names of Prof. Jean-Pierre Godding, Mr. Jayantha Jayewardene, Prof. Achmad Rofi'ie, Prof. Ashok Mathur, Dr. Juma Nagsongwa, Rajendra Naidu, and Mrs. Kokeya Rahman Rabeer. They have shown particular enthusiasm in bringing out this work and updating the material wherever necessary. Prof. Ashok Mathur's paper "Why Growth Rates Differ in India—An Alternative Approach'. was earlier published in the 'Journal of Development Studies'. I gratefully acknowledge the permission given by Frank Cass publishers, London to reproduce the above paper read by Prof. Mathur at the seminar. Mathur wishes to acknowledge his indebtedness to RCO, Matthews, Michael Lipton, Hans W. Singer and Suresh Tendulkar for their comments on the draft. Another debt which he wishes to acknowledge is Jeffrey G. Williamson as some of the ideas emerged following up his suggestion during a discussion. Further, the chapters on "participatory Action Research on Labour Co-operative Movement—A Field Action Report from Bundung" and "Participatory Action Research on the Informal Sector—A Field Action Report from Jakarta" are papers from Prof. Achmad Rofi'ie and have been published by the Institute of Development Studies, Lembaga Studi pembangunan. The suggestion from Rofi'ie to include these studies is welcomed with thanks. This was done with a view to enrich that area material contained in this work. Finally, I wish to express my gratitude to Prof. Michael Lipton for his immense help and support in finalising this work.

When it is estimated that 800 million people are in absolute poverty in the world, palliatives at least, if not remedies, are urgently needed. The rural-urban imbalance is continuing. At this juncture, it is hoped, that this work which contains the experiences of some of the under-developed and developing countries, will be of use in several countries of the world to planners, professors and students, Administration and the people interested at large.

K. PUTTASWAMAIAH

The Contributors

1 O.D. FAMURE, Professor, University of Maiduguri, Nigeria.
2 JOHN FARRINGTON, Professor, Department of Agricultural Economics and Management, University of Reading, United Kingdom.
3 JEAN-PIERRE GODDING, Senior, Community Development Officer, Rwanda.
4 MARTIN GODFREY, Professor, Institute of Development Studies, Sussex University, United Kingdom.
5 JAYANTHA JAYEWARDENE, Resident Project Manager, Mahaweli Authority of Sri Lanka, Galnewa, Sri Lanka.
6 KOKEYA RAHMAN RABEER, Social Organiser, Saptagram Women's Self-Reliance Movement, Bangladesh.
7 I.A. KIYAWA, Senior Lecturer, Department of Economics, Bayero University, Keno, Nigeria.
8 MICHAEL LIPTON is best known for his work on "urban bias" or the discrimination against rural poor in developing countries. He has also studied the interaction of credit, migration and health with rural efficiency and poverty.

Lipton has extensive field experience in Asian and African countries. He is currently president of the British South Asian Studies Association, a board member of the Development Economics Research Centre at Warwick University and is the director of the Food Consumption and Nutrition Policy Programme at IFPRI, Washington.

The author received his B.A., and M.A. degrees from the Oxford University and his doctorate from the Sussesx University. He has written on a wide variety of topics.
9 PROF. ASHOK MATHUR is Professor of Economics, Jawaharlal Nehru University, New Delhi.

10 J.N. MAWIYOO, Research Officer, Karen, Centre for Research and Training, Nairobi, Kenya.

11 J. MAYAKI, Assistant Director, Ministry of Agriculture and Natural Resources, Ilorin, Kwara State, Nigeria.

12 RAJENDRA NAIDU, Field Manager, Fiji Sugar Corporation Ltd., Suva-Fiji.

13 JUMA NAGSONGWA, Professor, School of Development Studies, Sokoine University of Agriculture, East Anglia.

14 K. PUTTASWAMAIAH has, following a brilliant academic career, worked in various capacities with the Government of Karnataka, in India. He has conducted several evaluation studies and formulated a number of projects to be aided by the World Bank and other international agencies.

The author has about fifteen-twenty books in English and in Kannada to his credit. He was awarded the University of Mysore First Prize for one of his Kannada books and he has also translated J.R. Hicks's—'Value and Capital' into Kannada. Being a Prolific writer, he has largely contributed to various periodicals of repute.

15 ACHMAD ROFI'IE, Director, Institute of Development Studies, Jakarta, Indonesia.

16 K.M SAEED, Planning Officer, Agricultural Planning Department, Ministry of Planning, Aden, Yemen.

17 ROGER SHOTTON Economic Adviser, Guinea Conakry, Brussels, Belgique.

18 PAULO SPELLER, Professor and Research Co-ordinator, Cidate University, Cuiaba, Brazil.

19 K.E. SRIRAMAPPA, Lecturer, Institute of Development Studies, University of Mysore, India.

CHAPTER 1

Aid to Agriculture and Rural Development

This paper has modest goals. It shows that, although increases in the share of aid which goes to agriculture and rural development (ARD) have taken place since the 1960s, such increases: (a) are smaller than official figures and categories imply; (b) are smaller for bilateral than for multilateral flows; (c) in total owe much to the shift of aid from bilateral towards multilateral flows; and (d) are under threat of reversal. This threat arises partly because recipient governments have sometimes stepped back from ARD where donors have stepped forward; partly because of the 'sector-project problem', discussed below; and partly because some recipients have allegedly not created the 'strategic environment'—of rural institutions, treatment, and other resource allocation to agriculture—necessary for the success of ARD aid projects.

STATISTICS ON SHARE OF ARD IN AID

Estimates of external resource flows to agriculture grossly overstate both the share of agriculture in such flows and the expansion of that share since 1960. There are three reasons for this.

First, FAO (and all others) 'reporting. . . is presently limited to "official flows" because sectoral data on private flows of external resources are not yet available'. It is agreed on all sides that much smaller and more slowly growing proportions of private net foreign investment—and, to the extent they are sectorally allocable, of bank loans and export credits—are for agricultural activities rather than for official flows.

Second, 'the data on official flows relate only to commitments' (FAO, 1981 : 21). The time lags between commitment and disbursement, and hence the erosion of the value of aid by delay and inflation, are greater for official flows to agriculture and rural development than to other sectors. Such time lags are also increased by learning processes when a sector is raising its share in official flows, as was ARD in 1965–80.

Third and most seriously, the OECD definitions of 'aid to agriculture' not only include too much, but do so by incorporating items that have expanded much more rapidly than aid which unambiguously benefits agricultural workers or farmers, and/or raises farm output. Already in 1968, 'assistance for agricultural development in less-developed countries . . . includes also assistance for direct processing, manufacture of agricultural inputs, forestry and fisheries, but excluding food aid' (OECD, 1968 : 11). Even broader is the current 'broad definition [which] includes . . . activities that are defined as "indirectly to sector" [viz.] forestry; manufacturing of inputs; agro-industries; rural infrastructure; rural development; regional development; and river development'—in addition to items in 'the narrow definition . . . "directly to sector" [viz.] appraisal, development and management of natural resources; research; supply of production inputs; fertilisers; agricultural services; training and extension; crop production; livestock development; fisheries' (FAO, 1981 : 21).

Why is this overinclusiveness so misleading? Above all, because aid to make fertilisers and pesticides is clearly aid to industry. It is to industry that the corresponding primary incomes accrue as wages and profits. Agricultural producers and output may incidentally gain from readier access to, or wider choice of, inputs —but have much more usually lost from artificial rises in farm input prices owing to domestic protection of the fledgling 'aided' industries against foreign competition. Similar arguments apply to aid for agro-industry that processes outputs, though here benefit to farming communities is rather likelier.

It is more defensible to include some components of 'rural development' programmes—primary rural health, education, transport, etc.—in aid likely to raise farm production and welfare. The problem, however, is that more and more borderline items get counted as aid to agriculture. This increases the *apparent* share of agriculture in aid, but of course does nothing for the true share. Thus, between 1968 and 1978, 'rural development and rural infrastructure, forestry, and regional and river projects' were added to the (already far too inclusive) broad definition of agriculture. In 1978, the narrow definition was confined to aid 'mainly relating to food production', but by 1981 production of fertilisers—formerly only in the broad definition—had been added to the narrow (OECD, 1968:11; FAO, 1978:1-49 to 1-50; 1981:20). Unfortunately, the borderline items absorbed ever-growing shares of total; crop and livestock production, for example, absorbed 50 per cent of multilateral commitments to 'broad' agriculture in 1973, but 36 per cent in 1980 (FAO, 1981:24).

In spite of these surely unnecessary data problems, some fairly clear conclusions emerge about aid and other official flows to agriculture and rural development. First, the share of these sectors in *bilateral* flows has risen only slightly since the 1960s. Second, their share in *multilateral* flows has increased substantially. Third, the rising role of multilateral in total official flows (both aid and non-concessional—and of Africa in multilateral commitments—has carried the share of agriculture in total sectorally allocable aid flows, bilateral plus multilateral, up somewhat. Fourth, this share nevertheless remains rather less than the share of similar sectors in the (sectorally allocable) domestically financed investment budgets—though more than in allocable domestic current budgets. (And the proportion of technical assistance person-years devoted to agriculture, etc., by aid agencies probably outweighs comparable proportions of LDC skilled public sector personnel by at least 3 to 1, and perhaps even 5 to 1.) Fifth, there are some signs that the modest uptrend in ARD's share of aid is being reversed. Sixth and most alarmingly, even the modest temporary rise in the share of official foreign finance going to support investment in Third World agriculture appears to be offset by a fall in the proportion of *domestic* finance for such investment. As these six quantitative results show, the uptrend in 'aid to agriculture'—apart from being imperilled by the threat to aid itself, which in 1981 fell in real terms for the first time for 10 years—is thus modest, temporary, and fungible. The critical need for country-specific strategies, especially as the focus shifts to Africa where the performance of both aid and agriculture in the 1970s has been relatively bad, is clear.

In 1965, some 12.6 per cent of all bilateral aid commitments went to agriculture 'broadly defined'—slightly above the 12 per cent average for 1962-67 (OECD, 1968 : 11-12). By 1976 it was 14.2 per cent of the 'total allocable by sector', and by 1980 and 1981 respectively 16.2 per cent and 17.0 per cent. This looks like a steady rise, but is it? In 1965, the proportion of 12.6 per cent appears to relate to all bilateral aid; in 1976, the 14.2 per cent relates to 'aid allocable by sector', which is only 54.6 per cent of bilateral aid, so that only 7.8 per cent of all such aid went to the agricultural sector; similarly in 1980-1981, but with about 70 per cent of bilateral aid sectorally allocable. Thus 11.5 per cent of total bilateral aid (sectorally allocable or not) went to agriculture in 1980, and 12.0 per cent in 1981, the same as in 1962-67 (OECD, 1978 : 224-5, 1982 : 230-1).

In absolute terms and at 1975 prices, official bilateral (including EEC) OECD/DAC commitments to support agriculture 'broadly' defined rose from $ 2.1 bn in 1974 to $ 3.1 bn in 1979, but fell to $ 2.8 bn in 1980. Over 95 per cent of these commitments were on aid terms. Supporting bilateral flows to agriculture (in 1975 prices) 'narrowly' defined rose far more slowly, from $ 1.69 bn in 1974 to $ 2.17 bn in 1979 and $ 1.96 bn in 1980—almost all aid (FAO, 1981 : 20, 23). The World Bank (1982: 51) records a big once-for-all rise in bilateral *aid* to agriculture ('broadly' defined) in 1979 prices from $ 1.6 bn in 1973 to $ 2.8 bn in 1974, a level maintained with fluctuations until 1977, when a further rise to about $ 3.4 bn occurred and was maintained with fluctuations until 1980. The latest OECD data suggest subsequent falls. In any case, it is clear that (a) both the narrow and (especially) the broad definition are too broad, and increasingly so; (b) that 'narrow' bilateral flows to agriculture have expanded far more slowly than 'broad' ones. The increasing tendency in the latter 1970s to incorporate many non-agricultural rural activities in general 'rural development' programmes—whatever its pros and cons—certainly tended to puff up the proportions of aid assigned to agriculture under the 'broad' definition, even if the change in the real structure of aid programmes was not nearly so large as it seemed.

This definitional inflation also affected aid to ARD from multilateral agencies (MAs)—most of which came through IDA, the concessional arm of the World Bank—but does not suffice to explain the big rise in MAs' aid to ARD even on the 'narrow' definition. In 1974, MAs supplied $ 721 mn of such aid; by 1980 it was $ 1,545 mn (all data in 1975 prices). If we add so-called non-concessional MA flows to ARD—mostly from the World Bank's IBRD counter, and still much cheaper than commercial borrowing—'narrow' ARD received $ 1,675 mn from MAs in 1974 and $ 2,892 mn in 1980: slower growth than for concessional MA flows alone, but still much faster than for bilateral aid to 'narrow' ARD. MA flows to 'broad' ARD grew faster still (though the disparity was less than for bilateral aid): from $ 2,228 mn in 1974 to $ 4,096 mn in 1980 (FAO, 1981 : 20, 23; 1974 : 1-49, 1-50).

The role of the MAs in agricultural support is much larger than it was, say, 10 years ago. This, however is concealed by (a) the use of 'broad' definitions that include some industrial and social-sector financing in flows to ARD plus (b) the convention that only the cheaper forms of money from the World Bank and the regional banks count as 'concessional' (aid) flows under OECD definitions, although there is a large concessional element even in their loans under standard terms. Hence the illusion that the multilateral share in non-OPEC *ODA* to *broad* agriculture at constant prices showed no clear trend—a freak 48 per cent in 1973, oscillating around 40 per cent since; 36 per cent in 1979; and 43 per cent in 1980 (World Bank, 1982 : 51). However, the MAs' share in (a) ODA to 'narrow' agriculture (now over 40 per cent), (b) all flows to 'broad' agriculture (up fairly steadily from 47 per cent in 1974 to 59 per cent in 1980) and (c) all flows to 'narrow' agriculture (about 50 per cent in the mid-1970s, about 60 per cent now) gives a clear picture of the growing importance of MAs to agricultural development finance (FAO, 1981 : 21, 23; 1978 : 1-49,   1-50).

Figures since 1980 are incomplete, but there is reason to suspect that the share of ARD is falling. The pressures, during recession, to tie aid to donor exports have led some, perhaps most, bilateral donors to reduce their stress on agriculture proper. Some have also weakened in their support of rural 'basic needs'—which require mainly local costs—or have directed it towards donor nationals' salaries, via technical cooperation and other commitments in the 'broad' rural sector. (Incidentally, 'rural development' in World Bank parlance refers to spending directed mainly at the poor; most of it is 'narrow' agriculture). Such pressures against agricultural aid are rather less important for MAs, but most donors, bilateral and multilateral alike, have felt their ARD programmes pressed down: by disillusionment with big, multi-ministry, coordinated rural development programmes; by blurring of the poverty-focus; and by downward pressures on *total* aid. In constant prices, this fell in 1981—for the first time for over a decade—and probably also in 1983.

By 1980, however, 'the share of ARD in the lending of the [MAs had risen] to nearly 30 per cent—or in the OECD's 'broad' sense to 37 per cent, from 26 per cent in 1973 (FAO, 1981 : 174; World Bank, 1982 : 51). But its share in *allocable* bilateral ODA from OECD was only 16 per cent, and in all bilateral ODA 11.6 per cent (OECD, 1982 : 231; FAO, 1981 : 174); OPEC flows of aid, and both OPEC and OECD official non-aid flows, were even less concentrated on agriculture. Altogether, in 1980, developing countries received about $ 38 bn in aid—$ 19 bn OECD bilateral, $ 9 bn OPEC bilateral and $ 8 bn multilateral— plus $ 5 bn from multilateral agencies and $ 2 bn of other official OECD capital (OECD, 1982 : 179). FAO concludes that in 1980 some 19 per cent of all net official aid inflows reached 'broad' agriculture; about 13 per cent went directly into 'narrow-definition' agriculture (FAO, 1981 : 174, 176). About 18-20 per cent of Third World investment appears to reach 'narrow' agriculture—a proportion generally agreed to be inadequate (albeit perhaps for compelling politica reasons). The contribution of official inflows, especially bilateral ones, to agricultural development is thus proportionately less—despite recent increases—than the contribution of LDCs themselves.

The latter contribution, as measured by the share of agriculture in total investment, has been falling for most LDCs with available data (FAO, 1978 : 1-54; UN, 1980). For several such LDCs, the expected (albeit inadequate) role of ARD in aid must have made a major impact. 'In the poorer African countries, aid accounts for 20 per cent of public investment in agriculture' (World Bank, 1982 : 52)—although this should be offset against the fact that net aid accounted in 1979 for 54 per cent of *total* gross investment, public and private, in all low-income countries of sub-Saharan Africa (OECD, 1981). If such public investment has stagnated or worse, while real aid to agriculture has expanded, the governmental willingness to allocate domestic savings to public investment in support of agriculture must, by definition, have declined. If so, aid expansion to agriculture must have proved *fungible* for governments, being used to permit domestic government outlay to be redirected away from ARD to other uses, good or bad.

For individual donors, the proportion of bilateral aid to agriculture shows huge fluctuation from year to year (UK, 1977, 15.4 per cent; 1980, 5.8 per cent—not a 'trend'). A few (predictable) smaller donors—Austria, Canada, Denmark, Netherlands, Sweden—regularly allocate 25 per cent or so of aid to ARD (FAO, 1981: 177).

However as suggested above, the uptrend in aid to agriculture, from all donors together, was clear, but is probably being reversed. Fashionable multi-sector projects have proved very hard to manage; software is very hard to tie to inefficient donor exports (yet it looms largest in rural activities); perhaps above all, the low cost loan sections of MDBs are ever harder to replenish. The major thrust of 'aid to Africa' appears to some to require, in agriculture, massive research and technical assistance, rather than capital aid. World Bank budgetary projections to the mid-1980s show a quite substantial decline in the share of ARD. Moreover, one cannot assume that, just because the proportions of domestic public (or total) investment in agriculture fell as aid to the sector rose, they will rise again if it falls.

Rather little is known about the composition of aid to ARD

a) Crop and livestock production accounted for 12½ per cent of official commitments to 'broad definition' agriculture in 1973-76, but only 9½ per cent in 1979-80. Research has remained steady, after a steep rise, at 3-4 per cent since 1977. 'Land and water development, including major irrigation-power projects like Mahaweli, averaged 20 per cent in 1973-6 but 24 per cent in 1977-80 (FAO, 1981 : 176)

b) In 1980, Asia and the Pacific received 46 per cent of total official commitments to 'broad-definition agriculture; Africa 22 per cent; Latin America, 25 per cent; and the Near East 7 per cent (FAO, 1981 : 25). Asia (excluding China and the Middle East) plus Oceania contained about 1380 mn persons, and Africa (excluding North Africa and RSA) about 320 mn. The bias of aid away from the 'big poor' South Asian countries is thus less serious for agriculture than for aid as a whole.

AID TO AGRICULTURE AND PUBLIC INVESTMENT IN THE RURAL SECTOR

The apparent fungibility of aid to agriculture is hard to understand. The two relevant 'great events' have been (a) a sixfold rise since 1972 (even after the downturn, *in dollar terms*, of 1982-4) in the real price of fossil energy, and (b) the demonstration since 1965 that, in large tropical areas, dramatic yield increases in cheap calorie sources can be labour-intensively achieved. These events should have stimulated even urban-biased governments to raise the salience of agriculture. High-yielding cereals raise the productivity of physical and human investment in agriculture—on any plausible assumption about prices, at least for non-exporters of cereals far away from the N. American surplus wheatlands. Dearer energy lowers the cost production of tropical agriculture: (a) relative to most other tropical production lines, (b) relative to temperate agriculture, and (c) *more* relative to costs of production in non-agriculture, than is 'the case for temperate developed countries where agriculture is often as energy-intensive, per unit of value added, as most non-agricultural components of GNP. Normally these three effects work almost as powerfully upon marginal costs as upon average costs.

One explanation of why more farm aid has nevertheless meant less, not more, proportionate farm investment out of LDC savings might be that industrialisation has been successful and attractive. This could be true of some Latin American countries, whose agricultural share in workforce and GDP is already low enough to indicate an industrialising path. Another explanation would be that the very success of agriculture in meeting domestic needs via higher cereal yields—plus the difficulty of expanding exports— has indicated a slower pace of farm investment. This could be true in some Asian countries, notably Thailand. Others, notably

Pakistan and India, are (nearly) 'self-sufficient' potential exporters, worried about glutting the world cereal market but only because their many hungry people are seldom getting the extra income needed to buy the extra food output. Such countries' prospects of improving nutrition through more food production—not for export, but for self-consumption on deficit farms— remain good.

Moreover, the central 'mystery area' is Sub-Saharan Africa (SSA). Aid to agriculture normally finances well below 10 per cent of Asian LDCs' farm investment; moreover, several Asian governments *have* responded to more aid-to-agriculture, in an environment of costly energy and of HYVs, by slightly raising domestic shares of savings going to that sector. Latin America has not received a great upsurge of farm aid. In SSA, aid now finances a large proportion of agricultural investment; yet *domestic* investment in agriculture has (in most cases) started low and seemingly declined, and food aid and agricultural output and availability per person, despite the prospects to apply HYV-based research (and despite rising energy costs of diverting resources to industry and infrastructure), have in most countries actually fallen. The key to the mystery may lie in the so-called 'sector-project problem'.

Nature of the Sector-Project Problem

This problem is defined by the curious coexistence of two facts. First, even before the two 'new events'—HYVs and energy crises —'narrow' agriculture showed substantially higher returns to capital, average and marginal, that the rest of the economy (as a whole) or its other major sectors. Such relationships must have been sharpened by those two events. And they must also apply to human capital and to 'broader' rural development. Typical urban doctor/patient ratios are three to eight times rural ratios, despite much higher rural incidence of preventable disease; this strongly suggests a much higher rate of return to doctors in rural than in urban areas. Similar indicators exist for education and other subsectors (Lipton, 1977, 1984).

One would, then, expect dramatic improvement in returns to aid, resulting from the shift towards ARD in the 1970s. Yet— while measurements are incomplete and often flawed—the economic rate of return to aid-financed investments in ARD has since 1970 been neither better nor worse than in other economic sectors. Aid invested in supporting agricultural research (Evenson and Kislev, 1976; Pinstrup-Andersen, 1982), and in providing seed capital for institutions to expand rural credit (World Bank, 1981), *has* achieved returns well above those from average aid. Other sub-sectors, particularly livestock development, have done substantially worse than that average (World Bank, 1981). In irrigation, 40 World Bank projects showed generally good returns, with an average and a spread probably close to those for non-farm projects (Notes in Carruthers, 1982). USAID's summary evaluations of aid to rural electrification and rural roads (USAID, 1981, 1982) also provide no evidence of substantial economic gains—or losses—from 'ARD-ward' aid shifting.

How can this apparent sector-project problem—'pre-shift' evidence that a shift of aid to ARD sectors should raise returns to aid and 'post-shift' evidence of little change from completed projects—be understood and tackled in ways that promise better economic returns to ARD aid in the future? Unless this is done, aid to ARD is under serious threat from: (a) changing fashions, (b) the thrust towards aid tying, (c) the persistent—though quite probably wrong (World Bank, 1983: 5, n. 1)—perception that the costs to aid agencies of administration and management are greater for rural, especially poverty-focused, projects than for non-rural ones, and (d) occasional crashing groundnuts-scheme-like failures. These, it will be argued below, are implicit in the future of most aid agencies to adapt their methods and styles of project management to the increasingly rural locus of their operations. It is the old story. Throwing money at rural poverty is necessary to conquer it, but not sufficient. Reductions in *allocative* urban bias in assigning funds—whether aid or domestic—to projects cannot achieve their aims, unless accompanied by reductions in *dispositional* urban bias: in the tendency to design and manage the project cycle for big rural outlays as if they were similar, in their requirements for access, to a steel-mill, metalled road, or power station with similar cost.

Before we can reasonably blame the sector-project problem on the aid agencies' mistaken transference of urban project techniques to rural projects, we should examine other possible explanations. Have ARD projects perhaps selected especially recalcitrant places, regions, or target groups? Even where they have, they have done no worse than conventional projects; in the World Bank. 'poverty-oriented' agricultural projects (termed by them 'rural development') have shown, if anything, slightly higher rates of return than other agricultural projects (World Bank, 1983: 7, n. 1). It is true that ARD aid (and other aid—Papanek, 1972, 1973— and indeed domestically-financed investment) appears to have done much less for growth in SSA than in Asia; but we saw above that ARD aid was *less* concentrated on Africa than other aid.

Is it, then, that unexpectedly bad price movements—perhaps in part arising out of the very successes of agricultural research in the 1960s—have damaged returns to ARD projects in ways that could not reasonably have been foreseen? Certainly the Bank's Operations. Evaluation Division's 'Project Performance Audits' regularly point to such price movements as grossly altering ARD project returns from the best estimates at appraisal. But (a) such movements are as often up as down; (b) in particular, hydroelectric irrigation-and-power projects have often been saved from disastrously 'underperforming' rates of return (vis-a-vis appraisal) by rising energy prices; and (c) ARD investment can often be partly saved, from the impact of falling prices of a particular output, by two techniques not so easily open to steel mills or power-plants: altering the crop-mix or self-consumption instead of sale.

Thus neither 'place' nor 'price' explains the failure of ARD aid to realise, so far, returns much better than other aid. Of course, agency and recipient policies for both place and price are capable of improvement. As regards 'place', a growing regional thrust of ARD aid into Africa urgently requires: (a) 'learning from Asia', above all through providing in African ARD aid recipients, as did the South and S.E. Asian countries that accelerated yield growth after 1960-65, local institutions for adaptive agro-economic crop research; yet (b) 'differentiating from Asia', above all through recognition—made tangible in project structures—that most African agricultures require several years of acquiring and testing local knowledge, and the cadres to implement and administer it, before major capital spending on the lines of, say Muda or Mahaweli is likely to succeed. As regards 'price', even the very best and

most competent international aid agencies has failed to coordinate
the effects of (a) its projects in different countries (as with World
Bank support for Brazilian cocoa expansion in the 1970s, though
poorer African producers lost much more revenue than Brazil
gained), and (b) its project and policy advice. Even now the Bank,
having recognised that it should not as a rule lend for cocoa and
coffee production lest it glut the markets, is advising producer
countries *separately* to raise growers' price-incentive, though if
all accept that advice all may lose, as the very price-responsiveness
of *each* country's farmers gluts the markets for *all*. Much, too,
could be done, via location-specific policies even at given prices,
to improve returns to ARD aid—but that applies to all sectors,
as does the requirement for supportive changes in government
policies and institutions if project returns, aided or domestic, are
to improve.

Project Evaluation—How It Should and Should Not Be Done

There is currently a burgeoning of new, more or less agricul-
ture-based, strategies for nationally led but donor-backed 'strategies' for African countries. Some implications of these strategies
are discussed elsewhere (Lipton, 1983). Here the question to be
asked is what needs to be done if donors' project cycles are to be
appropriately adopted to handle a further upsurge of ARD projects. The cycle comprises project identification, design, appraisal,
implementation, and monitoring and evaluation (Baum, 1978)
and the process commonly takes three to ten years, depending on
project size, novelty and complexity. Let us examine the final and
weakest link in the chain—monitoring and evaluation. Getting it
right will teach us how to strengthen the elements of the cycle.
Lessons for ARD go far beyond aid and embrace most domestic
ARD projects. There happen to be, ready to hand, almost ideal
examples, both involving highly competent persons from the same
university (Reading), of 'how to' and 'how not to' evaluate comparable aid (tractors) from the same donor (UK)—respectively to
Sri Lanka (Farrington and Abeyratne, 1982) and to India (Dalton,
1976). The central lesson is the need for, and difficulty of, prolonged on-the-spot fieldwork, with local and appropriate collaboration
but without biased interlocutors, if a rural project cycle is to be
well handled despite its inevitable urban origins. Farrington and

Abeyratne had the good fortune to be allocated sufficient resources to meet that need; Dalton did not. That lesson applies far beyond tractors, UK projects aid, South Asia, or indeed the evaluation component of project cycles.

Before looking at these two evaluations and drawing conclusions specific to ARD aid, we shall review the role of evaluation in donor project cycles. USAID and the World Bank are the only major donors, as far as I know, who build *genuinely independent* evaluation of *many or most* projects as *funded components* into the project cycle—though UK aid is moving in that direction. All three italicised components are important. In-house evaluation, as practised by most bilateral donors, cannot often escape the pressures to conform and to speak agreeably. (The Operations Evaluation Division of the World Bank is not 'in-house' except technically; the Chief of Division is a Vice President of the Bank, reports directly to the Board and the President, and cannot be fired by him, nor may he later accept any other post with the Bank Group). If only a few projects are evaluated—typically in a blaze of publicity after disaster has struck—lessons are unlikely to be learned and transferred efficiently. Unless adequate funds are made available—one to three per cent of project costs is not unreasonable—professionally adequate execution of evaluations, together with retrieval and use in later projects, is very unlikely.

This is not, of course, all there is to ARD aid project evaluation. Baseline surveys and control groups are needed. For best results, the evaluations should have close though independent contact with project management, and should stay in post long enough to see the project at work, not just to certify completion of works and re-estimate *expected* rates of return. *Residence in the project area, and intensive prolonged contact with poor and rich persons in it, is vital.* Expertise in economics—often, for big ARD projects, in macro-economics also—and in relevant physical disciplines (e.g., agronomy, medicine, engineering) should be represented on the evaluation team.

Last and perhaps most important, that team should increasingly consist, not of visitors from the aid agency—certainly not of flying accountants or auditors from European capitals, honest and serious but unskilled in developmental issues—but, increasingly, of experts from the developing country where the project is located. There are three reasons for this. First evaluation continuing after the project is completed, if persistently confined to representatives or even consultants of the aid agency, risks conflict with—and secretiveness from—departments of national governments, and may be seen as threatening national self reliance: not a good way to build working relations with a (possibly anyway reluctant) project management team, or to persuade it to accept advice based on evaluation surveys. Second evaluation by independent local experts, with plenty of relevant field experience, should eventually prove cheaper and more reliable than agency evaluations. Above all, the need for rural project evaluation is not confined to the part of ARD project money that is aid-financed. Few ARD outlays have higher long-run returns than those spent in building up institutions, reasonably independent of Ministries but trusted by them, able to undertake multidisciplinary evaluation of ARD projects, whether aided, tax financed, or even private.

A number of LDCs already have institutions capable of evaluating in this way, which are so used: Ahmadu Bello University in Northern Nigeria, the Agrarian Research and Training Institute in Sri Lanka and the teams evaluating PIDER in Mexico come to mind, among others. In some LDCs, a long institution-building period is required to develop such institutions. But most donors, for all their fine words, do not help much. (The International Fund for Agricultural Development, IFAD, has an outstanding document on evaluation, and good intentions, but a Charter that prevents it from employing sufficient field staff to realise them.) A steel mill or an urban motorway, can perhaps be evaluated by 'visiting firemen'; to discover whether tractors are benefiting the poor, or whether they obtain adequate return only thanks to hidden subsidies to local 'big men,' requires prolonged study of the affected area, and residence in it. To achieve their potential results—to escape the sector-project problem—rural projects require methods of management appropriate to rural needs. That lesson does not stop with evaluation, but until we get evaluation right we shall deceive ourselves about much else too.

Case of Tractorisation

In 1975, Dr. Dalton evaluated the aid-financed export of 3,850 British made tractors to India in 1971-74. His method was a small survey in August and September 1975 in which 177 of these tractors were located in the field and their owners interviewed. The states covered included the Punjab, Haryana and Western Uttar Pradesh, Maharashtra, Andhra Pradesh and Karnataka. . . The (tractor) distributors provided transport, interpreters and introduction to local dealers. This meant a good deal of suspicion on the part of the farmers was overcome, especially if the local dealer or one of his employees accompanied us on our visit to the farmers. The local dealers were also helpful in that they knew. . . the history of the tractors. . . The choice of which tractors to go and see was severely restricted by the proximity of the farms. A random element, however, also came into the choice in so far as quite a few tractors were either met on the road or were seen from it. . . A formal questionnaire. . . only acted as a check list [and] was not produced at the interview but brief notes were made to be written up afterwards. . . The disadvantage. . . is that it is not possible to carry out any statistical investigation of the results (Dalton, 1976: vii, 6-7).

No blame attaches to the author, who imaginatively sought to achieve his aims, e.g., to make some assessment of the social costs and benefits (using shadow prices) of these machines, including their effects on employment and food production (p. vii). What is unfortunate is the choice of such a low level of funding that the investigator was compelled to rely upon: (a) the casual empiricism of rapid trips to accessible places, and (b) interlocutors inevitably biased towards presenting a favourable picture of the impact of tractors.

A maximally favourable picture, indeed, is what emerges. Careful studies (Binswanger, 1978; Agarwal, 1980, 1984) establish beyond doubt that tractorisation in South Asia has in most cases greatly reduced workplaces; has not significantly raised output when other variables (such as the farmer's capacity to afford fertilisers) are held constant; and—except in the Punjab and Haryana—has not compensated for its unquestionably damaging effects on poor people by achieving acceptable social rates of return, but has proved privately profitable only thanks to hidden subsidies upon foreign exchange, fuel or credit. Dalton's unavoidable concentration on accessible farms and roadside tractors, and his time-limit which forced him to rely on facts and views presented by the tractor industry, seems to have come between his astute observations—which were not very different from the Binswanger or Agarwal studies—and his conclusions, which are an astoundingly complete justification of a policy that sent '3,850 tractors of five different makes' (p. vii) as aid to a country with massive rural unemployment and poverty, yet hardly any spare land that was economically arable. Indeed the tractors are claimed in this evaluation to be fully justified not only in the Punjab and Haryana—whose biggish, flat wheatfields create at least the ecological pre-conditions for tractorisation—but elsewhere, even in the tiny flooded rice paddies of Eastern Andhra Pradesh (p. 6).

Although relying on (accessible) farmers' reports, Dalton shares the caution of systematic studies showing that the switch from oxen to tractors generally does not affect yields (pp. 46-51, 75-6), but appears to believe that the benefits of 'timeliness' produce practical yield gains nevertheless. If that were so, one would expect 'timely' ploughing to produce major gains in cropping intensity. Yet Dalton's informants suggest that this depends more on 'supply of water and other inputs. . . than [on] the availability of power' (p. 52). Dalton adds evidence from several studies showing only small differences—some in each direction—in cropping intensity between tractor farms and ox farms (pp. 52-3). The claim of social benefit from tractors then rests mainly on (i) extra land cultivated, (ii) saved costs of oxen (and perhaps of pasture or fodder land that could be turned into crop land), and (iii) redeployment of labour. On (i), Dalton estimates that 'each tractor has reclaimed an average of five acres of land in the Punjab, Haryana, Western Uttar Pradesh (p. 55)—a claim that seems unsupported by these farmers' reports and in conflict with other evidence—but claims no land expansion elsewhere. On (ii) a social case perhaps can be made in those parts of the Punjab and Haryana where some fodder crops were previously grown, but hardly in Maharashtra where 'most bullocks are fed on [crop, residues] and graze on waste ground and common land' (p. 78)—typical conditions for most of India. On (iii) Dalton renders the case very implausible by making repeated claims that tractorisation of itself does not reduce employment per acre. There is now massive evidence against this (though it is unlikely to be obtained in unstructured discussions with tractor agents and big-farm employers). Unfortunately, however, unemployment rather than redeployment is the likely result—especially if tractors tend to raise average farm size via evictions (as confirmed by Dalton's respondents on p. 55, and by much other evidence), because bigger farmers are characterised by lower labour/land ratios.

Again it must be said that neither Dalton's results nor his methods can be criticised, *given the constraints placed on his evaluation.* He had to evaluate farms using British aid tractors, in isolation from the general tractorisation issue, in two months. These tractors were spread over many states and used year-round. Had I faced such an assignment, I should have come with a different mental set to Dalton's, but my conclusions and recommendations, while different, would have been no better based. Rural aid *deserves* better.

Now for the good news! It can be done, at reasonable cost, though it takes time. Based on ARTI Colombo, a joint Sri Lankan-British team evaluated *draught power alternatives* in a country characterised by repeated 'waves' of British tractor aid. The two-year, all-season surveys obtained and cross-checked data from tractor owners and hirers (and labourers) in environments with different options and costs regarding mechanical and animal power. Thus the surveys were able to reach clear conclusions. Tractor aid was justified in a few circumstances in Sri Lanka. However, the aid had been spread to places, seasons, and cropping and water use patterns where its benefit/cost was far below unity. Open and hidden subsidies, to make tractors popular with farmers despite very low or negative social rates of return, had supported this process. It enriched both local importers, who collected a monopoly rent, and British manufacturers and workers who would otherwise have faced lower demand. However, this 'aid,' while paid for by British taxpayers, did nothing to raise farm or non-farm output in Sri Lanka. There, the rich were made richer only by 'unemploying' the poor with the help of an inappropriate technique made artificially profitable (Farrington and Abeyratne, 1982; see also Burch, 1979).

Of course, there are many more optimistic evaluations of aid projects. Aid to ARD has, on most evaluations, produced respectable returns, as good as those of aid projects as a whole. But they should have been much better, in view of *sectoral* returns, as we have seen. Part of the problem has been that so much rural aid has gone into (a) farm mechanisation, and (b) heavy irrigation construction. Both sectors cover big, politically powerful producers (or contractors) in donor countries; potential owners of assets in recipient countries, also powerful, able to earn monopoly rent, especially if convertible currencies are made available to them to buy these 'aid' assets (tractors, deep tubewells, improved land) cheap from government; and fashionably 'modern' farm techniques that often displace labour. It is hard to deny that a major reason why aid to ARD has not attained higher project returns than other aid, despite the sector's low marginal capital/output ratio, is the concentration of such aid on (a) farm machinery, (b) large-scale irrigation systems (see Chambers, 1979, on the chronic underperformance of such systems).

The need to make evaluation local and systematic is the key example of the revamping of project-cycles required if ARD aid is to escape the sector-project problem and realise its full potential for growth and the alleviation of poverty. This is largely because self-satisfied, self-serving styles of evaluation are an important reason why the rest of the project cycle does not improve. The occasional scandal (call in the Court of Auditors!) actually preserves errors by creating the complacent illusion that we can improve matters by chasing out a few scoundrels. So do even cleverer formalisations of benefit/cost analysis (in itself an essential tool) which divert technical skills to appraisal away from the more urgent, but also more sensitive tasks of improving evaluation and design. We can easily see, however, how non-localisation and a 'visiting fireman' approach to ARD projects vitiates the early stages of the project cycle, too. Consider the reluctance to analyse local drilling rigs at the design stage for tubewells in Bangladesh in 1972-5; or, today, the failure to look behind the implausibly low 'expected' water-duties, fed by irrigation ministries to those appraising major irrigation projects, and hence the failure to perceive the realities of virtually uncontrolled top-end overuse.

CONCLUDING NOTES

Aid to agriculture and rural development grew substantially in the 1970s, even after allowing for definitional padding. However, the growth was much faster in MAs than from bilateral donors. If MAs receive less international support—as with IDA—and as donors seek aid linked to exports, the tide of aid to ARD may be receding. Especially in Africa, such aid has, to some extent, displaced local investment in the sector.

Aid to ARD, including aid to smallholders and support for rural health and education (see especially World Bank, 1980: 4), shows as good an economic rate of return as do other sorts of project. On the sectoral evidence, however, ARD should do much better, especially in a time of costly fossil energy and promising new cereal varieties. The surface signs of what is wrong are seen in the project cycle. Per unit of potential benefit, much less *on-the-spot* and (less indigenous) talent goes into identifying, designing, evaluating and operating projects in ARD than in steel, docks, or metalled roads. In particular, both donor agencies and LDC governments appear reluctant to meet the one to three per cent project costs needed for the localised, prolonged evaluations that alone can assess ARD projects.

Only when the project-cycle and staffing issues are addressed, through appropriate, priorities and career incentives for LDC nationals, will aid—and domestic investment—in ARD begin to realise its potential.

REFERENCES

Agarwal, B., 1980, 'Tractorisation, productivity and employment,' *Journal of Development Studies*, vol. 16, no. 3.
—————1984, 'Tractors, tubewells and cropping intensity in the Punjab', *Journal of Development Studies*, vol. 20, no. 4.
Baum, W., 1978, 'The World Bank project cycle,' *Finance and Development*, vol. 15, no. 4, December.
Binswanger, H., 1978, *The Economics or Tractors in South Asia*, ADC/ICRISAT, New York.
Burch, D., 1980, Overseas Aid and The Transfer of Technology, PhD thesis; University of Sussex.

Carruthers, I., 1982, *Aid to Irrigation*, OECD, Paris.

Chambers, R., 1981, 'In search of a water revolution: questions for canal irrigation management in the 1980s,' *Water Supply and Management*, no. 5.

Dalton, G., 1976, *British Aid Tractors in India: an Ex Post Evaluation*, EV36, ODM, London,

Evenson, R., and Y. Kislev, 1975, *Agricultural Research and Productivity*, Yale U.P., New Haven.

Farrington, J. and F. Abeyratne, 1982, *Farm Power in Sri Lanka*, University of Reading.

FAO, 1978, *State of Food and Agriculture, 1978*, Rome.

————1982, *State of Food and Agriculture, 1981*, Rome.

Lipton, M., 1977, *Why Poor People Stay Poor: Urban Bias and World Development*, Temple Smith, London.

————1983, 'African agricultural development: the EEC's new role,' *Development Policy Review*, vol. 1, no. 1.

————1984, 'Urban bias revisited,' *Journal of Development Studies*, vol. 20, no. 3.

OECD, 1968, *Aid to Agriculture in Developing Countries*, Paris.

————1978, *Development Cooperation 1978*, Paris.

————1982, *Development Cooperation 1982*, Paris.

Papanek, G., 1983, 'Aid, growth and equity in Southern Asia,' in J. Parkinson (ed.), *Aid and Poverty*, Blackwell, Oxford.

Pinstrup-Anderson, P., 1982, *Agricultural Research and Technology in Economic Development*, Longman, Harlow.

UN, 1980, *Yearbook of National Accounts Statistics*, New York.

USAID, 1980, *Rural Roads Evaluation: Summary*, G.W. Anderson et al., Working Draft, Washington.

World Bank, 1980, *World Development Report 1980*, Washington, DC.

————1981, *Agriculture and Rural Development Sector Survey*, Washington, DC.

————1982, *World Development Report 1982*, Washington DC.

————1983, *Focus on Poverty*, Washington DC.

CHAPTER 2

Foreign Aid as an Obstacle to Development: The Case of Rwanda's Rural Development Projects

INTRODUCTION

Rwanda's per capita income is one of the lowest in the world, estimated by the World Bank in 1982 at $ 200. Foreign aid has become one of the major assets of national development policy, with 85 per cent of development investment being financed from foreign capital, which is a sum higher than the country's ordinary budget. Being somewhat overwhelmed by this massive investment, the government seems increasingly to leave control of aid funds to foreign organisations which plan their own projects through a considerable number of experts and advisors (56 per cent of the total aid is foreign staff). Does this situation further development? Or does it lead rather to a kind of dependence and the undermining of development through foreign aid bias? The object of our analysis is to examine this process.

The Process of Designing Projects

We will here examine rural development projects only, though a large part of the analysis is valid in other sectors also. This is important, given that the government's target is to cover each commune with a 'great project,' which represents an investment of $ 10 mn for each commune of about 30,000 inhabitants, that is to say, $ 33 per inhabitant for a period of four years (or $ 83 per inhabitant per year, whereas the annual money income per farmer is less than $ 50). So local investment is apparently massive, but there are many questions to be asked about the use to which the money is put. It should also be noted that the role of international organisations in rural development ($\pm$ 25 per cent of aid programmes) allows the government to devote its attention to other problems: neither the ordinary budget nor the development budget provides more than 5 per cent of its expenditure for the agricultural sector.

IDENTIFICATION OF PROJECTS

This is normally carried out by the government (usually with the aid of resident experts, even at this stage). But as the requisite skilled staff are often not available only the outline of the project will be produced, with the foreign organisations left to work out the project files. There is a significant evolution here which is worth noting: up to 1976, most of the major projects concentrated on export crops, sometimes to the neglect of the food-producing sector. Since then, the number of projects aimed at intensifying agriculture has increased (a phenomenon which is probably related to the World Bank's change of policy). The country must follow this priority: the 1977-1981 Five-Year Plan gave priority to food-producing agriculture. But if we look at the proposed annual growth percentages, the picture is: 3 per cent for food-producing cultivation and 12 per cent for export.

PREPARATION OF PROJECTS

This stage of project implementation in particular prompts the question—in whose interests are projects carried out?

In Kigali, we see many expert missions arriving to spend two or three weeks in the country (sometimes less). After this, they are able to write up a lengthy report, sometimes containing several hundred pages. How can we characterise these experts' work? What follows is an outline of their operation:

Meeting with national officials: Welcome and presentation of the main targets by a higher official meeting with 'skilled' Rwandese technicians in order to elaborate the project through consultation delivery of the preliminary report to the higher official.

Meeting with foreign experts living in the country, who will often have initiated the mission. The newly arrived expert spends most of his time with a resident one, who gives him/her all the required information in the relevant field. These visits tend to become exchanges of contacts and favours. Mention may be made of X expert at the Ministry of Public Works who has special funds at his disposal for inviting advisors for short periods (never more than three weeks, usually less). Such an advisor may end up with a job as a resident expert, and then be able to reciprocate the invitation to the first expert back in France.

Collection and analysis of the existing statistics. Everyone in the country knows that they are inaccurate, but for the experts, as good economists, they are essential. It is strange to meet people on international organisation missions entrusted with the job of calculating the country's GNP in two weeks!

Visit to the project location, very often as a 'rural development tourist', as Chambers puts it. That is to say, a visit at a fixed time in the year, to a comparatively accessible place, and meeting only people who can speak French—in other words, local senior managers. Many examples could be mentioned: the case of an expert who was to study nutritional problems resulting from the intensification of coffee growing who could not even speak French, so that he was limited to discussions with other foreigners. I suggested a visit to the hills. His reply was: 'Oh! It is not necessary, I saw enough from the road.' Another example is that of an international organisation representative who, after visiting the location of an integrated development project, professed himself very satisfied and remarked: 'At last here work has been done; the houses for the top staff are really a fine achievement.'

These two examples are merely 'touristic', but some cases have negative ramifications when the expert takes himself so seriously as to want to write a fine report, as did the advisor who asked the Prefect to invite all the jobless youngsters living in town to a meeting. During the ensuing meeting, the expert asked them to express their wishes about finding a job in the future, so he could record them. Was this not a way of misleading these youngsters and falsely raising their expectations? The expert knew very well that he would not come back, and had no plans for a project.

Elements in previous experts' reports are looked up and summarised. These reports are very often borrowed, but practically
never brought back.

Sale of foreign technology, as represented by the expert, directly or otherwise. There is the case of an expert in alternative energy
sources who suggested that biogas plants should be built in
places where people in effect do not raise animals, and furthermore proposed that farmers' houses should be equipped with solar
waterheaters, in places where water must be fetched from considerable distances. The same expert recommended 'timbers of the
banana-tree' for heating, but that is another story. I must also
mention another advisor who was asked to design an important
rural project, and who proposed that levellers should be given to
communes. We should also recall how many international organisations are ready to launch major projects in fertiliser supply,
since they know there is no development without fertilisers, but
which fail to ask who is going to bear the long-term cost, or how an
exhausted soil and non-selected seeds will respond. Actually, of
course, as one local representative of an international organisation explained (a representative who had not left his office in the
capital for a year), it is just a question of assessing the economic
benefit of the project. This means that beyond the experts' experience and his universal European model, his calculating machine
must be his principal instrument. Do further yields which should
make the project feasible, involve adequate benefit, and scope for
refunding credit? If they do, it is a good project. It must also be
added that such a project will have to increase the income of the
poor rural population. This is a fashionable target, even if it turns
out there is no time to consult this population. But in a poor and
'egalitarian' country like Rwanda, this target seems (wrongly, as
we shall see later) obvious. And it is always pointed out that these
are only preliminary reports, with further survey and evaluations
recommended which provide scope for the experts to offer their
services again and maintain the system of experts' reports.

THE 'TECHNICAL PACKAGE'

Research centres. To plan and specify a project, a 'technical
package' is necessary for estimating the output at each stage.
What kind of 'technical package' should be suggested to transform

agricultural methods? That is the role of research centres. It is noteworthy that the experts who have set up such centres have mostly secured them against intrusion; but that is symbolic since they never leave their centres, never study traditional agricultural methods (intercropping etc.) which are automatically considered non-rational and non-profitable; they remain confined to their European specialisations, trying to reproduce their European laboratory 'ideal' conditions. Thus, new high-yielding varieties are worked out, a map of agricultures suitable to each area of the country is drawn and a theoretical, technical model of agricultural development worked out. Finally, this model is communicated to the Ministry of Agriculture to be diffused through the country, via agricultural extension.

Agricultural extension. As the model referred to above is supposed ideal, farmers are assumed to have no reason to refuse it. Any rejection will be regarded as proof of their 'irrationality'. But this term is no longer popular, the fashion now being to listen to farmers from a distance. The experts find it better, therefore, to criticise the agricultural extension and to point out that it is absolutely inappropriate and does not fulfill its role of spreading techniques. However, they are willing to excuse current agricultural extension workers on the grounds that they are undertrained, underpaid and not well backed up; but they think that if a 'modern' organisation with a strict hierarchy is established, with each agronomist in charge of only a restricted number of families, the message should spread (more easily); and they add that 'small demonstration farms' with wage-workers could also be set up to allow the peasants to see the 'ideal model'. But in the eyes of farmers, the fact that the small demonstration-farms are publicly financed completely alters the results.

The small demonstration farm in Rwanda. It is under these circumstances that the ISAR (Rwanda's Agronomic Sciences Institute) has settled its 1.0 ha demonstration farm, which is proposed as a model for the whole country and based on the 'marriage' of agriculture and breeding, i.e., cowshed where cows will be fed with the grass gained from erosion control, producing manure for different soils, each type being dedicated to a specific crop carefully planted in well-spaced rows. This model may seem more realistic. It is different from that of the experts, to whom agriculture is

unimaginable without fertilisers or machines, and who calculate
the number of bags of fertilisers which are to be supplied to each
family without counting the cost of foreign currency and transport, and the cost as each project comes to an end, and is inevitably followed by another one.

However, even this model remains quite inappropriate and is
relevant only to a statistical and static study of Rwanda's agriculture. It is true that the average area of a farm is more or less 1.0
ha, but more than 50 per cent of the farms are no longer that size,
and most important, such a farm is divided into many small lots
(may be as many as 30 on a 1.5 ha farm), according to the history
of the family. (I did not write 'according to the fortunes of history'
since when a father shares his land between his sons, he knows
quite well that in some places it is fertile for one kind of cultivation and elsewhere for others). Would a farmer walk half-an-hour
from home to cut a few clumps of grass for his cow? Besides, if
this grass fixes the soil correctly, it will tend to spread quickly
and form an unfarmable zone. When a man does not have enough
land to live on, he will find it difficult to leave one strip of his
land to protect the rest (without any insurance and with a comparatively slight risk of major losses in the traditional system).
Rwanda's traditional agriculture is very often based on intercropping, in which, for instance, maize is used as a support for beans
and combined with sweet potato; the whole ensures a permanent
soil cover.

When farmers are asked what is 'modern' agriculture, they reply
smiling: 'It is planting in rows,' but they never add (for fear that
they might have trouble with the person they are talking to) that
they have never understood the relevance of this technique which
requires more time for sowing, involves less yield and does not
cover the soil as thickly (erosion between rows), but it is difficult
for them to understand the problem of the economists entrusted
with the job of calculating the country's agricultural production
whose statistical methods are completely opposed to their kind of
cultivation.

Researcher and farmer meetings. Yet, without even taking
foreign experiences into account (training and visit system, Chinese researchers and farmers. . .), other forms of research have
been carried out in Rwanda. The PNAP (National Programme

for the Improvement of Potatoes), depending on the CIP (Lima's international potato centre), has started a very interesting seed-breeding programme, during which tests are carried out in connection with farmers' cooperatives. The meeting of the two genuine professionals was intriguing: on the one hand, the farmer, who knows all the practical method and diseases of potatoes, and on the other, the agricultural engineer, with his theoretical knowledge of the remedies to be used and all the forms of seed breeding. The farmers, who had just listened politely to the agricultural extensionist (who know no more than they did; and in particular could not explain anything) began asking the agronomists long series of questions. On their part, the agronomists were willing to hear about practical methods and the farmers' problems. However, the scope of a research centre which is limited to one type of cultivation, can only be restricted, since it cannot take the whole system into consideration.

AGRICULTURAL EXTENSION METHODS

Organisation chart. The study of the 'technical package' has raised this question before. What should the experts designing projects conserve? Since the technical package is considered reliable, unquestionably difficulties with intensification are assumed to lie with agricultural extension. Since there is doubt about whether farmers are adopting effective methods, it is felt that projects must plan to have a large number of training staff.

Working out an elaborate organisation chart is often one of the highest pleasures of the consultant adviser: at the top, so many A-1 agronomists and veterinaries, then the A-2, A-3, the agricultural monitors on the hills. As for the rest of the project, government officials do not have much to say; they just look forward to its realisation and do not interfere, as the experts tell them they would make things more difficult. But when the project is to start, it turns out that these agronomists and veterinaries are not available, simply because they are outnumbered by the multiplicity of projects. It is also worth examining how these agronomists are trained. When I met the headmaster (a Frenchman) of the national training-school for agronomists, he told me that the idea of discussing things with farmers as helpful was an out-of-date myth: 'The only effective process is to give them precise orders; orders which involve fines!' With this kind of training, we will never have pedagogues; especially as the programmes are based on foreign models, on the assumption of European technical superiority, and never on the study of traditional methods.

Agriculture instructors. For any major project, there will be agriculture extensionists, one for 600 families or even fewer. These instructors are one of the important 'investments' of the projects. They are local young people; they must be able to cope in French (since the experts cannot understand the local language) and will receive intensive training in agriculture for a few months (usually three), after which they are sent to 'the field'. They seem to be dynamic and interested, but they have never been asked what really interests them. They might have replied that they were not interested in agriculture, but just wanted a job. Furthermore, they do not themselves practise the methods they are teaching. They can understand French because they have spent a year or two at high school, after which they were sent back home. That is to say, their hopes to become intellectuals in the future have been frustrated, but they no longer see themselves as belonging to the rural community.

Teaching methods. What will happen to these young people, once the project has come to an end? Nobody asks this question. Will their commune be interested, and able to re-employ them? Or will they simply have to go back home? Neither has anyone asked how the farmers are likely to receive them, though it seems totally predictable when they bring ready-made solutions. Are the authorities not despising the farmer and all his experience in sending him a semi-trained youth who knows no more than himself about the potential of his land? Projects are always conceived from the top and according to foreign models. It seems that the first step should rather be to work with the old farmers, and listen to them, but this takes a long time, requires acquaintance with the country and the language, and cannot be quantified or standardised.

Given the large amount of attention devoted to the organisation chart (staff problems always rank first when planning is done from the top), the educational capacities of the staff, though essential, are not regarded as problematic, even though the relationship between field staff and farmers is, as a matter of fact, one of the major difficulties. On occasion, as in one German project, considerable funds will be provided for an educational thrust (demonstration farms. posters, felt boards. . .) including wage-workers to undertake applied work on the peasants' plots; and then the evaluation reports wonder about the absence of results. But what can farmers do if no one listens to them and if they are paid to work at home? They are bound to prefer to wait and see what will be paid for. Foreigners want to obtain results quickly.

Consultation with the Population

Having worked out the 'package,' there is sometimes a move to consult the local population, since 'participation' is in fashion and some interesting ideas might be suggested; but since the project itself is already planned, no important changes are possible. The experts entrusted with the job of planning the project, and the national executives who have to guide them, will organise a meeting with the local authorities, who are requested to report the next day at the regional office. In 45 minutes or so, the experts explain the project and especially the financial investment, the significance of which has been pointed out above (annual investment *per capita* of nearly double the farmer's average monetary income per year).

I should like to mention as an example, a local consultation in which I took part some time ago. The project aimed to destroy the last natural mountain forecast (badly damaged) in the area, plant pine trees on an area of 10,000 ha and establish cooperative pastures of 5,000 ha to settle the cattle which formally grazed in the forecast. The locals who were invited to the meeting and consulted, pointed out problems in relation to the ownership of these trees ('the project said it would be state property'), the control of water springs in this forest, which was regarded as a water tower for the area ('the experts said we have noticed from our experience in other countries that this kind of afforestation does not cause any water problem') and the relevance of some realism as far as cooperatives are concerned ('the project's view was they shall be open to any farmer').

But each of these questions involved so many components that it was impossible to discuss: farmers no longer owning wood would not respect a forest belonging to the state; the experience of clearing and planting eucalyptus had already involved the disappearance of springs; the farmers' cooperatives would be monopolised by some dominating individuals. What is the point of asking these questions when you are only asked to approve a project which has already been worked out? When the experts left, they were satisfied with their work, but probably not aware of the fact that they had initiated a process which could ruin local development.

Carrying out the Project

First stage: buildings, vehicles, premiums. The initial stages of a new project are always as follows: first, an expert entrusted with the job of building comes to ask local authorities the appropriate locations and at the same time apologises for not being able to give further information about the project, saying that the leader of the project must come for this purpose. But meanwhile, houses for the foreign experts must be built, large and luxurious enough to match their status. Houses must be built as well for the national executives involved in the project, and these must not be too different from those of the experts.

Afterwards, vehicles must be provided (they will rapidly become commercial vehicles). And the national executives involved in the project must also be paid special premiums by the project in addition to the salary paid by the government. This must allow them to have better working conditions, but it must especially help to reduce the tremendous gap between foreign experts' remunerations and those of their national counterparts. A recent study carried out in Rwanda showed that the income of the experts and foreign workers in this country was 33 times as high as the average local salaries, and that it represented 3.4 per cent of the personnel in the public sector, and 50 per cent of the money income of this sector (St. Marijesse, 1982). And yet some people wonder at the uneasy relations between these national workers and the peasants, from whom they are cut off.

Relations with the local authorities. Usually it is when the project has been started and when equipment or people are needed, or when a conflict arises, that the project managers realise that local leaders have not been consulted yet ('You must understand, there is no time because of the work of installation!'). *Then* they go to see these people; they explain to them the plan of the project and ask them for their 'total collaboration' to complete these 'noble objectives'. Sometimes their dealings will not go further than that: a recent five-year German project report did not even mention local leaders.

However the project may help to fulfill some local needs: For instance, equipping a water spring or building a school. We will see later how the majority of these 'gifts' do not allow people to take part in the implementation of such infrastructures. Sometimes it is through the local leader ('he must be involved') that those responsible for the project introduce themselves to the population. It is interesting to listen to the speeches of the experts who see themselves in the role of Santa Claus, announcing proudly to the population that they 'are leading a project of $ 20 mn dollars, that is to say 2,000 mn Rwandese francs, for the development of the area, and that they rely on everybody's contribution to complete the project properly'. The farmers then applaud, since they know experts like to be applauded. After this, how can one wonder at people not taking part in the project? Everything will in the end be given as a present. It is easy to understand those local officials involved in the project who are driven to make the most of this windfall which they know will not go on forever.

An example of this can be found in an important project for which nine people were taken on over 12 months for one post of accountant; the chief of the project checked his wage lists personally every month, but did not have time to visit the project location.

Other infrastructure provided. The other infrastructures provided for in the project can then be undertaken. We can mention among others:

> The establishment of social infrastructure (water supplies, primary schools, community clinics. . .). Their relevance should not be criticised, but rather the way they are established, which makes them gifts and does not involve the farmers. They will never see themselves either as owners or as responsible, which may be an acute disadvantage and become costly for the maintenance and efficiency of these services.

Road-making

Training and extension facilities, such as lecture halls or small demonstration farms, which may do no better than introduce cattle that are selected but not sufficiently resistant, so that they die after only a few days on the peasant's farm.

Implementation of a storage system: it is usually believed that farmers' storage systems incur considerable losses and that small businessmen are speculators. Projects usually include a storage component composed of big sheds and lorries with a working capital amounting to many millions of Rwandese francs—which can only be properly managed by a very competent technician, in practice a foreigner. This means, once again, frustration of possible local development based on the improvement of families' stocks and the establishment of cooperation.

To boost the role of local trainers involved in the project, such people are often paid premiums for any meeting they are asked to attend with the executives involved in the project. This undermines training throughout the area since the communes which are not covered by the project cannot afford to pay such premiums to the executives who, in such conditions, no longer work.

Some projects involving huge sums of money and not knowing how to use them, spend them on building offices for the agronomists.

The survival of projects. Thus we often see a major part of the project coming to an end without any direct and real impact upon the farmers. A recent survey conducted among farmers involved in one of the major projects, and financed by an international organisation, showed that farmers had gained on three counts (three years after the project had been started): the construction of buildings, road-making and the vehicles used for the project.

In this way it appears to be necessary to plan a second and even a third stage of projects which seem to form an endless chain.

Some projects are more specific: in recent years, the ILO has put emphasis on highly labour-intensive projects as a way of reducing seasonal rural unemployment and implementing infrastructures which are essential (roads, dikes and afforestation). The principle of these projects is interesting but their implementation may be dangerous, as can be explained by the example of a project of reafforestation on which 6,000 peasants were engaged for two years:

> The 6,000 peasants were, of course, satisfied at getting jobs, that is to say, regular wages.

> It is necessary to emphasise that the reafforestation must be carried out at the same time as the cultivation.

> The wages which are paid (the minimum national wage) do not allow the peasants to effectively make any investment, and in practice ensure that money will be spent mainly on drink (beer), with inflation as a result—all the more as these projects provide for no saving or credit systems, and do not set up shops which could provide small investment articles: building materials, tools etc.

> The final result of the project may be negative as far as wood is concerned: how can large plantations belonging to the state be settled on hills where farmers are short of timber, and where there is no place to plant trees?

> During the elaboration of the project, the target was to reach an additional income for the government, which would then lease the farming of the plantation to private firms. But in this case, farmers do not profit from the wood plantations. Are they not going to consider public property as theirs?

> But, above all, without any other organised structure suggested to the population, this kind of project may lead to its proletarianisation. Farmers, in effect, abandon their occupations and their emerging groups to join a project which will not help them either to become self-sufficient or to organise themselves, but will keep them dependent on less intensive work (how can one watch over 6,000 tree planters?), even if it is regularly remunerated.

The idea of this sort of major project derives from the Great Chinese Work, but when it is considered out of its organisational framework (workers delegated by their basic groups), it becomes another destructive element in the rural sector. The ILO experts are responsible for fund management; Therefore, their objective is to get the best investment for infrastructure. They look after realisable projects in the country, reckon their 'benefit,' import the necessary small materials (instead of studying their local production, to discover which is the more costly) and undertake the management of the works (together with specialised consultants). This approach, which is once again purely an 'economising' one, may result in serious effects for a population which becomes proletarianed rather than learning to become self-sufficient.

Food Aid

The intention here is not to consider the whole rationale for food aid, but only some of its effects on the agricultural sector when it is maintained for long periods (i.e., not, for example, when aid is offered in response to a bad harvest).

—Rwanda receives from the EEC and from Belgium, several thousand tons of wheat each year. Wheat can be grown in Rwanda, even though the soil is not good. The provision of food aid may be detrimental in two ways:

the taste for a product which may remain scarce, will be encouraged;
the food incentive to produce this cereal will be reduced and food dependence on foreign countries reinforced.

—The American Catholic Relief Service distributes maize, soya flour and cooking oil to women who come regularly to nutritional centres as an incentive. The aim of these centres is to observe children's growth curves each month, and to give nutritional courses to their mothers, so as to ensure a better-balanced diet, partly through agricultural improvements. But this distribution of food has little educational effect; it has attracted women's interest to such an extent that they only go to the centres when there are food supplies. These products, especially the cooking oil but also the two others are not traditional foods in Rwanda; even if women can get used to the flour, they still resell the cooking oil.

—All high-schools are boarding schools and are also supplied with soya flour, powdered milk and cooking oil by the CRS. This aid seems to be essential; to be short of it would, of course, be costly. But it has negative consequences:

> no school cultivates its own fields, despite pupils' permanent presence in the boarding schools;
> this aid to young people breeds new eating habits, such as dependence on bread, milk and oil, which may become too costly when the country has to import these products for the growing bureaucratic class.

Technological Aid

We must also consider the industrial sector, and its direct links with the rural environment.

In a country with a rural population density like Rwanda's where the area per family is less than 1.0 ha, it is essential to attempt to find a future for the young people. Since their parents cannot give them land, a rural employment policy provides the only means to avoid a massive rural exodus to the cities, where there are far fewer opportunities to succeed than in the country side.

However, such is not the policy of the foreign experts at the Ministry of Economy, who suggested that the Government should decide in favour of increasing the number of replacement industries with high technology and preferably locate them in the capital in order to reduce production costs and improve competitive productivity.

But once more, these economist experts, who have no time to leave their offices in the capital, are ruining the country's future by not being able to take its characteristics into account; its small area, the considerable density of population, its more or less practicable means of communication, the absence of urban structure.

Two examples can be cited: first the credit granted by the Government (the Rwandese Bank of Development), on these experts' advice, for an investment by an Asian who owns a small biscuit factory with automatic machinery imported from Australia. This ignored the fact that two small cooperatives had already started producing biscuits made by craftsmen (with wood-burning furnaces) one of which was located in the south, and the other in the west country. The former employs 2 or 3 technicians, the latter 15 people in the countryside (with actually a lower productivity, but that is not the essential point).

Secondly, there was the refusal by the National Bank to grant an import licence for second-hand carpentry machines: only new materials must be imported. This principle might be a proper end, but the recovery of old and solid foreign equipment, which is easier to maintain and less costly, represents a major opportunity for small rural craftsmen.

The desire to transfer a system of production and a model of technology which are completely different and related to very different living conditions, can only bring about costly failure. If some experts have understood this principle, they have already turned to the 'appropriate technology'. I do not want to discuss here the principles of a technology appropriate to the country, as these are explained elsewhere, but to consider the strange way in which some experts set up demonstrations and exhibitions of appropriate technology. It is a contradiction; the right way is to start with traditional technology, discuss with people the technical questions at issue, and try to find solutions together. If the expert identifies a problem and proposes his own answer, to which person shall the technology be adapted?

Two more cases come to mind:

— Implementation by UNICEF (in another country) of production of large cement jars to recover rain water; this technology has been proposed to Rwandese farmers, but it requires three bags of cement costing 2,000 Rwandese francs ($20) a bag, except when it is a donation, to make one jar.

— The study of alternative cookers proposed to farmers in Sri Lanka: engineers have made various tests, but without taking into account the difference of energy consumption and of time, and without studying the side-effects of traditional cookers. In other words, this is a typical case of a study by an expert who has no links with the community for whom he works.

CONCLUSIONS

Generalities

Our analysis of international aid for Rwanda's rural development allows us to draw conclusions which are quite clear: official
texts hardly refer to experts, they refer more often to local administration, and mention always the poor farmer, whom rural
development must be directed to. And yet people who profit by
it should be classified in the reverse order, since other data can
confirm the observation of the 'three-thirds' in foreign financing:
1/3 for the experts, 1/3 for the different services offered to the
national executive and 1/3 for the farmers.

EXPERTS, OFFICIALS, AND FARMERS' EXCLUSION

Experts. If the main rule of an expert is to calculate the economic benefit of a project, it is likely that he does not apply this
rule to himself. Otherwise his action would be quite limited;
according to the World Bank's estimation the monthly cost of an
expert in Rwanda was, in 1982, $ 10,000 inclusive, that is to say
$ 1 per minute of work (22 days a month × 8 hrs). The expert's
opinion must be very important to cover such a cost.

By controlling the financing agencies, experts not only control
the process of development, but they also form one of the only
groups able to control almost freely their own reproduction, by
determining research missions within the framework of development projects. Our study of Rwanda's rural development projects shows that the portion of the project's financing used to
remunerate experts and consultants varies from 1/3 to 1/4 (but it is
closer to 1/3); without taking into consideration the aid projects
for establishing files of projects, such as the latest project financed
by the World Bank in Rwanda; $ 6.3 mn is estimated solely for the
financing of foreign advisers for a period of four years.

Experts are very often economists and their basic instrument is
the calculator which enables them to evaluate a benefit (which
often only exists in theory) on the basis of inaccurate statistics.
This approach through figures reveals a misunderstanding and a
contempt for human beings, who are considered of minor importance.

Confined to this approach, experts have 'no time' to listen to rural people, whom they cannot understand (in a few hours) with no acquaintance with their language and their values. But meanwhile they have the wrong impression that they *do* hold a dialogue with rural communities through local executives (rural development tourism); they simply class the interests of the executives as those of the farmers.

These experts come from Europe ('Northern' countries) with a fixed idea of development which consists in 'transferring' the European model. The expert is to write up an integrated project as a technical package, the yield of which will be estimated as if he were delivering a ready-made factory. But with no link with farmers, such projects are doomed to failure.

The administration. It is remarkable how the local upper class is really concerned about the development of the rural population, trying to elaborate one project for each country.

Nevertheless, other popular national aims should be emphasised: peace and national unity, growth of exports (need for foreign currency), conservation and transport of basic food products between the regions (specially for the urban market) and multiplication of jobs.

There is always a danger in the attitude of some officials who try to benefit themselves through the infrastructure of the project, instead of being really in the service of the rural population.

Farmers. Since the foreign experts have not asked the farmers for their opinions or wishes, they are excluded from responsibility.

When they are asked for their opinions, they are aware that they are expected to give fixed answers.

A fundamental principle is that all of them work for themselves, but that they may not be helped to organise themselves.

Projects often lead to the proletarianisation of farmers, especially because of the labour-intensive nature of the work, where they are used as instruments for production in big enterprises, and not as people responsible for their own development.

A Possible Way Out

Aid conceived by foreign experts and conforming to their system will never enable farmers to ensure their development. Another way of proceeding is necessary:

Perhaps local executives, refusing an interesting job in the administration, should be able to start a 'development project' with farmers in their native region. But this process is difficult.

Or foreigners should contribute to the achievement of this undertaking, but this is not reliable as long as they come to impose their style of development, and do not understand the local population.

Finally, do not traditional 'good will and charity' lead to the same effects as the great projects? Giving something to people may be proof of feeling pity for them, but it is above all a way of creating a situation of dependence: it is teaching them to be dependent and not to be self-sufficient.

Three points seem to be fundamental in this collective process:

Listening. Listening must not be an intellectual appropriation (a typical danger of anthropological studies). I shall mention the case of a French researcher who carried out a wonderful study on a Rwandese Commune, in which he lived for a whole year for this purpose. When he was about to leave the country, his last words were: 'I shall never set foot here again.'

A very good report on the region's population will be set out but it will be limited to 'exploitation-knowledge', which will result in no collective action.

Listening must not be recording, which would mean that people were asked to describe their problems, and told that executives will do everything they can to find solutions; such a case would mean the undermining of people's responsibilities, the very opposite of increased participation, since when the farmers' problems have been solved, they will have nothing else to claim.

Listening must be a collective analysis of problems and ways of proceeding to find solutions, which takes into account what farmers say about the problems, though they do not say it in a systematised way. Their opinions must be summed up and given back to them as a whole, within their economic, social and political context, which will permit understanding of the origin of these problems, and unmask the real obstacles.

Collective undertaking. In order to go deeper, this listening has to be shared through a collective undertaking, the only means by which a person can prove his/her real motivation; not by implementing a technical package defined in a foreign laboratory, but by common research (trials and errors) which will relate the technician of the practice (the farmer) and the technician of the theories (the agronomist, for instance).

This collective undertaking must result in self-confidence among farmers as far as their responsibility for development is concerned; they will find out that methods which were appropriate sometime ago can now cause damage (for instance, the increase in Rwanda's population has resulted in suppressing fallows and in planting crops on steep slopes; thus new solutions have to be found). They will realise that nobody will 'bring them development if they do not work for it themselves.

This collective undertaking can be valid for farmers and craftsmen (not by bringing modern machines, but by consulting old craftsmen so as to see together how to control the new production processes); it can be valid for health services (by appointing elementary medical practioners); and for water boards.

Organisation. Listening and cooperation require organisation since, as they say in Rwanda, 'a forest cannot be made of one tree; a house cannot be built with one plank; a single man can do nothing'. Or, to quote Paulo Freire: 'You do not save yourself alone, you do not save the others, but you save yourselves all together.' Aid which is limited to consulting farmers will maintain a structure of power which is out of the isolated farmer's range; this structure can be broken only by a farmers' organisation. It might be possible to set up such an organisation on the basis of traditional structures (groups of mutual aid, villages) since they constitute a centre of deeply established relations. But this is possible on the condition that one is aware of the real structure of these traditional groups, which is often deeply inegalitarian. How can one manage to develop these traditional groups without some people seizing power? Or how can one manage to develop these groups, giving more or less regular mutual aid, into basic cooperatives? How to create new forms of grouping through collective action while, at an early stage, seeing that these groups select themselves, set themselves up and are not too big for self-management. Yet only with this type of organisation can the groups involved federate in order to tackle together regional development problems, contrary to any policy which creates cooperatives from the top and thus forms groups which will become instruments for controlling farmers, and manage to keep control over the organisation.

A Definition of Development

These different approaches are linked to definitions of development. It seems to be important to point out the contour of these definitions: the definition of development as the growth of the gross national product, though no longer officially used, has left traces in the economist's approach that links development to the analysis of statistics.

We shall not linger over the criticism against the approach which considers the value of GNP without taking into account what is produced, who produces it and who receives it. It seems to us however that the role of the experts in the analysis of projects of integrated rural development, is still linked to this sort of analysis, when their study focuses on a 'technical package' and on its economic benefit without consulting local people, without wondering who will really profit by this 'package'.

The definition by international organisations is at present mainly linked to 'basic needs'. This definition has brought about a reorientation of aid towards the poorest classes, at least theoretically. Thus the World Bank defines rural development as the improvement of the living conditions of the masses with low income living in rural areas, so that this process of development can go on by itself (Lele, 1979). The 'basic concept of rural poverty is alleviated by a steady growth of production and of the income of families and low wage rural workers' (World Bank, 1975). The basic elements seem to be the 'scientific, study (which means foreign) of 'needs' and the definition of the best 'technical packages' for a solution, a set which no longer includes only agricultural production but also water, health and basic education. It is acknowledge that the participation of the population is an incentive to carry out this policy, but only in a minor way, as is specified by Dudley Seers in his definition:

The questions which are to be asked about the development of a country are these: what has been done to counter poverty? What has been done to fight unemployment? What has been done to reduce inequalities? If there has been a considerable decrease in all these three sectors, then without any doubt, it has meant the development of the country involved. Although political freedom is to be considered as an important objective, it is of minor importance as long as a major part of the population is underfed and underemployed.

The author then contradicts himself by acknowledging that in general the absence of political freedom has not made easier the achievement of these three most essential objectives.

In fact, this political freedom is conceived as the possibility of establishing an opposition party based on a European model and not at all on the idea of people's participation as responsible for their development.

An interesting study by the *Institut Universitaire d'Etudes de Development* in Geneva (1980) has shown that this type of definition is not new but rather the same approach as that made by governments to the situation of the working class in Europe in the 19th century.

In some ways, this seems to be right (ensuring a living wage) but it is completely distorted, since the definition of needs as well as the definition of policies is drawn up outside the involved group, which is maintained in dependence, that is to say, in the impossibility of deciding, as far as its future is concerned.

A recent report on rural training in India (Shirastava and Tandom, 1982) has made these aspects clear by explaining that current official development programmes are characterised by the following elements:

i) No understanding of the economic, social, political and cultural bases of rural poverty.

ii) Technicians implement their programmes from the top without any prior analysis of the situation.

iii) In this strategy no importance is attached to the population living in rural areas; their role is limited to that of instrument for production.

iv) It is considered that it is the foreigners who are acquainted with the problems, and development is imposed from the top.

v) No concern for the distribution of power is apparent, which means that farmers are again excluded from it.

This definition of development by an Indian agriculture extensionist seems to be far more correct than all those given by the experts of the World Bank and other international organisations:

"The objective of development is to build up a human being with all his powers of reflection about himself and his real living conditions, to link him with others in a spirit of love and solidarity, to make alone one's decisions and to have confidence in oneself and in society (Shirastava and Tandom, 1982).

It will only be when farmers, and not experts, are asked to define 'development' that this word will acquire a meaning, not on a paper ensuring an expert's future, but in actual fact, which will finally enable farmers to be responsible for their future.

REFERENCES

Institut Universitaire d'Etudes de Developpment, 1980, *Il faut manger pour vivre* . . . . . , Paris.

Lele, Uma, 1979, *The Design of Rural Development*, Washington.

Shirastava, Om, and R. Tandom (eds.), 1982, *Participatory Training for Rural Development*, New Delhi.

St. Marijesse, 1982, Basic Needs, Income Distribution and the Political Economy of Rwanda. University of Antwerp (mimeographed).

World Bank, 1975, *Rural Development Sector Policy*, Washington.

CHAPTER 3

International Migration and Rural-Urban Balance

SCALE, PATTERN AND PROSPECTS

The number of people working outside their own countries is greater than is generally realised. Towards the end of the 1970s it was estimated at around 20 mn (World Bank, 1980). Of these, 6 mn were in the USA (mainly from Mexico) (Piore, 1979), 5 mn in Western Europe (mainly from Yugoslavia, Greece, Portugal, Spain, Turkey, Italy, Morocco, Tunisia and Algeria) (Paine, 1974; Bohning, 1979), and around 3 mn in the Arab region, particularly Saudi Arabia, Kuwait, Qatar, United Arab Emirates and Libya mainly from Egypt, Jordan, Yemen AR, Yemen PDR, the Sudan, Syria, India, Pakistan, South Korea, Taiwan and Bangladesh (Birks and Sinclair, 1979). In addition, there are longstanding migration systems in Southern Africa (to South Africa, from Lesotho, Botswana, Swaziland, Mozambique and until recently Malawi) (Colclough 1980) and Western Africa (to the Ivory Coast from Upper Volta, Mali, Benin and Guineas) (Amin, 1978).

The last two decades have seen great changes in levels and patterns of international migration. During the 1960s and early 1970s employers in the central economies, particularly those in labour-intensive industries, facing international competition, and those in the secondary sector of a dualistic labour market, facing difficulties in recruiting indigenous workers, enthusiastically recruited immigrant workers. For instance, the number of immigrants in the Western European labour force rose from 2 mn in the early 1960s to over 6 mn in the early 1970s.

Since then, however, there has been a drastic deterioration in the international labour market. Rates of economic growth in industrialised market economies have plummeted. Rates of inflation have increased and, most important for our topic, unemployment in the industrialised economies has risen to levels and rates unheard of since the 1930s; in the European Economic Community alone there were 10.7 mn out of work at the end of July 1982. At the same time large increases in the price of oil have unbalanced world trade and payments and generated excess demand for labour in oil-producing economies. As a result, growth rates in developing countries GDP and manufactured exports have begun to falter and net immigration into industrialised countries has fallen. Within Western Europe, for instance, the onset of recession, reducing the demand for immigrant labour, has coincided with the 'maturing' of the immigrant population, making it more difficult for employers to treat indigenous and immigrant labour as non-competing groups and more necessary for governments to increase provision of social infrastructure. The number of young Europeans entering the labour force has also been abnormally large. As unemployment has risen, political tensions, nurtured by right-wing organisations, have grown. During the 1970s, therefore, several European governments have followed a policy of 'stabilisation,' restricting new immigration, offering financial grants to those who wished to leave permanently and trying to integrate those who remained. The inflow of new immigrant workers has fallen dramatically; from 795,000 in 1973 to 141,000 in 1978 in West Germany, Belgium, France, Sweden, Switzerland and Austria. And in the five-year period 1974-78 more than $1\frac{1}{2}$ mn workers are estimated to have returned from Western Europe to their countries of origin (Lebon and Falchi, 1981). However, this has been offset by an increase in migration to the booming oil-producing countries. The stock of foreign workers in the Arab region alone is likely to have risen by more than a million between 1975 and 1981 (World Bank, 1981).

The prospects for future migration will tend to vary by type of destination. Although opinions differ about the outlook for economic growth in industrialised countries, it is realistic to expect that it will be considerably slower in the 1980s than it was in the 1970s (World Bank, 1982) and that un-employment will increase. If, as a result, wages in these countries increase more slowly and labour becomes more docile, this might be expected to further reduce the pressures behind the search for cheap labour. To an extent, having developed a sizeable reserve army of its own, central capital will have less need of an international reserve army. In addition, radical new developments in micro-electronic technology are expected by many researchers not only to erode the comparative advantage of peripheral surplus-labour economies in labour-intensive manufacturing, also to displace labour in industrialised economies, particularly in information-processing activities and generally in labour-intensive sectors (Hoffman and Rush, 1980; Kaplinsky, 1982). This can be expected to add to pressure for protection against imports and for control of immigration in industrialised countries. Europe will be additionally affected by the proposed enlargement of the European Economic Community during the 1980s to include Greece, Portugal and Spain, all of them labour-surplus economies (with 1.3 million migrant workers in the EEC in 1976) (Wedell, 1980). This suggests that while intra-EEC movement of labour may continue on a limited scale, the age of massive immigration into Western Europe is over.

In the capital-surplus oil-exporting countries, while the growth rate, though lower than it was, is expected to remain relatively high during the 1980s, there will be several new influences on their demand for immigrant labour (World Bank, 1979). The construction phase of their development is beginning to subside and demand for skilled workers, technicians and professionals is likely to grow in relative importance to that for unskilled and semi-skilled workers. At the same time, the number of unskilled and semi-skilled nationals of oil-producing countries entering the labour market is tending to increase. The demand for unskilled and semi-skilled immigrants is still likely to increase during the decade but at a slower rate, and a higher proportion is expected to come from South and Southeast Asian countries rather than other Arab countries. At high and middle manpower levels, however, where the bulk of the additional demand for immigrants is likely to be concentrated, the preference for Arabic speakers will still exert itself, to the detriment of workers from the poorer non-Arab States. Thus for any individual non-Arab economy the opportunities for exporting workers to the Arab region are likely to shrink, while some can actually expect a net return flow.

At any rate it is likely that the oil-producing economies of the Arab region will remain the most important destination for international migrants over the next ten years or so, although the flow of professionals from South to North (while much reduced from the peak levels of the early 1970s) is likely to remain significant.

Costs and Benefits of Exporting Workers

Before discussing the impact on rural-urban balance, it may be useful to undertake a brief general review of the broader costs and benefits of exporting workers, from the point of view of a low-income, labour-surplus economy.

If surplus unskilled workers are being exported, this should, by definition, have no effect on output in the labour-losing economy, but matters are rarely so simple. The proportion of totally unskilled migrants is likely to be smaller than expected; for instance, 62 per cent of foreign workers entering France between 1964 and 1968 were classified as skilled or semi-skilled (Ecevit and Zachariah, 1978: 34) and the comparable figure for Saudi Arabia in 1975 was 46 per cent (Ecevit and Zachariah, 1978: 37). Even when unskilled, a high proportion of migrants may be young males with key roles in the division of labour within the village economy; considerable reorganisation of work may be necessary to avoid a fall in output as a consequence of emigration. Thus the immediate costs of exporting workers may be higher than expected.

The benefits of strategy would be expected to come in two further stages, first through remittances and, later, returned migrants. The scale of emigrants' remittances as a source of foreign exchange has increased enormously over the past decade. By the end of the 1970s recorded remittances alone were estimated at around $ 24,000 mn, compared with less than $ 3,000 mn ten years earlier. For individual labour-exporting countries, the returns can be dazzling. For example, Yugoslavia alone received $ 1,728 mn from this source in 1976, equivalent to 22 per cent of its import bill. Yugoslavia is a relatively high-income country and at that time there were over 696,000 Yugoslavs working in Europe. equivalent to 16 per cent of those working in Yugoslavia. Lower-income labour-surplus economies such as Bangladesh can finance an even higher proportion of their foreign exchange obligations in this way from a much smaller proportion of their labour force. For instance, the 200,000 Bangladeshis working abroad in 1978-79 represented less than one per cent of the labour force, but their remittances of $ 180 mn were equivalent to around 40 per cent of the commercial import bill (Mahmood, 1981).

Again, however, all is not plain sailing. As migrants 'mature' (Bohning, 1972), lengthen their stay and are joined by their dependents, their propensity to remit tends to fall. Moreover, in market economies remittances can hardly be regarded as net additions to foreign exchange earnings available for socially optimal uses. Much is in the form of consumer goods rather than money; money remittances tend to be spent predominantly on consumer goods (usually with a high import content), housing, land and schooling. Clearly the lucky recipients benefit, but indirect effects may be negative. Appreciation of the exchange rate may affect the competitiveness of manufactured exports and the profitability of primary products. Land and other prices may rise and the demonstration effect of remittances may be strong. In areas where a high proportion of the labour force is abroad, this may come to be seen as the only route to higher incomes and spectacular consumption patterns, with a debilitating effect of the local economy.

Returned migrants might be expected to be an important source of skills to galvanise the rural and industrial economies to which they return. The extent to which this happens varies widely but in general experience has been disappointing. For instance, Piore reports of migrants into the United States that they 'have not been a significant source of industrial skills' for their home economies.

> The most skilled of the migrant workers are reluctant to return home. Those who do return often turn out to have acquired little in the way of industrial skills and are in any case, loth to enter in their home country the kinds of industries and occupations in which they worked abroad.

They also contribute further to the demonstration effect which their remittances have already generated.

Thus, if it is left to the free play of market forces, the strategy of exporting workers is likely to have a higher cost and to yield a smaller benefit in the short or medium term than a glance at the huge reserves of surplus labour available, the staggering figures of remittances and the apparent process of skill acquisition would suggest. In the longer run its impact on the productive capacity and rate of growth of the labour-exporting economy (as opposed to the consumption of some groups within that economy) may be minimal or even negative, tying the economy into chronic dependence on labour export rather than laying the basis for eventual growth towards full employment (Piore, 1979).

However, the stakes are too high to be rejected out of hand. There is a structured and centrally organised approach to exporting workers, pioneered by South Korea and much imitated by others, including the Philippines (with the slogan, the Philippines Overseas Employment Development Board 'delivers Filipino workers anywhere in the world') and even China. In the Korean version this involves construction and engineering contracts, using Korean contractors, materials, equipment and labour teams, thus maximising foreign exchange earnings in addition to workers' remittances. In the Chinese version, unskilled workers are employed by Italian corporations which pay a fee direct to the Chinese government which in turn pays the workers. Without going as far as this, governments of most labour-exporting countries now have schemes to encourage the channelling of at least some of the foreign exchange remittances into official hands. Such schemes, if efficiently devised and implemented, can go a long way towards making exporting workers a nationally profitable business. In short, there is a danger of expecting too much from a strategy of exporting workers. A well-managed migration policy, with remittances effectively channelled into productive investment, might well be a useful part of a *planned* development strategy. But this does not mean that emigrants' remittances and acquired skills will, in themselves, dynamise a stagnant economy. Indeed it may be more accurate in many cases to regard migrant workers as contributing primarily to the development of labour-importing countries.

Impact on Rural-Urban Balance: A Sri Lankan Survey

The best way to approach the question of impact on rural-urban balance may be through the statistics of a particular country. An official survey recently carried out in Sri Lanka will serve this purpose (Korale and Karunawathie, 1981). The survey was based mainly on the analysis of embarkation cards, which implies comprehensive coverage but some unreliability of detail (including probably a tendency to overstate occupational levels).

Table 3.1 summarises the distribution of migrants by occupational level and sex in 1979.

Table 3.1. Distribution of Migrants by Occupational Level and Sex, 1979

Occupational Level	Male		Female		Total	
	No.	%	No.	%	No.	%
High level	1,406	84.9	251	15.1	1,657	100.0
Middle level	1,993	84.0	381	16.0	2,374	100.0
Skilled	5,999	98.2	111	1.8	6,110	100.0
Unskilled	2,672	20.9	10,131	79.1	12,803	100.0
Not classified	1,563	53.3	1,368	46.7	2,931	100.0
Total	13,633	52.7	12,242	47.3	25,875	100.0

A notable aspect of the table is the high proportion of the migrants in the skilled and above categories—44 per cent of those for whom classifications are available. Interesting, also is the high proportion of female migrants, 93 per cent of them heading for jobs as housemaids. In contrast to females, thus concentrated in the unskilled category, only 13 per cent of males classified themselves as unskilled workers.

The majority of migrants described themselves as coming from urban rather than rural areas, as Table 3.2 shows, although this may reflect some temporary movement to urban areas during the process of recruitment.

Nearly 60 per cent of all migrants were from Colombo district, which provided even higher proportions *both* of high-level *and* of unskilled migrants. The proportion of housemaids from Colombo, at 64 per cent, was particularly high.

As for destination, 87 per cent (and an even higher proportion of the unskilled) were heading for the Arab region, as Table 3.3 shows.

Of the housemaids, 96 per cent went to the Arab region, particularly Kuwait. However, a more varied range of destinations is obviously still available to those in high-level occupations, including Africa and the traditional Northern destinations, particularly the UK.

All categories of workers considerably improve their financial position by emigrating, as the rough estimates of salary ranges in Table 3.4 show.

Finally, Table 3.5 shows the extraordinary scale of remittances from Sri Lanka's migrant workers—Rs 2,518 mn in 1980, equivalent to 14 per cent of export earnings in 1980 and 7 per cent of the import bill.

Of the remittances, 39 per cent came from the Arab region (which took 87 per cent of migrants in 1979). but substantial proportions are still accounted for by the USA (15 per cent), the UK (15 per cent) and West Germany (rise per cent), the predominant residences of expatriate Sri Lankan professionals (which took only two per cent of migrants in 1979). Sixty-two per cent of remittances are for the maintenance of relatives but 21 per cent are in the form of assets.

Interestingly, the category which apparently enjoys the biggest increase in salary as a result of migration is housemaids, which helps to explain the long queue of women looking for this kind of overseas work.

The cross-section picture of Sri Lankan migrants given by these tables is that, apart from the special category of housemaids, they are predominantly males in skilled and higher occupations. Most of them are from urban areas. Apart from professionals who retain their link with Europe and North America, most of them go to the Arab region. The private rate of return to migration is likely to be high, perhaps particularly so for housemaids. Professionals appear to account for a disproportionate share of remit-

Table 3.2. Distribution of Migrants by Occupational Level and District (1979:

District	High Level		Middle Level		Skilled		Unskilled		Not Classified		Total	
	No.	%	No.	%	No.	%	No.	%	No.	%	No.	%
1. Colombo	1,080	65.2	1,392	58.6	2,920	47.8	7,863	61.4	1,652	56.4	14,907	57.6
2. Gambaha	155	9.3	390	16.4	946	15.5	2,146	16.8	453	15.5	4,090	15.8
3. Kalutara	40	2.4	95	4.0	290	4.7	438	3.4	127	4.3	990	3.8
4. Kandy	69	4.2	83	3.5	263	4.3	484	3.8	129	4.4	1,028	4.0
5. Matale	12	0.7	26	1.1	73	1.2	106	0.8	15	0.5	232	1.0
6. Nurawa Eliya	03	0.2	11	0.5	47	0.8	36	0.3	14	0.5	111	0.4
7. Galle	24	1.4	49	2.0	460	7.5	370	2.9	104	3.6	1,007	4.0
8. Matera	06	0.4	17	0.7	111	1.8	87	0.7	33	1.1	254	1.0
9. Hambantota	05	0.3	02	0.1	32	0.5	123	1.0	21	0.7	183	0.7
10. Jaffna	159	9.6	148	6.2	355	5.8	266	2.1	115	3.9	1,043	4.0
11. Mannar	02	0.1	05	0.2	04	0.1	14	0.1	01	0.	26	0.1
12. Vavuniya	–	–	04	0.2	03	0.1	07	0.	01	0.	15	0.1
13. Mullaitivu	–	–	–		01	0.	01	0.	01	0.00	03	0.
14. Batticaloa	11	0.7	16	0.7	30	0.5	20	0.2	13	0.4	90	0.4
15. Ampara	07	0.4	05	0.2	30	0.5	13	0.1	07	0.2	62	0.2
16. Trincomalea	04	0.2	07	0.3	37	0.6	52	0.4	34	1.2	134	0.5
17. Kurunegala	23	1.4	30	1.2	115	1.9	139	1.1	34	1.2	341	1.3
18. Puttalam	13	0.8	23	1.0	79	1.3	124	1.0	29	1.0	268	1.0
19. Anuradhapura	–	–	04	0.2	14	0.2	31	0.2	12	0.4	61	0.2

20. Polonnaruwa	—	—	03	0.1	04	0.1	03	0.	—	—	10	0.
21. Badulla	03	0.2	12	0.5	36	0.6	74	0.6	23	0.8	150	0.6
22. Moneragala	—	—	—	—	07	0.1	03	0.	01	0.	11	0.
23. Patnapura	05	0.3	08	0.3	35	0.6	33	0.3	08	0.3	89	0.3
24. Kegalle	03	0.2	16	0.7	68	1.1	145	1.1	20	0.7	252	1.0
25. Address illegible	12	0.7	06	0.3	55	0.9	59	0.4	32	1.1	164	0.6
26. Address not stated	21	1.3	22	1.0	93	1.5	166	1.3	52	1.8	354	1.4
Total	1,657	100.0	2,374	100.0	6,110	100.0	12,803	100.0	2,931	100.0	25,875	100.0

Table 3.3. Distribution of Migrants by Occupational Level and Country of Destination

Country/Region	High Level		Middle Level		Skilled		Unskilled		Not Classified		Total	
	No.	%	No.	%	No.	%	No.	%	No.	%	No.	%
Middle East	544	32.9	1,743	73.5	5,171	84.6	11,502	89.9	2,020	69.0	20,980	81.0
Saudi Arabia	164	9.9	602	25.4	2,373	38.8	1,711	13.4	515	17.6	5,365	20.7
United Arab Emirates	126	7.6	444	18.7	620	10.1	3,032	23.7	422	14.4	4,644	18.0
Kuwait	31	1.9	136	5.7	225	3.7	4,303	33.6	465	15.9	5,160	19.9
Bahrain	50	3.0	171	7.2	344	5.6	1,158	9.1	354	12.1	2,077	8.0
Qatar	13	0.8	40	1.7	191	3.1	714	5.6	102	3.5	1,060	4.1
Oman	109	6.6	246	10.4	541	8.9	326	2.5	106	3.6	1,328	5.1
Other Middle Eastern Countries	51	3.1	104	4.4	877	14.4	258	2.0	56	1.9	1,346	5.2
Africa	316	19.0	41	1.8	—	—	01	0.	17	0.5	375	1.4
Nigeria	163	9.8	17	0.7	—	—	01	0.	03	0.1	184	0.7
Zambia	104	6.3	18	0.8	—	—	—	—	10	0.3	132	0.5
Other African Countries	49	2.9	06	0.3	—	—	—	—	04	0.1	59	0.2
Selected Countries												
Federal Republic of Germany	06	0.4	08	0.3	—	—	01	0.	08	0.3	23	0.1
United Kingdom	308	18.6	112	4.7	03	0.	31	0.2	39	1.3	493	2.0

United States of America	22	1.3	03	0.1	—	—	—	—	08	0.3	33	0.1
All Other Countries	318	19.2	302	12.7	474	7.8	537	4.2	586	20.0	2,217	8.6
Destination not stated	143	8.6	165	6.9	462	7.6	731	5.7	253	8.6	1,754	6.8
Total	1,657	100.0	2,374	100.0	6,110	100.0	12,803	100.0	2,931	100.0	25,875	100.0

Table 3.4. Comparison of Salaries in Sri Lanka and the Middle East, 1979
(Rupees per month)

	Sri Lanka	Middle East	Ratio of Median: Middle East/ Sri Lanka
Doctors	750—3500	15,000—25,000	9.4
Engineers	750—3500	10,000—15,000	5.9
Accountants	750—3500	12,000—20,000	7.5
Technicians	450—1000	3,000— 7,000	6.9
Clerks/Typists	250— 800	2,500— 5,000	7.1
Nurses	250— 800	2,500— 3,500	5.7
Drivers	200— 500	2,500— 5,000	10.7
Carpenters	250— 600	3,000— 5,000	9.4
Masons	250— 600	3,000— 5,000	9.4
Mechanics	250— 600	3,000— 5,000	9.4
Cooks	200— 500	2,000— 3,000	7.1
Waiters	100— 250	1,500— 2,500	11.4
Housemaids	50— 150	1,500— 2,500	20.0
Labourers	200— 400	1,000— 2,500	5.8

Source: Ruhunage, 1979.

tances.

If we add to this picture the tendency, noted in other countries, for remittances to be spent on consumer goods, housing, land and schooling, and for skills acquired abroad to be put to little effective use on return (both of which are hypotheses awaiting research in the Sri Lankan case), the implications for rural/ urban balance and for income distribution in general are not particularly encouraging.

Those who do emigrate from rural areas are likely to be from the upper echelons of income and asset distribution, to judge from the occupational composition. Thus the first-round effects of remittances are unlikely to improve intra-rural income distribution. The predominance of urban high and middle level emigrants is likely to stretch both intra-urban and urban-rural differentials as a result of remittances. Shortages of skilled workers, primarily urban-based, might be expected to widen personal income differentials as *scarcity rents* emerge.

Although there is an urgent need for government action to

reduce their vulnerability and to counteract the impact on children of single-parent families, the distributional effect of the emigration of housemaids is likely to be positive. They are predominantly from urban areas but are from one of the lowest income groups with most to gain (proportionately) from migration.

The nature of the 'subsequent-rounds' effects of remittances and of the longer-run returned-migrant effect will depend very much on the nature of the underlying process in the labour-exporting economy. In many such economies market forces are allowed to exert a powerful disequalising effect. As ownership of assets, particularly land, becomes more concentrated and as the higher paid exert their power to purchase more effective education and training, which secure continuing access for their families to the upper reaches of the wage and salary structure or to the professions, and as modern-sector employment grows relatively slowly, whole sections of the population may be *excluded* from the possibility of earning an adequate income, with the landless and the unemployed as the extreme cases.

There is a tendency in this situation for the already better-off individuals and districts to gain differential advantage from almost *any* new development, e.g., technological change such as the 'green revolution,' a government agricultural extension programme, an increase in educational expenditure, an improvement in commodity prices—and the sudden massive inflow of remittances from emigrant workers. The government can intervene either to *counteract* this disequalising process or to *reinforce* it. The long-run impact of international migration will largely depend on which course the government takes and with what effect.

A Note on the Effects of Brain Drain on Rural-Urban Imbalance

The emigration of professionals not only has implications for the incomes of the emigrants and their families, but also affects the welfare of those who thus lose the benefit of their services and products. *Given the existing job definitions of most professionals*, which are related to the pattern of effective demand in cities (e.g., for designers and builders of high-cost mortgage housing and curative hospital-based medical workers) and not be the pattern of need, the rural poor probably have little to lose from the international brain drain. It is, after all, only the operation at the

Table 3.5. Foreign Inward Remittances Classified by Purpose and Country—1980 (Rps 000)

Country/Region	Col. 1	Col. 2	Col. 3	Col. 4	Col. 5	Col. 6	Col. 7	Col. 8	Col. 9	Col. 10
United Arab Emirates	70,054	6,879	5,354	82,287	40	82,327	1,148	83,475	4.7	117,580
Saudi Arabia	273,784	31,013	26,481	331,278	155	331,433	1,331	332,764	18.6	467,731
Bahrain	23,542	4,150	1,798	29,490	—	29,490	04	29,494	1.6	41,104
Kuwait	112,234	6,987	7,500	126,721	58	126,779	102	126,881	7.1	178,401
Oman	37,224	5,180	2,979	45,383	27	45,410	64	45,474	2.5	63,615
Qatar	12,681	4,968	942	18,591	—	18,591	06	18,597	1.0	25,853
Iraq	5,624	1,234	867	7,715	—	7,715	—	7,715	0.4	10,618
Iran	2,105	616	568	3,289	—	3,289	—	3,289	0.2	4,740
Other Middle Eastern Countries	33,918	10,710	4,909	49,537	41	49,578	329	49,907	2.8	70,225
Sub Total	571,166	71,737	51,388	694,291	321	694,612	2,984	697,596	38.9	979,867
Nigeria	12,446	2,548	1,356	16,350	—	16,350	13	16,363	0.9	22,894
Zambia	3,495	1,386	1,232	6,113	—	6,113	—	6,113	0.3	8,290
Kenya	637	387	181	1,205	—	1,205	03	1,208	0.1	1,934
Other African Countries	3,744	1,545	537	5,826	—	5,826	01	5,827	0.3	8,004
Sub Total	20,322	5,866	3,306	29,494	—	29,494	17	29,511	1.6	41,122
Canada	11,601	3,695	3,807	19,103	105	19,208	3,156	22,364	1.3	31,797
United States of America	122,536	93,854	24,711	241,101	198	241,299	32,050	273,349	15.3	384,370

	1	2	3	4	5	6	7	8	9	10
United Kingdom	128,322	90,946	33,680	252,948	620	253,568	8,045	261,613	14.6	367,555
West Germany	76,645	27,524	33,705	137,874	218	138,092	18,624	156,716	8.7	219,846
East Germany	44	—	07	51	—	51	—	51	0.	66
India	4,385	2,617	708	7,710	371	8,081	924	9,005	0.5	12,633
Maldives	1,494	999	73	2,566	—	2,566	04	2,570	0.1	3,296
Singapore	20,554	8,740	4,118	33,412	16	33,428	1,132	34,560	1.9	48,347
Hong Kong	9,624	12,293	837	22,754	131	22,885	—	22,885	1.3	32,318
Japan	7,716	5,086	2,446	15,248	—	15,248	117	15,365	0.9	21,896
Australia	14,686	8,325	4,972	27,983	92	28,075	1,701	29,776	1.7	42,112
All Other Countries	120,815	37,430	32,729	190,974	642	191,616	45,392	237,008	13.2	332,791
Sub Total	518,422	291,509	141,793	951,724	2,393	954,117	111,145	1,065,262	59.5	1,497,027
Total	1,109,910	369,112	196,487	1,675,509	2,714	1,678,223	114,146	1,792,369	100.0	2,518,016

Key: Column 1 = Personal voluntary remittances for the maintenance of dependents
Column 2 = Transfer of assets
Column 3 = Other private donations, gifts
Column 4 = Total of Column 1, Column 2 and Column 3
Column 5 = Money order remittances, migrants transfers and private transfers for the purchase of motor vehicles
Column 6 = Total of Column 4 and Column 5
Column 7 = Private transfers for all other purposes
Column 8 = Total of Column 6 and Column 7
Column 9 = Relative share of the country (%)
Column 10 = Estimated value of foreign inward remittances

international level of the principle of supremacy of demand over need which already operates at the national level. Those who emigrate are not, on the whole, experts in eco-systems in low rainfall areas, small farm technology, basic food crops, pastoralism, nutrition, rural water supply, low-cost housing and preventive health care. Indeed most training systems produce few persons in these categories and the structure of most government services means that few could be absorbed if they were produced. This does *not* necessarily imply that producing, professionals for export makes sense as a national policy—merely that, until the content of training and the pattern of demand are reoriented, rural/urban balance may be, if anything, improved by government *not* trying to retain them or to attract them back home.

REFERENCES

Amin, S., 1978, *Unequal Development*, Harvester Press, Brighton.

Birks, J.S. and C. Sinclair, 1979, *International Migration Development in the Arab Region*, ILO, Geneva.

Bohning, W.R., 1972, *The Migration of Workers in the United Kingdom and the European Community*, Oxford University Press, Oxford.

————1979, 'International Migration in Western Europe: Reflections on the past five years,' *International Labour Review*, vol. 118, no. 4.

Colclough, C., 1980, 'Some aspects of labour use in Southern Africa—problems and policies,' *Bulletin* vol. 11, no. 4. IDS, Sussex, pp. 29-39.

Ecevit, Z. and K.C. Zachariah, 1978, 'International labour migration,' *Finance and Development* vol. 15, no. 4, pp. 32-7.

Hoffman, K. and H. Rush, 1980, 'Microelectronics, Industry and the Third World,' SPRU, University of Sussex (mimeographed).

Kaplinsky, R., 1982, *Computer-Aided Design Electronics, Comparative Advantage and Development*, Frances Pinter, London.

Korale, R.B.M. and I.M. Karunawathie, 1981, *Migration of Sri Lankans for Employment Abroad*, Employment and Manpower Planning Division, Ministry of Plan Implementation, Sri Lanka.

Lebon, A., and G. Falchi, 1981, 'New developments in intra-European migration since 1974,' *International Migration Review*, vol. 14, no. 4.

Mahmood, R.A., 1981, 'Migrants' Remittances as a Source of Foreign Exchange—the Experience of Bangladesh', IDS, Sussex (mimeographed).

Paine, S., 1974, *Exporting Workers: The Turkish Case*, Cambridge University Press, Cambridge.

Piore, M.J., 1979, *Birds of Passage: Migrant Labour and Industrial Societies*, Cambridge University Press, Cambridge.

Ruhunage, L.K., 1979, 'Migration of Sri Lankans to Middle Eastern Countries,' Ministry of Plan Implementation, Colombo.

Wedell, G., 1980, 'The enlargement of the European Community: implications for employment and free movement of labour,' in J.W. Schneider (ed.) *From Nine to Twelve: Europe's Destiny?* Sijthoff & Noordhoff, Alphen aan den Rijn, Netherlands.

World Bank, 1979, 'Research Project on Labour Migration and Manpower in the Middle East and North Africa,' *Interim Report*, Washington, December.

————1980, *Annual Report*.

————1981, *World Development Report*.

————1982, *World Development Report*.

CHAPTER 4

'Why Growth Rates Differ' within India:
An Alternative Approach

1. INTRODUCTION

This article is devoted to an explanation of variations in growth rates in India during the past three decades, both over time and across regions. There are essentially five types of approaches to this theme which can be discerned in the literature. The one from which the title of this article has been borrowed is based on Edward Denison's two major works (1962, 1967). It rests upon decomposition of growth into its sources, making use of the neo-classical marginal productivity theory of distribution. The second approach which is made use of, often implicitly, stems from Harrod's growth model (1948). In this approach, growth rates are explained in terms of the saving rate at the capital-output ratio. The third approach is that of Kaldor (1966), whose focus is on explaining performance in the manufacturing sector, which is taken to play a key role in determining overall growth rate. Irma Adelman and Cynthia Taft Morris (1967) have used factor analysis to study the role of a large number of socio-economic variables in economic development. And finally, Mancur Olson (1982, 1983) draws upon certain institutional attributes to explain variations in growth performance.

This article follows somewhat a different path from these approaches although many ideas in it have been imbibed from these works. The theme 'Why Growth Rates Differ' is viewed here from two angles, the first of which we call the 'Sources of Growth' approach and second the 'Determinants of Growth' approach. These are derived from the attributes of steady growth and its adaptation to non-steady character of the development process. In the first mode of approach the national and regional growth rates are decomposed into contribution made by a few basic sources of growth. While the 'Sources of Growth' approach as developed here shares with Denison the element of growth decomposition, the conceptual framework utilised for the purpose is a different one. We confine our attention to only three basic sources of growth but focus much more on the sectoral aspect. Moreover, estimation of source-wise contributions by itself cannot tell us much about the relationship of different sources to the rate of growth unless one goes a step further and studies association between variations in the contribution of different sources and corresponding variations in the rate of growth.

While the 'Sources of Growth' approach sheds valuable light on the pattern of growth at the national and regional levels, it does not go very far in pinpointing factors which might be considered to play a key role in determining the pace of development. We identify four sets of variables as determinants of the pace of development. Their role is then assessed empirically at two levels. First, it is assessed at the national level by correlating time series of the identified variables and of the national rates of growth of output. Second, their role is investigated by correlating regional values of the identified variables and the rates of growth of regional output.

Growth Rates Over Time and Space

First, a synoptic view of the factual record of growth of output, employment and productivity from 1951 to 1981 at the national and regional levels is presented here. Two points emerge from the decadal growth rates at the national level as given in Table 1.[1]

Table 1. All-India Sectoral Growth Rates

	1950s	1960s	1970s	1951-81
Primary sector	2.79	2.19	1.63	2.20
Secondary sector	6.05	5.29	4.21	5.18
Tertiary sector	4.82	4.98	5.09	4.96
Overall economy	3.81	3.55	3.30	3.55

Table 2. Growth Rates of Output, Employment and Productivity (1951-81)

	Overall			Primary Sector			Secondary Sector			Tertiary Sector		
	O	E	P	O	E	P	O	E	P	O	E	P
Andhra Pradesh	2.98 X	2.33	0.63	1.95 XI	2.32	−0.36	4.65 VII	2.04	2.56	3.94 VIII	2.56	1.35
Assam-Meghalaya	3.29 VI	2.41	0.86	2.00 X	2.25	−0.24	4.07 IX	2.95	1.09	5.54 I	3.01	2.45
Bihar	3.14 VII	2.12	1.00	2.04 VIII	1.91	0.13	4.74 VI	4.00	0.71	4.11 VII	2.47	1.60
Gujarat	3.46 V	2.47	0.96	2.54 III	2.34	0.19	4.77 V	3.04	1.68	3.76 XI	2.40	1.33
Kerala	3.01 IX	2.00	0.99	1.77 XIV	1.50	0.27	3.83 XII	2.57	1.23	4.65 V	2.52	2.08
Madhya Pradesh	2.91 XII	2.04	0.85	1.86 XII	1.84	0.02	4.35 VIII	2.46	1.85	3.79 IX	2.82	0.95
Maharashtra	4.30 II	2.16	2.10	2.94 II	1.77	1.16	5.14 III	3.06	2.02	4.73 IV	2.41	2.27
Karnataka	3.63 IV	2.51	1.09	2.40 V	2.38	0.02	4.82 IV	2.70	2.07	4.98 III	2.86	2.06
Orissa	2.93 XI	2.02	0.89	2.29 VI	2.05	0.24	3.89 XI	2.30	1.57	4.30 VI	1.74	2.52
Punjab-Haryana	4.49 I	2.08	2.36	3.71 I	1.90	1.78	6.05 I	3.63	2.34	5.32 II	1.83	3.17

	O	E	P	O	E	P	O	E	P	O	E	P
Rajasthan	3.07 VIII	2.02	1.03	2.53 IV	1.95	0.57	3.05 XIV	2.10	0.93	4.01 VIII	2.23	1.74
Tamil Nadu	3.67 III	2.42	1.21	2.20 VII	2.22	−0.01	5.19 II	3.03	2.10	3.37 XII	2.51	1.81
Uttar Pradesh	2.42 XIV	1.52	0.89	2.03 IX	1.64	0.38	4.07 X	1.54	2.50	2.65 XIV	0.90	1.73
West Bengal	2.53 XIII	2.17	0.36	1.80 XIII	2.39	−0.58	3.18 XIII	2.36	0.80	2.91 XIII	1.58	1.31
Average	3.31	2.08	1.20	2.32	1.98	0.34	4.58	2.61	1.92	4.08	2.11	1.91

Notes: O: Output   E: Employment   P: Productivity

(1) Roman numerals indicate state ranks.

(2) These states account for over 90 per cent of the national output. Tables 1 and 2, however, are not strictly comparable, for Table 1 is based on the CSO (Central Statistical Organisation) data while Table 2 is derived from SSB (State Statistical Bureaux) and NCAER (National Council of Applied Economic Research) data. Punjab-Haryana and Assam-Meghalaya are treated as one unit each on account of data problems. References in the text to Punjab and Assam pertain to these combined units.

For the period 1950-51 to 1980-1981 as a whole, the secondary sector has grown the fastest, followed by the tertiary and primary sectors. The primary and the secondary sectors reveal a tendency towards retardation in their decadal rates of growth.[2] The services sector registered an acceleration, but its offsetting effect was insufficient to prevent a retardation in the overall rate of growth.

The regional analysis is conducted in terms of 14 major states of India for which it is possible to build up relevant series going back to 1950-51. Compound rates of growth of output, employment (male work force) and output per (male) worker for the period 1951-1981 are given for each state as also for each sector in Table 2.[3] Punjab, Maharashtra, Tamil Nadu and Karnataka emerge as states with the four highest rates of aggregate output growth.

We now turn to composite regional performance in terms of growth of output, employment and productivity per worker. In order to comprehend simultaneously the behaviour of all these variables, we make use of an adaptation of a graphical technique which Walter Isard (1960) has proposed for the study of regional industrialisation. The Y-axis (Diagram 1) measures the average annual rate of output growth during period under consideration plus 100 per cent. O_y depicts zero rate of growth while the origin O depicts—100 per cent rate of growth. Scale of measurement below O_y is kept 1/100th of that above it, for use of a uniform of scale would cluster the observations within a tiny segment of the graph. Similarly X-axis depicts growth rate of employment plus 100 per cent. O_x represents zero rate of growth of employment. Scale to its left is 1/100th of that to its right.

A point on this graph depicts the rates of growth of output and employment (plus 100 per cent) of a region. It can be shown that when the axes represent growth variables in the form indicated above, the slope of radius vector of any point shall depict proportional growth of productivity per worker (plus unity) in a region.[4] The intersection of LL' & MM' at A depicts the average national rates of growth of output and employment (plus 100 per cent). The slope of OAP measures the national pace of growth of productivity (plus unity) while slope of OP' (45° line) indicates zero rate of growth of productivity.

In this diagram one can demarcate six zones. Zones above MM' show a superior composite growth performance than those below it, for the former zones (I, II and III) reflect an above-average performance in at least two variables while the latter (IV, V and VI) reveal an above-average performance in only one variable at the most. Within the former group, zone I depicts most dynamic growth, for it contains regions where rates of growth of output, employment and productivity have all been above the national average. As between regions in zones II and III, it is not possible to give a value free ranking, for among them there is a trade-off between productivity and employment growth in relation to their national averages. For the same reason, zones IV and VI within the worse-off group cannot be ranked. But they are both better-off than zone V where performance in all three variables is below the national average. Thus the regional hierarchy of composite growth performance can be put as zone I > (II, III) > (IV, VI) > V.

Graph 1(a) portrays composite growth performance in terms of the three variables for overall economy of each region while Graphs 1(b)-1(d) portray performance in primary, secondary and tertiary sectors during 1951-81. As may be observed from Graph 1(a), the states of Maharashtra and Punjab appear in the most dynamic zone (I). Karnataka, Gujarat and Tamil Nadu (zone II) also reveal an above-average performance except in respect of productivity. Andhra Pradesh, Assam, Bihar and West Bengal reveal an above-average performance only in employment expansion. The remaining states figure in the least dynamic zone (V). In the secondary sector (Graph 1c), Maharashtra, Tamil Nadu, Punjab and Karnataka appear in the zone of most dynamic industrial growth (zone I).

II. 'THE SOURCES OF GROWTH': A SUGGESTED FORMAT

The sources of growth analysis as developed here draws upon three characteristics of the process of development, when viewed in terms of the theory of steady growth.[5] First, economic development cannot be brought about through simple steady growth of the type associated with the original von Neumann model (1945) in which all inputs expand at the same rate, for the proportion

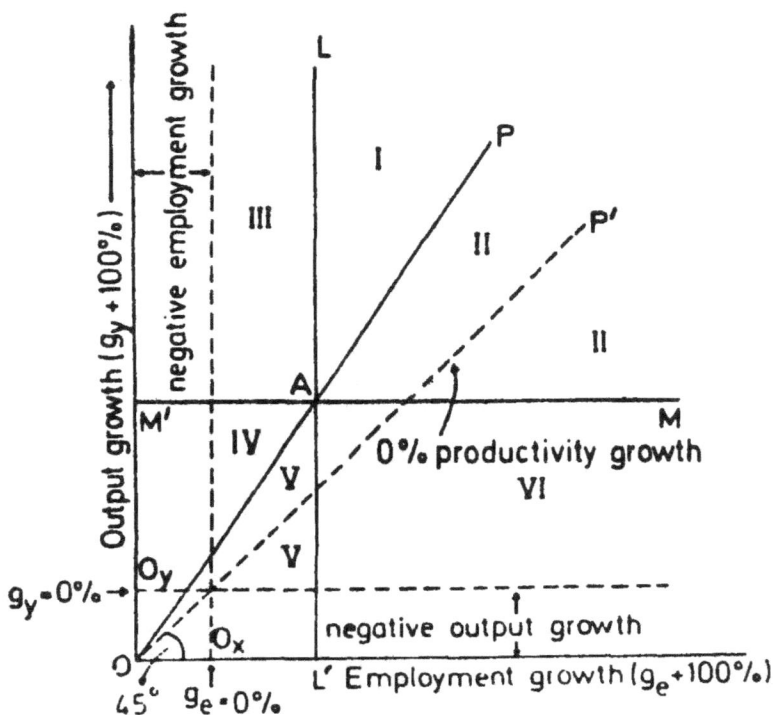

Diagram 1

and range of inputs needed in an underdeveloped economy and a technologically advanced economy are different. Development involves a faster pace of expansion of inputs needed for technological transformation of the economy towards an advanced economic system. Second, since most of the technologically superior inputs are produced in processes belonging to the secondary and tertiary sectors, it helps in bringing about a structural shift towards these two sectors, which is also a basic feature of economic development associated with the works of Colin Clark and Simon Kuznets. Third, it results in a rising level of average productivity per worker as well as of capital per worker. However, changes in these two variables are not brought about through operation of the law of variable proportions as in the neo-classical theory, but through a progressive shift from primitive to technologically advanced processes in the overall structure of the economy.

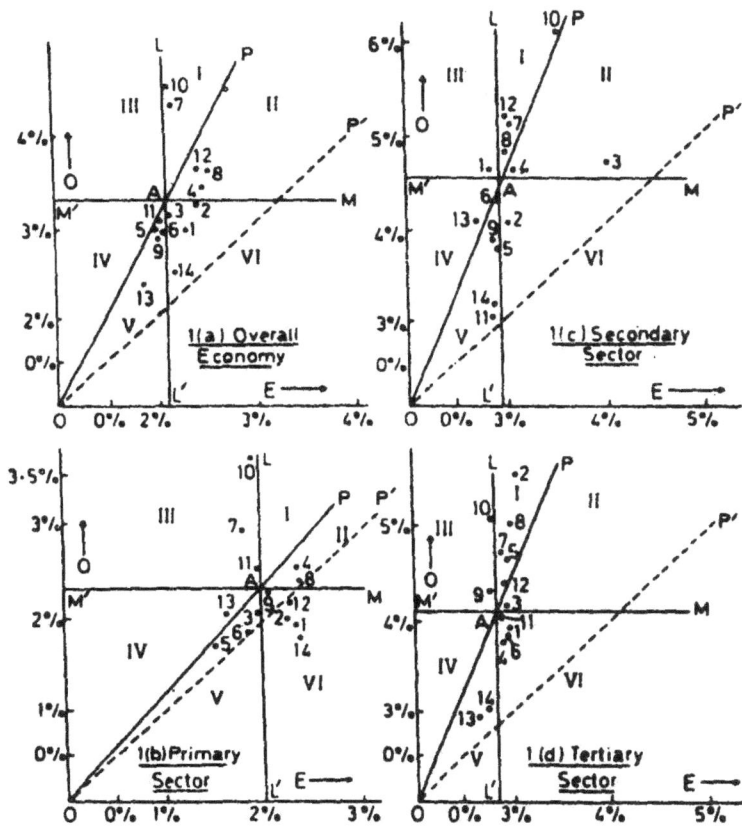

Graph I: Composite regional growth performance.

1 Andhra Pradesh 2 Assam 3 Bihar 4 Gujarat 5 Kerala 6 Madhya Pradesh
7 Maharashtra 8 Karnataka 9 Orissa 10 Punjab-Haryana 11 Rajasthan
12 Tamil Nadu 13 Uttar Pradesh 14 West Bengal

NOTE : While the axes measure $(g_e \cdot 100\%)$ ∩ $(g_y \cdot 100\%)$, the percentage
figures shown on the axes indicate the g_e ∩ g_y components of
$(g_e + 100\%)$ ∩ $(g_y + 100\%)$

The path of development is thus of a non-steady character,
but it can be viewed as being composed of a steady and a non-
steady component. We shall first elucidate the sources in a steady
growth state, as we see it. Under steady growth state an economic
system, at any level of technology, expands through joint effort
of all inputs used in it, and all inputs as also national income

expand at the same rate. As productivity levels in each process and proportional distribution of labour as well as other inputs among processes remain the same, all growth is contributed by expansion in the supply of inputs alone. But, as among the inputs, growth of output cannot be apportioned separately to different inputs. Entire growth in a steady growth state can thus be designated as the contribution of labour in conjunction with capital and other inputs.

However, once we cross into the threshold of non-steady growth, this picture undergoes a transformation. Technological change brought about through progressive intrusion of the high productivity processes results in a pattern of growth in which capital-labour ratio as also productivity per worker increase and distribution of labour and other resources shift towards sectors with higher productivity per worker. Thus growth of output associated with the process of development can be viewed as being composed of three distinct components.

a) The first is that part of growth in output which would materialise if productivity and sectoral distribution of labour were to stay at their initial level and employment were to expand at the same rate as that of output. This component can be characterised as the steady growth contribution of labour, in association with capital and other inputs, to total output growth for it conforms to basic characteristics of steady growth.

b) The second and third components of output growth can be ascribed to two sources associated with non-steady character of the development process. The first one among these pertains to contribution made by increase in productivity per worker. Since this is brought about essentially through higher input of capital per worker associated with shift to superior techniques, the role of capital deepening as a source of growth appears as a part of growth in output contributed by productivity increase.[6] Capital does not appear in our analysis as a separate source. This does not imply downgrading the role of capital accumulation in growth. But its contribution is viewed as being composed of two components. The base widening aspect of capital accumulation forms an inextricable component of the first source discussed above. The role of capital accumulation as the vehicle of technological change, which brings about a rise in capital-labour ratio, forms a part of the second source, which is under discussion. Technological change as measured here incorporates the effect on productivity of improvements in technique under a given state of knowledge as well as those arising out of new accretions to knowledge (cf. Kaldor, 1967).

c) Our third source is the increase in output contributed by change in the sectoral structure of labour force towards high productivity sectors.

We now turn to measurement of the contribution of these three basic sources to growth of output. In order to measure the contribution of the first source one has to compare initial sectoral output with the hypothetical level of output in each sector which would come about at the terminal level of aggregate employment if one assumed that its sectoral distribution and productivity stayed at their initial level. The difference between the two would yield an estimate of the contribution made by this source in each sector. Similarly in order to measure the contribution of increase in productivity, one would have to estimate that hypothetical level of output which would materialise if technological processes were those used in the terminal period, but the aggregate employment and its sectoral distribution were taken to be that of the initial period. And for estimating contribution of the third source, namely, structural change, the hypothetical level of output to be estimated would be that based on the terminal employment structure but initial aggregate employment and sectoral productivity levels. As in case of the first source, the difference between sectoral estimates of these two hypothetical output levels and the initial sectoral output would give the contribution of the second and third sources respectively. But the contribution of these three sources would not generally add up to the actual output growth, for there is also an interaction among them.

This estimation procedure may now be expressed mathematically. Let the initial aggregate domestic income and employment be denoted by Y (1) and L (I). $S_i(1)$, $T_i(1)$ and $Y_i(1)$ depict the initial proportion of labour employed in sector i, productivity per worker in sector i and domestic income of sector i. i = 1, 2, 3 represent primary, secondary and tertiary sectors. It can be seen that:

$$Y(1) = \sum_i^3 Y_i(1) = L(1). \sum_i^3 S_i(1). T_i(1) \tag{1}$$

The values of these variables in the terminal period (n) would be:

$$Y_i(n) = Y_i(1) + \triangle Y_i \qquad (2a)$$
$$T_i(n) = T_i(1) + \triangle T_i \qquad (2b)$$
$$S_i(n) = S_i(1) + \triangle S_i \qquad (2c)$$
$$L(n) = L(1) + \triangle L \qquad (2d)$$

Domestic product in the terminal period can be expressed as:

$$Y(n) = \sum_i^3 Y_i(n) = L(n). \sum_i^3 S_i(n). T_i(n) \qquad (3)$$

By substituting (2a) to 2 (d) in (3) and expanding, we get:

$$Y(n) = L(1). \sum_i^3 S_i(1). T_i(1) + \triangle L. \sum_i^3 T_i(1). S_i(1) +$$

$$L(1). \sum_i^3 \triangle T_i . S_i(1) + L(1). \sum_i^3 \triangle S_i . T_i(1)$$

$$+ [\triangle L . \sum_i^3 T_i(1). \triangle S_i + L(1) . \sum_i^3 \triangle T_i . \triangle S_i + \triangle L .$$

$$\sum_i^3 S_i(1) . \triangle T_i + \triangle L . \sum_i^3 \triangle S_i \triangle T_i] \qquad (4)$$

Subtracting (1) from (4) we get:

$$\triangle Y = \triangle L . \sum_i^3 T_i(1) . S_i(1) + L(1) .$$

$$\sum_i^3 \triangle T_i . S_i(1) + L(1) . \sum_i^3 \triangle S_i . T_i(1)$$

$$+ [\triangle L . \sum_i^3 T_i(1) . \triangle S_i + L(1).$$

$$\sum_i^3 \triangle T_i . \triangle S_i + \triangle L . \sum_i^3 S_i(1) .$$

$$\triangle T_i + \triangle L . \sum_i^3 \triangle S_i . \triangle T_i] \qquad (5)$$

Using notation which is self-evident, this equation may be abridged as:

$$\Delta Y = \sum_i^3 K_{1i} + \sum_i^3 K_{2i} + \sum_i^3 K_{3i} + \sum_i^3 K_{4i} \qquad (6)$$

This equation gives the decomposition of increase in output among four components. $\sum_i^3 K_{1i}$ gives steady growth contribution of labour, in association with complementary inputs, to overall growth. $\sum_i^3 K_{2i}$ gives contribution of technological change as reflected in productivity growth, $\sum_i^3 K_{3i}$ gives contribution of structural change and $\sum_i^3 K_{4i}$ gives contribution of interaction effect. In a similar fashion one can express the contribution of these sources to growth within each sector:[7]

$$\Delta Y_i = K_{1i} + K_{2i} + K_{3i} + K_{4i} \qquad (7)$$

Contribution of the Sources to National and Regional Growth in India

Based on the decomposition scheme derived above, Table 3 shows percentage contribution of the three sources and their interaction to growth in the national economy. For the three-decade period, the steady growth contribution of labour works out to be the highest (45.7 per cent) followed by that of technological change (28.0 per cent). Structural change contributed very little (0.6 per cent), but the interaction term accounted for a sizeable contribution (25.8 per cent).

As among the sectors, labour's contribution stands the highest (86.9 per cent) within the primary sector. The contribution of technological change emerges to have been the highest (40.7 per cent) in tertiary sector, followed by that in the secondary (27.9 per cent). There is also a considerable contrast among sectors regarding relative importance of these sources within the sectors. For example, while contribution of labour within primary sector far outweighs that of technological change, the position is reversed in the other two sectors.

Table 3 also gives source-wise contribution separately for each decade.[8] From the 1950s to the 1970s there was some decline in overall contribution of labour to growth from 67.1 per cent to 53.4 per cent. This was true of the two non-agricultural sectors but not of the primary. On the other hand, overall contribution of technological change to growth increased from 23.2 per cent to 30.0 per cent but this increase took place mainly in the tertiary sector. A noticeable change has occurred in the contribution of

Table 3. Source-wise Decomposition of All-India Growth

Period	Sector	Labour	Structural Change	Technological Change	Interaction Effect
			Percentage Contribution to Growth of		
1951-81	Overall economy	45.7	0.6	28.0	25.8
	Primary	86.9	−3.6	11.1	5.6
	Secondary	26.6	6.9	27.9	38.6
	Tertiary	25.7	0.0	40.7	33.6
1951-61	Overall economy	67.1	1.6	23.2	8.1
	Primary	88.8	−7.0	16.0	2.2
	Secondary	43.4	21.5	19.1	16.0
	Tertiary	52.0	0.1	36.8	11.2
1961-71	Overall economy	41.3	−2.5	55.8	5.5
	Primary	68.3	11.9	14.7	5.2
	Secondary	26.3	−14.6	85.5	2.7
	Tertiary	27.8	−6.9	71.5	7.6
1971-81	Overall economy	53.4	7.5	30.0	9.1
	Primary	122.0	−24.8	6.6	−3.8
	Secondary	41.8	36.3	10.7	11.2
	Tertiary	30.5	7.1	49.0	13.5

Notes: (1) Although referred to as the contribution of labour for sake of brevity, it should be borne in mind that it represents the 'steady growth contribution of labour in association with capital and other complementary inputs';

(2) CSO data on national income at 1970-71 prices have been used. Employment estimates for 1981, based on 1981 Population Census, include both main and marginal male workers.

structural change, which was quite insignificant (1.6 per cent) during the 1950s but became 7.5 per cent during the 1970s. Although still small in comparison to the role of labour and technological change, the 1970s marks the first decade in which it emerges to be of some significance.

The decade of the 1960s does not fit very well into this trend of transformation. While from the 1950s to the 1960s the trend of change in respect of the contribution of labour and technological change was broadly similar to that from the 1950s to the 1970s, the direction of change from the 1960s to the 1970s was almost the reverse. The shift from the role of labour to that of technological change was strong during the 1960s, but became feeble in the 1970s. The contribution of technological change within the secondary sector increased from 19.1 per cent in the 1950s to 85.5 per cent in the 1960s. But during the 1970s it registered a sharp decline to 10.7 per cent which is essentially a reflection of industrial retardation from the mid-1960s to the mid-1970s.

Spatial variations in the contribution of different sources to regional growth are summarised in Table 4. The contribution of labour to overall growth varied from 80.8 per cent in West Bengal to as low as 31.3 per cent in Punjab. In respect of the contribution of technological change, the highest-ranking state was Punjab (36.4 per cent), while at the other end were Bihar (12.9 per cent), Assam (13 per cent) and Madhya Pradesh (14.3 per cent). It may also be observed that in no state was the contribution of technological or structural change to overall regional growth higher than that of labour. But within the secondary sector, contribution of technological change was above that of labour in the case of Punjab, Andhra Pradesh and Uttar Pradesh.

Sources in Relation to the Pace of Growth and Levels of Development

The regional estimates of contribution of different sources by themselves cannot indicate whether a source which made the most prominent contribution to the growth of a state was the most growth promoting for it. In fact, within the framework of 'Sources of Growth' approach, be it of the type undertaken here or that in Denison's work, in order to answer the question 'Why Growth Rates Differ', one has to go a step beyond derivation of source-

Table 4. Source-wise Decomposition of Growth (1951-81): A Regional Analysis

State	Overall Economy				Primary Sector				Secondary Sector				Tertiary Sector			
	L	S	T	I	L_1	S_1	T_1	I_1	L_2	S_2	T_2	I_2	L_3	S_3	T_3	I_3
Andhra Pradesh	70.5	1.0	13.6	14.9	126.5	−0.4	−13.0	−13.2	34.1	−2.8	39.0	29.7	45.6	3.1	22.6	28.7
Assam	63.3	1.2	13.0	21.8	127.9	−5.6	−8.5	−13.9	44.9	7.5	16.6	31.0	25.7	4.8	26.5	43.0
Bihar	57.3	7.2	12.9	22.7	105.0	−7.1	4.8	−2.6	29.2	24.2	7.8	38.8	37.4	4.6	26.0	32.1
Gujarat	61.0	0.3	17.7	21.1	96.4	−3.3	5.2	1.7	35.4	6.0	21.2	37.4	53.3	−1.1	24.0	23.7
Kerala	56.8	−1.2	22.4	22.1	117.1	−20.0	12.2	−9.3	38.9	8.7	21.2	31.2	27.9	5.6	29.4	37.1
Madhya Pradesh	60.9	4.3	14.3	20.5	112.5	−7.7	0.9	−5.7	32.1	5.1	28.2	34.5	40.2	12.7	15.9	31.3
Maharashtra	35.4	2.2	29.3	33.2	664.7	−7.8	29.7	13.5	25.6	8.6	23.5	42.2	29.9	2.5	32.0	35.6
Karnataka	57.6	0.7	17.9	23.8	106.7	−3.7	0.6	−3.5	35.5	1.8	27.3	35.4	33.4	3.3	25.6	37.7
Orissa	59.7	−0.4	23.6	17.1	84.4	0.9	7.6	7.1	38.2	4.0	27.6	30.2	32.4	−3.2	43.8	27.0
Punjab-Haryana	31.3	0.4	36.4	31.9	43.2	−2.7	35.2	24.4	17.8	11.8	20.9	49.7	25.3	−2.1	45.9	31.2
Rajasthan	55.7	0.6	23.1	20.7	73.5	−1.8	16.7	11.6	56.1	1.8	21.8	20.4	36.5	2.9	30.1	30.6
Tamil Nadu	54.0	0.6	20.0	25.3	114.0	−6.4	−0.4	−7.1	29.5	5.4	24.3	40.8	40.3	1.0	27.4	31.3

Uttar Pradesh	54.6	−1.5	32.7	14.3	69.2	4.5	14.6	11.7	24.7	0.2	47.4	27.6	47.9	−14.0	56.5	9.5
West Bengal	80.8	−2.3	15.2	6.3	128.0	9.3	−22.5	−14.8	58.2	3.6	17.4	20.9	66.4	−11.8	35.1	10.3

Notation: L – Percentage contribution of Labour to growth (see note to Table 3).
S – Percentage contribution of Structural Change to growth
T – Percentage contribution of Technological Change to growth
I – Percentage contribution of Interaction Effect to growth
1981 Work Force (WF) includes main and marginal workers (male only)

Note: Whereas the sources of state incomes in this table are the SSBs (State Statistical Bureaux), the source in the case of Table 3 is CSO (Central Statistical Organisation). Hence Tables 3 and 4 are not strictly comparable.

wise contributions. It is quite possible that a source might be contributing a substantial portion of growth in a region, but the magnitude of growth in that region may be relatively low and vice versa. In order to gauge the influence of a source on regional growth rates, one would have to assess the extent and direction of correlation between regional growth rates and the corresponding estimates of regional contribution of that source.

The results of analysis along these lines (Table 5) are quite revealing. There is a strong statistical relationship between the

Table 5. Correlation Coefficients of Sources with Rates of Growth

Sector	Labour	Contribution of		
		Structural Change	Technological Change	Interaction Effect
1951-81				
Overall Economy	−0.79***	0.20	0.40	0.91***
Primary	−0.82***	0.03	0.76***	0.82***
Secondary	−0.86***	0.34	−0.07	0.95***
Tertiary	−0.85***	0.58**	−0.27	0.92***
1951-61				
Overall Economy	−0.56**	0.29	0.46*	0.68***
Primary	−0.79***	0.02	0.61**	0.81***
Secondary	−0.68***	−0.04	0.33	0.20
Tertiary	−0.70***	0.84***	−0.59**	0.84***
1961-71				
Overall Economy	−0.68***	0.32	0.20	0.50**
Primary	−0.44*	−0.33	0.50**	0.50**
Secondary	−0.74***	0.12	0.13	0.26
Tertiary	−0.25	0.38	−0.36	0.43*
1971-81				
Overall Economy	−0.59**	−0.43*	0.51*	0.86***
Primary	0.40	−0.41	−0.52**	−0.50**
Secondary	−0.83***	−0.38	0.69***	0.91***
Tertiary	−0.22	−0.93***	0.01	0.76***

Notes: (1) Asterisks indicate significance at the one per cent level (***), five
per cent level (**) and ten per cent level (*).
(2) Note given at the end of Table 4 is applicable here as well.

steady growth contribution of labour and the overall growth rates as well as between the former and the sectoral growth rates. But it is a negative relationship, thus confirming the doubts raised above. Labour does account for a substantial contribution to growth, but its relationship to growth, overall as well as sectoral, is not positive—at least in the context of a labour abundant economy like India.

The contribution of technological change and the overall growth rate (1951-81) are positively related, but their correlation coefficient is not very significant. This relationship is positive and significant in the primary sector but, surprisingly, it is insignificant in the other two sectors. The relationship between structural change and overall regional growth rates is also feeble. A striking result is that the interaction effect, which is generally considered to be non-significant, exhibits a strong positive relationship to growth rates. The fact that the interaction effect may not be all that unimportant was initially pointed out by R.C.O. Matthews (1969).

The basic sources whose contribution to growth we have just studied, can also be drawn upon to analyse the sources of differential levels of regional development as measured by per capita incomes—a step parallel to that undertaken by Denison as well within his framework of analysis. For this purpose, treating equation (1) as that pertaining to a region m and dividing it by population P_m of that region, after dropping the time suffixes, we get:

$$y_m = Y_m/P_m = r_m \cdot \sum_i^3 (S_{mi}) (T_{mi}) \qquad (8)$$

where $r_m = L_m/P_m$ is labour's participation rate in region m and y_m is per capita income of region m.

The corresponding equation for the national per capita income $\bar{y}$ can be expressed as:

$$\bar{y} = \bar{r} \cdot \sum_i^3 (\bar{S_i}) (\bar{T_i}) \qquad (9)$$

Subtracting (9) from (8) and expanding the right-hand side, we get:

$$(y_m - \bar{y}) = (r_m - \bar{r}) \cdot \sum_i^3 (\bar{T_i}) (\bar{S_i}) + \bar{r} \cdot \sum_i^3 (T_{mi} - \bar{T_i}) \cdot \bar{S_i} + \bar{r} \cdot$$

$$\sum_{i}^{3} (S_{mi} - \bar{S}_i) \cdot \bar{T}_i$$

$$+ \left[(r_m - \bar{r}) \cdot \sum_{i}^{3} (S_{mi} - \bar{S}_i)(\bar{T}_i) + \bar{r} \cdot \sum_{i}^{3} (S_{mi} - \bar{S}_i)(T_{mi} - \bar{T}_i) + \right.$$

$$(r_m - \bar{r}) \cdot \sum_{i}^{3}$$

$$(T_{mi} - \bar{T}_i) \cdot \bar{S}_i + (r_m - \bar{r}) \cdot \sum_{i}^{3} (S_{mi} - \bar{S}_i)(T_{mi} - \bar{T}_i) \left. \right] \tag{10}$$

Symbols with a bar at the top pertain to the national economy. Hence expressions within braces represent deviation between region m and the national economy for variables y, r, S and T. The deviation of a region's per capita income from the national per capita income can thus be treated as being composed of the contribution of the deviation in the participation rate, the contribution of sectoral productivity deviations, and the contribution of structural differences and their interaction (expression within brackets). Using (10), the contribution of these components to regional income differentials was estimated for all the states for 1951, 1961 and 1971. Thereafter source-wise percentage contributions were averaged for these states and are given in Table 6. As may be observed, the contribution of productivity differentials (over 80 per cent) emerges to be the most important source of per capita income differences whereas in the case of growth its percentage contribution was much less (see Table 3). The contribution of structural differences is also much higher than in the case of growth. On the other hand, average contribution of participation

Table 6. Contribution of Sources to Regional Per Capita Income Differentials

	Labour	Percentage Contribution of		
		Structural Differences	Technological Differences	Interaction Effect
1951	11.50	9.27	87.60	−8.38
1961	11.28	17.71	82.83	−11.82
1971	9.18	30.48	82.21	−21.88

rates, which corresponds to the role of labour in case of growth, is low (about ten per cent) whereas it was the most important source in case of growth. Thus the pattern of contribution of the basic sources to growth and to per capita income differentials emerges to be widely different.

The Anatomy of Interaction Effect

The significance of Interaction Effect revealed by the preceding section leads us to a discussion of three issues. First, what is the relative importance of its sub-components as given by equation 5? These are presented in Table 7. The bulk of this effect is contributed by the interaction of productivity increase and labour increase (89.5 per cent). This is true of each sector, although its force is weaker in the secondary sector. The contribution of the interaction of all three components is not much (4.3 per cent) but in the case of the secondary sector it is somewhat higher (12.7 per cent).

Table 7. Sub-components of the Interaction Effect (1951-81)

Sector	Percentage Contribution of Sub-components to Interaction Effect			
	$\Delta L . T_i(1) . \Delta S_i$	$L(1) . \Delta T_i \Delta S_i$	$\Delta L . S_i(1) . \Delta T_i$	$\Delta L . \Delta S_i . \Delta T_i$
Overall economy	1.82	4.37	89.47	4.34
Primary	-52.90	-6.76	165.19	-5.35
Secondary	14.74	13.00	59.56	12.70
Tertiary	0	0	100.00	0

Note: In the case of sub-components for the overall economy, the algebraical expressions given as column headings are supposed to be summation over i.

Second, why is the percentage contribution of the Interaction Effect (Table 3) much more substantial than expected, for example, on the basis of Denison's work. The answer is simple. The magnitude of Interaction Effect is very much a function of the time span over which growth is measured. Since we are analysing long-term growth using decadal periods, the interaction effect accounts for a much higher contribution than would be the case if growth were measured on an annual basis.

The third issue is the more enigmatic one, that is, how is it that the interaction effect is so highly correlated with growth rates. The essential explanation of this, we feel, lies in what may be called tremendous magnification power of the multiplicative effect which is inherent in the decomposition format of equation 5. For a simplified illustration of this point, let us ignore sectoral distribution aspect and express domestic income as the product of domestic employment and economy wide average output per worker. Suppose there are four regions, all with initial values of aggregate employment and productivity as 2 m and £ 2,000. In region A, employment expands by 50 per cent while in region B productivity rises by 50 per cent over a decade. The terminal domestic income of both would be 50 per cent higher. On the other hand, in region C where both variables grow by 50 per cent, domestic income (obtained through multiplication of the two component variables) should expand not by $50+50=100$ per cent, but by 125 per cent thus revealing how the interaction of the two together accounts for an additional 25 per cent ($=125-100$) growth. In region D, where both variables expand by 100 per cent, the growth of domestic income is not merely 200 per cent, but 300 per cent, leaving a 100 per cent increase as attributable to interaction. Thus, the more substantial and simultaneous the growth in employment and productivity, the steeper is output growth as is also the interaction effect indicating a high correlation between them. In this simplified illustration the correlation coefficient between growth rate and interaction effect works out to be $+ 0.90$.

When structural change is also brought into the picture, by the same logic, in a region where growth in productivity employment and structural shift are all strong and in the positive direction, the interaction effect and growth rate would be expected to be simultaneously high, and vice versa. For example, in the case of Punjab (Table 2) where productivity growth and structural shift are substantial, while employment growth is also near the all-India level, the interaction effect (Table 4) and growth rate are both near the top. West Bengal is an instance of the reverse type.

III. 'THE DETERMINANTS OF GROWTH' APPROACH:
A CONCEPTUAL FRAMEWORK

For locating causatory influences operating upon the pace of growth, one has to go behind the sources of growth and look at some of the explanatory variables involved in the process of growth in a developing economy. The first determinant to consider is savings generated, expressed as a ratio of some other variable—a determinant which has a long ancestry in economic literature. The second set of determinants is based upon the proposition that the overall growth rate of an economy would depend upon the pace at which the technologically advanced segment expands. The higher the allocation of resources for producing inputs needed in this segment, the higher the overall rate of growth of the economy is likely to be. This set of determinants therefore comprises rates of growth of certain basic inputs which are crucial for the expansion of this segment. The third set of determinants pertains to the initial availability ratios (IAR) of some selected inputs. This set is based on the attribute that for any particular growth path—be it a steady one of the Neumann type or a non-steady one—the inputs are needed in a specific proportion. If there is a shortfall in the availability of some input from the needed proportion it could tend to retard the growth rate. We shall express IARs in the form of availability of various inputs per worker.[9] Finally, certain institutional and environmental factors are taken as the fourth set of determinants.

Subsequent analysis for examining the role of these determinants falls into two parts. In the first part we shall study correlations between annual growth rates of output and time series of the determinant variables at the national level from 1950-51 to 1980-81. In using correlation analysis for this purpose, one has to bear in mind that the influence of many determinant variables on growth often takes time to operate, for example, the effect of an expansion in transport network may take a period of years to manifest itself. In view of this, we have estimated both short-term and long-term correlations. The short-term correlations have been obtained by correlating annual data on determinant variables and annual growth rate of output. The long-term correlations have been obtained by overlapping five-year periods—a methodology similar to that used by Kuznets (1946) for estimating long-term consumption function. The overlapping method as used here involves estimation of growth rates of output and of the explanatory variables for 1951-56, 1952-57,......1976-81 and correlating the resulting series, separately for the primary and secondary sectors. The second part of the analysis will examine significance of the selected determinants through correlation analysis across regions. For this purpose growth rates of primary, secondary and tertiary sectors have been estimated for the period 1961-81 for the 14 states studied here.[10]

Two variables based on CSO estimates of savings have been used for correlation analysis at the national level, namely: (i) the ratio of gross savings to national income, and (ii) rate of growth of gross savings (at 1970-71 prices). Estimates of regional savings were derived in a more circuitous manner on the basis of NSS consumption expenditure surveys for 1960-61, 1964-65, 1970-71 and 1973-74[11] and CSO's state income estimates.[12] These estimates for four time points were averaged and divided by male workforce to obtain average savings generated per worker (concept I). However, the actual investible surplus available within each region is modified through fiscal as well as non-governmental inter-regional transfers. Using George and Gulati's (1978a) estimates of total fiscal transfers to states, we obtained 'savings per worker net of fiscal transfers' (concept II). By adding to these Gulati and George's estimates (1978b) of state-wise flow of institutional credit, we finally got regional estimates of 'net savings per worker' (concept III).

In the case of second and third sets of determinants one has to identify key inputs needed for rapid growth of the technologically advanced segment. The Mahalanobis model (1955) underlines the crucial role of basic heavy industries for the long-term pace of growth. So also does the model of development strategies formulated by Gautam Mathur (1967, 1980), but with a simultaneous emphasis on essential consumer goods production. Raj and Sen model (1961) underlines the need for distinguishing between basic industries like steel and the machine-making industries. Hirschman (1958) focusses upon infrastructural *vis-a-vis* non-infrastructural type of basic investments. Taking a cue from these models, we have considered four types of key inputs, namely, infrastructural facilities, basic industries like steel, power generation, equipment making and some crucial intermediate goods like fertilisers. The specific variables[13] whose growth rates have been used for national level analysis are:

A) *Variables mainly relevant for secondary sector or overall growth*: 1(a) Power consumption; (b) Power generation; (c) Installed capacity. 2(a) Length of surfaced roads; (b) Registered goods vehicles. 3(a) Railway route length; (b) railway rolling stock; (c) Train kilometres. 4. Output of basic metal industries. 5. Output of (a) Non-electrical machinery; (b) Electrical machinery. 6. Output of transport equipment. 7. Output of cement.

B) *Variables mainly of relevance for primary sector growth*: 8. Irrigation infrastructure as measured by (a) Net irrigated area (percentage); (b) Gross irrigated area (percentage). 9. Output of fertilisers.

In the case of institutional and environmental determinants, at the national level only three variables have been used. The first one is an important environmental determinant of the agricultural sector, namely, rainfall, time series for which has been constructed by averaging the annual rainfall for all the meteorological subdivisions of India.[14] In addition, two indicators of industrial relations have been used, namely, (a) no. of workers involved in industrial disputes, and (b) no. of man-days lost in industrial disputes. For regional analysis, the following additional institutional variables have been used:

(1) Industrial organisation, measured by proportion of household to total industrial workforce. (2) Land tenure as indicated by the percentage of (a) area leased-out to owned area; (b) area leased-in for fixed produce to total area leased-in; (c) area leased-in for usufructuary mortgage to total area leased-in; (d) 'other area' leased-out to total area leased-out.[15] (3) Size structure of farms as indicated by area (percentage) occupied by: (a) Small farms < 5 acres; (b) Large farms > 30 acres. (4) Index of non-renewable resource endowment, measured by: (a) per capita mineral reserves; (b) Annual per capita mineral exploitation.[16] (5) Institutional Finance per capita.[17] (6) Institutional agricultural credit per hectare.[18]

Table 8. Growth Determinants: National Level Correlations

Determinant Variables	Dependent Variables					
	Five Yearly Growth Rates (Long-term relationships)			Annual Growth Rates (Short-term relationships)		
	g_D	g_s	g_y	g_D	g_s	g_y
I. Savings Generated						
(1) Savings-income ratio	−0.01	−0.13	0.02	0.08	−0.35*	0.02
(2) Growth of savings	−0.24	0.72***	0.02	−0.15	0.56***	−0.01
II. Growth Rate of Key Inputs:						
Infrastructural Inputs						
(1a) Irrigated area (net)	0.43**	—	0.30	0.05	—	0.10
(1b) Irrigated area (gross)	0.24	—	0	0.01	—	−0.02
(2a) Power consumption	−0.09	0.75***	0.12	0.16	0.46**	0.26
(2b) Power generation	0.12	0.63***	0.05	0.02	0.49***	0.12
(2c) Power (installed capacity)	−0.24	0.36*	−0.08	—	0.12	−0.04
(3a) Railway route length	−0.31	0.18	−0.33	—	0.11	−0.24
(3b) Railway rolling stock	−0.25	0.65***	−0.14	—	0	−0.03
(3c) Train kms.	−0.21	0.78***	0.15	—	0.31*	0.12
(4a) Road length	0.21	−0.44	0.02	−0.16	−0.23	−0.20
(4b) Goods vehicles (on road)	−0.06	0.76***	0.05	—	0.28	−0.06

III. Capital Goods					
(5) Basic metals	-0.04	0.58***	0.20	—	0.26
(6a) Non-elec. machinery	-0.10	0.67***	0	—	0.49***
(6b) Electrical machinery	-0.03	0.52***	0	—	0.55***
(6c) Transport equipment	0	0.70***	0.15	—	0.56***
Intermediate Goods					
(7) Fertilisers	0.41**	-0.42**	0.21	0.18	—
(8) Cement	0.14	0.49***	0.14	—	0.36*
IV. Institutional—					
Environmental Factors					
(9) Average rainfall	0.15	—	0.43**	0.46**	—
(10a) Industrial disputes (workers involved)	—	0.82***	—	—	-0.18
(10b) Industrial disputes (Mandays lost)	—	-0.66***	—	—	-0.21
V. Tertiary Sector Determinants		(g_t (long term))			g_t (short term)
(11) g_p (primary sector growth)		-0.05			0.34*
(12) g_s (secondary sector growth)		0.73***			0.74***

Notation: $g_{p,s,t,y}$ — growth rates of primary sector, secondary sector, tertiary sector and national income.

Empirical Results: The National Scene

The role of above variables as determinants of the trend of growth
in the Indian economy which emerges from short-term and long-
term correlation analysis is evident from Table 8. As surmised
earlier, there is a marked increase in the strength of relationship
of the relevant variables when we consider long-term growth. This
point is vividly brought out by the role of net irrigation as also
that of fertilisers in generating primary sector growth.[19] The same
point is revealed by the role of power generation, basic metals
(which includes steel industry) and the three equipment making
industries in promoting industrial growth.[20] This bears out the
essential point of the Mahalanobis model (1955). In respect of
transport infrastructure, the chosen variables are of two types,
one pertaining to its length and the other indicating availability
of vehicles. While the length of the transport system does not
emerge to be of great importance, availability of the means of transport, that is, the stock of goods vehicles on road and railway rolling
stock shows a strong long-term relationship to secondary sector

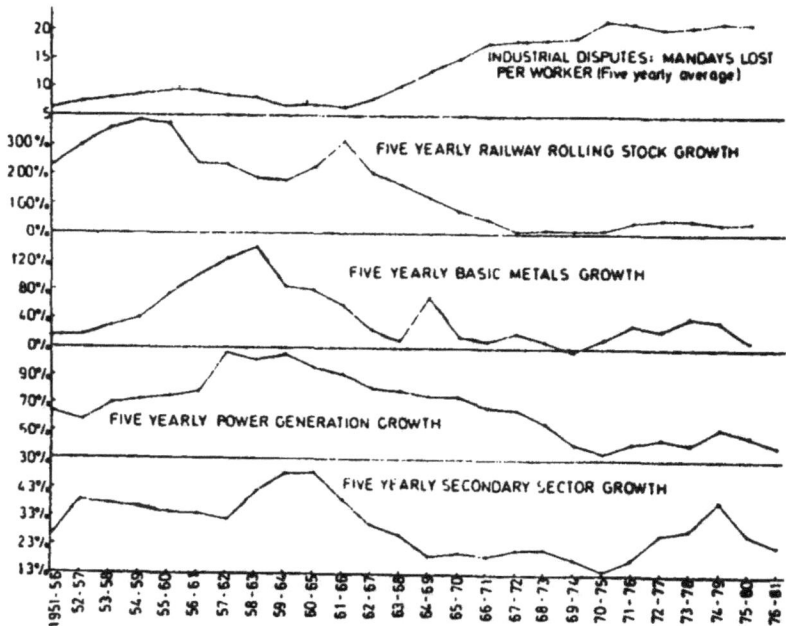

Graph 2: Trend of growth rates.

growth (r=0.76 and 0.65). Finally, it is worth noting that the two industrial disputes variables, which reflect the state of industrial relations, also exhibit a strong long-term relationship to the pace of secondary sector growth but, as expected, it is a negative one.

If we place the above relationships together with a dip in the trend of growth of power generation, railway rolling stock and basic metals (Graph 2), it appears that the declining momentum in the expansion of infrastructural facilities and some of the key industries was a prominent factor responsible for the slowing down of industrial growth. Periodic bouts of coal, power, steel and wagon shortages were a manifestation of this phenomenon. But some of the alternative explanations (see Nayyar, 1978 and Ahluwalia, 1985) could also have been operating simultaneously— or perhaps sequentially as suggested by Rangarajan (1982).

The short-term and long-term correlations of overall growth with respect to savings rate, which hold a central place in many models of growth and development, as also with respect to rate of growth of aggregate savings are poor. But secondary sector reveals a contradictory picture: while its correlation with growth of savings is negative. Savings therefore do not emerge as a clearly significant variable.[21] The factors which emerge to be more important determinants of the pace of long-term growth are the productive channels in which resources are utilised and the consequent pace of growth of the key inputs.[22]

We now turn to three issues concerning above analysis. First since we have used time series data, could our inferences have been distorted by the problem of auto-correlation? The DW statistic indicates absence of auto-correlation from most short-term correlations (except industrial disputes) as well as long-term correlations of primary sector determinants (Table 9). But the same is not the case with determinants of long-term secondary and tertiary sector growth. To eliminate the influence of auto-correlation from these, the long-term variables which emerged to be important on the basis of Table 8 were transformed and fresh regression results were obtained using the Cochrane-Orcutt two-stage procedure. Table 9 gives comparative regression results with these transformed long-term variables, the original long-term variables and short-term variables. Most new DW values (col. 8) are above tabulated d_u values (at 0.05 and sometimes 0.01 probability level) thus indi-

Table 9. Comparative Regression Results (Single Explanatory Variables)

	Short-term Variables			Long-term Original Variables			Long-term Transformed Variables		
	r (1)	DW (2)	b (3)	r (4)	DW (5)	b (6)	r (7)	DW (8)	b (9)
Primary Sector									
Net irrigated area	0.05	2.83	0.20 (0.26)	0.42**	2.05	1.18** (2.14)		Not required	
Fertiliser production	0.18	2.75	0.12 (0.89)	0.41**	1.77	0.10** (2.93)			
Secondary Sector									
Power generation	0.49***	1.77	0.42*** (2.90)	0.63***	0.67	0.28*** (3.95)	0.38*	1.47	0.21* (1.99)
Basic metals	0.26	1.42	0.10 (1.37)	0.58***	0.86	0.14*** (3.53)	0.27	1.23	0.06 (1.32)
Non-electrical machinery	0.40***	1.82	0.12*** (2.88)	0.67***	0.71	0.07*** (4.46)	0.47***	1.63	0.05** (2.57)
Electrical machinery	0.55***	1.71	0.26*** (3.38)	0.52***	0.56	0.12*** (3.00)	0.32	1.55	0.10 (1.63)
Transport equipment	0.56***	1.75	0.13*** (3.55)	0.70***	0.61	0.12*** (4.79)	0.58***	1.65	0.11*** (3.44)
Railway rolling stock	0.01	1.32	0.01 (0.02)	0.65***	0.77	0.62*** (4.13)	0.43**	1.53	0.51** (2.28)

Train kilometres	0.31*	1.76	0.28 (1.64)	0.78***	0.82	0.94*** (5.72)	0.54***	1.61	0.52*** (3.00)
Goods vehicles on roads	0.28	1.29	0.30 (1.45)	0.76***	0.88	0.41*** (5.46)	0.59***	1.39	0.32*** (3.40)
Saving rate	−0.35*	1.26	−0.43*	−0.13	0.47	−0.07	0.18	1.39	0.04 (0.89)
Growth of gross savings	0.56***	1.58	0.22*** (3.41)	0.72***	0.66	0.47*** (5.15)	0.60***	1.67	0.34*** (3.61)
Indust. disputes (workers involved)	−0.18	1.12	−0.06 (0.92)	−0.82***	0.91	−0.22*** (6.98)	−0.31	0.84	−0.06 (1.53)
Tertiary Sector								
Primary sector growth	0.34*	1.19	0.08* (1.94)	−0.05	0.34	−0.03 (0.23)	0.29	0.85	0.08 (1.44)
Secondary sector growth	0.74***	1.90	0.32*** (5.84)	0.73***	0.34	0.41*** (5.27)	0.71***	1.58	0.34*** (4.81)

Notes: r: Correlation coefficient   DW: Durbin-Watson statistic   b: Regression coefficient
't' values of regression coefficients are given within parenthesis
(***) indicates significance at one per cent level, (**) at five per cent level and (*) at ten per cent level.

cating that auto-correlation has been removed. The only exceptions are in the case of industrial disputes and primary sector
growth as a determinant of tertiary sector growth. The new values
of correlations are generally lower than correlations with original
long-term variables, as may be observed from a comparison of cols.
4 and 7. In the case of transport variables and secondary sector
as a determinant of tertiary sector growth, reduction is only of a
minor order. The main reduction occurs in the case of basic metals,
electrical machinery and industrial disputes. But, as subsequent
analysis reveals, although correlation with transformed long-term
variables is weak, lagged correlations of basic metals and industrial
disputes (Table 10) and short-term correlation of electrical machinery (col. 1, Table 9) are significant and free of auto-correlation
problem.

Second, the long-term data were tested for possible existence of
heteroscedasticity. It was found to be absent. In case of no variable the Spearman's rank correlation test for heteroscedasticity
revealed a coefficient between ranks of residuals (ignoring sign)
and of an explanatory variable to be beyond 0.17.

Third, a general limitation of correlation analysis is that by itself it cannot disentangle the cause and the effect. It needs to be
noted in this context that inputs are broadly of two types: those
where existence of demand for them can be expected to overcome
input shortage by inducing a supply response, and those where
investment requirements are so lumpy and time-consuming that
unless production capacity for them is pre-existing, activities based
on their input use would be unable to come up. This is identical
to the distinction between 'growth promoting' and 'growth thwart-
ing' shortages proposed earlier (Puttaswamaiah, 1966). In the case
of the latter type of goods, if there is observed to be a strong correlation between growth of an 'input' and growth of sectoral 'output', on *a priori* logic one can assert that the basic causative variable is 'input' growth. Further, in the case of those inputs where
the supply is basically the result of public sector investment and
not subject to endogenous determination, the initiating role would
again be that of input growth. Going by these criteria, the direction of causation would run from that of growth of electric supply,
basic metals, railway rolling stock, irrigation and fertilisers to
output growth.

An attempt is also made to see if empirical analysis can shed some further light on this issue. The approach used is that of estimating lagged correlations from annual growth rate series by introducing lags first in the dependent (output growth) and then in the explanatory variable (Table 10). The presumption is that in case an explanatory variable is the primary causative agent and that some lags do exist, the correlation coefficient with the lagged dependent variable would be higher than the corresponding correlation coefficient with lagged explanatory variable. In Graph 3 a few of these values are portrayed visually. The continuous line shows correlations when an explanatory variable precedes output growth and a hyphened line shows the reverse situation. The most important indicator is the relative magnitude of correlations for a one-year lag in either direction, but where the continuous line is above the hyphened one for most of its length, the evidence in favour of an explanatory variable being the cause would become further strengthened. It may be noted that in the case of industrial disputes the continuous line would have to be below the hyphened one in order to confirm the causatory role of the explanatory variable, since industrial disputes are inversely related to output growth.

Using these criteria, our earlier conclusions stand confirmed in respect of the role of power generation, basic metals, transport equipment, both types of machinery, industrial disputes and train kilometres traversed. However, the difference between correlation coefficients for positive and negative lags (cols. 10 and 11, Table 10) passes the 'z' test of significance only in case of basic metals, transport equipment and industrial disputes. In the case of growth of savings, the results for one-year and two-year lags pass the 'z' test of significance of difference in correlation coefficients, but the difference is in the reverse direction indicating savings to be following secondary sector growth rather than the other way around. In the case of fertilisers, irrigation and goods vehicles, there are two possible reasons for the absence of a clear picture of causation. First, reverse influence from the demand side, induced by output growth, could be operating simultaneously resulting in mutual causality. Second data may not be reliable enough or time series sufficiently long to indicate the direction of causality in a firm manner in some cases.

Table 10. The Structure of Lagged Correlation Coefficients

The Variable which is Lagged (2)	No Lag r (3)	One Year Lag r_d/r_e (4)	DW (5)	Two Year Lag r_d/r_e (6)	DW (7)	Three Year Lag r_d/r_e (8)	Four Year Lag r_d/r_e (9)	(r_d-r_e) for a Lag of one year (10)	two years (11)
Primary Sector									
Net irrigated area									
Dependent	0.05	0.21	2.83	−0.27	2.56	0.07	−0.24	−0.01	−0.49*
Explanatory	0.05	0.22	2.82	0.22	2.54	−0.55***	0.12		
Fertiliser production									
Dependent	0.18	0.13	2.73	0.11	2.65	−0.13	0.05	+0.03	+0.40
Explanatory	0.18	0.10	2.88	−0.29	2.92	−0.15	0.01		
Secondary Sector									
Power generation									
Dependent	0.49***	0.41*	1.89	0.26	1.46	−0.10	−0.37**	+0.30	+0.25
Explanatory	0.49***	0.11	1.50	0.01	1.11	−0.09	0.12		
Basic metals									
Dependent	0.26	0.50***	2.07	0.48***	2.01	0.20	−0.19	+0.75***	+0.63**
Explanatory	0.26	−0.25	0.93	−0.15	1.16	0.05	0.18		
Non-electrical machinery									
Dependent	0.49***	−0.36*	1.78	0.06	1.52	−0.12	−0.07	+0.09	+0.30
Explanatory	0.49***	0.27	1.06	−0.24	0.97	−0.02	0.02		
Electrical machinery									
Dependent	0.55***	0.32*	1.68	−0.11	1.49	−0.26	−0.07	−0.05	+0.04
Explanatory	0.55***	0.27	1.06	−0.15	1.01	−0.16	0.09		
Transport equipment									
Dependent	0.56***	0.55***	2.00	0.15	1.58	−0.12	−0.05	+0.63**	+0.51*
Explanatory	0.56***	−0.08	1.06	−0.36*	0.94	−0.18	−0.05		
Railway rolling stock									
Dependent	0.01	−0.12	1.42	0.14	1.56	0.36*	0.30	−0.40	−0.34
Explanatory	0.01	0.28	1.10	0.48***	1.21	0.27	−0.05		

Train kilometres	Dependent	0.31*	0.34*	1.64	0.07	1.57	-0.03	-0.21	+0.09	+0.01
	Explanatory	0.31*	0.25	1.25	0.06	1.12	-0.04	-0.25		
Goods vehicles on road	Dependent	0.28	0.19	1.56	0.07	1.58	0.19	-0.20	+0.14	-0.23
	Explanatory	0.28	0.05	1.16	0.30	1.09	0.09	-0.06		
Savings rate	Dependent	-0.35*	-0.28	1.64	-0.12	1.58	-0.06	-0.07	-0.26	-0.39
	Explanatory	-0.35*	-0.02	1.04	0.27	1.12	0.39**	0.06		
Growth of gross savings	Dependent	0.56***	0.01	1.49	-0.43**	1.57	-0.16	-0.05	-0.66***	-0.62**
	Explanatory	0.56***	-0.67***	1.88	0.19	1.23	-0.20	-0.35*		
Indust. disputes (workers involved)	Dependent	-0.18	-0.52***	1.47	-0.34*	1.89	-0.22	0.16	-0.47*	-0.29
	Explanatory	-0.18	-0.05	1.11	-0.05	1.05	0.03	0.06		
Tertiary Sector Primary sector growth	Dependent	0.34*	0.02	1.38	0.02	1.55	0.09	-0.27	-0.46	+0.10
	Explanatory	0.34*	-0.44**	1.15	-0.08	1.02	-0.11	-0.14		
Secondary sector growth	Dependent	0.74***	0.32*	1.86	0.12	1.56	-0.24	-0.14	+0.08	+0.39
	Explanatory	0.74***	0.28	1.56	-0.27	0.89	-0.26	-0.40**		

Notes: r_d: Correlation coefficient when dependent variable is lagged.

r_e: Correlation coefficient when explanatory variable is lagged.

Asterisks have the same connotation as in Table 9. b coefficients and their t values are not given here. Since this Table is based on single independent variable regression analysis, the significance level of b values is identical to that indicated for the r values. The DW values indicate, as in the case of lagless correlations (Table 9), the absence of auto-correlation when dependent variable is lagged. But when explanatory variable is lagged, auto-correlation is often present.

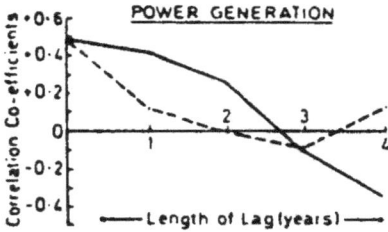

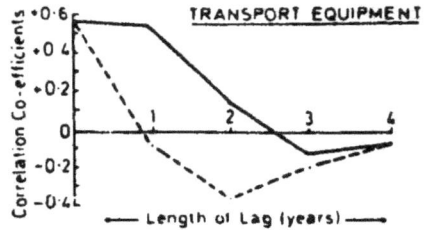

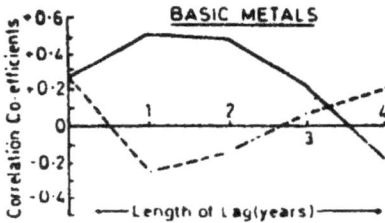

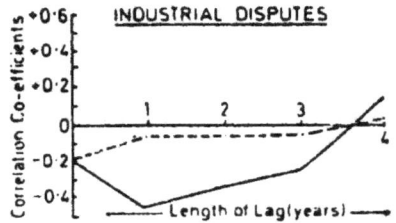

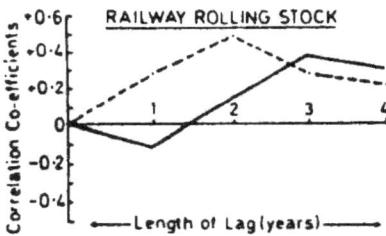

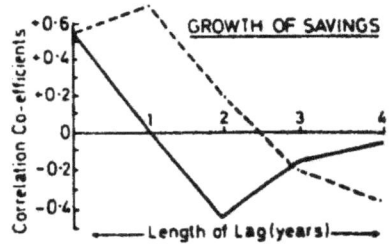

Shows Correlation Co-efficients when dependent variable is lagged —————
Shows Correlation Co-efficients when explanatory variable is lagged — — — — —

Graph 3: A visual picture of some lagged correlations.

A Consolidated Picture

The collective effect of the above variables on long-term growth was assessed through a combination of factor analysis and step-wise regression. The number of variables is large in relation to the number of observations and many of the variables have high inter-correlation. Therefore, some of the variables were composited into a single one in the form of the first principal component.[23] In the secondary sector the following variables were reduced to single determinants:

a) Five-yearly growth rates of all capital good industries $(=x_3)$;
b) Five-yearly growth rates of transport infrastructure variables $(=x_4)$;
c) The indicators of industrial disputes $(=x_5)$.

As there was high inter-correlation between x_4 and growth of power generation, which resulted in a negative regression coefficient for transport infrastructure in step-wise regression, x_4 has been omitted from regression equations for secondary sector growth. The regressions are given below:

Primary Sector

$$g_p(n) = -4.62 + 1.383^*x_1 + 0.005x_2 \qquad \ldots 11(a)$$
$$(1.52) \qquad (0.07)$$
$$\bar{R} = 0.405^{**} \qquad DW = 2.18$$

$$g_p(n) = -1.05 + 1.182^{**}\, x_1 \qquad \ldots 11(b)$$
$$(2.14)$$
$$\bar{R} = 0.375^* \qquad DW = 2.05$$

Secondary Sector

$$g_s(n) = 6.95 + 0.461x_3 - 0.213x_5 + 0.335^{***}x_6$$
$$(0.41) \qquad (0.10) \qquad (2.67)$$
$$+ 0.190^{**}x_7 \qquad \ldots 12(a)$$
$$(2.02)$$
$$R = 0.830^{***} \qquad DW = 0.95$$

$$g_s(n) = 6.30 + 0.517x_3 + 0.340^{***}x_6 + 0.198^{***}x_7 \qquad \ldots 12(b)$$
$$(0.54) \qquad (2.93) \qquad (3.62)$$
$$\bar{R} = 0.839^{***} \qquad DW = 0.95$$

Tertiary Sector

$$g_t(n) = 15.68 - 0.004\ g_p + 0.405^{***}g_s \qquad \qquad \text{...13(a)}$$
$$(0.05) \qquad (5.15)$$

$$\bar{R} = 0.717^{***} \qquad DW = 0.35$$

$$g_t(n) = 15.63 + 0.406^{***}g_s \qquad \qquad \text{...13(b)}$$
$$(5.27)$$

$$\bar{R} = 0.719^{***} \qquad DW = 0.35$$

$g_p(n)$, $g_s(n)$ and $g_t(n)$ are five-yearly growth rates of primary, secondary and tertiary sectors at the national level; x_1 is a five-yearly growth rate of net irrigated area; x_2 is a five-yearly growth rate of fertiliser production; x_6 is a five-yearly growth rate of gross savings; x_7 is a five-yearly growth rate of power generation; asterisks have the same connotation as in Table 9.

The values of DW statistic for equations 12(a) to 13(b) reveal the presence of auto-correlation. Hence these were re-estimated using Cochrane-Orcutt procedure. The revised equations are:

Secondary Sector

$$g_s(n) = 8.15 + 1.167x_3 - 2.028x_5 + 0.192x_6$$
$$(0.85) \qquad (0.64) \qquad (1.20)$$

$$+ 0.109x_7 \qquad \qquad \text{...14(a)}$$
$$(0.80)$$

$$\bar{R} = 0.715^{***} \qquad DW = 1.84$$

$$g_s(n) = 4.91 + 1.320x_3 + 0.247^{**}x_6 + 0.181^{**}x_7 \qquad \text{...14(b)}$$
$$(1.00) \qquad (1.86) \qquad (2.40)$$

$$\bar{R} = 0.725^{***} \qquad DW = 1.95$$

Tertiary Sector

$$g_t(n) = 2.85 + 0.048\ g_p + 0.323^{***}g_s \qquad \qquad \text{...15(a)}$$
$$(1.26) \qquad (4.60)$$

$$\bar{R} = 0.702^{***} \qquad DW = 1.48$$

$$g_t(n) = 2.80 + 0.338^{***}g_s \qquad \qquad \text{...15(b)}$$
$$(4.81)$$

$$\bar{R} = 0.693^{***} \qquad DW = 1.58$$

In these regression equations the DW values are above the tabulated d_u at 0.01 significance level, thus indicating absence of auto-correlation from the transformed variables. In the primary sector, the addition of fertiliser growth to irrigation improves $\bar{R}$. In the secondary sector, the highly intercorrelated industrial relations variable (x_5) has been dropped in equation 14(b). This in fact improves considerably the significance level of the remaining variables and $\bar{R}$ marginally from 0.715 to 0.725. 't' values indicate growth of power generation to be the most significant determinant.[24] In the case of tertiary sector growth, the hypothesis is that growth of service activities is essentially dependent upon the pace of growth of the other two sectors. Equations 15 (a) and 15(b) as well as Table 8 reveals that the dominant determinant of tertiary sector growth, at the national level, is growth of the secondary sector and dropping primary sector growth reduces $\bar{R}$ only very marginally.

Empirical Results: The Regional Scene

Data about agricultural implements are available at the State level and hence inputs of iron ploughs, tractors, oil engines and electric pumps, which depict the use of superior technology, have been incorporated among the regional determinants. But we have excluded output of capital goods industries, which are akin to Leontief's (1953) 'national commodities', partly because their overall impact transcends regional boundaries and partly due to data problems.

We may now indicate the manner in which IARs have been built into the subsequent analysis. The underlying assumption of subsequent analysis is that variation in the 'required input proportion' across regions is small, particularly in comparison to variation in actual availability ratios. Therefore a region where actual availability ratio for some input is low compared to its national average, this would have a retarding effect on growth of that sector of the region for which this input is crucial. Second, growth in the regional availability of this input would not be able to exercise its full influence on regional growth, for a part of this input growth would go towards bridging the gap between the actual initial and 'required' availability. Given this 'catching up' effect, the influence of high regional growth rate of any key input on regional growth would get diluted if the IAR of that input in a region were low and vice versa. S.K. Rao (1971) reached almost an identical conclusion but along a different route and his analysis was confined to irrigation. His logic rested on what may be called 'the small base effect' that is, at low level of input availability, even a minor addition to it would show up as a high percentage increase in it. The explanatory power of input growth as a determinant of regional growth would thus be expected to improve if regional input growth rates were adjusted for IARs. To test this hypothesis we have estimated two sets of correlations between regional growth rates and growth rates of key inputs—one, before adjusting the input growth rates and the second, after adjusting them (Table 11). The adjustment is done through the multiplication of the input growth rates by an index of initial input availability,[25] so that for states where this index is low, the input growth rate gets deflated and vice versa.

The determinants of the pace of regional development are revealed by Table 11. Correlation of savings generated with regional economic growth (0.27), although higher than the corresponding national level correlation, is not significant. Inclusion of fiscal transfers does not improve the explanatory power of the savings variable. But regional flow of institutional finance is highly correlated with pace of regional growth ($r = 0.74$) and its inclusion within savings (concept III) raises the correlation to 0.44. Thus non-governmental finance flows appear to have been growth promoting, but reverse causation resulting in funds getting attracted to the more dynamic regions cannot be ruled out.

For the majority of inputs the explanatory power of growth of key inputs in accounting for differences in regional growth increases substantially when IARs are incorporated (Table 11), thus confirming our hypothesis.[26] Our analysis also confirms Rao's [1971] explanation of relation between irrigation and regional agricultural growth. The relationship of primary sector growth and growth of gross irrigated area is weak ($r = 0.12$), but it becomes significant ($r = 0.54$) when its IAR is incorporated. However, in assessing the full significance of irrigation for regional development one has to incorporate an additional dimension of water availability, namely, the influence of rainfall. The significance of extension of irrigation is expected to be greater in dry regions than in high rainfall regions. This is confirmed by the correlation of primary sector growth with what we call 'rainfall adjusted irrigation growth'. In this variable regional growth rates of gross irrigated area are deflated by an index of average regional rainfall.[27] The correlation, which is only 0.12 between primary sector growth and growth of gross irrigated area, goes up to 0.36 when irrigation growth is adjusted for regional rainfall and further to 0.66 when IAR is also incorporated. The pattern revealed by relationship between technologically superior agricultural implements and primary sector growth is also parallel to that for irrigation. In contrast, the correlation between growth in wooden ploughs, which symbolise an antiquated technique, and primary sector growth remains negative (−0.41) even after incorporating its IAR.

The relationship of regional growth to growth of power generation is surprisingly weak. The mystery surrounding this relationship, which also intrigued Alagh *et al.* (1983), disappears once the IAR effect is incorporated. In respect of transport infrastructure, whereas at the national level extension in length of road network was not important, in respect of regional development it shows up as a significant variable. This is essentially a reflection of the fact that whereas for the country as a whole the existing network may not be too weak, when considering the regional scene there are areas where the transport network is very unsatisfactory and extensions in it hold considerable importance for their development (cf. Raj Krishna, 1980).

Among institutional factors, the land tenure system is a very important one. Tenancy is generally supposed to exercise an inhibitive effect on enterprise through warping of the incentive mechanism. However, if one looks at the relationship of land leased out for cultivation and primary sector growth, it is positive (r = 0.40). A possible reason for the reverse sign may be that the contractual arrangements under which land is leased out are more important than total area leased out. This is borne out by negative correlation (−0.34) between primary sector growth and the extent of fixed rent payment. In fact, the direct influence of most institutional variables, except institutional finance, on growth emerges to be rather feeble. This may be a consequence of data problems. But, as pointed out by Dantawala (1978), the absence of the ex-

Table 11. Growth Determinants: Regional Correlations

Determinant Variables	Correlations with Non-adjusted Determinant Variables — Dependent Variables			Correlations with IAR Adjusted Input Growth Rates — Dependent Variables		
	(1) g_p	(2) g_s	(3) g_r	(4) g_p	(5) g_s	(6) g_r
I. Savings						
1. Savings generated (Concept I)	0.07	−0.07	0.27			
2. Savings net of fiscal transfers (Concept II)	0.11	−0.25	0.20			
3. Net of all flows (Concept III)	0.26	−0.03	0.44			
II & III. Growth Rates of Key Inputs:						
Infrastructural Inputs						
(4a) Irrigated area (net)	0.26	—	0.14	0.42	—	0.33
(4b) Irrigated area (gross)	0.12	—	0.16	0.54**	—	0.49*
(4c) Irrigated adjusted for rainfall	0.36	—	—	0.66***	—	—
(5a) Power consumption	−0.04	−0.12	0.06	0.37	0.40	0.61**
(5b) Power generation	0.11	−0.27	0.07	0.44	0.41	0.68***
(5c) Power (inst. capacity)	0.21	−0.38	0.26	0.46*	0.37	0.62***
(5d) Road length	0.59**	0.50*	0.70***	0.22	0.52*	0.42
(5e) Goods vehicles on road	0.11	0.71***	0.47*	0.27	0.33	0.68***
Capital Goods						
(6a) Tractors	0.09	—	0.20	0.74***	—	0.65***
(6b) Oil engines	0.20	—	0.08	0.78***	—	0.75***
(6c) Iron ploughs	−0.06	—	−0.15	0.41	—	0.57*
(6d) Electric pumps[1]	−0.25	—	−0.20	0.37	—	0.79***

	Primary (p)	Secondary (s)	Tertiary (t)	Overall (y)
Intermediate Goods				
7. Fertilisers	0.55**	—	—	0.41[a]
IV. Institutional-Environmental Factors				
8. Percentage employment in household industries[3]	—	-0.35	—	—
(9a) Industrial disputes (workers involved)	—	-0.16	—	—
(9b) Industrial disputes (mandays lost)	—	-0.20	—	—
(10a) % area leased-out	0.40	—	—	—
(10b) Area leased-in for fixed produce	-0.34	—	—	—
(10c) Area leased in under usufructus mortgage	0.51*	—	—	—
(10d) Area leased-out (other terms)	-0.36	—	—	—
(11a) Holdings < 5 acre	-0.26	—	—	—
(11b) Holdings > 30 acre	+0.07	—	—	—
(12a) Instituitional Finance per capita	—	—	0.48*	0.74***
(12b) Agricultural institutional credit per hectare	0.39	—	—	—
Tertiary Sector Determinants				
1. g_a	—	—	g_t 0.42	—
2. g_p	—	—	0.71***	—
(13a) Resource reserves per capita	—	—	-0.32	-0.30
(13b) Resource exploitation per capita	—	—	-0.23	-0.36

Notes: $g_{p,s,t,y}$ — growth rate of primary sector, secondary sector, tertiary sector and overall regional incomes. Asterisks indicate significance at one per cent level (***), five per cent level (**) and ten per cent level (*).

1. Excludes Tamil Nadu
2. IAR is for 1971
3. Excludes West Bengal

pected type of statistical relationships cannot be considered in any way to reduce the importance of a policy for institutional reform. For a wide-ranging analysis of some institutional forces in shaping India's development, a reference may be made to Bardhan (1984).

Finally, indices of resource endowment and of resource exploitation both exhibit a negative but insignificant correlation. This supports the view that the existence of natural resources by itself cannot ensure economic growth.

As at the national level, the collective influence of determinant variables on regional growth was evaluated by compositing four groups of variables with the help of factor analysis. The results of step-wise regression are not given here for reasons of space, but it may be mentioned that in the case of primary sector growth the composite IAR-adjusted growth of superior agricultural implements emerged as the dominant determinant while the composite infrastructure variable emerged as the dominant determinant of secondary sector growth.

IV. CONCLUSIONS

The core of this article is based on the need to distinguish between the sources of growth and the determinants of growth. Both are important for the empirical analysis of growth but they address themselves to different issues. The sources of growth analysis reveal three important points. First, the steady growth contribution of labour accounts for a substantial portion of growth, but it is negatively related to the pace of growth in India. Second, the interaction effect which is generally considered to be unimportant, emerges to be of substantial significance both in terms of its percentage contribution to growth and its positive relationship with the long-term rate of growth. Third, the structure of contribution of the sources to growth and to regional per capita income deviations differ markedly.

The analysis of determinants of growth at the national level rests on a study of correlations and regression analysis using short-term variables, long-term variables and lagged variables. Empirical results do not bear out the importance of a savings ratio as a key determinant of the pace of growth. What emerges to be much more important is the directions in which savings are utilised. To mention just a few of the important results, the determinants of growth approach brings out the role of expansion of machine-producing and basic metal industries and some of the infrastructural activities, especially power generation and irrigation, in having exercised a dominant influence on the pace of long-term growth in India. The need for adequacy of investment in these activities is thus an important policy prescription which emerges from an empirical analysis in this article. When we come to regional level analysis, it shows the significance of the initial availability ratio (IAR) of various inputs in explaining regional growth patterns. Once the IAR effect is incorporated, some of the anomalies between national and regional level results disappear. Lastly, it should be borne in mind that all our empirical conclusions need not necessarily hold in case of the developing countries which, unlike India, are small-sized economies. In their case external factors—an area outside the purview of this article—may play a dominant role.

NOTES

1. The compound growth rates per annum have been estimated for each decade by averaging the income estimates, at 1970-71 prices, of three years at the terminal points, namely, 1950-51 to 1952-53, 1959-60 to 1961-62, 1969-70 to 1971-72 and 1978-79 to 1980-81 in order to eliminate the influence of short-term fluctuations on decadal growth rates.
2. As argued by K.N. Raj (1984), it is possible that a periodisation other than a decadal one may yield different results.
3. For data up to 1975, see Ashok Mathur (1983). States for which latest figures were available for 1979-80 at the time of preparing this article, figures for 1980-81 were estimated. Male workforce estimates have been used since it is generally recognised that for inter-decadal comparisons, census of population based total workforce estimates are less reliable. Further details about estimates can be provided on request.
4. If O' and E' depict output and employment in period t_a while O and E denote their values in t_0, the Y-axis shall measure $(g_y + 100\%) = 100.(O' - 0)/0 + 100 = (0'/0).100$ and X-axis shall measure $(g_e + 100\%) = 100.(E' - E)/E + 100 =$

$(E'/E).100$. Slope of radius vector of any point shall depict the ratio of these two, that is, $(0'/0).100/(E'/E).100 = (0'/E')/(0/E) = P'/P$ where $P' = 0'/E'$ and $P = 0/E$ are productivity per worker in periods t_n and t_o. But $P'/P = 1 + (P' - P)/P$, where $(P' - P)/P$ depicts proportional growth of productivity per worker.

5. See Gautam Mathur (1965, 1979). For the Neumann strand of analysis, see also Dorfman, Solow and Samuelson [1958] and Hahn and Matthews (1965).

6. The contribution of increase in productivity to growth is supposed to measure, in our approach, the combined effect of increase in capital intensity, scale economies, education and health.

7. It may be pointed out that within each sector labour's contribution is measured as that of total L and not of increase in labour employed within each sector. This procedure has been followed to separate the effect of structural change from that of growth in employment at the sectoral level.

8. An inter-decadal comparison has to be qualified by the remark that the inter-censal definitions of workforce have not remained the same. But we have undertaken adjustments to make data comparable.

9. However, there are some exceptions, for example, irrigation is expressed as a percentage of area irrigated to the input of cultivated area.

10. The growth rates have been worked out by the averaging sectoral outputs for the base period from 1960-61 to 1962-63 and for the terminal period for the last three years in order to eliminate the effect of short-term fluctuations on growth rate estimates.

11. The data were obtained from the National Sample Survey, *Tables with Notes on Consumer Expenditure*, Report Nos. 101, 209, 231 and 240.

12. See Fifth, Sixth and Seventh *Reports of the Finance Commission* and *National Accounts Statistics 1970-71 to 1976-77*, Central Statistical Organisation, New Delhi, Appendix 2.

13. Most of the data required for their computation were taken from annual volumes of *The Statistical Abstract of India*, CSO, and relevant volumes of the Census of Population of

India, 1961, 1971 and 1981.

14. One can validly question the meaningfulness of an estimate of average annual rainfall for India. Despite its limitations, the average estimate does not appear to be completely off the mark, as subsequent results show.

15. Data are based on National Sample Survey, *Tables with Notes on Some Aspects of Land Holdings in India*, 26th Round (1970-71), all-India Report No. 215 and its state tables (mimeographed).

16. Based on data compiled by a Jawaharlal Nehru University, research student, Tapan Das.

17. Based on data taken from Gulati and George (1978b).

18. Data are taken from Tara Shukla (1971).

19. Rainfall is one of the few variables whose short-term correlation is visibly higher than the long-term one. This reflects the short-term dependence of fortunes of agriculture upon vagaries of the monsoons whereas long-term agricultural growth is much more dependent upon man-made irrigation facilities.

20. One may be inclined to query the significance of these high correlations since these industries form a part of the overall industrial structure. To dispel this doubt, we may note the weights of these industries in the index of industrial production which are: Basic Metals—8.84 per cent; Electrical Machinery—5.30 per cent; Non-Electrical Machinery—5.55 per cent; Transport Equipment—7.39 per cent. Thus the share of none of these is above nine per cent.

21. The absence of the expected relationship between savings and growth in the Indian economy has also been noted by V.K.R.V. Rao (1980). Shetty and Menon (1980) and a Reserve Bank of India study (1982). It may be pointed out that savings do not emerge as a determinant of long-term growth in the Mahalanobis model (1955). Regarding this point, also see K.N. Raj (1961).

22. Conventionally, following the Harrodian approach, in addition to the savings rate, capital-output ratio is taken to be the other main determinant of growth rate. However, the use of capital-output ratio as a key variable is open to certain objections (Reddaway, 1962 and Myrdal, 1968). It may be noted that some of the empirical results of this article run

counter to those flowing from the capital-output ratio criterion. For example, within the Harrodian framework, aggregate capital-output ratios as a determinant would be negatively related to growth rate. But some of the activities which show a strong positive correlation to secondary sector growth in our empirical analysis, for example, power generation, have a high capital-output ratio.

23. The first principal component is a weighted linear combination of individual variables expressed in the standardised form $(x - \bar{x})/\bar{o}_x$. The weights are derived so as to maximise the sum of the square of correlations between individual variables and the composited variable obtained with the help of these weights. For details see Harman (1960). It may also be noted that the purpose for which factor analysis has been used here is different from that of Adelman and Morris (1967). They have used it for identifying variables which could be clustered together and communalities have been used as a measure of explanatory power. We have used factor analysis for compositing of variables and explanatory power is measured as in standard multiple regression.

24. One should also bear in mind that although growth of savings is included here as a determinant and it emerges to be significant, in terms of sequential correlation analysis of the previous section there was an indication that its direction of causation is a reverse one.

25. The index of availability of its input in region k $(= I_i^k)$ is defined as $I_i^k = R_i^k / \bar{R}_i$, where R_i^k ($=$ Input i used/labour employed) is the IAR of input in region k and $\bar{R}_i$ is the all-India IAR of input i.

26. There are some exceptions, for example, in case of road infrastructure variables and fertilisers. A possible reason for this could be that our assumption regarding variation in 'required input proportion' across regions, indicated earlier, does not hold in the case of these inputs.

27. Index of average rainfall for region n may be defined as $I_n = F_n / F$ where F_n is normal annual rainfall in region n and F is the average of regional normal rainfalls as reported in *Report of the National Commission on Agriculture*, Ministry of Agriculture, New Delhi, 1976.

REFERENCES

Adelman, Irma and Cynthia Taft Morris, 1967, *Society, Politics and Economic Development*, Baltimore, MD: Johns Hopkins University Press.

Ahluwalia, Isher J., 1985, *Industrial Growth in India: Stagnation Since the Mid-Sixties*, New Delhi: Oxford University Press.

Alagh, Y.K., Kashyap, Shah and Awasthi, 1983, 'Indian Industrialisation: Regional Structure and Planning Choices', *Man and Development*, Vol. V, No. 1.

Bardhan, Pranab, 1984, *The Political Economy of Development in India*, Oxford: Basil Blackwell.

Dantawala, M.L., 1978 'Future of Institutional Reform and Technological Change in Indian Agricultural Development', *Economic & Political Weekly*, Vol. XIII, Nos. 31-33.

Denison, Edward F., 1962, *The Sources of Economic Growth in the United States and the Alternatives Before Us*, New York: Committee for Economic Development.

Denison, Edward F., 1967, *Why Growth Rates Differ*, Washington, DC: The Brookings Institution.

Dorfman, R., P.A. Samuelson and R.M. Solow, 1958, *Linear Programming and Economic Analysis*, New York: McGraw Hill.

Gulati. I.S. and K.K. George, 1978a, 'Inter-state Redistribution through Budgetary Transfers', *Economic & Political Weekly*, Vol. XIII, No. 11.

Gulati, I.S. and K.K. George, 1978b, 'Inter-state Redistribution through Institutional Finance', *Economic & Political Weekly*, Vol. XIII, Nos. 31-33.

Hahn, F.H. and R.C.O. Matthews, 1964, 'The Theory of Economic Growth: A Survey', *Economic Journal*, Vol. LXXIV.

Harrod, R.F., 1948, *Towards a Dynamic Economics*; London: Macmillan.

Harman, H.H., 1960, *Modern Factor Analysis*. Chicago: Chicago University Press.

Hirschman, A.O., 1958, *The Strategy of Economic Development*, New Haven, CT: Yale University Press.

Isard, Walter, 1960, *Methods of Regional Analysis*, Cambridge, MA: MIT Press.

Kaldor, Nicholas, 1957, 'A Model of Economic Growth', *Economic Journal*, Vol. LXVII.

Kaldor, Nicholas, 1966, *Causes of the Slow Rate of Economic Growth of the United Kingdom*, An Inaugural Lecture, Cambridge: Cambridge University Press.

Krishna, Raj, 1980. 'The Centre and the Periphery: Inter-state Disparities in Economic Development', *Economic Times*, 14, 15 and 16 May.

Kuznets, Simon, 1946, *National Product Since 1869*, New York: National Bureau of Economic Research.

Leontief, W.W., 1953, 'Inter-regional Theory', in W.W. Leontief *et al.* (eds.), *Studies in the Structure of the American Economy*, New York: Oxford University Press.

Mahalanobis, P.C., 1955, 'The Approach of Operational Research to Planning in India', *Sankhya*, Vol. 16, Pts. 1 and 2.

Mathur, Ashok, 1966, 'Balanced vs. Unbalanced Growth: A Reconciliatory View', *Oxford Economic Papers*, Vol. 18, No. 2.

Mathur, Ashok, 1983, 'Regional Development and Income Disparities in India: A Sectoral Analysis', *Economic Development and Cultural Change*, Vol. 31, No. 3.

Mathur, Gautam, 1965, *Planning for Steady Growth*, Oxford: Basil Blackwell.

Mathur, Gautam, 1967, 'Investment Criteria in a Platinum Age', *Oxford Economic Papers*, Vol. 19, No. 2.

Mathur, Gautam, 1979, 'The Capital Theory Base of Development Economics: Editorial Observations,' *World Development*, Vol. 7, No. 10.

Mathur, Gautam, 1980, 'National Strategy for Economic Development', Allahabad: *National Academy of Sciences*, Golden Jubilee Annual Number, Part I.

Matthews, R.C.O., 1969, 'Why Growth Rates Differ' *Economic Journal*, Vol. LXXIX.

Myrdal, Gunnar, 1968, *Asian Drama* (Vol. III, App. 3), London: Allen Lane/The Penguin Press.

Nayyar, Deepak, 1978, 'Industrial Development in India: Some Reflections on Growth and Stagnation', *Economic & Political Weekly*, Vol. XIII, Nos. 31-33.

Neumann, J. von, 1945, 'A Model of General Equilibrium', *Review of Economic Studies*, Vol. XIII, No. 1.

Olson, Mancur, 1982, *The Rise and Fall of Nations: Economic Growth, Stagnation and Social Rigidities*, New Haven, CT: Yale

University Press.

Olson, Mancur, 1983, 'The Political Economy of Comparative Growth Rates', in Dennis C. Mueller (ed). *The Political Economy of Growth*, New Haven, CT: Yale University Press.

Raj, K.N., 1961, 'Growth Models and Indian Planning', *Indian Economic Review*, Vol. V, No. 3.

Raj, K.N., 1984, 'Some Observations on Economic Growth in India over the Period 1952-53 to 1982-83', *Economic & Political Weekly*, Vol. XIX, No. 41.

Raj, K.N. and A.K. Sen, 1961, 'Alternative Patterns of Growth under Conditions of Stagnant Export Earnings', *Oxford Economic Papers*, Vol. 13, No. 1.

Rangarajan, C., 1982, 'Industrial Growth: Another Look', *Economic & Political Weekly*, Vol. XVII, Nos. 14-16.

Rao, S.K., 1971, 'Inter-regional Variations in Agricultural Growth, 1952-53 to 1964-65: A Tentative Analysis in Relation to Irrigation', *Economic & Political Weekly*, Vol. VI, No. 7.

Rao, V.K.R.V., 1980, 'Savings Capital Formation and National Income', *Economic & Political Weekly*, Vol. XV, No. 22.

Reddaway, W.B., 1962. *The Development of the Indian Economy*, App. C. London: George Allen & Unwin.

Reserve Bank of India, 1982, *Capital Formation and Saving in India*, 1950-51 to 1979-80.

Shetty, S.L. and K.A. Menon. 1980, 'Savings and Investment Without Growth', *Economic & Political Weekly*, Vol. XV, No. 21.

Shukla, Tara, 1971, 'Regional Analysis of Institutional Finance for Agriculture', *Indian Journal of Agricultural Economics*, Vol. XXVI, No. 4.

CHAPTER 5

Planning and Implementing a Development Programme for the Poor: A Case Study from the Mahaweli Development Programme in Sri Lanka

Sri Lanka has an area of 25,332 square miles and is separated from the Indian subcontinent by a narrow strip of shallow water, the Palk Strait. Aside from India, the nearest neighbours of Sri Lanka are the Maldive Islands to the West, and the Nicobar and Andaman Islands to the East and Northeast respectively. The greatest length of the island North to South is 270 miles and the greatest breadth 140 miles.

The topography of the island comprises a mountainous area along the central part, with an altitude of 3,000 to 7,000 feet, which is surrounded by an upland belt of 1,000 to 3,000 feet, with a coastal plain occupying the rest of the island.

The Portuguese arrived in Sri Lanka in 1505 and conquered the maritime parts of the island. They were the first to introduce Christianity to this country. Subsequently, the Portuguese were ousted by the Dutch, who ruled over the island from 1640 until 1706, when the British conquered the Dutch. In 1815 Sri Lanka became a British Colony after the entire island had been conquered. The island gained its independence in 1948. Sri Lanka at present has a democratic socialist form of government patterned after the British and is a member of the British Commonwealth.

Sri Lanka is an agricultural country. The agricultural structure consists of a plantation sector and a peasant or small-holder sector. The plantation sector consists mainly of tea, rubber and coconut and is characterised by large holdings, intensive capital application, organised labour, and relatively high productivity. This sector accounts for almost 70 per cent of the Foreign Exchange earnings of the country. The plantation sector covers about 60 per cent of the island's agriculturally developed acreage.

The peasant sector of the island consists mainly of small holdings of both paddy land and highland where mainly food crops are cultivated. This sector is characterised by low levels of productivity, a high incidence of tenant cultivators, indebtedness, neglect of the highland, dependence on family labour, and mainly subsistence production.

New development programmes [are being implemented in Sri Lanka in the dry zone of the island. This is an area that receives relatively low rainfall and that, too, at a particular time of the year. During the rest of the year this area becomes parched and arid and no use can be made of the land. The peasant in the dry zone cultivates paddy in the low-lying areas under rainfed conditions. He also grows subsidiary food crops on the slash and burn (chena) system in the higher areas, where there is a secondary forest, during the rainy season. In this way he has to eke out an existence entirely dependent on the monsoon rains for all his activities. The average size of a holding is about 1.5 acres.

Most developing countries have recognised the need to formulate and implement development programmes to benefit the poor. The Accelerated Mahaweli Development Programme is one of these projects, wherein a serious attempt is being made to benefit the impoverished.

What does the Accelerated Mahaweli Development Programme set out to achieve? Generation of power; settlement of landless people in lands in the dry zone of Sri Lanka (made irrigable by water diverted from the Mahaweli River); reducing unemployment; and increasing agricultural production, with emphasis on achieving self-sufficiency, especially in rice. These are some of the purposes for which the Government embarked on this massive and ambitious programme.

Much thought and consideration was given to these ideas prior to the formulation of definite plans. The concepts of this scheme were fully understood by the Planners before this conceptualisation was transformed into feasible plans that could be implemented with the resources available.

The next step was to turn these plans into work programmes that the people in the field could interpret, understand and put into effective operation. It was apparent that the officer in the field had to be an important cog in the machinery that was to be put in motion to make the concepts, plans and programmes a tangible achievement in the field. If this Field Officer is to play such an important part in the Accelerated Mahaweli Development Programme, he must be aware of what the programme sets out to achieve, its concepts and, more important, what his specific role in this whole operation is. It is also necessary that his superiors likewise know what is expected of him if a co-ordinated effort is to be made to ensure the success of the programme. In this respect strong and relevant training and orientation programmes were necessary.

The envisaged development programme for these new settlement areas is the largest simultaneous operation that this country and probably the whole of Asia has ever undertaken. Since this is the first development scheme of this magnitude and with varied objectives in this country, the operations and management agencies had no past experience to draw upon in the implementation of these programmes. Initially the Mahaweli Development Board started off the work in System 'H', which was the first area to be developed under the then Mahaweli Diversion Scheme. With the Government's decision in 1978 to accelerate this scheme and telescope the proposed work of thirty years into six years, the Accelerated Mahaweli Development Programme, as it has now come to be known, took on new dimensions and greater purpose. Maps of the Accelerated Mahaweli Development Programme and System 'H' are shown in Figures 5.1 and 5.2 respectively.

The Mahaweli Development Board at first undertook the construction of the irrigation infrastructure and the social infrastructure facilities, and the settlement and post-settlement work. This they did quite efficiently. With the accelerated programme gaining momentum however, it was found that it was too much to expect one organisation to carry out all the functions in a pro-

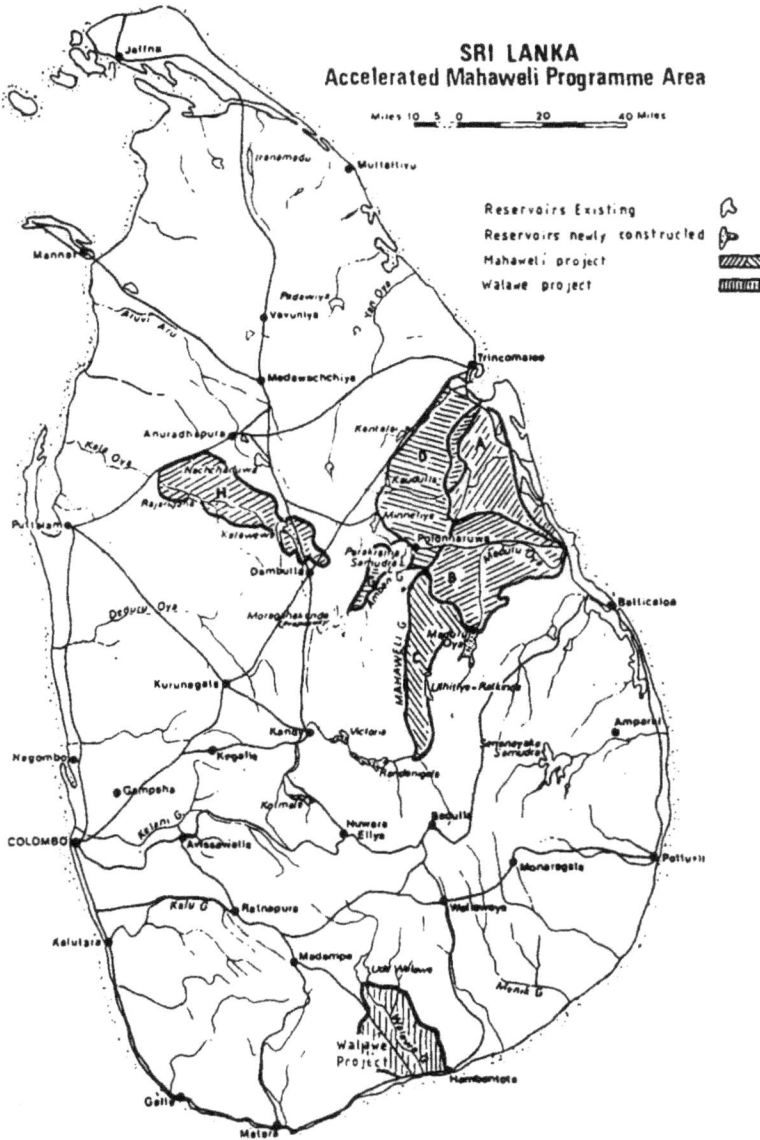

SRI LANKA
Accelerated Mahaweli Programme Area

Fig. 5.1

MAP OF SYSTEM - H

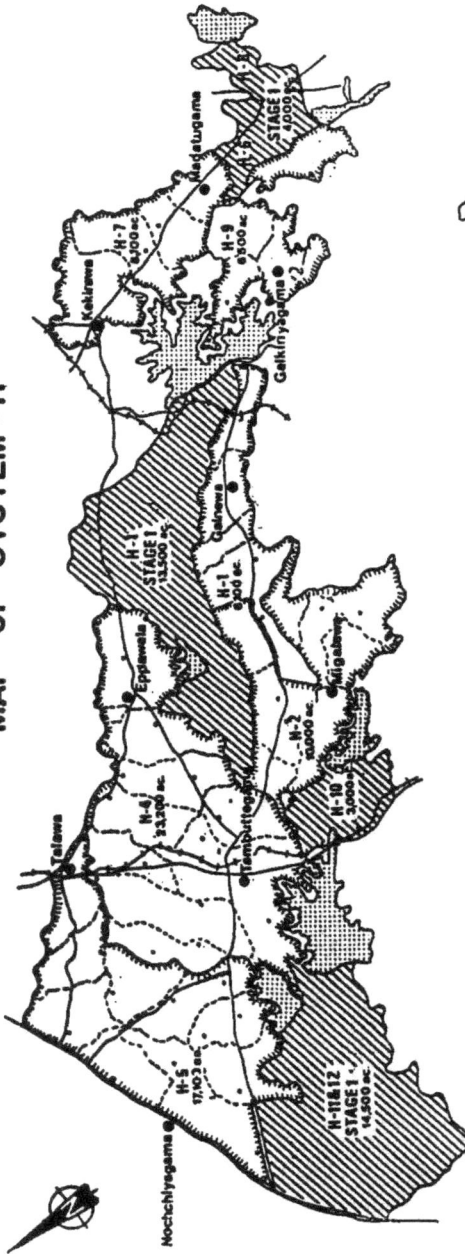

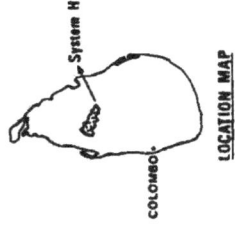

SCALE - 1 : 264 000

LOCATION MAP

LEGEND
Block Boundary
System Boundary
Main Road
Railway
Township   ● GALNEWA
Previously developed area
Main Reservoirs

Fig. 5.2

ject area. It became too unwieldy for one organisation to handle. It was therefore decided that the Mahaweli Development Board would continue to do the construction of the irrigation and social infrastructure and that the Mahaweli Authority of Sri Lanka (Settlement Branch) would do the settlement and post-settlement work, since this was a different aspect of the implementation of the overall plan. The Mahaweli Economic Agency now handles all the settlement and post-settlement aspects.

This arrangement became even more necessary when the Hon. Minister of Mahaweli Development, Mr. Gamini Dissanayake, wanted greater emphasis placed on post-settlement work than had been done in the earlier settlement or colonisation schemes. It was found that the main reason the earlier schemes were not achieving their set objectives fully, was the fact that there was little or no post-settlement work done. A little Community Development work was done in earlier schemes but in the Accelerated Mahaweli Development Programme equal emphasis is given to Community Development and to Irrigation, Agriculture, Land Administration, and so forth.

System 'H' was the first area to be settled under the Mahaweli Development Programme. The scheme started in 1975 with the settling of approximately 500 families in the area. This programme of settlement was accelerated from 1978 by the present Government.

System 'H' is an irrigated settlement scheme where a total of 24,000 families have now been settled. The project area consists of a total of 108,000 acres, of which 72,000 acres have been taken up for settlement under the Accelerated Mahaweli Development Programme. The balance of 36,000 acres falls under old Colonisation Schemes, coming under the command area of System 'H'. The Mahaweli Economic Agency is not involved in the total management of these old schemes, but assists in some specific functions, such as Water Management and Marketing.

Three types of settler families have been allocated land in the 'H' area under the present scheme. They are:

a) *Re-settlers*: These are people from within the area who have been re-settled under the new scheme. Some of these people lost land which they had earlier owned in this area. They have been compensated in terms of cash and land.

b) *New settlers:* One hundred landless families from each electorate in the Central Province were chosen and settled here. The selections were made by the Government Agents concerned in consultation with the local Member of Parliament.

c) *Evacuees:* These are people whose lands come within the Bowatenne, Victoria and Kotmale dam sites of the Mahaweli Scheme and whose lands were lost as a result of inundation.

Each settler is given an irrigation allotment of two-and-a-half acres and a highland allotment of half an acre. In instances where the settlers owned land within the 'H' area which was taken over, they were initially given up to a maximum of seven Blocks in the initial stages, but now a maximum of three Blocks of irrigable and highland lots are given. This is because it was found that farmer families could not conveniently cultivate more than this holding due to problems of labour, etc. The new settlers are entitled to only one allotment each.

When the settlers first arrive in the Project area they are housed in temporary camps that have the basic amenities, until they can construct their own dwellings on their highland allotments. The Mahaweli Authority provides them with the following assistance to enable them to make a good start.

a) An allowance of Rs. 1,500/- to build a house. This allowance at the initial stages was only Rs. 300/- but due to rising costs has been increased in three stages to the present figure. Free transport is also provided for the settlers to bring their own building materials, furniture, etc. when they come.

b) Free issues of dry rations for five members of a family for one year under the World Food Programme.

c) Free seed paddy for the first cultivation.

d) Free agricultural implements, such as mammoties, crowbars, axes, knives.

e) Free plants, such as coconuts, mango, and citrus for planting in the highland plots.

Hamlet settlement is now on the cluster-type as it was found that there were problems of communication, transport, and so forth in the ribbon type of settlement practised earlier. About 100-200 families are settled in a hamlet. Each hamlet is provided with a co-operative store, post box, day care centre and, wherever necessary, a primary school. A Village Centre is built to cover 8 or 10 such hamlets. A Village Centre consists of a rural bank, registered co-operative, community training and development centre, junior school, sub-post office, a weekly fair, and commercial allotments for the private sector to provide for the sale of consumer goods. Besides these facilities, land is allocated for persons with technical aptitudes to start industries such as bicycle repairs, tractor repairs, smithies, small-scale rice mills, and so on.

A Township serves two to five village centres. A Township consists of, in addition to the commercial services, a secondary school, rural hospital, banks, police station, marketing department, co-operatives, fisheries stall, co-operative complex, fuel station and other facilities needed for an agricultural town. Plots of land are given in the Townships to businessmen and entrepreneurs to set up various businesses, and trades.

A number of Town Centres are planned for the 'H' area. They are Galnewa, Meegalewa, Madatugama, Galkiriyagama, Eppawela Talawa, Tambuttegama, Kekirawa and Nochchiyagama. Of these Meegalewa, Galnewa and Galkiriyagama are entirely new towns, whereas the others were existing towns whose infrastructure has been strengthened to cater for the increased population.

Water diverted from the Mahaweli River at Kandy (Polgolla) is fed, via another diversion at Bowatenna, into three main storage tanks that serve the 'H' area. The tanks are Kandalama, Dambulu Oya and Kalawewa. An intricate irrigation network carries the water to the farthest point of the scheme so that it can be evenly distributed amongst all the land beneficiaries.

This being an irrigated agricultural settlement scheme, the emphasis is naturally on maximum agricultural production. Though there is sufficient water, it has to be managed and distributed properly if maximum utilisation is to be made of the land that has been given to the farmers settled in the project area.

There are two cultivation seasons. One is the *maha* or main season in which rain water that falls during the Northeast monsoon, from October to January, is used. Irrigation water supplements the rain-fed cultivations of the *maha* season. The other season is the *yala*, during which cultivation is done from May to August and the water requirement is met mainly from irrigation.

The main crop cultivated here is paddy. Almost 100 per cent of the cultivation in *maha* is paddy and, if permitted to do so, the farmers would cultivate paddy in *yala* as well. However, as water is a limiting factor during the *yala* season, the authorities have tried to wean the farmers away from the cultivation of paddy in the *yala* season and have encouraged them to grow other field crops instead. Crops that can be grown successfully are chilli, cowpea, soybean, gingelly, black gram, green gram, and groundnut. The consumption of water in the cultivation of other field crops is much lower than for paddy. Now we find that an increasing number of farmers are taking to the cultivation of other field crops in *yala*. The main reasons that motivate the farmers to change over are those of economy, in that when convinced that their incomes will be better, they make the change.

The main purpose of the Mahaweli Economic Agency continuing the management of this scheme after settlement is to ensure the social and economic development of the families settled here. It is obvious from the experiences gained from the earlier colonisation schemes, that this cannot be achieved from irrigated agriculture alone. It is necessary for the community to develop along with the development of the land. This has not happened in earlier schemes. Therefore the Mahaweli Economic Agency has a separate division for community services and equal emphasis is given to this work as is given to agriculture, water management, and so forth.

In earlier settlement schemes, once settlement was over, the department or organisation which initially showed the farmers their lands and provided the irrigation facilities, went away. This left the new settler alone in an alien environment to fend for himself. He had to go to the various government departments for the numerous services and inputs he needed and also to have his problems solved. This meant that he wasted considerable time going from pillar to post in order to get his work done—time which could have been better spent in farming and other settling-down activities.

Hence the new settlers were not able to do proper cultivation and the whole process of settling down got off to a bad start. In the Mahaweli Settlement areas it is intended that the officers whom the farmers encounter when they first arrive, will continue for quite sometime until the new settlers are on their feet. It is also the intention of the Mahaweli Economic Agency to supply the new settlers with their inputs and other needs through these officers only. No other departments or agencies will function within the Mahaweli Department areas.

Community Development plays a very important role in the management of System 'H'. The Community Development Division has as its main objectives the social and economic development of the settlers, not only as individuals but as cohesive groups. The Mahaweli Economic Agency is working towards a time in the future when the settlers will be able to manage all their affairs by themselves, and their dependence on the Government and other agencies will taper off.

The management system that the Mahaweli Development Board adopted for the settlement areas of system 'H' was based on range, region and project level administration. This system worked well in the initial stages of the project. When the Mahaweli Economic Agency took over the management functions of System 'H', it based its management on the unitary system. This evolved from the agency's experience gained in a Pilot Management Project carried out in the 'H' area. Organisational charts of the two management systems described above are attached (appendices I and II). Appendix II-A is the organisational structure in a block within the project area.

A look at the Mahaweli Development Board's management system shows that each range had a set of officers from each of the disciplines, such as land administration, agriculture, irrigation, and so forth.

These officers had a role or part to play. At the next level too (regional) there was a hierarchy of officers for each of the operative disciplines. At the top or project level also there were Deputy Resident Managers for agriculture, water management, land administration, community development, marketing and credit. The senior staff were strengthened by an Accountant and an Administrative Officer. This, broadly, was the staff that assisted the Resident Project Manager in running the project.

An evaluation some time later showed that all the settlers were not getting the full benefits of the development effort and were not receiving all the inputs. The services provided were not accessible to some settlers and some did not seem to receive their benefits fully.

RESIDENT PROJECT MANAGER (KALAWEWA) ORGANISATION CHART

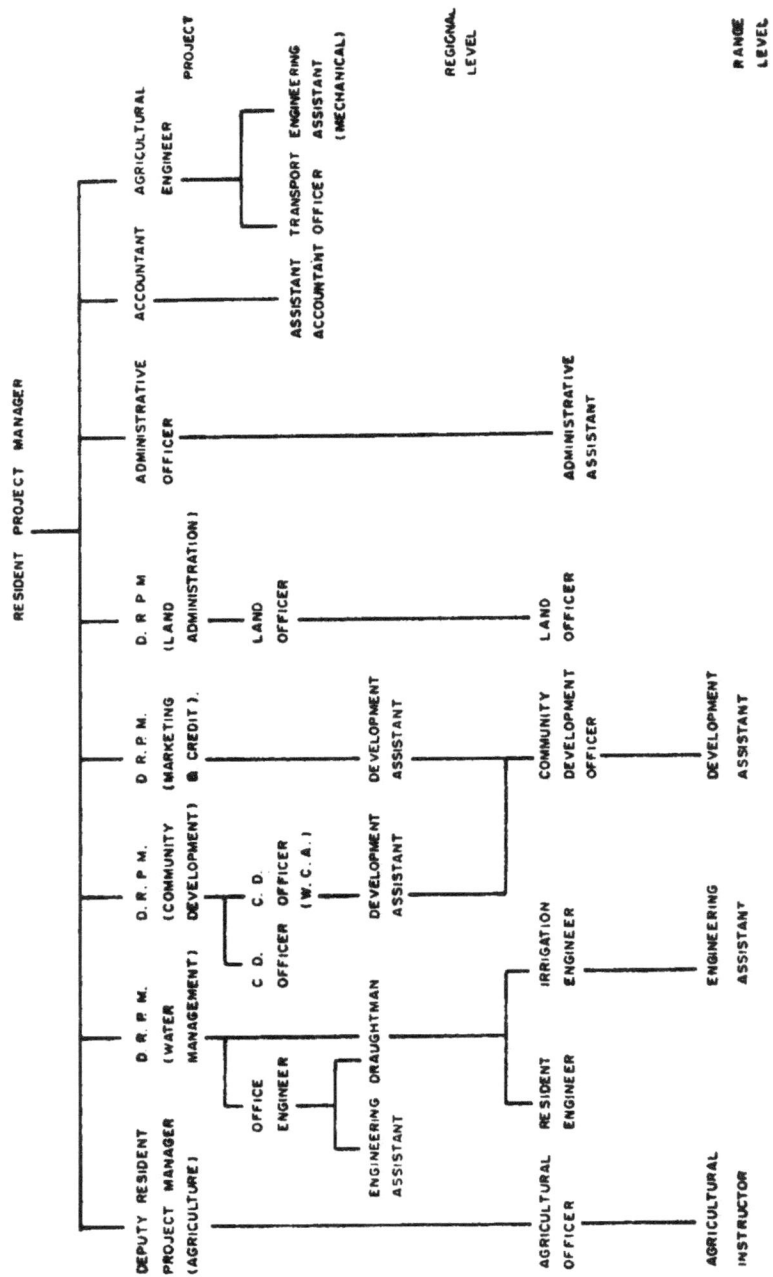

RESIDENT PROJECT MANAGER

REGIONAL LEVEL:

- AGRICULTURAL ENGINEER (PROJECT)
  - ASSISTANT TRANSPORT OFFICER
  - ENGINEERING ASSISTANT (MECHANICAL)
- ACCOUNTANT
  - ASSISTANT ACCOUNTANT OFFICER
- ADMINISTRATIVE OFFICER
- D.R.P.M. (LAND ADMINISTRATION)
  - LAND OFFICER
- D.R.P.M. (MARKETING & CREDIT)
  - DEVELOPMENT ASSISTANT
- D.R.P.M. (COMMUNITY DEVELOPMENT)
  - C.D. OFFICER / C.D. OFFICER (W.C.A.)
  - DEVELOPMENT ASSISTANT
- D.R.P.M. (WATER MANAGEMENT)
  - OFFICE ENGINEER
  - ENGINEERING DRAUGHTMAN ASSISTANT
- DEPUTY RESIDENT PROJECT MANAGER (AGRICULTURE)

RANGE LEVEL:

- ADMINISTRATIVE ASSISTANT
- LAND OFFICER
- COMMUNITY DEVELOPMENT OFFICER
  - DEVELOPMENT ASSISTANT
- IRRIGATION ENGINEER
  - ENGINEERING ASSISTANT
- RESIDENT ENGINEER
- AGRICULTURAL OFFICER
  - AGRICULTURAL INSTRUCTOR

APPENDIX I

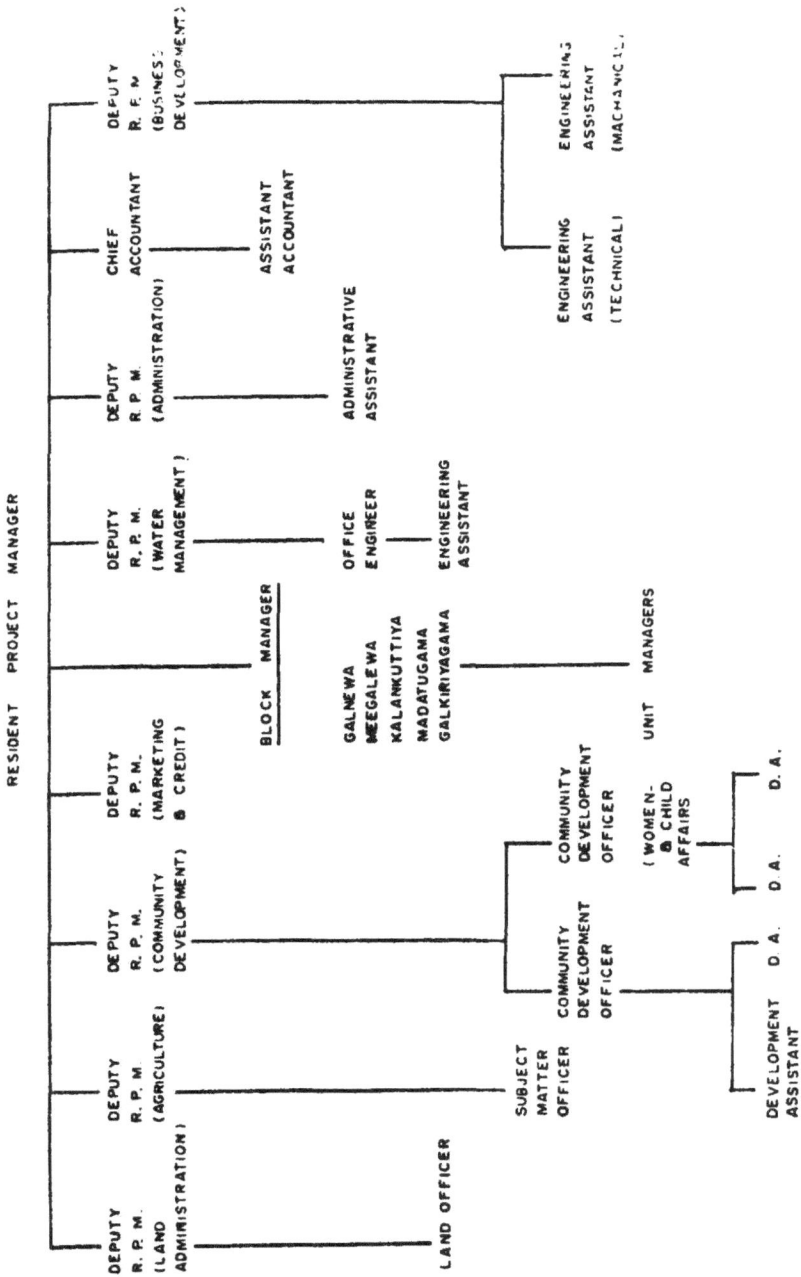

RESIDENT PROJECT MANAGER

- DEPUTY R.P.M. (LAND ADMINISTRATION)
  - LAND OFFICER
- DEPUTY R.P.M. (AGRICULTURE)
  - SUBJECT MATTER OFFICER
- DEPUTY R.P.M. (COMMUNITY DEVELOPMENT)
  - COMMUNITY DEVELOPMENT OFFICER
    - DEVELOPMENT ASSISTANT
    - D.A.
  - COMMUNITY DEVELOPMENT OFFICER (WOMEN- & CHILD AFFAIRS)
    - D.A.
    - D.A.
- DEPUTY R.P.M. (MARKETING & CREDIT)
  - BLOCK MANAGER
    - GALNEWA
    - MEEGALEWA
    - KALANKUTTIYA
    - MADATUGAMA
    - GALKIRIYAGAMA
    - UNIT MANAGERS
- DEPUTY R.P.M. (WATER MANAGEMENT)
  - OFFICE ENGINEER
    - ENGINEERING ASSISTANT
- DEPUTY R.P.M. (ADMINISTRATION)
  - ADMINISTRATIVE ASSISTANT
- CHIEF ACCOUNTANT
  - ASSISTANT ACCOUNTANT
- DEPUTY R.P.M. (BUSINESS DEVELOPMENT)
  - ENGINEERING ASSISTANT (TECHNICAL)
  - ENGINEERING ASSISTANT (MECHANICAL)

APPENDIX II

ORGANISATION CHART FOR THE BLOCK MANAGER'S OFFICE

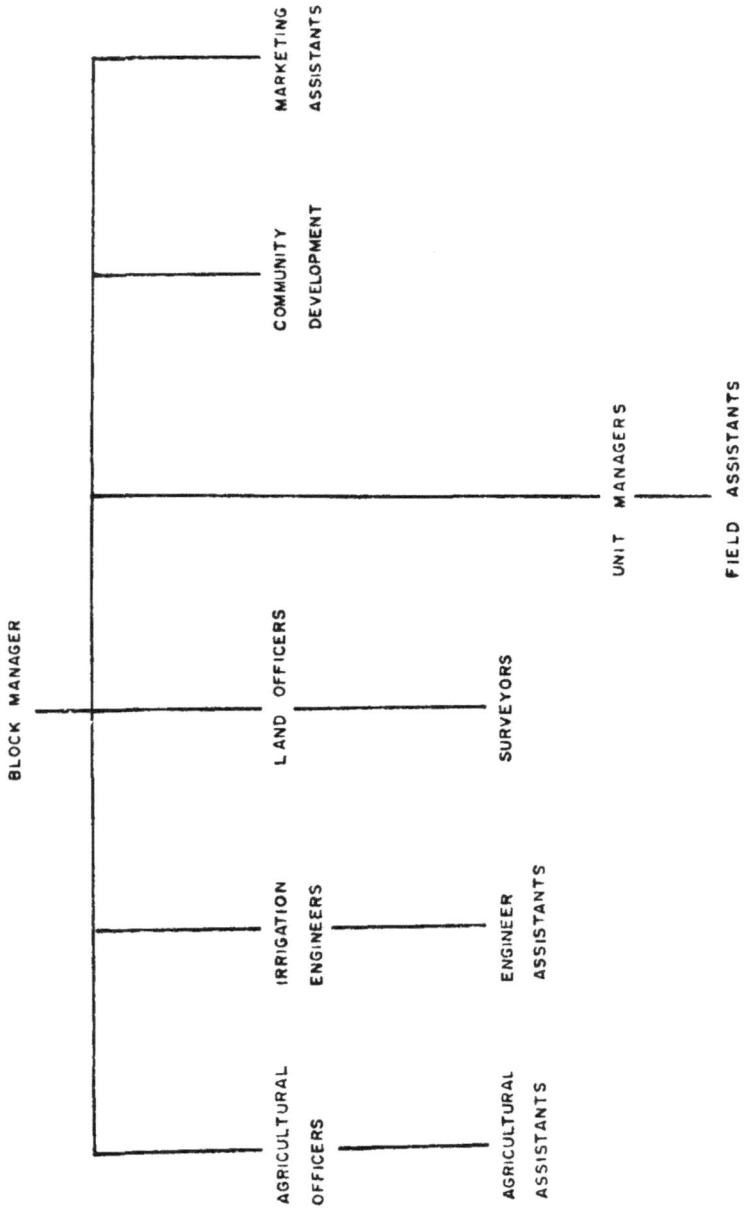

BLOCK MANAGER

AGRICULTURAL OFFICERS

IRRIGATION ENGINEERS

LAND OFFICERS

UNIT MANAGERS

COMMUNITY DEVELOPMENT

MARKETING ASSISTANTS

AGRICULTURAL ASSISTANTS

ENGINEER ASSISTANTS

SURVEYORS

FIELD ASSISTANTS

ONE UNIT MANAGER FOR 200 FARMER FAMILIES.

EACH UNIT MANAGER HAS TWO FIELD ASSISTANTS.

APPENDIX II-A

The reason for this state of affairs seemed to be that the farmers were not geared to receive these benefits and make the best use of them. These farmers did not have sufficient productive and management skills individually to receive the benefits of the services that were available to them. It was necessary to upgrade these skills in the farmers. It also seemed that effective servicing was only possible through group action. It was through group action that the basic skills in the farmers could be upgraded. Group action was also necessary to get the community to participate in the planned programmes of the project. It was found that the communities did not continue to function effectively if they were organised only to benefit from the social and welfare programmes of the project. It has been my experience that farmers are initially interested only in productivity, i.e., agriculture, land and water. Only after consolidation of these project benefits and successful cultivation do they become fully interested in social, cultural and religious activities. Only then do they participate together as a community in project activities or programmes with respect to environmental sanitation, community health, nutrition, clean drinking water, day-care centres, and so forth. Without community participation, no programme can be carried to successful completion.

In System 'H', as in most other irrigation settlement projects, water is the key to the success of the project, and in the eyes of the settlers the most valuable commodity. Since all attention is focused on water and since the irrigation design provides for a turnout area with groups of 12-20 farmers, it was decided that this should be the base of a farmer organisation. The irrigable area was broken up into blocks of 30-50 lots of irrigable land where the water was given to these farmers in bulk. The planners hoped that the farmers in this turnout area would manage their water equitably amongst themselves. In actual practice, this did not happen. The farmers could not organise themselves effectively to distribute water and to maintain the field channels and irrigation works. Farmers cannot form themselves into groups and co-operate in group activities unless their skills in management and organisational ability are developed to an effective degree. Because the distribution of water was not equitable and due to the non-co-operation amongst the farmers, some farm plots received little or no irrigation water for successive cultivations. As a result, the damage to irrigation structures and channels was very high. As mentioned earlier, turnout groups were then organised, initially for water management.

The turnout group was asked to elect two representatives from among themselves to be trained in water management and in agriculture. These representatives, elected by their fellow farmers, were then given formal training by the project officers not only in water management and agriculture, but also in community development, marketing and credit, land matters, etc. These training sessions were held at the community centres located in each range. Where there were no community centres conveniently, located, these meetings were held in the nearest school.

The response of the farmers to the formation of turnout groups and the attendance of their two representatives at the bi-weekly training sessions were very heartening. Their attendance was regular, they paid close attention to the proceedings, they kept notes and records, and also participated very keenly in the discussions. These two farmer leaders or representatives were then supposed to return to the other farmers in their turnout group and disseminate the knowledge and training they received at these fortnightly sessions.

With the organisation of the turnout groups and the election of their leaders for purposes of training, it was necessary to assess the training needs of these farmers. It was felt that any form of training must be relevant to the situation in the field and therefore discussions with the farmers themselves and the field officers was necessary. The purposes of these discussions were to identify the problems that the farmers faced and to equip them to solve these problems together with the project officers. The training was to be geared to upgrading the skills of the farmers so that they could be used effectively in the solution of these problems. As mentioned earlier, the project management had all the different disciplines represented at different levels or tiers by the officers in the field. There were officers for water management, agriculture, community development, and so forth at the project, regional and range levels.

It was therefore necessary that all these levels be represented in the discussions with the farmers lest the list of the problems facing the farmers not be complete. This also meant that the constraints felt by the project staff at all levels would also be identified. It was necessary first to find ways and means of eliminating the problems and constraints faced by the staff, if these people were to be fully involved in the solution of the farmers' problems.

Another important aspect of farmer training was that, considering the number of farmer leaders involved, it was not possible logistically for one group of trainers to train all the farmer leaders. It was therefore necessary to have a number of trainers, a group of whom could work regularly and continuously with a particular group of farmer leaders. In this context the best possible trainers were the field level officers themselves. But now we had to consider the question of training the officers to be trainers. This too was organised. A foundational course was held and regularly bolstered by a monthly two-day follow-up course.

The main problems with regard to water management that were identified at these discussions are given below. The initial training of farmers had to be geared to the solution of these problems.

a) Poor and unequitable distribution of water by farmers amongst themselves in a turnout area.

b) Poor maintenance of field drains and ditches by farmers within a turnout area.

c) No solution to problems with respect to land preparation, irrigation, and so on.

Because there was no organised system of water distribution within the turnout area, much water was being wasted and the consumption levels of water for cultivation were far in excess of the projected levels. Contrarily, in some instances no water whatsoever was reaching the fields of some of the farmers.

It was acknowledged at the discussions that the field level officers could not solve these problems by themselves, nor could the farmers do so without some form of organisation within their turnout area. It was clear that the co-operation of both officers and farmers was necessary for the solution of these problems. It was equally clear that the participation of the farmers in this exercise would be confined to their turnout areas. In System 'H', where nearly 72,000 acres of new lands were being developed for

24,000 families, there were 1,734 farmer turnout groups.

Problems with regard to agricultural extension were also identified. Studies of previous settlement schemes had very clearly shown the importance of agricultural production in the success of these schemes. Both agricultural extension and agricultural inputs are important. It seemed that relatively few resources were being devoted to agricultural inputs and some of these inputs, like tractors and heavy machinery, were not appropriate to the needs of the farmers. High costs of oil and spare parts had increased the need to use draught animals for farm power. It was also found that the extension education pertaining to agricultural production was weak.

A close look at all these problems revealed that there seemed to be very little co-ordination between the various project activities like agriculture, water management and community development.

The little co-ordination evident occurred at the top, i.e. at project level, whereas it was equally important to have some cohesion and co-ordination closer to the grass roots. Furthermore, there was very little participation by the community in the implementation of these programmes. Community participation, to my mind, is not merely keeping the community informed of the development programmes, but getting the community to actively participate in the implementation process. This also includes taking into consideration their views and satisfying their needs even though such may not be in the original plan. Unfortunately, community views are generally not obtained in the pre-planning stage.

One of the primary needs for agricultural settlement is to have the necessary infrastructure. There are basically three types of infrastructure. In our case the physical infrastructure was almost complete—buildings, irrigation channels, etc. The administrative infrastructure was also organised to facilitate the provision of advice, inputs and other services easily to farmers. This administrative infrastructure was found to need certain changes, however, to keep up with decisions on changes in our operational methods. The social infrastructure, or the building of communities, had as yet to be created. A social infrastructure is necessary to organise farmers and to improve their production, through co-operatives and other organisations, women and childrens' programmes, etc.

The social infrastructure must be so designed that it does not merely give the farmer security in the life he lives or regarding the land he owns, but also contributes to high productivity. The purpose of the development programme under discussion was to make the farmers increase production, thereby enabling them to raise their level of existence, and not merely to create more subsistence farmers.

In this respect, just as training is needed for the officers, the farmer too needs training and education. This training and education is very necessary if he is to increase production. Furthermore, increased production and increased income do not necessarily mean that his money is spent in the best possible way. He may have confused priorities. This is where not only the farmer but his wife as well, needs suitable education and guidance.

The Mahaweli authorities have, as mentioned earlier, placed considerable emphasis on community development and the participation of farmers in the operation of these programmes. This approach needs intensive training as it is a departure from the normal bureaucratic approach of the past settlement schemes. Such training has to be intensive. All the more so when one finds from evaluations that there are shortcomings in the implementation of proposed plans and programmes, especially with respect to farmers receiving the benefits directed to them

One of the main reasons for these shortcomings in the project under discussion was that there was no co-ordinated effort between the officers of the various disciplines at range or regional level. The Resident Project Manager had to co-ordinate all the work in the project. The line of command went straight down with no co-ordination between, say, agriculture and water management. As a result, it was not possible to have an integrated, interdisciplinary programme. Planning such a programme at the project level by the Resident Project Manager and his senior staff proved no problem, but implementing it in the field was difficult because no single officer had been made responsible for all the staff at the range or regional level.

Thus it appeared very necessary that there should be some coordinator at a very low level of the management structure. Breaking the management system into too many small co-ordinated units would nullify the purpose in co-ordinating managements' activities at the lowest level in the field. These groups have to be co-ordinated as close to the grass roots as possible, but not to the extent that there would be almost as many co-ordinators as those co-ordinated.

The Settlement Branch of the Mahaweli Authority of Sri Lanka, which was going to take over the settlement and post-settlement work in System 'H' and subsequently in all the Mahaweli settlement areas, therefore experimented with a new management system in a pilot project in the H_5 area. This unitary system of management was akin to the management system obtaining in the tea and rubber plantations in Sri Lanka. It is a system that has evolved over a hundred years. It was basically this system that was adopted in H_5. Obviously, it was necessary to make a number of modifications in this system to satisfy the set objectives of the Mahaweli Scheme. The management system tried out in H_5 seemed to work well and it was decided that with certain modifications and with further experience through operation, this management system could be adopted in the other settlement areas as well.

The Settlement Branch of the Mahaweli Authority of Sri Lanka (the forerunner of the Mahaweli Economic Agency) took over the management functions in System 'H' from the Mahaweli Development Board on the 1st January 1981. In April 1981 the management system as shown in appendices-II and II-A was adopted. Under the new system unit- and block-level management replaced range- and regional-level management. The management system at project level remained almost the same. This new management system has worked quite well. Intensive orientation and training programmes had to be conducted in order to give the officers a full and proper understanding of what was expected of them and to enable them to carry out their duties and functions properly and effectively.

It is very essential in development schemes such as this one that evaluations be made from time to time to ensure that the purposes and objectives of the programmes are being met. Such evaluations become even more important when the development programmes are for the benefit of the people and designed to improve their quality of life. Spending large amounts of money on a project does not necessarily guarantee its success. Constant evaluations must be carried out to ensure that this money is being utilised in the best possible way and that the target group has received maximum benefits from these efforts.

In a recent evaluation the following points were noted:

AGRICULTURE

There seems to be a trend toward increased yields in paddy season by season. There is also a noticeable increase in the use of fertiliser in the cultivation of paddy.

More and more farmers are taking to the cultivation of other field crops, especially chilli, during the *yala* season. This is because of the good prices they have realised for their products and the easy marketing facilities that are available.

The acreage of paddy that is transplanted is increasing each year. Weed control is more effective. This shows that farmers are receptive to the advice of the agricultural extension officers.

WATER MANAGEMENT

Taking successive *maha* and *yala* seasons separately, it was found that the water consumed per acre for cultivation has decreased progressively.

Farmers are taking a greater interest in water management. They are co-operating in the distribution of water and in the maintenance of the irrigation system. Very little damage is done to the irrigation structure now, as opposed to the past.

In the *yala* season, when water is limited, it is heartening to note that farmers get together and cultivate in equal shares the limited land that can be cultivated according to the water available.

This shows that the farmer training sessions, both in the field and in the classroom, have had a definite impact on the farmers.

COMMUNITY DEVELOPMENT

By their attendance and responses shown in many ways, it is obvious that the farmers have realised the benefits of farmer training and group action in not only the solution of these problems but also in carrying out their cultivation work.

The response of the farmers is exemplified by the participation of the farmers in our programmes. We have over 350 health volunteers who serve in each of the hamlets entirely on a voluntary basis. They render first-aid, distribute anti-malaria tablets, and pass out milk to the children daily as a part of our nutrition programme. They maintain registers and records of the work they do.

At the training sessions for farmer leaders it was mentioned that the farmers needed a place to keep their children during the day so that their wives could also work. The project management responded immediately and, with assistance from UNICEF, seventeen day care centres were started, with another thirteen opened in 1983. In most instances the affairs of these day care centres are managed by the Parents' Association formed for each day care centre. Another pleasing feature is that one parent brings a day's meal for all the children in a centre on a rotational basis.

Another matter brought up by the farmers was that the single well presently provided for every 20 families was not suitable and inconvenient to use. It was suggested that a smaller well to cater for six families be built. Here again, the management, with UNICEF assistance, responded quickly to the request of the farmers and over 4,000 wells have already been completed. The actual excavation of a well is done by six farmers who will benefit from that well.

As an added measure, to strengthen the turnout groups, I have requested my officers to give all contract work on maintenance and repairs of a particular turnout to that turnout group itself. Apart from working together and earning extra money, the farmers will ensure that the work is done to their satisfaction. This means that no reports of poor quality work will come back to the management.

On the first evaluation it was found that a number of farmers were not receiving the full benefits of our programme and in some instances some farmers were receiving no benefits at all. It was then that the management decided to see what the constraints and problems were. To overcome most of these constraints and problems we secured the active participation of the farmers. It was also decided that a co-ordinated effort should be made by their programmes. Farmer and officer training was planned as the key to this new approach. From the results of my subsequent evaluation, it is quite obvious that the new approach has paid very good dividends. This is mainly the result of the active participation of the farmers in our programmes. The active participation of the farmers was brought about by the management's quick and effective response to the needs and aspirations of the farmers.

The problems are certainly not over but much headway has been made. As long as we are sensitive to not only the needs, but the changing needs, of the farmers and our responses to them are positive, we cannot really go wrong.

CHAPTER 6

Economic Inequality between Top-enders and Tail-enders in Sri Lankan Irrigation Schemes

This paper presents the inequalities in economic gains between the top-enders and tail-enders in earlier Sri Lankan irrigation settlement schemes, or colonisation schemes as they were then called. The causes and reasons for such a situation developing are examined and the methods of correction and effective solutions implemented to prevent similar situations developing in the future are discussed, especially with reference to the Accelerated Mahaweli Development Programme.

In an irrigation scheme, water stored in a reservoir, commonly called tank in Sri Lanka, is distributed by means of channels of varying length and size to agricultural lands for the cultivation of short-term crops. In Sri Lanka, paddy is the main crop cultivated in these irrigation schemes. There is now a tendency, however, to grow other crops, such as chilli, soybean, pulses, and others. This change has been suggested and encouraged by the authorities because the consumption of water is less for other crops than for paddy. The income from other crops is equal to or better than that of paddy as is quite evident in the case of chilli.

Top-enders are those who receive water at the beginning of a distributary canal and tail-enders those whose farm plots are at the end of these canals. An irrigation system is diagrammatically illustrated in the appendix to this paper.

The first peasant colonisation schemes were started in Sri Lanka in the early 1930s. Moore defines a peasant as 'the small family farmer operating at a relatively low level of technology and in an environment of relative poverty'.

The main purposes of colonisation schemes were to:

a) Settle landlass peasants in irrigated lands to enable them to engage in profitable agricultural activity.

b) Try to solve the problems of feeding an increasing population by increasing paddy production.

c) Try to increase the incomes of the colonists.

d) Make better use of the land and other resources in the dry zone where these schemes were all located.

e) Ease the population pressure in the wet zone of the island by moving some of the people to the less densely populated dry zone.

Later studies of the working of these schemes and an evaluation of their performance revealed the following grey areas.

a) Apparently, insufficient attention had been paid by the planners to local variations in physical conditions, such as soils, salinity, and lands that would be unirrigable.

b) These schemes were mainly planned by the Irrigation Department and therefore other considerations, such as agriculture, community development, marketing and credit, were not given sufficient importance.

c) Officials instrumental in settling the peasants in various schemes left soon after settlement. This meant that the farmers were left to their own devices when various initial problems arose. They were left to the whims and vagaries of the officials of various government departments that operated as in other parts of the country. As a result, much time was wasted that could well have been spent by the farmers in the cultivation of their lands. Due to poor cultivation, the incomes of the farmers suffered consequently.

d) Farmers were given no proper training in water management. This led to considerable wastage of irrigation water, resulting in an insufficiency of water to be distributed to all the farmer allotments. The absence of strong farmer organisations was one of the main causes of poor water management. Most of the blame for inefficient water management fell on the farmer when, in fact, the officials should have shouldered part of the blame.

e) Due to the fact that all colonists were not from the same place of origin there were certain ethnic differences; hence the farmers were not able to organise themselves easily for 'group action' which is very essential for efficient water management in these irrigation schemes.

Studies and observations showed that those farmers whose fields are at the top ends of the irrigation canals developed much faster economically than those farmers at the bottom or tail ends of these same canals. This also meant that with better incomes, those farmers at the top ends are able to purchase more of the necessities for a better life and also able to accumulate capital.

Tables 6.1 and 6.2 give data from farmer samples covering four schemes which together account for a large area under the larger irrigation projects.

The inequality between the top-enders and the tail-enders was mainly caused by the following:

a) Bad irrigation design and construction and poor water management practices. This also includes misuse and under-utilisation of the irrigation facilities.

b) Problems that arose in land settlement and construction of the social infrastructure.

c) Problems in the layout and design of the social infrastructure.

It was found that the top-enders were always able to obtain more water for cultivation, generally at the expense of the tail-enders. Due to various faults in the irrigation system, water did not reach the tail-enders in sufficient quantity and sometimes not at all. Also the quantity of water sent down an irrigation canal is greatest at the top end of the canal. It follows therefore that the top-enders will receive their full quota first and whatever water remains will flow towards the tail-end.

The lack of adequate water for cultivation is not the only reason for large economic disparities between top-enders and tail-enders. Various other factors have contributed to this disparity noticed in most Sri Lankan Settlement Schemes.

The first objective of these schemes was to distribute land. The planners thought that the other objectives listed earlier would be achieved automatically. This did not happen. It was only in the 1960s that any attention was paid to better use of land and better agricultural techniques adopted. In the 1970s more efficient use of water was accentuated, now konwn as water management. Ini-

Table 6.1: Economics of Paddy Production according to Field Location on Three Irrigation Schemes

Scheme Field Location within Scheme		Uda Walawe		Kaudulla		Padaviya		
		Top	Tail	Top	Tail	Top	Middle	Tail
No. of farmer samples.	a	76	29	49	48	21	45	18
Average yields, bushels per acre, Maha 1979-80 and Yala 1980 seasons	b	52	38	65	58	83	69	62
Average fertiliser use, Ibs per acre, Maha 1979-80 season	c	95	48	163	133	66	165	43
Cost of production of paddy, Rs. per bushel, both seasons[1]	d	27	32	32	38	28	29	37
Net returns per hour of family labour inputs in Rs. both seasons[2]	e	5.1	3.2	4.8	4.5	5.3	6.5	3.5

[1]This figure includes the cost of family labour computed at the local wage rate.

[2]Labour of different kinds (i.e., according to gender and age) and in different occupations has been adjusted to adult male equivalents as explained in Farrington and Abeyratne, 1982: 108.

Source: Farm Power Project Survey.

Table 6.2: **Economics of Paddy Production according to Field Location on Three Sub-systems of the Gal Oya Project**

		Uhana-Mandur Sub-system			Left Bank Main Channel		Gonagolle Channel	
		Top	Middle	Tail	Top	Tail	Top	Tail
Average yield in bushels per acre[1]	a	53	46	33	48	33	45	37
Cost of Production[2] (per acre)	b	1231	1155	1416	1230	1522	1106	1182
In Rs. (per bushel)	c	35	49	53	30	53	29	55
Net returns per family Labour day in Rs.[2,3]	d	+27	+34	−48	+28	−11	44	−8

[1]Figures relate to the average of four seasons from Maha 1979-80 to Yala 1981, and were collected through sample crop cutting.
[2]Figures relate only to the Maha 1979-80 season.
[3]These figures have been adjusted to adult male equivalents.
Source: Data from a sample of 536 farmers. The ARTI's Water Management Group.

tially, the Land Commissioners Department handled the settlement, and the design and layout was done by the Irrigation Department. These two Departments did not think there was more to settlement than bringing in the settlers and giving them irrigated lands.

One of the main considerations in the implementation of the settlement schemes was that costs had to be kept as low as possible. This resulted not only in poor construction but also in various channels being designed and constructed to serve larger areas than was practically possible. It is necessary to have the proper infrastructure by way of channels, structures, control gates, and measuring devices for equal distribution of the available water to

all the farmers' fields. The annexation of more land to the irrigable area after the design and construction of the system aggravat-
ed a bad situation further. This was due mainly to influential
landowners exerting pressure to obtain irrigation water for their
lands. This resulted in some areas of most colonisation schemes
receiving no irrigation water at all. In addition, there was very
little control of water once it was released down the main channels. This meant that the top-enders were able to take all the
water they wanted and more, leaving very little or no water for
the tail-enders.

Obviously the ones adversely affected by the above situation
were the tail-enders, most of whom found it difficult to do even
subsistence level farming. Many encountered economic losses and,
as a result, abandoned these schemes altogether and returned to
their places of origin, or in some cases to urban areas in search
of any form of employment. In almost every instance these lands
were grabbed by an encroacher, who faced the same difficulties.

When a settlement scheme is started, all construction etc. starts
at the source of the water used for irrigation, which is at the
reservoir or tank. A bund is built or an old bund renovated as
the case may be.

Sluices and main canals leading from the tank are then constructed. The main camps where the engineers and workers live
are constructed in close proximity to the original construction
sites. These camps, over time, become the centre or hub of activity since in most cases no proper spatial planning is done nor
provision made for towns or villages. Here, too, it is the tail-
ender who suffers because he has to travel the farthest to obtain
any of his needs or to meet officials.

In some settlements, even though a promising start was made
with respect to provision of various social infrastructure facilities,
due to the Government having to make certain economies or due
to a change in policy, a reduction in the provision of these facilities has occurred. With settlement going down from the top or
reservoir end of the scheme, the tail end of the scheme bore these
reductions.

In times of water shortage, especially during *yala*, top-enders
were able to organise themselves to do a 'bethma' cultivation but
the tail-enders could not due to the absence or insufficiency of

water. A 'bethma' cultivation is one in which all land allottees cultivate an equal portion of that land which can be cultivated depending on the water available.

It is now opportune to consider what is being done in Sri Lanka's new Irrigated Settlement Schemes, especially in the Accelerated Mahaweli Development Programme, to try and eliminate the economic differences that develop between top-enders. and tail-enders.

It is obvious that first and foremost the irrigation infrastructure must be so constructed and maintained that it can carry sufficient water to all the irrigated land under its command, especially the tail end. Together with this, efficient water management must be practised to ensure equitable distribution. It is also important that cultivation loans be made available in time for cultivation. All inputs, such as farm power, seed material, fertiliser, and agrochemicals should be readily available and on time, thereby enabling the farmer to engage in timely cultivation.

New schemes are now carefully planned and construction of the entire scheme executed as planned, thereby ensuring no differences in the infrastructure facilities provided to the top-enders and the tail-enders.

It is easier to talk of efficient water management than to actually practice it. In the Mahaweli Scheme we have organised the farmers on a distributary channel and turnout basis for water management purposes. A turnout area consists of a number of irrigable plots grouped together where the water is finally distributed in bulk; this is illustrated in the appendix. As this water is given to a turnout in bulk, the farmers in that turnout area have to distribute this water amongst themselves equitably. Each turnout was asked to elect a leader and all turnout leaders along a distributary channel constituted a group given intensive training in water distribution and management. This group was also asked to identify problems in the construction and maintenance of their particular turnout area. Each farmer leader in the group was expected in turn to disseminate his knowledge to the other 15 to 20 farmers in his turnout area.

We have also trained these farmer leaders to try, insofar as possible, to encourage 'group 'action' amongst the farmers in their turnout area, especially along these lines:

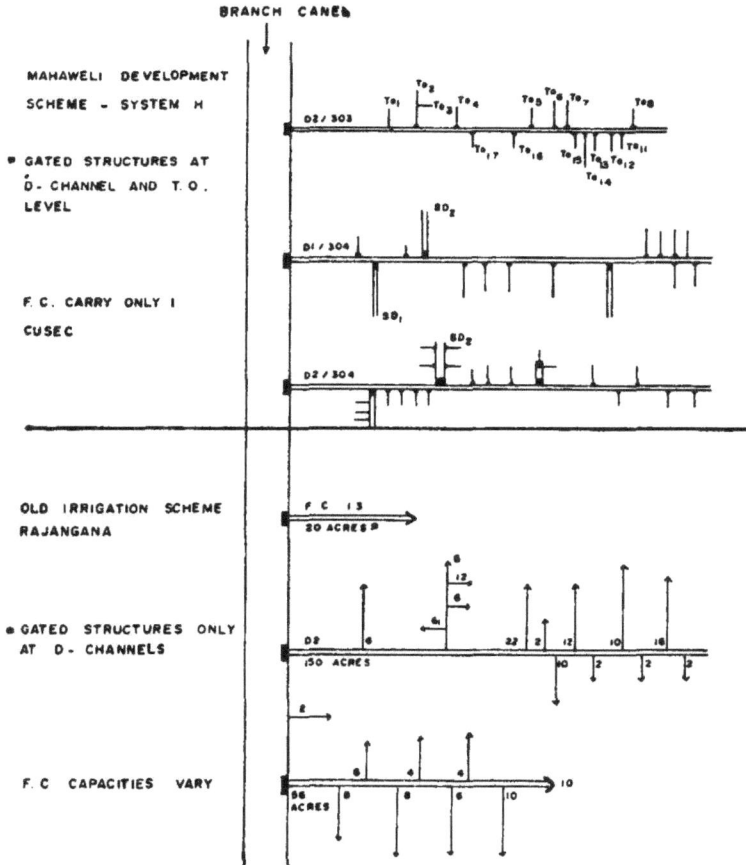

APPENDIX: Water Distribution in the Mahaweli Development Scheme (System H) and the Rajangana Irrigation Scheme.

a) Sharing out the farm power available among themselves.

b) Having just a few nurseries per turnout area instead of each farmer having his own nursery.

c) Joining together with other farmers and their families to operate a common programme of transplanting, harvesting and so forth.

The training programme has also tried to encourage leadership amongst the farmers to better organise themselves and better articulate their problems and needs. Fairly good results have been obtained by the programme in that greater co-operation was evident amongst the farmers within their turnout areas this current *maha* season, especially at the time of transplanting. Before the season started and water issues made, maintenance work on the irrigation system was carried out. This work programme was based mainly on the farmers listing their problems on a turnout basis.

This *maha* season water is being issued to the tail ends of the main channels first so that farm power etc. could be concentrated there. Once the initial work of land preparation is completed, the farm power will be moved up according to the water issues. The purpose of this season's arrangements are to ensure that the tail-enders get water and also to assist them in engaging in timely cultivation. It was difficult to get the top-enders to agree to allow the water to pass their allotments and go down to the end of the channel. However, with assured water in the tank, seasonal rains and much persuasion, we were able to achieve the present water arrangement. This is a major breakthrough and if we get through the season with no serious water problems, making similar arrangements in the future will not be so difficult.

A form of supervised credit has been organised in order to ensure that farmers repay their cultivation loans and, as a result, will continue to remain credit worthy. One feature of this scheme is that the seed material, fertiliser, agro-chemicals, and so forth are given in kind and not in cash. This reduces the farmers' temptation to utilise his loan for something other than cultivation.

We have also launched an effective community development programme whereby we are trying not only to develop the community in terms of health, nutrition, education etc., but to organise it to manage its own affairs. This will enable the community members to reduce their dependency on the Mahaweli authorities and other Government officials; it is our hope that this dependency will eventually taper off.

Intensive training in agriculture is given to the farmer leaders. The training and visiting system is working quite well and has also proved very useful to farmers in improving their agricultural skills.

The Mahaweli Economic Agency continues to manage the settlement areas after the settlers are brought in. The management system provides for one Unit Manager and two Field Assistants to look after the well-being of each unit of 250 farmers. This means that all the programmes, training, and so forth carried out by the project authorities are directed to the farmers through the Unit Manager and his Assistants. On the other hand, all problems confronting the farmer are taken up with the Unit Manager. This makes it much easier for the farmer in that he has only one person to deal with at all times. The Unit Manager lives within the unit and thus is readily available to the farmer.

These measures seem to be having the desired effect in that there are no inequalities apparent between top-enders and tail-enders in the new schemes. Future evaluations, however, will give us a definite indication of the effects of these new measures, implemented to eliminate any inequality that might arise between these two groups of farmers.

CHAPTER 7

Options in Irrigation System Management and Their Implications for Farm Technology in Sri Lanka*

This paper examines the options for future interaction between water management and farm technology, and the constraints likely to be faced, with particular reference to mechanisation. After a brief introduction, the main characteristics of current trends in water management and farm power use are highlighted (section 2). Set against likely developments in the agrarian framework (section 3), the scope for improvement in water use and related technologies through administrative action is explored (section 4). Such action might take several forms: improved water management without major physical or institutional change; promotion of organised staggering of cultivation or promotion of early land preparation and sowing. Finally, conclusions are drawn, focusing on constraints requiring early removal if progress in this area is to be achieved.

1. INTRODUCTION

The prospects for improving water management on large-scale irrigation schemes in Sri Lanka have recently attracted a spate of

*This paper draws partly on material prepared for the ARTI/Reading University Farm Power Study by M.P. Moore. The author is indebted to him for this and for comments on an earlier draft.

attention from engineers, social scientists and administrators. Earlier reports on the desirability of improving water use-efficiency (Chambers, 1975a, 1975b) were followed by expressions of concern by aid donors,[1] departmental memoranda within the Sri Lanka administration,[2] voluminous reports on the construction of new irrigation schemes—or the rehabilitation of existing ones— stressing the interaction between physical and institutional requirements for improved water management[3] and, most recently, the implementation of field trials designed to explore alternative ways of reducing water consumption.[4,5]

Much interest and enthusiasm have been devoted to the potential for improving water management. But to assess whether widespread practical improvements can be achieved in the field, and what implications these might have for the joint use-efficiency of farm power and water, requires careful prognosis based on a firm grasp of existing physical and institutional conditions in major irrigation schemes.

2. CURRENT WATER MANAGEMENT AND FARM POWER INTERACTION

In brief, the following characteristics appear to constitute the essence of present physical systems and practices:

1) Most existing major systems, excluding only those constructed or rehabilitated in recent years, incorporate the following design characteristics: open channel conveyance of water down to the individual allotment; subject to this constraint, capital cost minimisation per acre of land served, leading to long distributary channels (henceforth D-channels) and field channels (henceforth, FCs), wide variations in length and area commanded, lack of rigid and clear distinctions between main canals, branch canals, D-channels and FCs, and the feeding of some FCs directly from main or branch canals; placing of channels at a minimal slope across contours to maximise command area; and lack of designed re-use of drainage water.[6] One consequence of this design, and especially of long D-channels and FCs, is the difficulty of ensuring water delivery to the tail ends of D-channels and FCs. It is so easy for farmers near the tops of channels to appropriate water (and many systems are in such bad physical repair), that

extra water fed into the tops of channels may not reach the tail ends.

2) In recent years a new design has been developed in response to the above problems and to the opportunity for innovation presented by the creation of a separate Mahaweli Development Board. The physical core of this design is the standard FC of 0.028 cu mhos (one cusec) capacity. This is designed to serve about 16 ha of land in continuous flow for three days per week. Field channels are consequently relatively short, each serving between twelve and twenty farmers (each with paddy land allotments of 1.0 ha). The system is designed for rotations within distributary and field channels, with two farmers only receiving water at any one time. Outlet pipes to individual fields are 15 cm it diameter, larger than the 7-10 cm of the older designs because of the need to cope with a larger rotational flow in a shorter period of time. D-channels are designed with a capacity adequate only to serve all FCs at the designed flow capacity on a continuous basis. The system is intended to deliver just enough water to meet estimated needs. Evidence suggests that this new 'Mahaweli design' has reduced problems of inequitable access to water within field channels but that, because water is still appropriated beyond designed capacities, the brunt of water scarcity has fallen more squarely on field channels at the end of D-channels. One might note that by designing for rotational issues within FCs, the new design puts more emphasis than before on FC-level institutional devices for managing rotations.

3) Considerable inequalities exist between top- and tail-enders with respect to yields, income from cultivation, wealth, access to government offices, farm power, and political influence.[7] It is not known to what extent, if at all, these originated in the ability of more powerful or wealthy settlers to obtain land allotments at top ends. The greater access to water of top-enders and their location near main roads, commercial centres and government offices have certainly exacerbated any original inequalities.

4) The public organisations which construct, maintain and operate large-scale irrigation systems—the Irrigation Department, the Mahaweli Development Board, and the River Valleys Development Board—are, at the professional level, very strongly rooted in the discipline of civil engineering. This is associated with a

marked bias toward training, interest, perception, experience and reward in favour of construction-related activities (investigation, design and construction) and away from the functions of main-tenance and to an even greater degree, water management. Pro-fessionally-trained field staff (Engineers and Technical Assistants) are subject to continual transfer and thus generally fail to develop local field knowledge of either the physical system or the social situation. This kind of knowledge is possessed by more junior staff, especially Works Supervisors, who generally supervise the management of water on a day-to-day basis.

5) There are two main sets of decisions related to water manage-ment. The first, taken formally at the seasonal Water Meeting of farmers and officials, relate mainly to the opening and closing of the head sluices from tank to main canal: cropping patterns; dates for first issue of water; period of time for which a full flow of water is given for land preparation; date of termination of water issue. Decisions about rotations between D-channels may also be taken at this meeting. The second set of issues relate to the im-plementation of the agreed schedule and its modification accord-ing to circumstances. These affect mainly the opening and closing of gates to D-channels and FCs, and are handled mostly by junior staff, often on a day-to-day basis.[8]

6) The practice of water distribution bears the distinct imprints of the Irrigation Department's historical pattern of involvement in the question and of the physical limitations of systems. These imprints include: a prime focus on the manipulation of head sluices; enforcement of rotations as an emergency measure in situations of water scarcity; a general preference for limited con-trol of water below the level of the head sluice; and ad hoc alloca-tion of water in response to visible and/or articulated need, rather than according to contract, measurement of quantities delivered; or strict enforcement of rotational schedules.

7) With this focus on water control via manipulation of the head sluices, existing systems have not been designed for any sys-tem of intermediate storage between the main tank and fields, nor for separate intermediate storage tanks fed from the main channel, nor the practice of impounding water in main canals and operating in such a way as to maintain constant water level. It is argued that the short length of the main canals permits rapid

delivery of water from the main tank to any part of the command area. In practice the delivery time may be a multiple of design estimates, mainly because of the poor physical state of systems.

8) Lack of maintenance, deliberate destruction or bypassing of bunds and control structures, and erosion caused by overloading of canals have combined to seriously impair the capacity of most existing systems to deliver water in a controlled fashion.[9]

Given the uncertainty in timing and volume of water issues implied by these physical and institutional constraints, coupled with the irregularity of rainfall distribution at the start of the monsoon, the farmer's reaction is to delay land preparation until sufficient water is impounded in the reservoir to guarantee a regular flow both for land preparation and throughout the season. Once started, land preparation and planting commonly take five to eight weeks, the degree of staggering varying across schemes according to such factors as the time-requirement for water conveyance to the tail ends, and the size of the farm power stock (but not the proportion of tractors in the stock).[10] Tractors and buffaloes thus perform essentially the same tasks in near-universal wetland tillage, the individual farmer's demand for them is articulated in an imperfect and inefficient hire-market.[11] Little spontaneous effort appears to have been made by farmers to differentiate the tillage techniques of tractor and animal draught according to the individual horsepower capacities of each, or to adapt animal draught to semi-wet ploughing.

3. CHANGING TECHNOLOGICAL AND ECONOMIC CONTEXT

To examine potential changes in farm power and water use on the assumption that no other medium-term changes in the farmer's environment will take place would be simplistic: some developments can be predicted with reasonable certainty as extrapolations of existing trends; others are more speculative. In all events, the more likely developments need to be identified and collated in a scenario against which changes in the two main variables can be analysed.

The most likely medium-term developments are:[12]

1) An increase in the purchase price and running costs of tractors relative to those of animal draught, and relative to the farm gate price of paddy.

2) An increased likelihood of import restrictions on tractors resulting from official awareness that the tractor market is saturated and that deteriorating international terms of trade and balance of payments crisis prevent the continuation of existing levels of imports.

3) A continuing tendency, given the imperfect behaviour of draught hire markets, for tractor owners to pass on a high proportion of cost increases to hirers, and for buffalo owners to follow suit by increasing their hire rates despite a slower increase in their operating costs.

4) A corresponding desire among non-owners to avoid the burden of these cost increases by themselves acquiring a power source, the buffalo being relatively attractive in view of its lower capital outlay and enhanced earnings potential in times of rising hire charges.

5) A slow increase in the proportion of irrigated land under non-paddy crops in the *yala* season, as self-sufficiency in paddy is approached and the prospects of exporting rice remain poor.

6) The widespread introduction of appropriate zero or minimal tillage techniques on irrigated paddy lands, probably dependent on greatly improved irrigation and drainage control, and requiring smaller stocks of draught power than hitherto.

7) The breeding and adoption of a short duration paddy variety with vigorous leaf canopy, which would both inhibit the weed competition currently experienced in the *maha* dry sowing of paddy, and permit subsequent early planting of a *yala* or inter-monsoon crop.

The agrarian context within which improvements may be made in the joint efficiency of farm power and water use is therefore unlikely to remain unchanged: a relative shift in favour of animal draught may impair the prospects of a dry-sowing strategy for economising on water; a shift towards non-paddy crops may, on the other hand, reduce the need for tractor power[13] in both land preparation and threshing, and correspondingly increase that for human[14] effort in preparing ridges, beds, etc. The balance of opportunities for more efficient use of farm power and water may be altered by advances in both plant breeding and, more dramatically, in zero tillage techniques.

4. ADMINISTRATIVE ACTION TO IMPROVE WATER USE AND RELATED PRACTICES

The physical and institutional barriers to improved water use have been the subject of extensive research.[15] It is possible to summarise only the main prospects for improvement here.

Improved Water Management without Major Physical/Institutional Change

It is important to record that more efficient water use would in itself increase the efficiency of the use of the farm power stock without requiring a high proportion of tractors in the stock. A more reliable and predictable supply of irrigation water would allow and encourage farmers to put more effort and more inputs (fertiliser, labour, etc.) into production, and thus lead to higher output and higher returns per unit of all inputs used, including farm power. Insofar as better water management could save water in the *maha* season and thus permit the extension of the cultivated acreage in the *yala* season, this would provide greater opportunities for the use of farm power stocks which are currently unemployed or under-employed at that time [see Chapter 6.2, Farrington and Abeyratne (1982)]. This would permit an increment in annual use-intensities from the present low level. The more intensive use of capital assets (i.e., tractors) thus implied, would permit either more rapid recoupment of capital outlay at existing profit margins per hour of use, with the prospect of faster re-investment of the surpluses generated, or a reduction in hourly charges and recoupment of capital outlay at the same rate, with a consequent shift in the terms of trade to the advantage of (economically vulnerable) non-owners of draught power, or some combination of the two. Furthermore, any such increase in the demand for farm power which is not seasonally concentrated, would tend to increase a return to (and thus the attractions of owning) those types of farm power which (a) have few or no alternative uses outside agriculture and (b) tend to deteriorate more according to age rather than to cumulative use rates. In other words, *yala* cropping would increase the attractiveness of owning buffaloes rather than tractors, and 2wt rather than 4wt.

It is rather outside the scope of this paper to discuss in any detail the ways in which standards of water management might feasibly be improved. It is useful however to provide an illustrative example. The research conducted on the Kaudulla scheme since 1978 by the UK Hydraulics Research Station and the Sri Lanka Irrigation Department has revealed that a considerable quantity of water could be saved in the *maha* season if irrigation water were issued only when rainfall was inadequate. Because water management is not sufficiently sensitive to a reduction in irrigation issues where rain has occurred, most rainfall is lost as run-off.[16] To save rainfall is not possible without the investment of certain resources and efforts; otherwise it would be standard practice. A major point to consider is the evidence produced in the same study of the enormous local variability of rainfall even on a scheme covering only some 11,000 acres of paddy land. This is a product of the shower pattern of the monsoon rains. The present practice of closing the main sluices from the tank when it rains hard *there* is a very inadequate and possibly counter-productive method of attempting to adjust for rainfall. It may deprive water to those areas which have received no rain at all, especially if they happen to be on the tail end of the scheme. Because no control is exercised over the level of water in the main channel, the level drops as soon as the head sluice is closed. Even after the head sluice is re-opened it may take several days before the main channel is sufficiently filled to push water down to the tail ends of the main and distributary channels.

To save rainfall efficiently and without damaging crops in some areas would require, from the physical and procedural point of view: operational procedures for the water level in the main channels to be kept constant at all times to make possible rapid and effective responses to local water requirements; the existence and use of cross-regulators in the main channels and efficient gates from main channels to distributary channels; an effective system for reporting regularly and rapidly on rainfall and crop conditions on a tract by tract basis; and a procedure for utilising this information. In essence, what is required is more *informed control* of water; this is necessary whatever the precise techniques of water management chosen.

Apart from the inadequacy of the physical infrastructure in many schemes, there are pre-conditions to the adoption of such water-saving procedures which are organisational, attitudinal, and still in large part unfulfilled. They include recognition that low water use—efficiency is more the result of the lack of (or mis-) management of the *irrigation system* rather than of poor water use practices by farmers at field level; acceptance that irrigation management is about the *control* of water after it has left the main sluice; and the creation of a climate of sufficient trust between farmers and water managers that the former will be prepared to accept the enforcement of rotations and limits on water use without resorting to political pressure or to damaging the physical infrastructure.

The reaping of high potential benefits from improved water management[17] thus requires action on several fronts: in the conception of what water management is; in the effective representation of farmers in decision-making; in farm organisation; in physical rehabilitation; in the creation of effective communication systems, procedure and discipline within management organisation; and in the psychological climate at field level on irrigation schemes.[18] Because of the complexity of the interaction between these factors and the importance of such unpredictable variables as attitudinal and organisational change, it is not possible to predict likely future rates of progress. The progress which has been registered in recent years has largely been in the recognition of the nature and magnitude of the problem. Few, if any, concrete improvements in water use—efficiency appear to have been achieved except in one or two intensive pilot schemes (see Moore, 1980a). However, having recognised the problem, Sri Lanka is in a better position now than it was a few years go to tackle it. There are encouraging signs that water management is becoming a focus of attention in the Agriculture and Agrarian Services Departments. These, alongside of Mahaweli Authority, are beginning to provide what may prove very stimulating competition in water management to the department 'traditionally' concerned with this subject—the Irrigation Department. It is therefore possible to be cautiously optimistic about the possibilities of progress.

Organised Staggering of Cultivation

The 'staggering' of cultivation within a single irrigation scheme— i.e., wide differences between different plots and farmers in the timing of land preparation and sowing—has been the subject of much complaint, has often been attributed to a scarcity of farm power, and has thus been used as evidence of a need to increase power stocks, especially via tractor imports. In turn, this has contributed to the neglect of possible alternative strategies, including an increment in use intensity of the existing farm power stock and strengthening the seasonal flows of migrant labour from wet to dry zones. More important, it distracts attention from a central component of the problem: where strong rapport exists between farmers and the Irrigation Engineer, it is possible to achieve both early and synchronised cropping with wet-land techniques.[19] Where mutual trust and confidence are lacking, the reverse may occur.

It is surprising that, to the best of my knowledge, no attempt has been made to combine a stronger management of draught hire market and of water supply in a system of 'organised staggering', which is likely to reduce the overall time taken for land preparation to below even the five weeks or so achieved under favourable irrigator/farmer relations and a high density of farm power stock.

Such a practice should, in fact, be relatively easy to implement given the physical shape of most of Sri Lanka's large irrigation projects. The typical scheme comprises a bund across a shallow valley and two main channels, one running down each side of the valley.[20] In most cases each channel is served by a separate sluice in the tank bund. It seems quite feasible that, at the beginning of the season, water could be issued to one main channel sometime—say, two weeks—before the other. This would permit owners of farm power to concentrate first on one locality and then the other, extending the amount of work done by each unit, and thus reducing the overall number of units required.

There are, of course, potential obstacles to such a plan. Farmers would need to see the rationale and to approve. Arrangements would perhaps have to be made to change from year to year the turn to cultivate first—although this might not be feasible where the sluices are not at the same level, because then only the farmers served by the lowest sluice could draw on the last few inches of water in the tank at the end of the year. Where there is only one main channel the same principle could be pursued by staggering between tracts, although this might be physically more difficult to enforce.

It is difficult, however, to see any objection to attempting such a practice, at least on an experimental basis, in most schemes.

Draught hire markets, on the whole, are highly imperfect. If a system of 'organised staggering' were introduced, it would follow that: (a) the sequential concentration of demand for farm power hire in one locality after another should in itself help to make the market run a little more smoothly; and (b) that there is a good case in principle for some kind of public action to increase communication between potential hirers and potential contractors. This might, for example, take the form of a public register, renewable daily, of those with power for hire and those seeking it.

Some approximate calculations permit the broad order of magnitude of benefits derivable from a reduction in staggering to be assessed: estimates from various sources[21] suggest that land preparation involves the issue of 915 m³/ha of water per week when it is issued continuously for land preparation,[22] i.e., for typically five weeks in *maha* and seven weeks in *yala*. At a typical scheme where 15,000 and 24,000 m³/ha are consumed over the entire season for *maha* and *yala* respectively,[23] the amount saved by a one-week reduction in water issue during land preparation would permit irrigation of an additional 6.1 per cent of the *maha* paddy acreage, i.e., an additional 245 ha on a typical 4,000 ha scheme, or 15,000 ha over the dry zone as a whole. A simple example illustrates that a water saving of this order should be feasible with only a 2-week staggering and with no higher tractor use-intensity. Consider a 4,000 ha scheme with 80 tractors where land preparation typically takes 5 weeks, involving a work-rate of 10 ha/tractor/week. Dividing the scheme (and tractor population) into two equal parts (A and B) staggering by two weeks, and reducing the land preparation period for each half from 5 to 4 weeks would have the following effect:

> The first side (say, A) to receive water would have the attention of all 80 tractors for the first fortnight, the 80 would split between the two halves for the second fortnight, and then concentrate on side B for the final fortnight, giving a total of 480 tractor-weeks of work over the 3 fortnights, and a reduced work-intensity of 8.3 ha/tractor week necessary to

complete the whole 4,000 ha. Given the low current use-level of tractors,[24] and the scope for official assistance in facilitating hire contracts,[25] an increase of this order appears feasible.

Promotion of Early Land Preparation and Sowing[26]

The concept: In recent years a considerable degree of interest has been shown at the level of both research and experimental action projects, in the idea of advancing the cultivation calendar in dry zone irrigation projects. Experimental action projects have been undertaken both on village tanks (the work at Walgambahuwa Tank of the Cropping Systems Research Project at Maha Illuppallama Research Station) and on large schemes (the Tank Irrigation Modernisation Project on five tanks in the North-Central and Northern Provinces). The core notions behind these experiments are:

1) At present a great deal of valuable irrigation water and rainfall is wasted by the standard practices in irrigation schemes of delaying land preparation until the tank is full or nearly full, using lavish quantities of water for wet-land preparation and generally failing to use rainfall as a substitute for stored tank water either for land preparation or during crop growth.

2) The area cultivated, total agricultural production, and production per unit of scarce irrigation water could all be considerably increased through a modified set of agricultural and irrigation practices involving:

a) early preparation (ploughing) of land in a semi-dry condition at the onset of pre-*maha* rain showers in September;

b) sowing of the rice crop in October on semi-dry land, using only rainfall and not irrigation water;

c) use during the *maha* season of only the minimal quantities of water required to meet moisture deficiencies arising from inadequate rainfall;

d) saving the bulk of stored irrigation water to make possible a large *yala* crop, either of irrigated paddy or lightly irrigated non-paddy crops;

e) reliance on herbicides for weed control instead of maintaining a minimum depth of standing water.

Within this general strategy there are a number of elements which may be varied. Some are discussed in more detail below, while those that are not discussed[27] further include:

1) The question of the duration of the paddy variety chosen for the *maha* season. The potential advantages of the strategy can best be reaped if a short duration variety is chosen. Not only does this reduce the period over which irrigation water might be required in the *maha* season, but it also makes possible an early *yala* season, and thus minimises the loss of irrigation water which otherwise occurs when the season coincides with the month of high evapo-transpiration rates in June to August. However, the paddy variety chosen for the *maha* season must additionally be able to overcome strong weed competition (see below). At present there is no suitable high-yield paddy variety which is both of short duration ($3\frac{1}{2}$ months) and robust in the face of weed competition.

2) The question of whether the early sown *maha* paddy be broadcast or line sown. At present broadcasting is likely to be the only popular option.

3) The question of whether it is desirable to encourage farmers to use little or no fertiliser in the *maha* season, when much of it may be washed away, and to save resources for a high-input, high-output *yala* of paddy or non-paddy crops.

Early land preparation and farm power: Because it has been tested and promoted in large-scale irrigation schemes under the Tank Irrigation Modernisation Project (TIMP), the technique of early land preparation and sowing has become associated with a strategy of tractorisation, especially the use of 4wt.

Inadequacy of farm power was identified as a constraint on early and speedy land preparation and an initial component of the project was the supply of additional tractors. It has been argued by the TIMP staff that early dry or semi-dry land preparation cannot be completed without prime reliance on 4 wt because of the speed at which they operate. It has further been convincingly argued that (a) 4 wt are more efficiently used in semi-dry land preparation that in mudland preparation, since in the latter case they suffer wheel-slip, require more fuel per acre, and deteriorate more quickly; and (b) that the relative economic efficiency of 4 wt vis-a-vis draught animals (and 2 wt) is greater in semi-dry tillage than in mudding.

These points collectively appear to highlight two very divergent land, water and power use-strategies in large irrigation schemes:

the one (TIMP) involving greater use of 4wt to increase cropped area, output and water use-efficiency; and the other (mudding and later land preparation) involving greater reliance on animal power at the possible cost of a lower cropped area, total output and output per unit of irrigation water. If the difference between these strategies were clear, we could proceed straight to examining data relevant to the choice between them: their relative practical feasibility, and relative socio-economic benefit-cost ratios. Unfortunately, the difference between the two strategies is not necessarily quite so clear as the above summary would suggest.

As promoted to date, the TIMP strategy involves the ploughing of land at the onset of the pre-monsoon showers in September. The land should be sown before the end of October. Before the onset of the pre-monsoon showers the soil will be too hard to plough, or at least to plough by buffalo or 2wt. If there has been a *yala* crop, the soil will be bare, exposed and hardened for a month or two, or if there has been no *yala* crop, for up to six months. However, as the TIMP staff have themselves suggested, the initial tilling need not be immediately before the *maha* crop but at the end of the *yala* crop, thus benefiting from moisture remaining in the soil. This would be all the more feasible if the *yala* crop has been a paddy crop, and therefore relatively heavily irrigated, because more residual moisture would be available. In principle, the major attraction of tilling after the *yala* crop on residual moisture is that this spreads the tilling operation over time. Thus there would no longer be such a strong imperative to invest in 4wt in order to complete pre-season tillage in a brief period in September and early October. In those months it should be possible to complete a second and final tilling using animal draught. There is an additional potential advantage to tilling on residual moisture: it promises to conserve rainfall to make the early pre-*maha* rains more effective. At present, very deep fissures commonly open up in the more clayey soils during the period when there is no crop. Early rainfall tends to fill these fissures and thus is not effectively available to soften the top soil for early tillage. If tilled after the *yala* crop, clay soils would be less prone to cracking, and early rainfall would thus be more effective.

As will become clear below, there are obstacles to the adoption of tillage on residual moisture, which are certainly no less severe than the obstacles to the adoption of early tillage/sowing. They relate above all to risk, to the farmers' unwillingness to pursue the practice in the absence of any guarantee or confidence that others will do the same, and to the problems of obtaining finance in time. And, since tillage on residual moisture has not been intensely promoted, like tillage on early pre-*maha* rains, one can be even less certain of its technical feasibility, benefits and attractiveness to the farmers. Therefore for the purpose of the discussion below of benefit-cost ratios of the different strategies, it will be assumed that early tillage means simply tillage on pre-*maha* rains, and that this will create a pressure for rapid land preparation and therefore for 4wt. This assumption is suggested only to clarify the somewhat complex issues involved in evaluating these alternative strategies. It is not intended to imply that the strategy of tillage on residual moisture can or should be ignored. On the contrary, it would seem to require more rigorous investigation and experiment.

Practical feasibility of early sowing: Early land preparation and sowing—'kekulan' in Sinhalese—is not a new concept for dry zone farmers. Even in irrigation schemes it is regularly practised on high-lands that receive no irrigation water and by farmers on the tail ends of schemes who have little faith that irrigation water will actually reach them [see the discussion of timing of tail-end cultivation in Chapter 3.4, Farrington and Abeyratne (1982)]. It is in fact a 'traditional' practice which has been partly supplanted by the introduction of large scale irrigation. Ignorance of *kekulan* is no major barrier to its adoption. To see what those barriers are it is useful to look first at some of the advantages of the usual practice of delayed mudland preparation. From the farmers' point of view, there are two main advantages of established practice:

a) delaying land preparation until there is a large volume of water in the tank guarantees some kind of crop and thus provides insurance against the loss of the resources invested in land preparation and sowing.

b) The practice of mudland preparation and the use of large quantities of irrigation water provides what is to the farmer (if not necessarily to the national economy) the easiest, cheapest and most reliable protection against a major cause of poor paddy yield—weed competition.

There are three further advantages to conventional practices accruing to those responsible for organising supporting services;

1) By beginning to issue water only when the irrigation tank is well stocked, those responsible for water issues (irrigation staff and the Government Agent) are secure, at least in the *maha* season, against irrigation water scarcities and thus against the need to enforce physically and politically troublesome and difficult tight institutional water-issue schedules.

2) Decisions about the timing of agricultural credit advances and the varieties of paddy seed to be supplied can continue to be made, with minimal effort, in the 'water meeting' held a few weeks before the season commences.

3) Where a crop is fully irrigated, the basis of indemnity under the national crop insurance scheme is clear. If a partial reliance on rainfall is introduced, the responsibility for yield losses resulting from water stress cannot always be unequivocally attributed to failure of irrigation supply, and so the process of compensation becomes much more complex. This issue was the subject of protracted negotiations at Mahakandarawa in *maha* 1980-81.

The main obstacles to the adoption of early land preparation and sowing are more or less implicit in this list of the advantages of conventional practice. It is however, useful to detail these disadvantages. Although they interact with one another, they are more conveniently treated as five separate points:

a) From the point of view of the individual farmer, the adoption of *kekulan* involves a greater risk of loss of crop through weed competition.[28] It is not clear how far this risk can be reduced through improved skill and techniques on the part of the farmers. For example, it is argued that with good and careful land preparation, weeds may be dealt with effectively even under semidry conditions. This will depend in part, however, on the occurrence of rainless spells during which the weeds dry out and can be removed or burned. Again it is possible that the effectiveness of weedicides—which will normally be necessary with *kekulan*—may be greatly improved by the use of correct dosages and better spraying methods.[29]

b) Information collected by the TIMP staff and apparently corroborated by our own brief field enquiries suggests that an important reason why farmers do not adopt *kekulan* is lack of confidence that other farmers will do the same. For the advantage of the strategy can only be reaped if all farmers follow suit; otherwise it will not be possible to save water during *maha* by giving only short and rare rotational issues. The problem then becomes the lack of means to persuade or coerce all farmers into taking simultaneous action.

c) *Kekulan* is not equally attractive to all farmers. Quite predictably, the poorer cultivators are more averse than others to incurring the additional risk involved, insofar as they have a choice between *kekulan* and a reliably irrigated crop. As discussed above, those without reliable irrigation supplies have no alternative but to adopt early (rainfed) planting. The fact that *kekulan* with 4wt generally requires less labour (in land preparation) than 'mudding' with buffaloes, is of more consequence to those who hire labour than to those who have adequate supplies of family labour. Those who for various reasons have never fully levelled their fields or who have fields supplied by drainage water from other fields, face the prospect of receiving inadequate irrigation water during *maha* when only slight water issues are made to meet the inadequacies of rainfall. None of these inter-farmer differences would be very significant if it were not for point (2) above the need for simultaneous adoption of *kekulan* by all (or most) farmers.

d) The success of early sowing depends on the availability and use of both the physical and institutional means to control water, issue it sparingly and evenly, and to prevent large scale 'illegal' impounding of water by those intent on 'mudding'. Some success in water management was undoubtedly achieved by the TIMP on the Mahakandarawa scheme in the *maha* 1980-81 season, but in the context of a recent physical rehabilitation programme, a large administrative effort fired by a great deal of special interest and support from higher echelons and a very unusual degree of co-operation between separate government departments.[30] Such special efforts may be almost essential if progress is to be achieved. But, to the extent that they demonstrate what is possible, they also reveal why this is not achieved in normal conditions. Even if the necessary institutional effort and cooperation could be reproduced on a wider scale, one encounters the problem of the dearth of physical means to control water. At the opposite end of the scale to the newly rehabilitated Mahakandarawa are schemes like Gal Oya, where physical means to control water are very scarce, and where water even physically cannot be delivered to some tailend tracts.[31] In between area series of schemes wherein the physical potential to control the volume and/or timing of water deliveries is highly variable, even *within* the individual scheme.

e) Compared to 'mudding', *kekulan* requires both more support from government agencies in the form of credit, crop insurance, and early supplies of fertiliser and weedicides and, in the case of credit in particular, certainty about whether or not this will be available, in what quantities and at what times. Present rhythms for the supply of these agricultural inputs tend to be attuned to the normal timing pattern for mud cultivation. To ensure that they arrive on time for early land preparation and sowing requires a special effort. This special effort is possible only in the context of a special project which has a special over-arching management structure to coordinate the activities of the separate government agencies—the Agriculture, Agrarian Services, Irrigation and Land Commissioner's Departments, the banks and the Agricultural Insurance Board. In the absence of such special management, there is no institutional provision at scheme level to plan and coordinate the supply of inputs and to put pressure on the separate departments to ensure that they perform better than they would otherwise. The implication of these points was seen early in the life of the TIMP: a special integrated, authoritative management structure is required in each scheme, not unlike that now adopted for the newly developed Mahaweli areas.[32]

The supply of agricultural credit constitutes a special subcategory within this general problem area. Its peculiarity arises from the combination of three factors: (1) the enormous uncertainty about whether and in what quantities credit will in principle be offered to the locality and to the individual (in part the result of continually changing policies with regard to past defaults); (2) the great complexity of the procedures for obtaining credit; and thus the risk that even the nominally eligible individual will for some reason fail; and (3) the fact that, because of low interest rates and low repayment rates, agricultural credit is, once obtained, very valuable.

At our study locations the reliance on official credit was very low, although informal credit channels involving interest charges of up to 10 per cent per month were an important source of funds, particularly to cover 'distress' requirements. In view of previous defaults on repayment, most farmers are forced to manage without official credit in the typical season. It is clear however, and was especially evident at Mahakandarawa in the 1981-82 *maha* season, that the prospect that they *might* gain access to this almost free resource tempts some farmers to delay land preparation rather than to obtain the resources from elsewhere, i.e., friends, relatives or private moneylenders, and thus get on with the job.

In sum, the main obstacles to the widespread adoption of early land preparation and sowing lie in lack of confidence on the part of the individual farmer that he will not lose his crop to weeds, that other farmers will also follow the same strategy, and that irrigation water and other inputs will be available in the necessary quantities at the correct time. To overcome this lack of confidence requires a management and planning effort which is greater and more integrated between separate agencies than that currently practiced.

Costs and benefits of early land preparation and sowing. As detailed above, early land preparation and sowing appear to offer, compared to conventional 'mudding' techniques, the prospect of increases in area cropped, total agricultural production, and agricultural production per unit of scarce irrigation water. Without being able to assign quantities to the economic variables concerned, it is convincingly argued that the potential benefit-cost ratio to the national economy is high, even allowing for the increased dependence on tractor cultivation. The practice of early sowing is also promoted in the belief that it is in the economic interests of the average farmer. However, since farmers incur the additional risk of suffering reduced yields with no compensating reduction in water-use cost, the subjectively perceived benefit-cost ratio will be somewhat less to them than to the national economy, and it seems only in areas (such as the trial location, Mahakandarawa) where irrigation water is frequently inadequate for a full *maha* crop under mudland tillage that *kekulan* has a chance of adoption.

It may however be misleading to end the analysis by looking at the potential costs and benefits to the average farmer. There are fairly wide socio-economic differences among cultivators in irrigation schemes.[33] To some degree these differences determine the attractiveness of early land preparation to the individual farmer and thus affect the practical feasibility of the early sowing strategy as a whole (see above). For example: poorer farmers are less able and willing to take the increased risks involved in early sowing; those who depend mainly on family rather than hired labour are less attracted by the fact that early sowing tends to save on labour in the *maha* season; those whose land is near the tail end of main or distributary channels may fear that, if there is aı delivery in the irrigation rotation system, the light irrigation water issues made during the *maha* season would be less likely to actually reach their fields than the normal issues.

In addition to factors of this kind, there are other ways, not necessarily evident to the farmers themselves in which the early land preparation and sowing strategy might threaten to *increase* economic inequalities between rural households: (a) early land preparation places a premium on ploughing by 4wt rather than by buffalo and thus, for reasons given above, tends to accentuate the growth of inequality. The ownership of tractors leads to wealth and land accumulation more rapidly than does the ownership of buffaloes. Since ownership of tractors is concentrated near the top ends of irrigation schemes, the opportunities for access to hire services may be weighted against tail-enders; and (b) early land preparation and sowing is not compatible with the practice of transplanting paddy. Given the general slow island-wide trend towards the wider adoption of transplanting as the man: land ratio increases, it becomes clear that, if it became widespread, *kekulan* would be labour replacing *in this operation*. Whether it would reduce or increase the overall demand for labour—and thus the incomes of the rural poor would depend on how much extra land could be cultivated each year as a result of water saving in *maha*. However, even if the aggregate labour demand were to be the same or greater than in mudding, there would still be a new loss of job opportunities to poorer rural women. There is a high degree of gender specialism in paddy labour, land preparation is almost entirely men's work. Women are engaged mainly in transplanting, hand weeding and harvesting. Insofar as the very poorest rural households are those which depend mainly on the wage earnings of unskilled female labour,[34] then their living standards are threatened by agricultural techniques which reduce the demand for labour in transplanting and hand weeding.

In conclusion, there are doubts about the income distribution consequences—and thus the desirability—of early land preparation and sowing which may not have been foreseen by those engaged in promoting the practice. Those are secondary however to the more difficult question of whether the strategy is feasible as a substitute for mudland preparation. The answer to this depends ultimately on evaluation of the possibility of changing the structures and procedures of local level administration in order to achieve the kind of integrated, activist, competent and planned managerial interventions necessary for the strategy to succeed (see above). The constraints are organisational and ultimately of much the same kind as those facing any attempt to make government intervention more effective in promoting development at the local level. There are contradictions which are neither new nor trivial, between the type of official action needed and the normal operating procedures of government agencies.

Perhaps the most confident general conclusion one can reach about the prospects for the spread of early land preparation is that it will at best be slow, and is likely to be limited to those schemes where:

a) water for a *yala* crop is regularly scarce, and seen to be scarce;[35]

b) the physical infrastructure for water management is well developed and maintained (which in most cases means after an effective rehabilitation programme); and

c) the practice of mudland tillage followed by paddy transplanting is not already well established. This may mean in effect that, at best, there is little prospect in the foreseeable future of early land preparation becoming the standard technique outside (some of) those five schemes currently covered by the Tank Irrigation Modernisation Project.

5. CONCLUSIONS

The lack of adequate and regular supplies of water is the major constraint to increased agricultural production in the dry zone; yet the prospects for saving water by reducing its consumption in

areas currently under paddy are complex and permit only mode-
rate optimism. Certainly, the search for a technology-based solution, relying on the innovative impact of tractors to reduce
staggering and encourage early cultivation, was misguided: in the
absence of institutional pressures—and appropriate physical structures through which they could be channelled—towards more
sparing use of water, the impetus of tractorisation was dissipated
in its replication of traditional buffalo tillage techniques.

Further, the strategy of tractorisation was counterproductive
insofar as it distracted attention from necessary institutional
reform. It is only now—more than 25 years after the commitment to mechanisation—that attention is returning to the essential
task of improving the performance of institutions—and their relations with farmers—in water management.

Such improvement is a prerequisite to any of the strategies for
reducing water consumption outlined in this paper. That achieved, the precise choice of strategy will depend mainly on the hy-
drological characteristics of individual locations, where water is
generally adequate for a full *maha* and partial *yala* cultivation,
it seems logical to progress from the relatively simple steps needed to generate enough farmer confidence for early and synchronised mudland cultivation, relying principally on irrigation water
through an organised staggering, perhaps ultimately to dry-sowing followed by an inter-monson high-input paddy crop. In areas
where water is sometimes inadequate even for a full *maha* crop,
there seems little alternative to early introduction of dry-sowing, provided the necessary organisational effort is forthcoming.
Variations on this theme include tillage on residual moisture, the
planting of a proportion of the *maha* command area under non-
paddy crops and the choice of paddy or non-paddy crops for
yala according to water availability.

These innovations demand of irrigation administrators a sound
practical knowledge of delivery systems, a commitment to managing
water for increased crop production and mutual sympathy between
irrigation engineer and farmer. The fostering of adequate motivation however requires some prior attention to broader problems.
These include the historical bias towards construction and design,
and away from water management, in the irrigation profession:
poor living conditions in some of the remote major schemes

and a consequent reluctance to accept postings to such areas, and a high turnover of senior staff at practically all locations.

Above all, perhaps, fresh recognition is required by politicians and professionals of the enormous production potential of each major scheme, and of the key role of irrigation staff in realising this potential. An increase in their concern for improved water management could therefore appropriately be exemplified by such practical steps as more frequent visits to (especially) remote schemes, a deeper commitment to understanding the practical environment in which senior staff operate and the adoption of responsible mediating roles in improving staff-farmer relations.

NOTES

1. World Bank, quoted in *Cabinet Memorandum*, 1978, pp 2-3.

2. e.g., *Cabinet Memorandum*, Department of Irrigation, 1978.

3. e.g., Ch 2 M. Hill Inc. 1979, *Hunting Technical Services Ltd.*, 1979b; UNDP/FAO, 1975.

4. e.g., *Hunting Technical Services Ltd.*, 1979a; Merriam, 1979.

5. A particularly noteworthy research study on water management is that currently conducted by the Agrarian Research and Training Institute, in collaboration with USAID, and their reports, in the form of Yearbooks, to be published by ARTI in Colombo.

6. With very few exceptions, such as part of Stage I at Kaudulla.

7. See Moore *et al*. (in press).

8. The inadequacies of the Seasonal Cultivation Meeting as a forum for detailed and binding agreement on the season's cropping and water management patterns are discussed by Murray-Rust and Moore (in press).

9. Whilst highly objectionable in principle, much of the illicit appropriation of water, damaging of structures and delay in starting cultivation by farmers is a subjectively rational response conditioned by past experience of uncertainty in the timing and volume of irrigation supplies. The enforcement of sanctions against these parties is unlikely to be effective without simultaneous improvement in water supplies.

10. Land preparation took the relatively short time of five weeks at Padaviya (a scheme with abundant farm power) in both

maha 1978-79 and *maha* 1979-80, despite the large increase in tractor stocks between the two seasons (Farrington and Abeyratne, 1982). Additional data on land preparation/planting time requirements were supplied by Sri Lanka/IRRI/IDRC Cropping Systems Study for *maha* 1978-79 at Minneriya, Kaudulla and Mahaweli System H (personal communication).

11. For examples of constraints in the hire market and their implications for tractor use-intensity, see Farrington & Abeyratne, 1982, Ch. 6.2.

12. For elaboration of these points, see Farrington & Abeyratne, 1982, Ch 6.4.

13. Equipped, as it currently is, with such a crude implement as the nine-tine tiller.

14. In the continuing absence of appropriate implements and operator skills which would permit animal draught to perform these operations.

15. See, particularly, Moore, 1980a, 1980b, (in press); Murray-Rust & Cramer, 1979; Murray, Rust Moore, (in press); Farrington *et al.*, 1980, Ch. 3. 4; ARTI/USAID (in press).

16. D.W. Holmes *et al.*, 1980.

17. For example, the *preliminary* estimates of the Kaudulla study, covering four seasons beginning *yala* 1978, are that each year actual water issues are 41 million m³ in excess of computed minimum requirements (see D.W. Holmes, *et al. op. cit.*). If one values this water at the estimated current cost of providing new irrigation water—Rs. 0.24 per m³ (P. Russell, private communication)—then the cost of the water wasted on this scheme amounts to Rs. 10 million per year, or about Rs. 1,235 for each ha of land irrigated.

18. See, for example, Moore, 1980a.

19. See the case study reported in Farrington & Abeyratne, 1982, Appendix 3. 4.

20. See Map Appendix 8.

21. Especially Murray-Rust and Cramer (1979) for Minneriya and Kaudulla. For other sources see Farrington & Abeyratne, 1982, Ch 6. 4.

22. All volumes are estimated as headworks discharges.

23. *Cabinet Memorandum*, 1978, pp 2-3.

24. See Farrington & Abeyratne, 1982, Appendix 6. 4.

25. Such assistance at Mahakandarawa by the Tank Irrigation Modernisation Project in *maha* 1980-81 involved the revival of official credit schemes and the grouping of farmers into contiguous blocks for land preparation.

26. This section owes a great deal to valuable conversation with the staff of the Tank Irrigation Modernisation Project, papers supplied and field observations of their project. The TIMP staff are not responsible however, for the interpretation put forward here, and may indeed disagree with aspects of it.

27. Although clearly they have implications for agronomic and agricultural engineering research.

28. Note that the risk is all the greater because, due to lower seed germination rates and losses to birds and other pests, seed requirements for dry-sowing are greater than for 'mudding'.

29. Our own field investigation revealed that farmers tend to blame the ineffectiveness of weedicides on the lack of adequate moisture in the few days after application. This view is apparently held by many agricultural officers, but it is not clear how valid it is.

30. Rotational schedules and other agricultural matters were overseen on a tract basis by joint teams formed from officials of the Agrarian Services, Agriculture, Irrigation and Land Commissioner's Departments. Associated practices were detailed rotation schedules worked out for each plot and posted on signboards fixed at the heads of distributary channels.

31. Information on the paucity of physical controls over water flows in the Gal Oya scheme may be found in the contribution by H. Murray-Rust to the first Yearbook of the ARTI Water Management Project to be published by the Agrarian Research and Training Institute, Colombo.

32. See R.N. Parker, 1978, Management of Major Irrigation Schemes in the Dry Zone, TIMP (mimeographed).

33. See Farrington & Abeyratne, 1982, Appendix 8.

34. M P. Moore & is Wickremasinghe, 1980.

35. It may prove very difficult to introduce early land preparation and sowing in schemes which can receive irrigation water from the Mahaweli programme. Without a radical change in the methods and environment for water management, farmers will generally prefer to agitate politically for Mahaweli water.

REFERENCES

Agrarian Research & Training Institute, USAID, in press, *Yearbook of the Sri Lanka Water Management Project*, ARTI, Colombo.

Chambers, R., 1975a, 'On substituting political and administrative will for foreign exchange: The potential for water management in the dry zone,' in: S.W.R.A. de A. Samarasinghe (ed.), *Agriculture in the Peasant Sector of Sri Lanka, Ceylon Studies Seminar*, Peradeniya.

——, 1975b, *Water Management and Paddy Production in the Dry Zone of Sri Lanka*, ARTI, Occasional Publication no 8, Colombo.

Farrington, J. and F. Abeyratne, 1982, *Farm Power in Sri Lanka*, Department of Agricultural Economics and Management Development Study no. 22, University of Reading.

——, F. Abeyratne, M. Ryan and S. Bandara, 1980, *Farm Power and Water Use in the Dry Zone (Sri Lanka)*, pt 1, Research Study no 43, ARTI, Colombo.

Holmes, D.W., R. Woodridge, H. Gunston and C.H. Batchelor, 1980, *Water Management Study at Kaudulla Irrigation Scheme, Sri Lanka*, II, Interim Report Covering Seasons Yala 1978 to Maha 1979/80, Hydraulics Research Station, Wallingford, UK.

Hunting Technical Services Ltd., 1979a, *System C, Mahaweli Development Project, Feasibility Study 1979, Proposals for Irrigation System Trials in Block 404 System H*, Ministry of Mahaweli Development, Colombo.

——, 1979b, *System C, Mahaweli Development Project, Feasibility Study*, Interim Report, Borehamwood.

M. Hill Inc., 1979, Chapter 2: Proposed Water Management Program for Major Irrigation Schemes in Sri Lanka. Prepared for USAID (n.d.).

Merriam, J.L., 1979, Pilot Project Program, Mahakandarawa Left Bank DIO, Tank Irrigation Modernisation Project, Anuradhapura (mimeographed).

Moore, M.P., 1980a, *Approaches to Improving Water Management on Large-Scale Irrigation Schemes in Sri Lanka*, ARTI, Occasional Publication no 20, Colombo.

——1980b, 'The management of irrigation systems in Sri Lanka:

A study in practical sociology,' *Sri Lanka Journal of Social Sciences*, 2.2, Colombo.

——(in press), 'institutional adaptiveness and succession: The case of irrigation in Sri Lanka,' submitted to *Journal of Agrarian Studies*, Colombo.

——, F. Abeyratne, R. Amerakoon and J. Farrington (in press), *Space and the Generation of Socio-economic Inequality on Sri Lanka's Irrigation Schemes* (draft, mimeographed).

——and G. Wickremasinghe, 1980, *Agriculture and Society in the Low Country (Sri Lanka)*, Colombo.

Murray-Rust, H. and R. Cramer, 1979, An Evaluation of Water Management and Water Use Organisations in Three Selected Irrigation Schemes of Sri Lanka, USAID, Colombo (mimeographed).

——and M.P. Moore (in press), *Managing Sri Lanka's Irrigation Schemes: The Role of Cultivation Meetings* (draft, mimeographed).

CHAPTER 8

Farm Power and Water Use in Sri Lanka

INTRODUCTION

Pressures for an official strategy of small farm mechanisation in Sri Lanka began to emerge in the late 1940s and early 1950s. These coincided with an accelerated programme of population re-settlement from the wetter (southwest) to the drier (north and east) parts of the island, with the twin objectives of reducing reliance on imported food[1] and of relieving population pressure in the wet zone.[2] Some 180 irrigated major colonisation schemes have been established for this purpose in the dry zone since 1940, totalling 228, 378 ha in 1979.

Tractorisation was seen as the solution to the two major problems which emerged in the early days of settlement policy: first, when land allocations under settlement schemes were relatively large, at some 3 ha of irrigated land, settler families had to rely heavily on hired labour in the peak seasons of land preparation/ planting and harvesting/threshing. The necessary labour was not readily forthcoming, since many potential labourers preferred to obtain their own allotments—then abundantly available—on settlements. Furthermore, at that time seasonally migrant labour at peak periods had only just begun to emerge. Second, security-oriented strategies initially evident in dry zone village irrigation, but subsequently carrying over to settlement schemes, required irrigation tanks to contain adequate water for a full season's irrigation of paddy[3] before land preparation should start. This meant the loss of potentially productive rainfall whilst the tank was filling, and reduced water availability for subsequent minor-season cropping.[4] Tractors were seen as a means of advancing and synchronising cultivation to permit increases in the productivity of irrigated land.

The strategy of tractorisation—initially with 4-wheel, but since 1970 also with 2-wheel tractors—was pursued vigorously, with the result that Sri Lanka now has a tractor density approaching that of the Punjab in India[5] and some 45% of annual paddy acreage is tractor-ploughed.

POLICY MEASURES

The support of tractorisation was characterised by an initial period of direct government intervention, followed by (less direct) support for private ownership and use.

Tractor Pools

Some 350 4-wheel tractors were deployed in tractor hire pools by cooperatives, the Food Production Department and the Department of Agriculture in 1952-56. Thereafter, only the lastmentioned agency continued to operate, on a reduced scale, up to the late 1960s. Charges, at the equivalent of some 100 kg of paddy per hectare for ploughing, were substantially below those for animal draught, and the demand for hire services initially outstripped supply. However, revenues were inadequate to cover even running costs, so that tractor pools showed a total loss on current account of some Rs. 12 mn in the period 1952-65 and of almost Rs. 6 mn on the capital account.[6] Data limitations prevent precise calculations, but the official hire charges during this period are unlikely to have amounted to more than one-third of the real cost of ploughing, the remainder comprising the subsidy implicit in these losses.[7]

Private Ownership

Official tractor pools operated a larger number of tractors than the private sector only in the period 1952-55. In 1956, of the 855 tractors available for small farm use, 475 were in private hands. Total registrations increased to 2,080 by 1962 and 12,873 by 1976, whilst the number of pool tractors in operation steadily declined from the 350 or so available in 1956. Official support for private sector ownership included, at various times and to varying extents since the early 1950s: preferential rates of import duty, preferential allocations of foreign exchange, an over-valued exchange rate, subsidised credit, tax allowances and fuel subsidies.

THE STUDY

In view of the heavy burden imposed on public finances through tractorisation, and of inadequate information on the scale of benefits in relation to these costs,[8] a survey focusing on the impact of small farm tractorisation in major irrigated settlement schemes was conceived jointly by ARTI and Reading University in 1979. It covered both *maha* (main) and *yala* (minor) monsoon seasons between August, 1979, and October, 1980, collecting data on farm power use from samples of 240 owners of 4-wheel and 2-wheel tractors and buffalo, and on agricultural resources productivity from a sample of non-owners of similar size. The samples were drawn equally from three major schemes: Uda Walawe, Kaudulla and Padaviya, selected to reflect varying resource pressures, infrastructures and levels of economic opportunity.

Characteristics of Draught Power Ownership and Use

The ownership of tractors, but not of buffalo, was biased towards the top ends of irrigation command areas, reflecting higher levels of income and wealth there. Variations in mean buffalo herd size were wide, and corresponded with differences in husbandry, with stall-fed herds being small compared to those under open grazing.

The farms of both owners and non-owners are small, generally 1-2 ha, so that tractors can only be kept fully occupied through hiring out, and the scope for this, in turn, is limited by the difficulty of arranging multiple hire contracts within a day. An equally, substantial obstacle to efficiency lies in the small size of the bounded plot—around 0.04 ha—within which tractors operate.

Tractorisation and Agricultural Production

The assembled evidence suggests that the use of tractors in the mudland tillage systems, practiced almost universally in major irrigation, has not contributed to an improvement in the timing or synchronisation of paddy cultivation. Even in years when rainfall in the *maha* monsoon is heavy enough to permit mudland tillage prior to the opening of irrigation sluices, it is, in fact, the start of irrigation water issues that continues to mark the beginning of agricultural activity on paddy allotments. A major factor preventing tillage in the early rains is the farmers' lack of conviction that irrigation issues will be made to compensate for any lack of rain. If water is to be saved in this way, much depends on the creation of a climate of confidence between irrigation engineers and farmers, and on the sensitive administration of water as a means to the end of agricultural production. Set against these factors, the influence of 4wt on the timing of cultivation in major irrigation is negligible.

Paddy seasons are marked by the start and finish of water issues. The *maha* harvest will generally be complete before *yala* issues begin. In these circumstances, a higher annual cropping intensity (i.e., a higher percentage of the available land cultivated during *yala*) will stem only from improved timing and synchronisation of the *maha* crop, which, as argued above, has not emerged.

Irrigated paddy yields are some 250 kg/ha higher on the average among tractor owners than among non-owners. However, the quality of tilth and control of weeds achieved under tractorised ploughing show no advantage over traditional systems. Nor can yield differences arise from improved timing of cultivation. The higher yields of tractor owners are accounted for by better access to irrigation water, heavier fertiliser applications and higher levels of transplanting.

As far as current systems of production are concerned, tractors show a clear advantage over traditional draught systems only in the cultivation of large expanses of rainfed land. These, however, are comparatively rare; the predominant method of rainfed cropping involves 'slash and burn' techniques.

Tractorisation and Labour

Tractors displace labour both from agriculture directly and from the activities associated with animal draught maintenance. One 4wt displaces between 500 and 1,000 days of work per annum in total, depending on whether the animal husbandry methods replaced are intensive or extensive. The displacement effects of 2wt are approximately 50% less severe. More than two-thirds of the labour displaced is farm family, not hired labour, and this is re-deployed into other activities only among the owners (and not the hirers) of draught power. Whilst tractorisation represents some benefit through reduced drudgery, it adds to the lengthy periods of low activity already enjoyed by paddy farmers and, on balance, represents a withdrawal of productive resources from the economy.

Overall, the substitution by tractors for family and not hired labour runs counter to the expectations of administrators, and any cropping constraint attributable to hired labour shortages is unlikely to have been relieved by tractors. In fact, labour constraints appear to have been relieved by three other developments: first, the growth of seasonal labour migrations between wet and dry zones at times of low opportunity cost to the migrants; second, the increased population density in major agricultural areas with, particularly, the emergence of a second generation of settler families; and third, a reduction in average holding size per settler family from 3 ha to 1 ha since 1948. The early official promotion of the first of these could have alleviated labour shortages more successfully and cheaply than the adopted strategy of tractorisation.

Tractorisation and Distribution of Income and Wealth

With the advent of tractors, certain previously equitable practices for the shared use of draught power were displaced. These included herd pooling arrangements and deferred 'in-kind' payments for hire involving labour services or a share of the crop, which was reduced in years of poor harvest. The high recurrent costs of tractor operation (fuel, drivers' wages, etc.) caused the emphasis on immediate cash payments for hire—coinciding with a time of season when the hirer was normally in deficit—to increase markedly. Thus, tractorisation generated a higher risk of chronic indebtedness, forfeit of assets (especially land) to moneylenders and subsequent impoverishment.

At the opposite end of the spectrum, tractors offered the potential for obtaining particularly high returns to those with adequate capital. Tractor capital, in turn, was frequently obtained from unearned income such as the economic rent from favourably watered plots and the financial gains obtained by those in a position to exploit opportunities for fraud. Tractors have thus contributed strongly to a polarisation in rural communities in which tractor owners occupy one extreme and those owning no draught power occupy the other.

Social Costs and Benefits of Mechanisation

The extensive subsidies on tractors, and the fact that much of the private gain derives from re-distributive rather than from net productive effects, imply that social benefits are likely to be lower than the substantial private profits which are reflected in rates of return of some 20 per cent per annum on 4wt. Preliminary calculations suggest that 4wt in the period 1953-79 have generated higher social costs than benefits: a net disbenefit of some Rs. 2,400 mn over the period has been incurred, implying that only 70 per cent of the costs of importing tractors has been recovered through productive gains.[9] Tractors would have had to generate benefits some 50 per cent higher than those estimated, with no corresponding cost increase, if social costs were to have been covered by social benefits in the period 1953-79. This analysis—for the national tractor fleet, not merely those used in the dry zone—suggests that two-thirds of the benefits realised originate in non-agricultural work, a result far removed from the anticipated benefits in agricultural applications expressed in early mechanisation policy.

If this generation of social disbenefits is to be reduced for those tractors currently in use, the following steps will have to be taken:

1) to restrict severely the future volume of tractor imports;

2) to increase the use-intensity of the existing tractor stock from the low observed levels (497-734 hours per year for 4wt, according to location, and 340-486 hours per year for 2wt);

3) ensure that such increased use-intensity represents a net contribution to production by tractors, and not merely the substitu-

tion of (expensive) tractor draught in operations which (cheaper) animal draught can perform adequately;

4) promote a more balanced rural infrastructure, so that transport work in construction, crop extraction and storage, and other rural industries is available for those tractors currently based in agriculture during the off-season;

5) ensure adequate maintenance and spare parts facilities so that loss of tractor time through breakdown is avoided.

Two further points deserve emphasis: use-intensity remains low partly because of inefficiencies in the hire market and tractor charges are perceived as fixed and owners make no effort to sell their services. Assistance in organising work for owners during both peak and off-peak periods could help to increase use-intensities with a possible reduction in hire charges. Second, the fact that animal draught owners have followed tractor owners' hire-charge lead in raising their own hire rates has prevented the demand for tractor services from falling substantially. But it has also shifted the terms of trade against those who own no form of draught power, thus increasing the attractiveness of *owning* a power source.

In view of their limited resources the ownership of draught animals must present itself as an attractive proposition to many farmers.

Farm Power and Water Use

The prospects of increased efficiency in the consumption of stored water in major irrigation through earlier and unstaggered tilling were of particular appeal in early tractorisation strategies. However, the available evidence suggests that it is decisions concerning timing of water issue which determine the starting point of the agricultural season under conventional mudland tillage, regardless of the availability of tractors. The motivation and efficiency of the irrigation bureaucracy acts therefore as a major influence on productivity. Whilst the degree of staggering may be related to the overall volume of farm power, it does not, under current and foreseeable systems of water management in major irrigation, depend on the size of the tractor stock alone.

Only in one set of early tilling strategies currently under investigation (the 'kekulan' or 'dry' sowing under the Tank Irrigation Modernisation Project) does a high degree of reliance on tractor tillage appear necessary. The degree of organisational effort required for the success of these strategies, however, makes their early or widespread implementation improbable.

Where a high proportion of irrigated land is commonly cropped in *yala* immediately preceding *kekulan* sowing in *maha*, it appears that ploughing by buffalo on moisture residual from the *yala* crop, followed by a light (buffalo or tractor) second ploughing prior to sowing, offers an intuitively appealing alternative which merits widespread agronomic appraisal.

Major improvements can, however, be made in water use-efficiency under current mudland tillage systems, which are independent of the type of draught power used. Some of these require modest infrastructural investment; all require (to varying degrees) improvements in organisational efficiency. These are discussed in more detail in the recommendations below.

RECOMMENDATIONS

1) Some limited role for tractors in agriculture and transport exists, but this requires a national tractor fleet far smaller than the present one. Future imports of tractors should therefore be severely restricted.

2) If net benefits are to be obtained from a diminished tractor stock, use-intensities will have to be higher than at present, and the proportion of directly net productive work (as opposed to that involving merely the substitution of tractors for animals) will have to be higher. Opportunities for increased productivity lie in early tilling under rainfed conditions, and in off-season transport. Official assistance to increase the supply of these opportunities appears necessary.

3) For the bulk of tillage operations in which tractors are currently involved, a (socially) less expensive and more equitable alternative exists in the broad-based ownership of small herds of draught animals. It is recognised that a return to animal draught may be difficult to accept in some areas and for some farmers. The national costs of not doing so, however, are high, and evidence from some areas in the present study indicates aspirations for the ownership of animals but correspondingly weak, or non-existent,

institutions through which they may be purchased. Official assistance through credit programmes, breeding, calf-rearing, and the re-location of working animals is therefore necessary.

4) In many parts of the dry zone, herds of draught animals are large and the number of owners correspondingly small. This ownership pattern is accompanied by low levels of husbandry, extensive grazing and low use levels inimical to the high land use-intensities implicit in the current large-scale development of major irrigation. The widespread ownership of small herds (one or two pairs) of draught animals, following the pattern observed at Kaudulla, should therefore be pursued as the more desirable of these alternatives.

5) Widespread discrepancies exist between those located at the upper and lower ends of major irrigation schemes in levels of income and wealth. The ownership of tractors is also heavily biased towards the top end. Strategies developed to expand the role of animal draught should therefore attempt partly to redress, in favour of the tail-ender, the currently adverse bias of resource access opportunities.

6) Whilst draught animals might initially be fed (as currently done in a few parts of the dry zone) on grass cut from verges and reservations, for the medium term an officially sponsored strategy of promoting low-cost feed of adequate protein and caloric content from both crop residues and fodder crops grown on land of low opportunity needs to be pursued, along with appropriate extension and training.

7) With increasing emphasis on the need to conserve irrigation water through the cultivation of non-paddy crops in *yala* and, in land preparation, through efforts at dry or semi-wet ploughing, strategies to encourage a shift in the composition of animal draught herds away from water buffalo and towards bullocks might usefully be considered. The latter work at a faster pace than buffalo, require fewer rest periods, are not dependent on water for 'wallowing' and can conveniently be used in haulage. Their introduction requires careful monitoring, however, since their feed requirements are traditionally regarded as more exacting and their acceptance for field work may depend upon a change in socio-cultural attitudes in certain areas.

8) The search for improved water efficiency both generally and

with particular reference to land preparation, should attempt to include these aspects in the following order of priority:

a) increased awareness among those responsible for scheme level irrigation administration that on-farm water use is a major and legitimate area of their concern, and that farmer confidence in the permanence and impartiality of their concern is imperative;

b) introduce the necessary physical structures, information network and procedures essential to the finely regulated supply of water to distributary and field channels;

c) promote an organised staggering of cultivation so that draught and labour resources can be concentrated in one part of an irrigation scheme and then in another; and

d) discover methods for making more efficient use of early monsoon rains, which do not involve the severe income distribution penalties of heavy inputs of 4-wheel tractors. These might, in particular, involve ploughing on soil moisture residual from the previous season's crop, a practice urgently in need of field research and demonstration.

NOTES

1. Food imports have been necessary since at least the mid-nineteenth century, and have increased in volume to some Rs. 6,000 mn per year (approximately 20 per cent of the value of all imports) at present (Central Bank, 1980; Snodgrass, 1966; de Silva [ed], 1973).

2. Over 500 persons/sq km in some wet zone districts, and under 100/sq·km in the dry zone.

3. Paddy is virtually the only irrigated crop grown by small holders in settlements. Attempts to diversify into other grains, legumes and vegetables have failed, principally because of higher risk, more exacting cultivation and heavier capital requirements. Marketing and input supply have also been poor (Wijayaratna, 1982).

4. It has proved impossible to price water at the farm gate and hence consumption cannot be constrained by the market.

5. At approximately one tractor per 100 ha of cultivated land (NCAER, 1980).

6. Burch, 1980.

7. Calculated from data in Burch, 1975 and 1980.

8. The only previous broad-based, but comparatively unknown, study of mechanisation in Sri Lanka was undertaken by Carr (1975). Her samples for the dry zone farming sector are small and hence it is difficult to generalise findings. On the whole her findings indicate little net productive impact, but severe distributional effects of tractorisation, which are not consistent with the findings presented here.

9. For discussion of methodology, see Farrington & Abeyratne, 1982, Appendix 6.2.

REFERENCES

Burch, D., 1974, Agricultural Tractor Pools in Ceylon, 1952-56- Seminar paper, Institute of Development Studies, University of Sussex, 7th November 1974 (mimeographed).

—— 1980, Overseas Aid and the Transfer of Technology: A Case Study of Agricultural Mechanisation in Sri Lanka. Ph.D Thesis (unpublished), Institute of Development Studies, University of Sussex.

Carr, M.N., 1975, Patterns of Tractorisation in the Major Rice-Growing Areas of Sri Lanka. Ph D Thesis (unpublished), Institute of Development Studies, University of Sussex.

Central Bank of Ceylon, 1981, *Annual Report, 1980*, Colombo. de Silva, K.M., 1973, *History of Ceylon*, vol III, *From the Begining of the Nineteenth Century to 1948*, University of Ceylon Press, Peradeniya.

Farrington, J. and F. Abeyratne, 1982, *Farm Power in Sri Lanka, Development Study No. 22*, Department of Agricultural Economics and Management, University of Reading.

—— and W.A.T. Abeysekera, 1979, *Issues in Farm Power and Water Use in Sri Lanka*, Agrarian Research and Training Institute, Occasional Publication No. 17, Colombo.

—— *et al.*, 1980, *Farm Power and Water Use in the Dry Zone*, pt 1, *Research Study No. 43*, Agrarian Research and Training Institute, Colombo.

Harriss, B., 1977, 'Tractors, profits and debts in Hambantota District,' in B. Farmer (ed.), *Green Revolutions*, MacMillan, London.

National Council of Applied Economic Research, 1980, *Implications of Tractorisation for Farm Employment, Productivity and Income*, 2 vols, New Delhi.

Plumbe, A.H. and H.M. Byrne, 1981, *The Role of Agricultural Tractor in Road Haulage in Sri Lanka, Report No. LR 1007*, Transport and Road Research Laboratory, Crowthorne, UK.

Ryan, M.J., F. Abeyratne and J. Farrington, 1981, Animal Draught —The Economics of Revival, Agrarian Research and Training Institute, Occasional Publication no. 23, Colombo.

Siriweera, W.I., 1981, Water Resources and Buffalo and Cattle Rearing in Sri Lanka: an Historical Perspective. University of Peradeniya (mimeographed).

Snodgrass, D., 1966, *Ceylon: An Export Economy in Transition*, Richard D. Irwin, Inc., Illinois.

Wijayaratna, C.M., 1982, *Crop Diversification in the Mahaweli Research Study Series*, Agrarian Research and Training Institute, Colombo.

Wirasinha, E.C., 1974, 'A pilot project for the introduction of 2-wheel tractors for rice cultivation in Sri Lanka,' in H. Southworth and M. Barnett (eds.), *Experience in Farm Mechanisation in South East Asia*, Agriculture Development Council, New York.

World Bank, 1976, *Sri Lanka: Appraisal of the Tank Irrigation Modernisation Project, Report 951a-CE (November)*.

CHAPTER 9

Observations from a Bangladesh Village

Komarpur, the village under study, is a fairly prosperous village situated in the northwest part of Faridpur District (which is in the southwest part of Bangladesh) and is about 4 miles from the district headquarters. The main highway connecting Faridpur to Dhaka (capital of Bangladesh) passes through the village, dividing it into two parts. The village covers an area of 1,060 acres and it's total population is about 4,356 (437 households).

Komarpur village, despite it's landless population of 38.9%, is a fairly prosperous village with good communications to the district headquarters in Faridpur Town. It has benefited considerably from an easy access to public sector resources, i.e.,

Table 9.1. Distribution of Households by Cultivable Land in 1979

Land category (in acres)	No. of H.H.	% of H.H.	Total area owned	% of total area owned
0 acre	170	38.9	nil	nil
0.01-0.99	92	21.05	46.52	5.43
1.00-1.99	55	12.59	77.62	9.06
2.00-2.99	21	4.81	47.37	5.06
3.00-3.99	27	6.18	89.34	10.43
4.00-4.99	20	4.58	89.60	10.46
5 +	52	11.90	506.09	59.09
Total	437	100.00	856.54	100.00

communication, electricity, fertiliser, pesticide, as well as the availability of low-interest loans from the Krishi (agriculture) Bank and the Co-operative Bank. There are several low-lift pumps and one deep tubewell in the village, rented out to farmer co-operatives by the Bangladesh Agricultural Development Corporation at subsidised rates.

Since Independence in 1971 there has been a dramatic increase in the cultivation of HYV rice, both amon and boro (autumn and winter) crops. Until 1979, Komarpur could have been described as a predominantly IRRI rice-producing area. However, in 1979 an acute drought took place, accompanied by a wide-scale failure of electricity. The effect on those who had planted IRRI rice was disastrous. The heavy reliance of these crops on adequate water supply at critical moments of the growing cycle led to the failure of crops and considerable losses were incurred among all levels of cultivators. In response to this experience, many farmers moved away from such water-dependent crops. The nature of the choice facing them was dictated by a number of factors related to the kind of support agriculture received from the government. In the last decade there has been a steady increase in the prices of all inputs in the technology associated with the HYV package. From 1980 the rate of price increment has accelerated, as is shown in Table 9.2. (Although the price of pesticide is not shown, the order of increase was almost the same.)

To make any kind of profit, it was necessary for the farmers to shift into crops which economised on the use of these inputs. This did not mean, however, a return to the traditionally established pattern of agriculture, dominated by traditional varieties of rice and by jute. Instead Komarpur farmers chose sugar cane and wheat. To understand the choice of sugar cane, it is necessary to understand the government policy towards the production of sugar cane. The sugar cane industry has always been a nationalised one and the government has always extended considerable support to growers of sugar cane. Farmers who produced sugar cane received fertiliser, seeds and low-interest loans from the Agricultural Ministry. Moreover, the government mills bought sugar cane directly from the cultivators at prices settled beforehand. Risk was therefore considerably minimised in the cultivation of sugar cane.

Table 9.2. Increase in Prices in Technological Inputs (1968-82)*

Fertilisers

Year	Urea	Triple Superphosphate	Muriate of Potash
1968	Tk. 9	Tk. 9	Tk. 7
1974	Tk. 83	Tk. 83	Tk. 65
1980	Tk. 120	Tk. 120	Tk. 90
1982	Tk. 135	Tk. 135	120

Electricity

Year	
1968	Tk. 0.25 per unit
1980	Tk. 1.20 per unit
1982	Tk. 1.45 per unit

Diesel Fuel

Year	
1968	Tk. 0.90 per gallon
1980	Tk. 25.00 per gallon
1982	Tk. 36.00 per gallon

*Data collected from the farmers.

Since sugar cane cannot be grown for more than two consecutive years on the same piece of land, the HYV variety of wheat, which uses much less water than its main winter competitor, boro rice is alternated after every two years. Even those small farmers who gave up IRRI and reverted to traditional aus and amon, replaced boro rice cultivation with winter HYV wheat. When asked, farmers gave these reasons for opting for HYV wheat as a winter crops:

1) Same amount of water will adequately support about five times as many acres of wheat as in the case of boro rice.

2) HYV wheat produces more maunds (80 1bs per maund) per acre than boro rice does.

3) Though the price of wheat is about two-thirds that of paddy, this loss is compensated by higher yields per acre of wheat.

4) Wheat is a winter crop. Its full growing cycle is about 100/115 days, whereas boro rice usually requires 150/180 days. Hence wheat can be harvested in time to allow the land to be prepared for a broadcase aus rice crop.

One very interesting phenomenon is the drop in production of jute. In Komarpur, the average acreage devoted to jute has fallen at an alarming rate. In the last few years, jute production has steadily given way to other crops, even though it remains Bangladesh's main export crop. One possible explanation may be the inadequate level of support extended to jute by the government, which makes it a poor choice. Up to 1971 jute was in the private sector and hence outside the government's scope of interest of intervention. However, even after nationalisation in 1972, a policy of neglect towards jute characterised the government's attitude (justification for this may lie partly in the depressed international prices for the commodity, but this is a fairly recent phenomenon). Private middlemen still dominate the marketing of raw jute. The inability of small cultivators to hold their crop until its price goes up—a few months after the harvest—means that they are crucially dependent on whatever prices prevail at the time of harvesting. It is hardly surprising, therefore, that small farmers are switching over to the traditional varieties of rice, which they can at least use for personal consumption.

Another repercussion of the recent developments in the relative input prices is evident in the pattern of tenure among farmers. Traditionally it was customary for those with inadequate holdings to supplement them by renting land from rich farmers. There is now an increasing tendency among marginal farmers to sharecrop their land to large landholders and become hired agricultural labourers. There arises an unequal relationship between the marginal farmers and the wealthy and often powerful farmer, whereby the traditional share of 50 per cent of harvest from the sharecropped land is frequently ignored and the allocation is determined at the whim of the powerful partner. The transformation of this large layer of marginal farmers into wage labourers means that a major portion of their food consumption has to be purchased on the market. As a consequence, many of them have been pushed into debt, often to those to whom they rent their land. The inevitable result of this is loss of land through the inability to pay off debts, and therefore an acceleration in the growth of landless. A 1982 survey of Komarpur revealed almost 42 per cent landless versus 38.9 per cent in 1979.

Although there may be some differences in underlying causes, there is a great similarity between the national picture and what is occurring at the village level. Tables 9.3 and 9.4 present some data on the land distribution and the cropping pattern at the national level.

Table 9.3. Distribution of Agricultural Land (1981)

Distribution of Agricultural Land in 1981	
10% largest landowners own	48%
10% smallest landowners own	1%
Rural households owning no land	50%
Distribution of Income	
Top 20% of population take	41% of national Income
Bottom 20% of population take	7% of National Income

Table 9.4. Rice, Wheat, Sugar Cane and Jute—Area and Production
(1969-81)*

Year	Area in Hectare	Production in Metric Ton
1969-71	9,842,000	16,540,000
1979	10,160,000	19,599,000
1980	10,309,000	20,822,000
1981	10,100,000	20,000,000
Wheat		
1969-71	121,000	103,000
1979	265,000	494,000
1980	433,000	823,000
1981	591,000	1,093,000
Sugar Cane		
1969-71	165,000	7,551,000
1979	155,000	6,937,000
1980	151,000	6,676,000
1981	149,000	6,599,000
Jute		
1969-71	878,000	1,115,000
1979	768,000	1,095,000
1980	642,000	904,000
1981	530,000	868,000

*FAO, *Production Year book*, 1981, Vol. 35; *Statistics Series* No. 40, 1982.

Bangladesh is one of the most densely populated countries with 90 per cent of its population living in rural areas. There is very little cultivable land left for the expansion of agriculture. The only choice is to raise per-acre productivity through a more efficient use of land. While the potential for this exists with the use of improved seeds, the introduction of an expensive capital-based technology into an environment of subsistence holdings inevitably links its adoption to the ability to command credit. The consequence has been an intensification of the process of marginalisation through a cycle of bad harvest, debt and land loss. It appears necessary to achieve a more equitable distribution of resources in the country before it will be possible for the new technology to make a proper contribution to Bangladesh's development.

NOTE

1. The trend in the agriculture pattern of a village is presented in this short paper. Interest was aroused by what appeared to be an interesting change in the cropping pattern during the years 1976-82, years in which the author worked there in a rural development project. A change in the traditional land tenure system occurred concomitant with the changing trend in the agriculture pattern.

CHAPTER 10

Employment: An Indonesian Portrait

INTRODUCTION

Since Indonesia entered into the New Order era, most people have appeared optimistic and enthusiastic in facing national development. Unlike the Guided Economy, managed under the Old Order era, which appeared almost non-helpful to the people, the New Order has promised to create healthy social and economic conditions. The government managed to build up confidence in the development of the country through *Repelita* (Five-Year Plan). The achievements gained through two *Repelita* (1969-74 and 1974-79) have, in some respects, exceeded those of the entire attempts in the previous era, through the implementation of long-term planning.

Repelita I emphasised food production and infrastructure rehabilitation, while both *Repelita II* and *Repelita III* (1979-83) emphasised employment and distributional equity as well as economic growth. However, up to the final year of *Repelita III* (1982-83) the New Order government faced many difficulties, particularly the employment problem. The projection of a work force, as reported by the Central Bureau of Statistics in cooperation with the Department of Labour Force has shown that the growth rate of the work force is 2.2 per cent per annum. Meanwhile, the population growth rate is 2.3 per cent per annum.

Of the economic growth gains of 6 to 8 per cent per annum, a substantial proportion is enjoyed by the modern (industrial) sector. According to *Sakernas* 1976 and 1978 (Labour Force Survey), the industrial sector in 1978 absorbed around 12 per cent of the total employment, which means a decrease of 1 per cent from 1976. The industrial policy in Indonesia tends to emphasise the prospects of modern large-scale firms, even though they do not provide many jobs, and it is probably a mistake to expect the industrial sector to absorb a substantial proportion of new entrants to the work force. The responsibility of modern manufacturing in Indonesia is to introduce and to adapt new technologies into Indonesian economy as well as to provide as many jobs as possible.

The industrial growth in the past decade has done only a little to alleviate Indonesia's unemployment problem. Against the annual increase in the Indonesian work force of around 1.5 million, the recorded increases in employment in the modern sector in recent years have been small. According to the government's policy during the last decade, the creation of employment was considered the most important objective of industrial growth. Official priority was given to employment and equity in *Repelita III*, and job creation will probably be given even higher emphasis in the next few years. Since the relationship between industrial policy and employment has attracted much attention in Indonesia in recent years, it may be worthwhile taking a more detailed look at the issues involved. The likely consequences of a continuation of present policies will be considered before turning to a review of possible alternative strategies.

AN OVERVIEW OF THE LABOUR FORCE

Employment

The Central Bureau of Statistics has published some data on employment from the 1980 Census which can be compared with previous censuses to obtain a picture of labour force changes over the past two decades. Table 10.1 shows labour force participation rates disaggregate by age and sex from the 1961 and 1971 Censuses, the 1976 Intercensal Survey (*Supas*), the 1976-78 Labour Force Surveys (*Sakernas*) and 1980 Census. The definitions used in the 1980 data are broadly consistent with those used in the 1971 preliminary (Series S) data. A comparison of the 1980 data with those from 1976 *Supas* and the 1976-78 *Sakernas* surveys suggest that both these surveys give rather overestimated labour force participation rates for both males and females, the *Supas* data in particular are 1980 estimates. It is likely that household-based sample surveys have an inherent bias in favour of settled households with a stronger labour force attachment. Although such surveys are invaluable for exploring differences between defined groups in the population, they become problematic when used to estimate aggregate changes.

The 1980 data on participation rates show little change compared to the 1971 Series C estimates except for the youngest age groups where rates have decreased due to the increased provision of primary school facilities. However, when the 1980 data on the industrial classification of the labour force are compared with those from the 1971 Census (Series C), some important changes are evident. The share of agriculture in the labour force fell from 66 per cent in 1971 to 56 per cent in 1980, and the rate of growth of agricultural employment was lower than for any other major industry (see Table 10.2). Nevertheless, because agriculture accounts for such a large proportion of total employment, even with a low rate of growth it accounted for an appreciable proportion of total employment growth.

2) Industrial Distribution

One possible reason for the slow employment growth in manufacturing in Indonesia in the 1970s is that the expansion of other employment opportunities (particularly in construction) drew labour away from the inefficient and unproductive cottage industrial sector. Such growth as occurred was concentrated in the modern sector. In addition, the industrial development strategy which Indonesia has followed over the past decade has been directed towards supplying the domestic market. Although incentives to export have increased this year, a more export-oriented outlook among manufacturers could improve the employment outlook in two ways. First, increased exports would open up employment opportunities in the exporting firms. Second, by leading to the development of an internationally competitive industrial structure

Table 10.1. Labour Force Participation Rates 1961-1980

	1961 Census	1971 Census		1976		1977-78 Sakernas[c]	1980 Census
		D	C	Supas[a]	Sakernas[b]		
Males							
10-14	22.7	18.3	18.3	26.1	16.7	16.5	12.6
15-19	66.7	52.8	48.9	66.4	58.8	58.9	47.6
20-24	87.2	79.2	76.5	88.3	87.1	87.1	79.3
25-44	95.5	93.6	92.3	98.2	98.6	98.2	94.3
45-54	95.6	91.6	90.1	97.0	95.4	96.1	87.7
55-64	89.6	82.2	81.1	90.3	85.3	85.7	81.1
65+	72.8	62.2	60.6	69.6	60.9	62.6	54.3
Total	79.8	70.3	68.7	77.1	73.8	73.6	68.2 (67.8)[d]
Females							
10-14	15.6	13.7	14.4	20.9	10.9	10.1	9.5
15-19	30.6	30.8	28.7	45.4	34.2	35.4	31.1
20-24	27.4	33.4	31.9	48.5	37.5	37.2	33.2
25-44	29.6	39.5	38.2	55.2	45.8	47.5	40.0
45-54	39.8	44.0	43.3	61.7	50.5	52.2	45.5

55-64	39.1	37.2	36.3	51.2	40.3	41.9	34.1
65+	27.8	24.0	22.8	30.9	20.0	23.8	18.8
Total	29.4	33.1	32.1	46.5	36.8	39.8	32.2 (32.0)[d]

[a]March-April.
[b]September-December.
[c]Averages for February, May, August and November.
[d]Adjusted to exclude those only working one day per week.

Sources: Census 1961: Population Census 1961. Those currently working and those who worked for 2 months or more in the past six months were counted as 'working'. Census 1971: Series C and D. Those working 2 days or more in the reference week were defined as 'working'. *Supas* and *Sakernas* 1976 and 77-78: Intercensal Survey and National Labour Force Survey respectively. Those working for at least one hour in the reference week were counted as 'working'. Census 1980: Derived from Series S No. 1. Those working at least one hour in the reference week were defined as 'working'.

Table 10.2. Employment Growth by Industry, 1971-80

	1971		1980		Percentage increase[a] (annual rate) 1971-80	Share of total increase[a]	Percentage annual growth in output per worker 1971-80
	(000)	(%)	(000)	(%)			
Agriculture etc.	24,963.9	65.9	28,040.4	55.5	1.0	20.6	2.9
Mining, quarrying	90.6	0.2	369.4	0.7	16.5	2.4	−13.8
Manufacturing	2,949.6	7.8	4,360.7	8.6	4.1	11.5	9.3
Utilities	38.1	0.1	84.6	0.2	8.9	0.4	4.2
Construction	740.6	2.0	1,573.1	3.1	8.4	7.0	6.6
Transport and Communications	919.2	2.4	1,467.8	2.9	5.0	4.5	6.9
Trade	4,143.8	10.9	6,611.4	12.1	5.0	20.4	1.3
Finance	95.5	0.3	232.5	0.5	10.1	1.2	3.4
Community, Social & Personal Services[a]	3,939.7	10.4	7,739.3	15.4	7.5	32.1	1.7
Others[a]	1,603.6[a]	—	712.8[a]	—	—	—	—
Total	39,474.5	100.0	51,191.5	100.0	2.9	100.0	4.8
(Male)	(26,357.5)	(66.8)	(34,486.0)	(67.4)	(3.0)	(69.4)	—
(Female)	(13,117.0)	(33.2)	(16,705.5)	(32.6)	(2.7)	(30.6)	—

[a]Others distributed proportionately among other industries.
Sources: 1971 Census (Series C); 1980 Census Series S, No. 1.

those manufactures would be available on the Indonesian market at prices more likely to attract a mass market.

3) Urban-Rural Employment Structure

The Census data of 1971 shows that one-quarter of those working in rural areas (about 7.9 million people) find their livelihood outside agriculture (i.e., trade, services and manufacturing, see Table 10.3). Even more, 76 per cent of all manufacturing employment in Indonesia is in rural areas, including activities such as

Table 10.3. Total, Urban and Rural Employment by Major Industry Group, 1971[a][b]

Major industry group	Total		Urban		Rural	
	Absolute numbers ('000)	Per cent	Absolute numbers ('000)	Per cent	Absolute numbers ('000)	Per cent
Agriculture, hunting, forestry, and fishing	24,930	67.1	582	11.3	24,347	76.2
Mining and quarrying	80	0.2	37	0.7	43	0.1
Manufacturing	2,571	6.9	591	11.5	1,980	6.2
Electricity, gas, and water	34	0.1	24	0.5	11	0
Construction	637	1.7	249	4.8	387	1.2
Trade, restaurants, hotels	4,073	11.0	1,354	26.3	2,719	8.5
Transport, storage, and communication	898	2.4	482	9.3	416	1.3
Financing, insurance, real estate, and business services	87	0 2	73	1.4	14	0
Community, social and personal services	3,852	10.4	1,763	34.2	2,089	6.5
Activities not adequately defined	428	b	102	b	327	b
Total	37,590	100.0	5,255	100.0	32,334	100.0

[a]Irian Jaya is excluded.

[b]Persons with activities not adequately defined, who constituted 1.9 per cent of the total employed population in urban areas and 1.0 per cent in rural areas, have been allocated to industry groups pro rata before calculating percentages.

Source: BPS, 1971 (Population Census, Series D, Tables 45 and 45A).

batik-making, brick-making, repair of bicycles and agricultural implements, and weaving of mats and hats. Not all rural manufacturing is small scale, in recent years many of the large plants built with foreign capital have been located in urban fringe areas outside city boundaries.

Rural areas provide more than half of all employment in services and construction and two-thirds of all employment in trade. The major industrial sectors in which a clear majority of total employment is provided in urban areas are transport, storage and communication and the two relatively insignificant sectors (from an employment point of view) of public utilities and finance, including insurance, real estate, and business services. When we add to these figures the large but unknown number of rural dwellers who move to the cities to obtain work on a temporary or casual basis but are classified by the census as working in agriculture, it is clear that a substantial fraction of all work engaged in by rural dwellers is in the non-agricultural sector. This is of some importance in planning for ways to cope with the inevitable expansion of the rural labour force over the remainder of this country.

Table 10.3 shows that as many as 11 per cent of those employed in urban areas are in agriculture. This percentage rises higher in the smaller towns; if we exclude Jakarta from the urban population, the agricultural employment in the remaining urban areas of Indonesia rises to 13.5 per cent. Many urban dwellers also do seasonal work in agriculture at busy times of the year. Therefore we must view the Indonesian employment structure as a continuum from large urban to small urban to rural, with agricultural employment penetrating into the cities and non-agricultural employment very important in rural areas, rather than sharply dichotomised between urban and rural areas.

When the figures are separated for Java and the rest of Indonesia, some noteworthy findings emerge. One is that there is a great deal more agricultural employment in the urban areas of the Outer Islands than of Java—21.6 per cent of total employment in these areas compared to 7 per cent in urban Java. No doubt this difference is partly due to the larger size of cities in Java, cities with a population about one million constitute 53 per cent of the urban population of Java, whereas there are no such cities in the Outer Islands. The boundaries of cities outside Java also appear to encompass large rural areas more often than is the case in Java. Rural areas of the Outer Islands are also much more agricultural than those in Java. Agriculture absorbs 84 per cent of the labour force in the Outer Islands compared to 72 per cent in Java. Manufacturing and trade employ 18 per cent of those employed in rural Java but only 8 per cent in rural areas of the Outer Islands.

4) Employment Dilemma

As seen in Table 10.2, the relationship between employment and output growth shows that over the decade all industries demonstrate an increase in real output per person employed (except the figure for mining and quarrying, which might be a suspiciously low employment figure for 1971). The industry with the highest rate of growth of output per person employed is manufacturing. Its rate of growth is higher than in most industry, and is probably attributable to the largely unmechanised nature of much Indonesian manufacturing at the beginning of the decade. It is noteworthy that manufacturing had the lowest rate of increase among other sectors, except agriculture. As a result, its contribution to employment growth over the decade was relatively small.

Table 10.3 shows that the employment figures for the agriculture sector is 67.1 per cent of the total employment, followed by the service sector (total, 24 per cent), which means the service sector absorbs the largest number of workers after agriculture. The manufacturing sector as well as the extractive and other modern sectors do not absorb much of the labour force due to capital-intensive approaches. If we add to the figure for the service sector those in the 'informal sector,' a worse condition might appear. This is a situation in which a relatively high percentage of the labour force in the service sector does not represent the outcome of the dynamic evolution of either an effective demand structure within the domestic economy or increase in productivity.

The service sector in Indonesia includes a large proportion of low-paid activities of various sorts which are in large supply, such as domestic and personal services of various descriptions, peddling, cart transport and clerical workers who crowd the government offices. The Indonesian service sector does not comprise the educated professionals employed in this sector due to the prevalence of effective demand from other economic sectors.

Jobs available in the sub-sectors of large and medium industries (mostly comprising import substitution with the purpose of employing cheap and unskilled labour) largely offer low career prospects and low wages. Here, workers are poorly paid because they have no other alternatives and most of them are those who have been pushed out from the traditional agricultural production system.

CONCLUSION

The issue of employment creation and human resource development is receiving considerable attention in preliminary discussions on Indonesia's *Repelita IV* which commences this year. There are two factions, one consisting of those who lobby for the expansion of production which will serve export markets, and the other those who argue that a drastic expansion of employment opportunities in itself is central to the elimination of poverty and to the generation of effective demand for manufactured products. The concept that employment generation is integral to the development process is now being advanced.

NOTES

1. The main difference in them is that in 1971 a person had to have worked at least two days during the week to be classified as 'employed,' while in 1980 the time period was one day. However, if those who worked just one day a week in 1980 are excluded from the labour force, the decline in overall participation rates for both males and females is minimal (as shown in Table 10.1).

REFERENCES

Arief, Sritua and Adi Sasono, 1981, *Indonesia: Ketergantungan dan Keterbelakangan*, Lembaga Studi Pembangunan, Jakarta.
Booth, Anne and Peter McCawley (eds.), 1981, *The Indonesian Economy During the Soeharto Era*, Oxford University Press, Kuala Lumpur.

Central Bureau of Statistics, various issues of Facts and Figures for Citation, Jakarta.

Djojohadikusumo, Sumitro, 1980, *Dasawarsa 1980*: *Prospek dan Tantangan*. Paper presented on the 25th Anniversary of the ISEI, Jakarta.

Scherer, Peter, 1982, 'Survey of recent development' in: *BIES* vol. XVIII, No. 2, ANU, Canberra.

Tjiptoherijanto, Prijono, 1982, *Pokok-pokok Pikiran Mengenai Pengembangan Sumberdaya Indonesia*, Jakarata, (mimeographed), Suroto, 1982, *Masalah Ketenagakerjaan dalam Repelita IV*, Jakarta (mimeographed).

CHAPTER 11

Participatory Action Research on the Informal Sector: A Field Action Report from Jakarta

BACKGROUND

It is now widely recognised in Indonesia that 72 per cent of the work force is employed in the so-called 'informal sector', the remaining 28 per cent working as civil servants or for medium to large-scale firms in the formal sector.

Not only do most people work in the informal sector, but it rather than the formal sector must absorb annual additions to the national labour force. Population growth has resulted in two million new additions to the work force annually, but the depressed state of the Indonesian economy, limited government funds for financing new job creation in the formal sector, and other factors have actually reduced the percentage of jobs available in the formal sector. The projected maximum employment expansion of the formal sector for the next five years is three million, which will leave seven million workers no alternative but to look for work in the informal sector.

In spite of the importance of the urban informal sector to the national economy, there have been no concerted attempts to co-ordinate or integrate government job creation programmes for the two sectors. Generally, the informal sector has received little positive attention from the government: wages are depressed and education and skill levels remain low. All too frequently people in the informal sector have failed to benefit from national development programmes, which usually extend only to people and activities in the formal sector.

SPATIAL PROCESS OF THE INFORMAL SECTOR

Urbanisation might generally be recognised as a continuum between rural and urban sectors. The rural characteristics brought by migrants gradually fade under the strong influence of urban characteristics. Subsequently, the migrants tend to polarise into formal and informal sector participants.

These two sectors are not dichotomous. They exist automatically due to the development model chosen by the government, wherein the 'modern and formal' sector benefits from the policy of privileged services for general infrastructural investment as well as from the allocation of development resources. Meanwhile, the 'traditional and informal' sector, which is not progressive, receives no such benefits.

The theoretical model shown in Figure 11.1 locates the informal sector in a paradigm. If development inclined to concentrate on modernisation, the informal sector activists would increase. The modernisation process tends to cause migration.

A characteristic of informal sector activities is that its labour relations are very flexible. Labour activity, which begins with a simple desire to be gainfully employed in the marketplace, generally gives way to unhealthy competition among informal sector traders. There is no real competition between modern and informal business interests since it is impossible for very small groups to fight more powerful ones. Among these small groups, however, there is intense competition and even conflict. Hence, the informal sector activists become powerless and receive little, if, any, benefit from the existing system (see Figure 11.2).

LSP's Informal Sector Development Programme

In 1983, the informal sector programme was established at LSP to focus on improving the socio-economic situation of selected target groups, such as street hawkers, *becak* drivers, and

Modern Sector

− capital intensive
− high skills
− fixed pattensr

Village Unit
Cooperative

RURAL | − − − − − − − − −·− − − −·− − + − − − − − − − − − | URBAN

Rural Informal Sector
−agrarian destitution
−property sharing
−patron-client

Urban Informal Sector
−village phenomenon
−street vendors, etc.

Informal Sector − − − −·−   − − − −·− − Informal Sector

−uncertain income
−insecure business
−consumption flexibility
−self-employment
−very small scale
−credit proliferation for all

−labour intensive
−transitional skills
−consumption flexibility

Traditional Sector

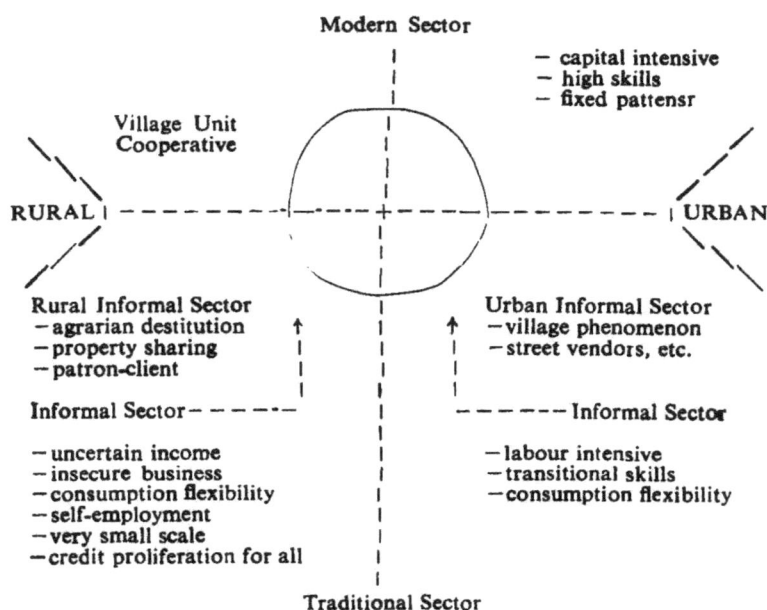

Figure 11.1: Spatial process of the informal sector

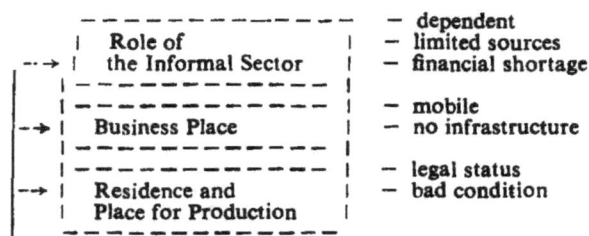

	Role of the Informal Sector		− dependent − limited sources − financial shortage
	Business Place		− mobile − no infrastructure
	Residence and Place for Production		− legal status − bad condition

Figure 11.2: Informal sector characteristics

noodle vendors. The thrust of this programme was to bring together people working in one activity and to help than establish
and manage a cooperative unit which could become the vehicle
for achieving the group's objectives.

LSP regards the institution-building process as crucial to successful development because it is through this process that participants acquire both an appreciation of the democratic process
and skills in working together to solve difficult socio-economic

problems. As part of its programme strategy, LSP runs a participatory action research programme (PAR) which incorporates a
series of stages to achieve the institution building described above.
Initially, institutions are little more than informal social or religious groups, meeting regularly as a forum for members and
LSP motivators to exchange ideas and discuss mutual problems.
Once group members gain experience and confidence in this form
of organisations more formal organisations such as pre-cooperatives can be established with statutes, administrative boards and
specific programmes. The institution-building process does not
end until a firm foundation for sustaining development has been
established.

LSP uses cooperatives or pre-cooperatives as a vehicle to
address development problems for several reasons, the most important of which are: they are endorsed by existing legislation as
an appropriate way to pursue economic development, they can
legally operate their own credit schemes for the benefit of members, they serve as rallying points for collective action by members to defend their interests, and they promote and sustain
bottom-up development by encouraging democratic participation
and the growth of accountability among members (see Figure
11.3). It has been LSP's experience that close cooperation between members can lead to the development of long-term solutions to the social and economic problems of the group.

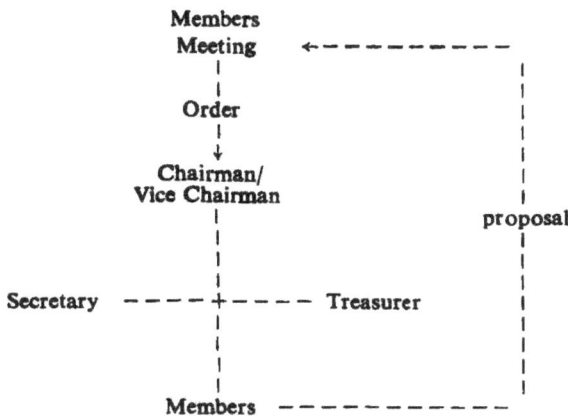

Figure 11.3: Group organisational structure

PURPOSES

The programme introduces various innovative aspects for enterprise development, organisational skills and technical know-how, as well as marketing organisation. These are indeed a long-term investment for human resource development.

The programme creates an institution in the form of a multipurpose cooperative society, which can comprehensively function as an agent of development, viz., economic, social, cultural and educational development, and also serve as an agent for equal distribution of the benefits of development. Over the long term, the institution will assure a process of continuous development in which multiple effects and benefits will constantly be created.

The programme was developed as a model for enterprise development for the urban poor. Since it is monitored and recorded it can contribute valuable experience and be a model of people-centred development which might be applicable to other areas.

It is evident that the (pre-) cooperatives offer one way of improving the socio-economic conditions of the poor without requiring a top-down approach: initiative for change proceeds from the participants' realisation that they must be actively involved in altering their situation; the small-scale nature of these collective units encourages democratic participation and enhances member understanding of the participatory process.

It is also true that the government of Indonesia regulates the involvement of NCO's in national development, permitting them to engage only in certain kinds of development efforts; cooperatives represent one acceptable form of involvement.

PROGRAMME APPROACH

LSP's participatory action research programme in the informal sector not only seeks to establish strong cooperatives, but to improve the socio-economic position of the poor. This requires augmenting their incomes through increased productivity, higher profit margins and better marketing techniques; teaching them to participate democratically in a collective organisation; and helping them to found strong organisations which can become a vehicle to defend and represent their interests.

PAR is carried out in five stages (see Figure 11.4):

```
                           LSP                              LSP
                           Monitoring                       Final
                           Evaluation,    — — — — — —        Evaluation
                           and                              and
                           Reporting                        Reporting
                              |                                |
         — — — · — — — — — — — + — — — — — — —                 |
         |                  |                  |              |
         ↓                  ↓                  ↓              ↓
Stage 1:— →  Stage 2:— →  Stage 3:— →  Stage 4:— →  Stage 5:
Observation  Target        Organisational  Institutional  Programme
and          Group         Skill and       Development    Evaluation
Research     Consolidation Technology
                     ↑     Transfer
                     |         ↑
                     |         |
         — — — — — — + — — — — — · — —
                     |
                     |
                  LSP—                      LSP
                  Sponsored                 Financial
                  Training    — — — — — →    Assistance
                  and
                  Technical
                  Assistance
```

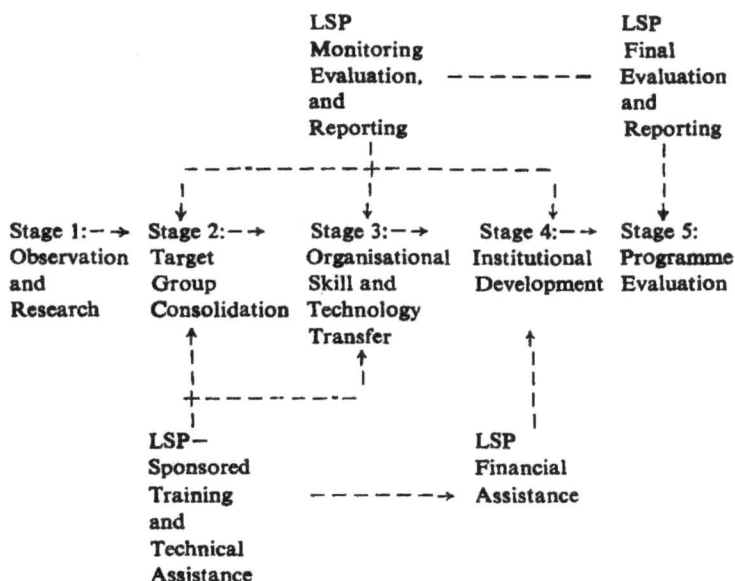

Figure 11.4: Programme implementation network for PAR

Stage 1: Observation and research

LSP identifies an activity in the informal sector which needs assistance; research includes constructing a community profile and finding a key person to act as group spokesman.

Researchers identify people whose incomes are low, averaging US $ 52.50 per month. LSP's target is to help these people increase their incomes by 35 per cent in the first year of participation in an income-generating programme.

Stage 2: Target group consolidation

Orientation meetings are sponsored by LSP at which prospective members are briefed about LSP's purpose in fostering cooperative development for participants; LSP field staff assist participants in discussing the group's common problems and ways to address them.

Stage 3: Organisational skill and technology transfer

An educational phase includes LSP-sponsored training sessions for cooperative coordinators on how to manage a cooperative,

plus training for members in book-keeping, appropriate technology, and problem-solving techniques. Business-related training
teaches individual participants how to run their businesses more
efficiently.

Stage 4: Institutional development

LSP assists each cooperative in instituting a compulsory savings and loan programme and in establishing regular board meetings and other aspects of responsible cooperative management;
members are encouraged to participate in the running of training
programmes and other activities intended for their benefit.

Individual cooperatives may set up food, materials, or equipment cooperatives as a service to members who benefit by reduced rates of up to 15 per cent on these items as a result of bulk
purchasing. Reductions in the cost of these items contribute
significantly to lower business expenses for members.

Stage 5: Programme evaluation

LSP reviews each cooperative's progress with members. Written
progress reports from the cooperative managements and comments from LSP field staff supplement information gained at
these meetings.

NOTES

The process of institution building and evaluation is a cyclical
one as each cooperative matures. At the individual level, PAR
contributes to a gradual improvement in the economic well-being
of members through training and self-help programmes which
help them to increase their gross monthly incomes while decreasing their expenses for raw materials, finished products, equipment rentals and for capital.

These benefits, together with the participants' growing confidence, in turn contribute to the members' faith in the cooperative and their support of its programmes. It is LSP's experience
that, with time, cooperatives expand their programming to include new services for members, such as housing improvement
programmes. External monitoring by LSP and regular internal
evaluations by members help to ensure that programmes really
meet the members' needs and promote their interests.

ORGANISATION OF THE INFORMAL SECTOR
DEVELOPMENT PROGRAMME

Since PAR is applicable to all activities regarding informal sector development programmes at the target group's level, LSP plays the dual role of facilitator and bridgehead for promoting not only economic growth, which is essential in efforts to eradicate poverty, but also social improvement. Hence the target groups in the development programme should develop a broader understanding of democratic principles and practices.

In the implementation plan of the programme, three main activities are mentioned:

1) consolidation of target group organisations;
2) Transfer of organisational skills and technical knowledge; and
3) Institutionalisation and motivation.

In this implementation plan, the division of tasks between LSP, the implementing organisation, and the target group, LSP will conduct surveys; make contact with particular key figures (informal leaders, government officials); introduce and discuss the guiding principles of the programme; and bring about the necessary agreements. LSP will also organise meetings with the target groups to elaborate the proposals and to organise the legal formalisation of group formation. The target group is expected to prepare and participate in meetings and to disseminate information on the programme to other members of the target group.

With respect to the transfer of organisational skills and technical knowledge, LSP will give training in management to the officials of the groups and information on cooperative principles to all members of the group. LSP will also organise training in leadership techniques, group administration and book-keeping for the officials of the groups.

The target groups will follow training courses, organise savings and loan programmes for members of the cooperatives, and provide monthly reports.

Institutionalisation and motivation will be reached by LSP in providing supervision and consultancy on organisation management and development; loans will be extended on the basis of plans approved by the umbrella target group organisation. LSP will carry out feasibility studies with regard to proposed activities and organise additional training in management techniques.

The target group are expected to introduce organisational structures based on the cooperative principle, to develop collective activities based on feasibility studies, and to improve the quality of the administrative systems of the groups.

To a certain extent, the revolving fund will enable an independent development of the programme. Furthermore, the creation of a service-rendering institute for the informal sector will reduce the part played by LSP.

Summarising the project activities, LSP assists the new groups in the identification of their problems and in discussing them, because the major obstacle in the activities of the target group is the inability of the members to see their problems as legitimate. LSP also tries to inspire confidence in the groups that their problems will be dealt with, if the members of the target group are prepared to school themselves and to act together. In this process LSP facilitates, i.e., provides transfer of knowledge and technology, advice and credit facilities not only to improve productivity and income on short notice, but particularly as part of a process of transfer directed toward autonomous organisation of these services. LSP also plays an important role as intermediary between the target groups and the local authorities, lawyers, scientists and the mass media.

Figure 11.5 describes the organisation wherein the parties involved will have an opportunity to implement works through a learning process which encourages mutual communication and reflection on problems emerging in the field. The main programme activities are: (1) to intensify the current processes of organisation building with 10 of the groups organised in the Joint Cooperative of TGC; (2) to increase the informal sector network in Jakarta by incorporating about 10 new groups into the programme; (3) to strengthen the organisational network between the groups organised in the Joint Cooperative of TGC; (4) to set up an effective line of communication between the informal sector network and the local authorities and services; (5) to run and monitor a small-scale credit programme in the form of a revolving fund for more than 1,700 small merchants and producers in the informal sector organised in 22 member organisations; and (6) to start a process of institutionalising services rendered, in order to reduce dependency on external institutions (such as LSP and funding agencies) and to set up service-rendering institutions of their own in the informal sector.

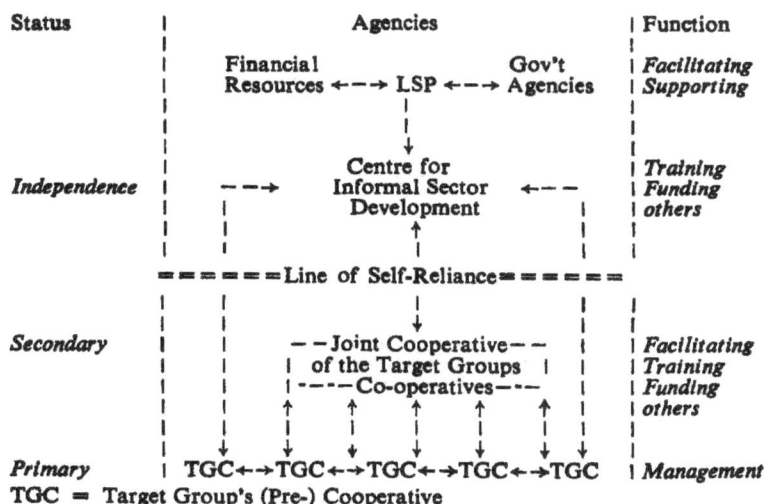

```
Status      |                    Agencies                    | Function
            |                                                |
            |    Financial                     Gov't         | Facilitating
            |    Resources ←— → LSP ←— → Agencies            | Supporting
            |                     |                          |
            |                     ↓                          |
            |               Centre for                       | Training
Independence|      — —→     Informal Sector     ←— —         | Funding
            |       |       Development          |           | others
            |       |            ↑               |           |
            |       |            |               |           |
   == == == ==Line of Self-Reliance== == == ==
            |       |            |               |           |
            |       |            ↓               |           |
Secondary   |       |   — —Joint Cooperative— —  |           | Facilitating
            |       |    | of the Target Groups |            | Training
            |       |    |— —·—Co-operatives—·—  |           | Funding
            |       |    ↑   ↑    ↑     ↑   ↑    |           | others
            |       ↓    ↓   ↓    ↓     ↓   ↓    |           |
Primary     | TGC←→TGC←—→TGC←—→TGC←—→TGC←—→TGC   | Management
TGC  =  Target Group's (Pre-) Cooperative
```

Figure 11.5: Collective organization to implement programmes

Profile of TGC

By the end of 1985, LSP and the target groups had actively built up 22 (pre-) cooperatives or collective small enterprises, an increase of 4 new units from 1984; there were 1,728 members in December 1985, up from 939 in 1984. Total savings at the end of 1985 were Rp 34,225,250.00, up from Rp 15,926,398.75 in 1984.

Figure 11.6 shows the location of the target groups on the map of Jakarta. They are: (1) Koppkalimaja/East Jakarta; (2) Bumi Membangun/West Jakarta; (3) Rahrja Lestari/West Jakarta; (4) Hondrowino 1/West Jakarta; (5) Semangat/West Jakarta; (6) Produsen Peti Kemas/West Jakarta; (7) Sari Kencana/East Jakarta; (8) Ibu Sejati/East Jakarta; (9) Tunas Mekar/Central Jakarta; (10) Hondrowino 3/North Jakarta; (11) Berkah/South Jakarta; (12) UBET/West Jakarta; (13) Langganan Tetap/Central Jakarta; (14) Konpeksi Kemayoran/Central Jakarta; (15) Rumah

Susun Penjaringan/North Jakarta; (16) Kakilima Tanah Abang/ Central Jakarta; (17) Persatuan Pedagang Kakilima Karet Teng-sin/Central Jakarta; (18) Simpay Mimitran Parikrama/East Jakarta; (19) Pedagang Kakilima Pasar Tanah Abang/Central Jakarta: (20) Pedagang Kakilima Kramat Jati/East Jakarta; (21) Al-Mukhlisin/West Jakarta; and (22) Puskosin/East Jakarta.

By the end of 1985, 157 people had been trained in the following programmes:

a) managing cooperative/collective enterprises;
b) managing small businesses; and
c) training in small business administration.

This select group of 157 subsequently became trainers for other members of their respective (pre-) cooperatives. In the meantime routine activities were held by field staff, including consultation with the cooperatives concerning organisational, business, and administrative problems and skill-training programmes.

From the start of the programme to the end of 1985, LSP had made loans totalling Rp 93,500,000.00 to the participating collective organisations; through the same period, repayment of principal amounted to Rp 18,276,337.00 and interest payments approximately 3 per cent of the total credit disbursement in 1984-1985. The following is a summary of the members' participation in credit programmes up to the end of 1985:

Loans made by LSP to (pre-) cooperatives:

1984 : Rp 58,800,000.00
1985 : Rp 34,700,000.00
Total : Rp 93,500,000.00

Repayment by (pre-) cooperatives to LSP on loans:

1984 : Rp   2,898,480.00
1985 : Rp 15,377,857.00
Total : Rp 18,276,337.00

A description of each (pre-) cooperative monitored up to May 1986 is as follows:

1) *Koppkalimaja*: Total Members: 203 (Street Vendors); Total Savings: Rp 2,307,500 (Base), Rp 9,295,000 (Obligation), Rp 3,021,373 (Others); Activities: Saving & Borrowing, General

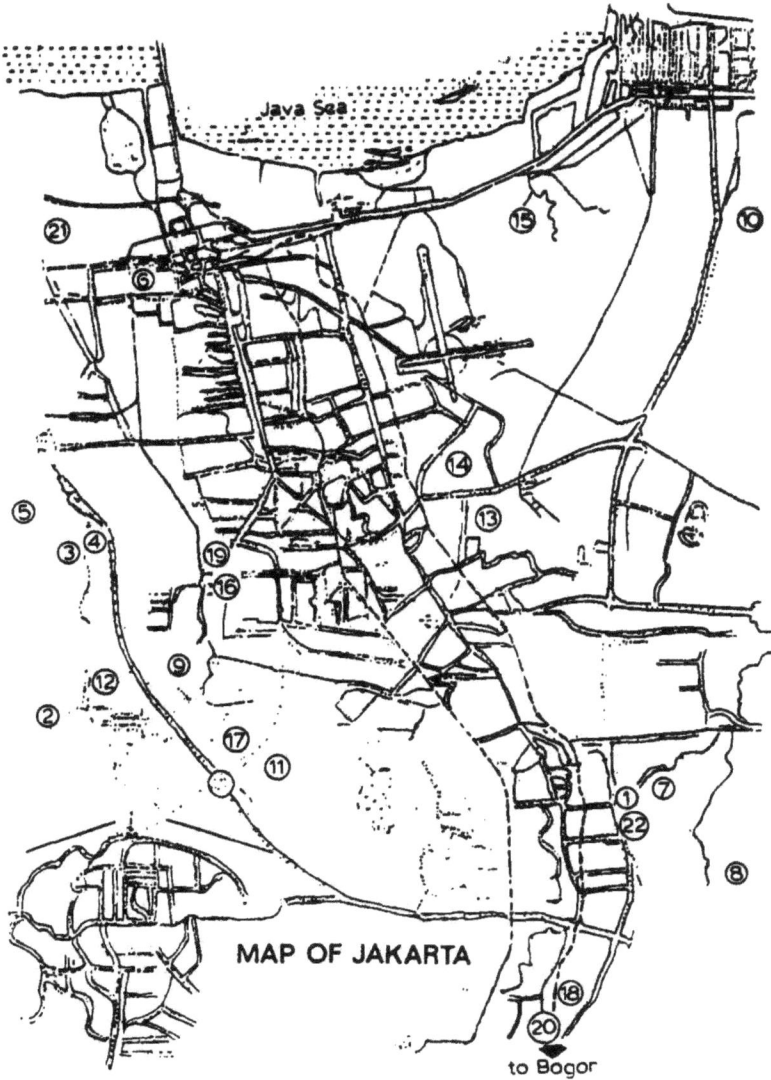

Figure 11.6: Location of target groups.

Trade, Joint Capital Investment, Photocopy Service; Economic Profile: 1983-84 Good, 1984-85 Declining (Mismanagement), 1986 Consolidation; Socio-Politically: Excellent, Recognised as a Pioneer Cooperative.

2) Bumi Membangun: Total Members: 51 (Flower Planters, Garment Makers); Total Savings: Rp 482,000 (Base Rp 868,000 (Obligation). Rp 855,850 (Others); Activities: Saving & Borrowing, Electric Bill Services, Petty Trade: Economic Profile: 1984 Good, 1985-86 Decreasing (Members & Activities); Socio-Politically: Excellent, Extended to higher level, Recognised by the Local Government.

3) Raharja Lestari: Total Members: 32 (Unskilled Labourers, Meat Ball Soup Sellers); Total Savings: Rp 320,000 (Base), Rp 95,000 (Obligation), Rp 0 (Others); Activities: Welding Workshop, Saving & Borrowing; Economic Profile: 1984-85-86 Good; Socio-Politically: Average.

4) Hondrowino 1: Total Members: 50 (Noodle Soup Sellers); Total Savings: Rp 91,000 (Base), Rp 327,475 (Obligation), Rp 306,025 (Others); Activities: Noodle Production, Saving & Borrowing, Trade, Push Cart Rental; Economic Profile: 1984-85 Good, 1986 Slightly Declining, Urgent to Consolidate; Socio-Politically: Average.

5) Semangat: Total Members: 86 (*Becak* Drivers, small Traders); Total Savings: Rp 760,700 (Base), Rp 263,900 (Obligation), Rp 0 (Others); Activity: Saving & Borrowing; Economic Profile: 1984-85-86 Good; Socio-Politically: Poor ('*Becaks*' have been phased out by the Local Government).

6) Peti Kemas: Total Members: 130 (Wood Container Makers); Total Savings: Rp 1,275,000 (Base), Rp 897,500 (Obligation), Rp 1,083,200 (Others); Activities: Saving & Borrowing, Wood Trade (Raw Material); Economic Profile: 1983-84-85-86 Average; Socio-Politically: Good.

7) Sari Kencana: Total Members: 48 (Housewives); Total Savings: Rp 111,000 (Base), Rp 127,250 (Obligation), Rp 42,265 (Others); Activities: Saving & Borrowing, Petty Trade; Economic Profile: 1984-85-86 Good; Socio-Politically: Average.

8) Ibu Sejati: Total Members: 53 (Housewives); Total Savings: Rp 132.500 (Base), Rp 371,000 (Obligation), Rp 14,758 (Others); Activity: Saving & Borrowing; Economic Profile: 1984-85-86

Good; Socio-Politically: Average.

9) Tunas Mekar: Total Members: 43 (Junk Dealers); Total Savings: Rp 384,000 (Base), Rp 64,500 (Obligation), Rp 0 (Others); Activity: Saving & Borrowing; Economic Profile: 1984-85 Poor, 1986 Good; Socio-Politically: Average.

10) Hondrowino 3: Total Members: 393 (Noodle Soup Sellers); Total Savings: Rp 1,910,000 (Base), Rp 1,260,000 (Obligation), Rp 1,273,400 (Others); Activities: Wheat Supplies (Raw Material), Sauce Trade; Economic Profile: 1985-86 Good; Socio-Politically: Excellent.

11) Berkah: Total Members: 40 (Small Traders); Total Savings: Rp 20,000 (Base), Rp 40,000 (Obligation), Rp 0 (Others); Activities: Saving & Borrowing, Consumer Goods Supplies; Economic Profile: 1985-86 Good; Socio-Politically: Average.

12) UBET: Total Members: 42 (Small Traders); Total Savings: Rp 548,460 (Base), Rp 211,000 (Obligation), Rp 117,655 (Others); Activity: Saving & Borrowing; Economic Profile: 1985-86 Good; Socio-Politically: Average.

13) Langganan Tetap: Total Members: 67 (Unskilled Labourers, Small Traders); Total Savings: Rp 670,000 (Base), Rp 0 (Obligation), Rp 0 (Others); Activity: Consumer Goods Supplies; Economic Profile: 1985-86 Good; Socio-Politically: Average.

14) Konpeksi Kemayoran: Total Members: 27 (Small Traders, Garment Makers); Total Savings: Rp 521,000 (Base), Rp 97,000 (Obligation), Rp 98,440 (Others); Activities: Garment (Home) Industry, Trade; Economic Profile: 1985-86 Good; Socio-Politically: Average.

15) Rumah Susun Penjaringan: Total Members: 82 (Small Traders, Unskilled Labourers); Total Savings: Rp 396,500 (Base), Rp 247,5000 (Obligation), Rp 858,205 (Others); Activities: Saving & Lending; Economic Profile: 1985-86 Good; Socio-Politically: Average.

16) Kakilima Tanah Abang: Total Members: 36 (Street Vendors); Total Savings: Rp 255,000 (Base), Rp 206,000 (Obligation), Rp 0 (Others); Activity: Saving & Borrowing; Economic Profile: 1985-86 Good; Socio-Politically: Average.

17) Persatuan Pedagang Kakilima Karet Tengsin: Total Members: 120 (Street Vendors); Total Savings: Rp 600,000 (Base); Rp 3,291,400 (Obligation), Rp 101,975 (Others); Activities: Sav-

ing & Borrowing, Trade; Economic Profile: 1985-86 Good; Socio-Politically: Excellent, Extended to Subdistrict Level.

18) Simpay Mimitran Parikrama: Total Members: 42 (Small Traders); Total Savings: Rp 283,000 (Base), Rp 83,000 (Obligation), Rp 34,700 (Others); Activity: Saving & Borrowing; Economic Profile: 1985-86 Good; Socio-Politically: Average.

19) Pedagang Kakilima Pasar Tanah Abang: Total Members: 76 (Street Vendors; Total Savings: Rp 742,000 (Base), Rp 2,242,500 (Obligation), Rp 2,300 (Others); Activity: Saving & Borrowing, Economic Profile: 1984-85-86; Socio-Politically: Average.

20) Pedagang Kakilima Kramat Jati: Total Members: 82 (Street Vendors); Total Savings: Rp 393,000 (Base), Rp 409,500 (Obligation), Rp 62,850 (Others); Activity: Saving & Borrowing; Economic Profile: 1985-86 Good; Socio-Politically: Average.

21) Al-Mukhlisin: Total Members: 25 (Unskilled Labourers, Small Traders); Total Savings: Rp 25,000 (Base), Rp 96,000 (Obligation), Rp 0 (Others); Activity: Saving & Borrowing; Economic Profile: 1985-86 Good; Socio-Politically: Average.

22) Puskosin: Total Members: 21 (Pre-/Cooperatives); Total Savings: Rp 0 (Base), Rp 0 (Obligation), Rp 0 (Others); Programmes: Increasing Members (Pre-/Cooperatives) Participation Especially in Saving Activities, Facilitating Business Activities to Support Members' Economic Growth, Conducting Other Activities such as Production, Distribution, Services including Construction, Trade which is not conducted by Members, Supplying Market Information, Facilitating Training of Related Efforts, Acting as a Consulting Agency for Technological Know-how, Production, etc. and acting as Financial Institute to Facilitate People's Economy; Economic Profile: 1985-86 Consolidation; Socio-Politically: Average.

POINTS TO PONDER: LEADING NOTES

LSP's overall policy is guided by the principle of development from the bottom-up concerning marginal groups, based upon creating internal solidarity and organisational development through the encouragement of common interests. In Indonesia this is rather difficult to deal with. This is mainly due to the strong exertion of state bureaucracy in the process of develop-

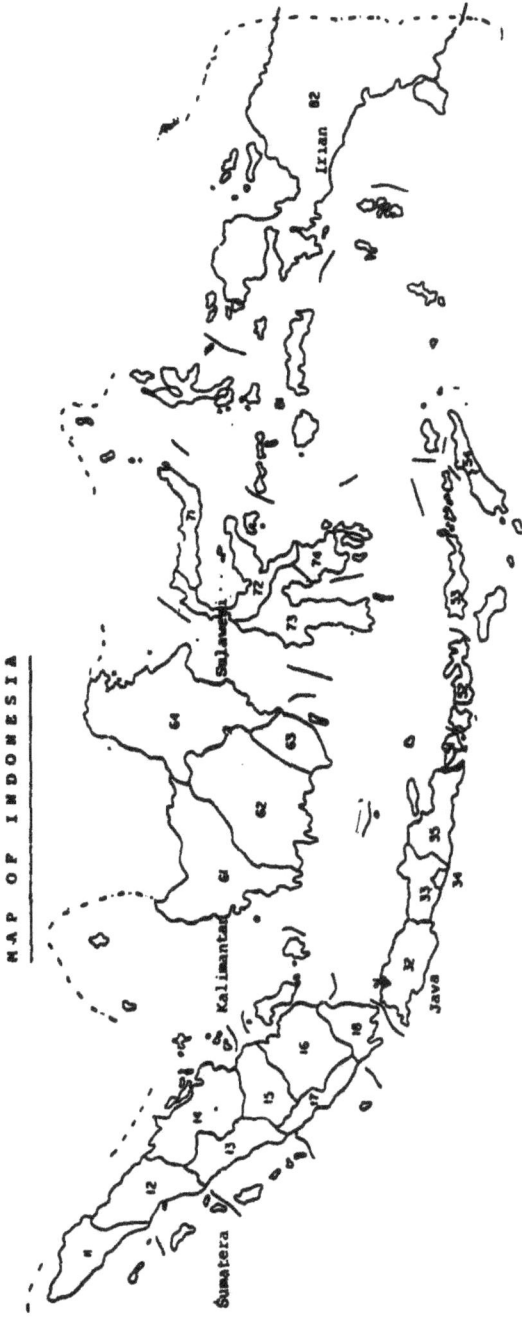

MAP OF INDONESIA

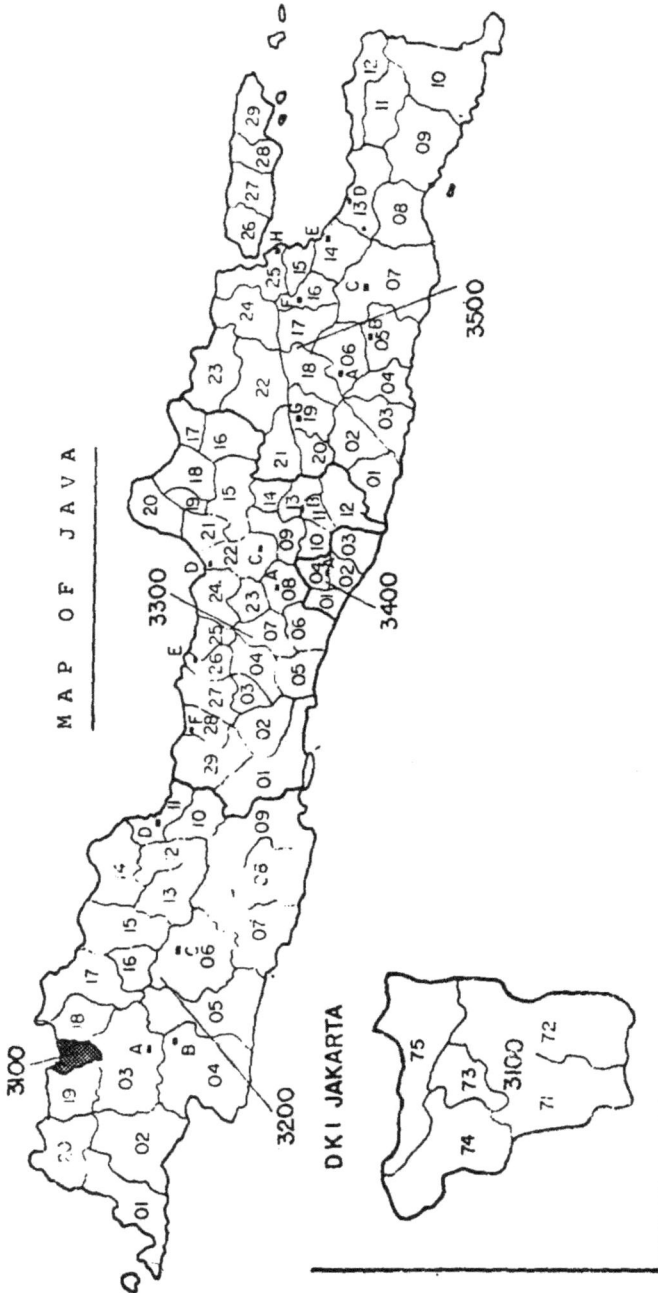

MAP OF JAVA

DKI JAKARTA

3100. DKI JAKARTA

71. Jakarta Selatan
72. Jakarta Timur
73. Jakarta Pusat
74. Jakarta Barat
75. Jakarta Utara

3200. PROP. JAWA BARAT

1. Kab. Pandeglang
2. Kab. Lebak
3. Kab. Bogor
4. Kab. Sukabumi
5. Kab. Cianjur
6. Kab. Bandung
7. Kab. Garut
8. Kab. Tasik Malaya
9. Kab. Clamis
10. Kab. Kuningan
11. Kab. Cirebon
12. Kab. Majalengka
13. Kab. Sumedang
14. Kab. Indramayu
15. Kab. Subang
16. Kab. Purwakarta
17. Kab. Karawang
18. Kab. Bekasi
19. Kab. Tangerang
20. Kab. Serang
71. Kodya Bogor (A)
72. Kodya Sukabumi (B)
73. Kodya Bandung (C)
74. Kodya Cirebon (D)

3300. PROP JAWA TENGAH

1. Kab. Cilacap
2. Kab. Banyumas
3. Kab. Purbalingga
4. Kab. Banjar Negara
5. Kab. Kebumen
6. Kab. Purworejo
7. Kab. Wonosobo
8. Kab. Magelang
9. Kab. Boyolali
10. Kab. Klaten
11. Kab. Sukoharjo
12. Kab. Wonogiri
13. Kab. Karang Anyar
14. Kab. Sragen
15. Kab. Grobogan
16. Kab. Blora
17. Kab. Rembang
18. Kab. Pati
19. Kab. Kudus
20. Kab. Jepara
21. Kab. Demak
22. Kab. Semarang
23. Kab. Temanggun
24. Kab. Kendal
25. Kab. Batang
26. Kab. Pekalongan
27. Kab. Pemalang
28. Kab. Tegal
29. Kab. Brebes
71. Kodya Magelang (A)
72. Kodya Surakarta (B)
73. Kodya Salatiga (C)
74. Kodya Semarang (D)
75. Kodya Pekalongan (E)
76. Kodya Tegal (F)

3400. DI YOGYAKARTA

1. Kab. Kulon Progo
2. Kab. Bantul
3. Kab. Gunung Kidul
4. Kab. Sleman
71. Kodya Yogyakarta (A)

3500. PROP. JAWA TIMUR

1. Kab. Pacitan
2. Kab. Ponorogo
3. Kab. Tranggalek
4. Kab. Tulung Agung
5. Kab. Blitar
6. Kab. Kediri
7. Kab. Malang
8. Kab. Lumajang
9. Kab. Jember
10. Kab. Banyuwangi
11. Kab. Bondowoso
12. Kab. Situbondo
13. Kab. Probolinggo
14. Kab. Pasuruan
15. Kab. Sidoarjo
16. Kab. Mojokerto
17. Kab. Jombang
18. Kab. Nganjuk
19. Kab. Madiun
20. Kab. Magetan
21. Kab. Ngawi
22. Kab. Bojonegoro
23. Kab. Tuban
24. Kab. Lamongan
25. Kab. Gresik (Surabaya)
26. Kab. Bangkalan
27. Kab. Sampan
28. Kab. Pamekasan
29. Kab. Sumenep
71. Kodya Kediri (A)
72. Kodya Blitar (B)
73. Kodya Malang (C)
74. Kodya Probolinggo (D)
75. Kodya Pasuruan (E)
76. Kodya Mojokerto (F)
77. Kodya Madiun (G)
78. Kodya Surabaya (H)

ment, but is also caused by vertical dependency relations within the semi-feudal structure, which to a certain extent still exists. Yet, it has been observed that the process of marginalisation has gone so deep in the society that even these structures no longer afford protection.

This erosion of vertically structured dependency relationship is striking especially among that part of the rural population which is trying to earn a living in cities and towns. Their only survival is seeking job opportunities in the so-called informal sector.

So the current process of modernisation within the framework of the existing politico-economic system of Indonesia causes a process of expulsion of the most vulnerable groups in the society.

As well as; the landless and marginalised farmers in the rural sector, this group of marginalised urban dwellers has become a major LSP target group in Indonesia. It is LSP's aim to contribute to an improvement of living conditions as well as to a strengthening of the bargaining power of the members of these groups, who are in fact already cut off from traditional redistribution mechanisms and do not (yet) participate in modern state mechanisms.

The Jakarta Informal Sector Development Programme of LSP is considered a useful channel for supporting the above-mentioned target groups. Although LSP generally stresses an integrated development approach, the sectoral approach of LSP applied in the informal sector development programme is more or less taken for granted. This is due to the intended targeting on the weakest groups in the society.

With regard to the rather substantial difference in socio-economic status between the (pre-) cooperatives involved and the fast-growing programme, there is a need to define potential target groups to be formed into (pre-) cooperatives. This is in consideration of LSP's goal of reaching low income groups.

The evaluation mission team has observed a wide range of (pre-) cooperatives, the so-called *Usha Bersama* (UB). This ranges from *Ibu Sejati*, located in the government organised housing complex of East Jakarta, being more a social gathering of wives of civil servants than an UB, to *Peti Kemas*, located on a 1.25 ha piece of filled swamp land in West Jakarta, which is a quite well established legalised UB of manufacturers of boxes, pallets and furniture from used wood.

The members of *Ibu Sejati* have thus far established a saving-loan system, but are not benefiting from production activities, while *Peti Kemas*, formerly illegally occupying a green belt area in the middle of a highway, performs at a high level of production *Peti Kemas* has already engaged a salaried manager. The main problems presented to the evaluation team were marketing and purchasing of used wood as raw material. The latter problem is due to the shift from wood-packed imported goods to containerised transportation.

Problems of marketing and production are caused by the business of sub-contracting. Through this system of business the main profits are earned by the contractor. But in the case of 10,000 crates ordered by a beer factory—a direct contract on recommendation of the Department of Industry—*Peti Kemas* could not meet the qualifications. They produced at a loss. This cooperative was in need of a qualified sales manager. To a large extent *Peti Kemas*, established in 1979, and now performing in a stable manner, is an example of formalisation within the informal sector.

Comparing the *Bumi Membangun* cooperative with the UB *Kakilima Tanah Abang*, the differences observed were striking, which indicate also the wide range of target groups. *Bumi Membangun* is localised within a well-defined and rather neatly developed village area in West Jakarta. The general impression of the village is very pleasant, and not just because the people are involved in the production and trading of decorative plants. The members of *Bumi Membangun* live at their place of work, although the selling of their products also takes place at different locations in the city. For this reason, they sometimes move to better situated selling locations along the main roads of Jakarta after starting and developing their business in an area of West Jakarta. This is the reason also that they leave the cooperative.

For the people who sell second-hand textbooks along the busy crossroads of Mansyur street in Tanah Abang, Central Jakarta, the outlook is completely different. They are the street vendors who come from many places of West Java and Central Java to find a livelihood in the city. Their position is highly uncertain and unstable. They have placed their trading stalls and small food shops along the sidewalks, thus causing pedestrians to use the road, which in turn causes traffic congestion. This forces the local authorities to issue harsh temporary measures from time to time. At present, the local government is planning to widen the road and to relocate the street vendors in a new market to be established at the existing bus terminal of Tanah Abang.

Although the members of UB *Kakilima Tanah Abang* are not opposing these plans, they have strong doubts concerning the relevance of this solution as it relates to their problems. Firstly, plots in the new market will only be allocated to traders who possess official identity cards (this is mandatory) and an official trader's licence for the Tanah Abang market, which most members of the KTA do not possess. Lacking these credentials they will not be allowed to join the *Bedagang Kakilima Pasar Tanah Abang* group, another cooperative of more legalised small business traders at Tanah Abang. Secondly, investment costs for one kiosk in the new market are as high as Rp 2,000,000 or about US $ 1,761—a sum of money they cannot afford.

The evaluation team also observed quite a different attitude on the part of the local government towards the relatively higher socio-economic status groups.

Bumi Membangun, which originated in 1980 from a former religious gathering called *Majelis Taklim*, was in fact welcomed by the local authorities because of this group's economic orientation for the well-being of the community. This background has also created a general acceptance of the cooperative in the village, which has been enriched with a cooperative store, where non-members can also buy daily necessities. Non-members are allowed to pay in cash only, whereas members are allowed to buy on credit. That their cooperative is well integrated within the local socio-political environment is proven by the fact that the Jakarta authorities want to establish *Bumi Membangun* as the only multi-business cooperative in the area. The process of legalisation is expected to be finalised soon. Furthermore, *Bumi Membangun* is expected to be chosen as one of the pilot project cooperatives of the city government of Jakarta. LSP is relying on this cooperative to be one of the five strong and legalised Joint Cooperative members.

The outward performance of this cooperative is rather good, although the integral development is rather slow and could even be called stagnant from the point of view of cooperative ability. Still the members do the buying and selling of their inputs and outputs on an individual or small group base. Only the payment of their electricity bills is, for reasons of efficiency, organised in a collective way. Leadership tends to be paternalistic and thus participation of the general membership is, in fact, decreasing. The cooperative is missing motivation for the development of economic activities towards a higher integrated level.

The *Kakilima Tanah Abang* did not start from a common spiritual background and its pre-cooperative was only recently established. The members are highly motivated by a common interest—to improve their low and uncertain living conditions.

UB *Semangat*, started in July 1984, has just recently solved several of its problems. This group suffered from distrust among the members of the board. The role of a certain person narrowly related to LSP gave rise to conflicts up to December, 1985. Since January 1986, a newly established board has clarified the financial situation. Meanwhile, the UB is deeply involved is seeking alternatives for their member *becak* drivers, due to the policy of the city government of Jakarta, which has discontinued *becak* as a means of local transport.

Another UB, *Konpeksi Kemavoran*, with 27 members, has established a rather high bargaining position. The cooperative's ability is quite well developed, as evidenced by collective purchasing at the local market even on credit. This has improved the profit margins of its members significantly.

Due to the wide range of types of UBs and target groups and their scattered locations throughout the city of Jakarta, LSP's involvement in them is not uniform. Furthermore, within and between the different UBs a wide range of social and economic conditions, from well-to-do to poor, exists. Some UBs perform at a high level of cooperative ability, while others are struggling through the conflicting interests of their members.

CONCLUSIONS

It is evident that the approach applied in the informal sector development programme—that is PAR—is time-consuming, since the process of problem-solving and problem-identification with target groups is informal. In addition, each (pre-) cooperative progresses differently, according to its members' skills and available resources.

Monitoring of the (pre-) cooperatives by LSP has demonstrated that the PAR program had mixed results. Positive results include: improvement in individual and group capability in problem-solving, improvement in individual member's incomes, an enhanced awareness of participatory democracy among (pre-) cooperative members, the development of administrative skills by group leaders, and the creation of training courses and credit programme. On the other hand, the (pre-) cooperatives continue to be dependent upon LSP for counselling, financial assistance and programme monitoring rather than becoming self-supporting entities.

Some of the problems which have emerged can be attributed to the relative youth of the organisations and lack of experience among the members and leaders in collective enterprise participation and management. Other problems could be overcome with improvements in PAR methodology. For instance, a longer or more intense period of social preparation is needed, which would include more experience in problem-solving and conflict-resolution.

Recommendations are now being discussed with regard to both long and short-term objectives; these are listed below.

First Long-term Objective

The programme will increase the level of knowledge and awareness of groups of small merchants and retailers operating in the informal urban sector of Jakarta. It also hopes to increase the community's level of knowledge and awareness through a community-based programme. *Hondrowino 1* (West Jakarta) and *Hondrowino 3* (North Jakarta) have been proposed as pilot projects.

Second Long-term Objective

The programme will enlarge the organised basis of the economic activities of the target group in light of the creation of a centre for the development of the informal sector. The Joint Cooperative of TGC has already been depicted in Figure 11.5.

Third Long-term Objective

The programme will improve the income of the target group. In some cases, e.g. *Konpeksi Kemayoran*, this objective has already been achieved, while in others, especially *Pedanang Kaki-lima Kramat Jati* and *Bumi Membangun*, income could be increased if cooperative ability were developed to a higher level. Among the less consolidated groups, such as *Semangat* and *Kakilima Tanah Abang*, an improved income situation has yet to be realised.

It has been observed that through the saving-loan system the cooperatives can generate lower interest rate capital. Production costs could therefore be reduced. This would also mean less dependency on outside money lenders. Obviously, cooperative members would feel happy, especially with the lower interest rates, but this does not automatically mean an increase in business activities. However, it must be stressed once again that the objective is to improve living conditions, as opposed to augmenting income only. In so doing, the scope of the programme will be broadened from the purely economic aspect to encompass social and physical conditions as well.

Fourth Long-term Objective

The programme will increase the assertiveness of the target group with regard to the dominating political economic system. LSP found a rather contradictory situation. On the one hand, the strengthening of horizontal, sectoral-based organisational structures was observed, through an increased number of target groups, an improved bargaining position, and an increased solidarity based on the awareness of common interests. On the other hand, the integration of vertical structures was striking, with an emphasis on legalisation and the obtaining of official locations. Obviously, this kind of integration is strongly related to the formalisation process of a part of the informal sector in Jakarta. LSP is strongly involved in the policy preparation concerning this development.

First Short-term Objective

The programme will help organise sectoral groups of retailers and producers in cooperative associations and, if possible in vertical structures.

Until now, LSP has succeeded in setting up 22 UBs. In achieving this objective, LSP has relied strongly on the creation of as many (pre-) cooperatives as possible. Two major goals are to widen the scope from sectoral to community-based development, and to diversify approach in order to better meet the needs of different groups. Notwithstanding this, it is acknowledged that the economic and financial interests of the (pre-) cooperative members are of great importance.

It is also acknowledged that rather than an increase in the number of cooperatives, the consolidation process of the target groups has to be intensified through a profound intervention strategy in light of the social preparedness of the target group.

Second Short-term Objective
The programme will institute training centres for the informal sector in general management enabling the community to set up and run the cooperatives itself.

LSP has carried out several types of training, e.g., in book-keeping, management of cooperatives, and marketing. In the future, training activities may be extended to include common members as well as board members, in order to create cadres, as well as to stimulate the process of democratised control and decision-making as the main principles of a cooperative organisation. This is especially relevant in the development of social abilities.

Third Short-term Objective
The programme will render services to small businesses and cooperatives. Although LSP has rendered services by means of training, consultancy and providing credits, highter skilled and more experienced field workers are needed because the project envisioned is broad. The tasks of field workers will become even greater as the scope of community development activities is extended. Cooperation with female field workers must be expanded because specific women's groups are included in the programme. In order to perfect the rendering of services, motivators have to be recruited from the target groups and trained by LSP.

Fourth Short-term Objective
The programme will strengthen the umbrella organisation's structures. This is an important point. As seen in Figure 11.5,

the Joint Cooperative of TGC should be developed according to the real needs of the participating primary cooperatives. Each of these cooperatives should function as an intermediary institute, rendering services to its (potential) members in order to lessen dependency on LSP.

Final Note

As the success of the implementation programme is largely dependent upon target group support and participation, LSP is aware that the programme will take at least five to six years to reach maturity. It is convinced that the ultimate aim has to be the establishment of self-reliant organisations, whether these are cooperatives with full legal status or (pro-) cooperatives without that status. The objectives are improvement of bargaining positions and improvement of living conditions. Subsequently the self-reliant organisations will operate beyond LSP's intervention.

CHAPTER 12

Participatory Action Research on the Labour Cooperative Movement: A Field Action Report from Bandung

BACKGROUND

The framework of labour relationship in the Indonesian economic system can be observed critically through the structure and mechanism of the prevailing labour market. The structure of the labour market is illustrated in Figure 12.1.

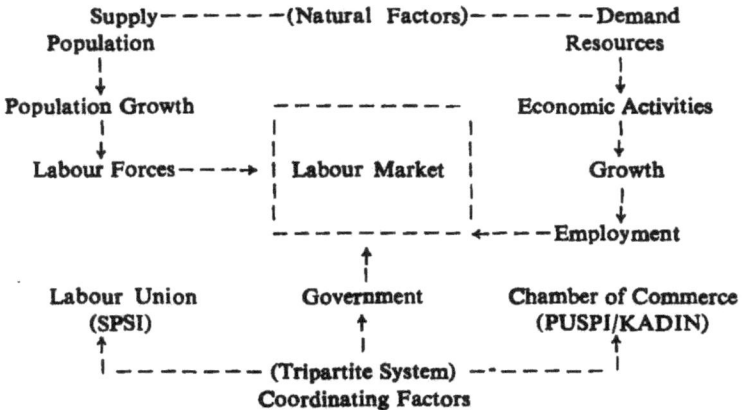

```
     Supply─ ─ ─ ─ ─(Natural  Factors)─ ─ ─ ─ ─Demand
    Population                                  Resources
        |                                          |
        ↓                                          ↓
 Population Growth     ─ ─ ─ ─ ─ ─ ─      Economic Activities
        |              |           |               |
        ↓              |           |               ↓
  Labour Forces─ ─ ─→  | Labour Market |         Growth
                       |           |               |
                       |           |               ↓
                        ─ ─ ─ ─ ─ ─ ─ ─  ←─ ─ ─Employment
                              ↑
                              |
  Labour Union           Government         Chamber of Commerce
    (SPSI)                   ↑                 (PUSPI/KADIN)
      ↑                      |                      ↑
      | ─ ─ ─ ─ ─ ─(Tripartite System) ─·─ ─ ─ ─ ─ |
              Coordinating Factors
```

Figure 12.1: Structure of the labour market.

There are two main points which must be considered at the outset as variables in labour consolidation. First, the demographic and socio-economic situations of the community as a natural factor, and second, the existing labour system that acts on factors coordination, control and institution.

The estimated economic growth rate for Indonesia in the next five years is 5 per cent p.a. Meanwhile, the maximum capacity of job creation in both formal and informal sectors is about 6.1 million or 70 per cent of the new labour force, excluding cummulative quantities of existing unemployment.

Besides the natural factor, the tripartite system has become another dominant factor in composing and controlling the effective labour market. Thus the real market mechanism never occurs. Furthermore the tripartite system has agreed that SPSI (All Indonesian Labour Organisation) will be the only coordinating labour organisation. Other organisations will be strictly prohibited.

Since there are very long queues of the unemployed, with no protection against oppression, the labour force ranks in the lowest position in the system of the labour market. In addition, prohibition of an effective trade union establishment outside SPSI resulted in:

—the failure of trade union development, which subsequently cannot protect labourers effectively;
—a very low bargaining position for employees vis-a-vis employers;
—the disorganisation and degradation of efforts to build labour solidarity.

LSP'S LABOUR COMMUNITY PROGRAMME

Due to the constraints of the foregoing limitations, the main problem faced by the labourers is the need to develop another legal and acceptable institution which will be able to increase labour solidarity, thereby strengthening their collective bargaining position.

The method of approach applied by LSP is to develop a labour community's small estate holdings. This should be carried out through the development of integrative workers' settlements and cooperatives. The following are the considerations:

1) The labour community will function as a supporting basis to strengthen the weak position of labour and will solve the problems together with LSP.

2) The labour community may also function as a centre of activities in:

labour education;
organising cooperation among themselves;
the effort of labour protection; and
improving labour welfare collectively.

3) A functional labour community could be developed through labour settlement development.

4) A labour settlement with a low-cost housing scheme should be based on full community participation through a functional housing cooperative, which is also a formal corporate body that can be established by the workers.

The Bina Karya Housing Cooperative

The approach used by LSP is to assemble and create an organisation of labour as a basis for activities. A low-cost housing programme was chosen as the focus for bringing a group of workers together. Figure 12.2 shows the role of LSP in helping to establish

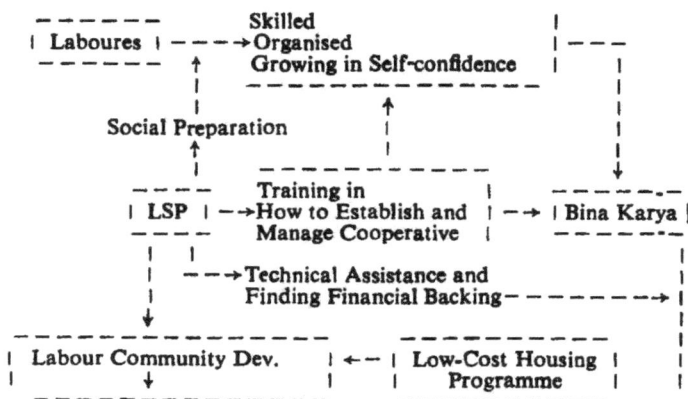

Figure 12.2: Establishment of Bina Karya Cooperative.

the Bina Karya Housing Cooperative and its community programme.

Since 1980, LSP has worked jointly with Bina Karya in establishing programmes in cooperative management and vocational
training seminars. These programmes have helped the cooperative to become firmly established and have enhanced individual
member job opportunities on a part-time or full-time basis. LSP's
role has been to carry out training, to act as a community-action
motivator, and to serve as a go-between with government sources
and financial sponsor.

Bina Karya is a mutual-ownership cooperative, i.e., the co-
operatiye owns legal title to entire property; the board collects
monthly carrying charges from members for mortgage debt service,
taxes, maintenance costs and other programmes (see Figure 12.3—
Organisational structure of Bina Karya, Figure 12.4—Membership representation, and Figure 12.5—Settlement development
team).

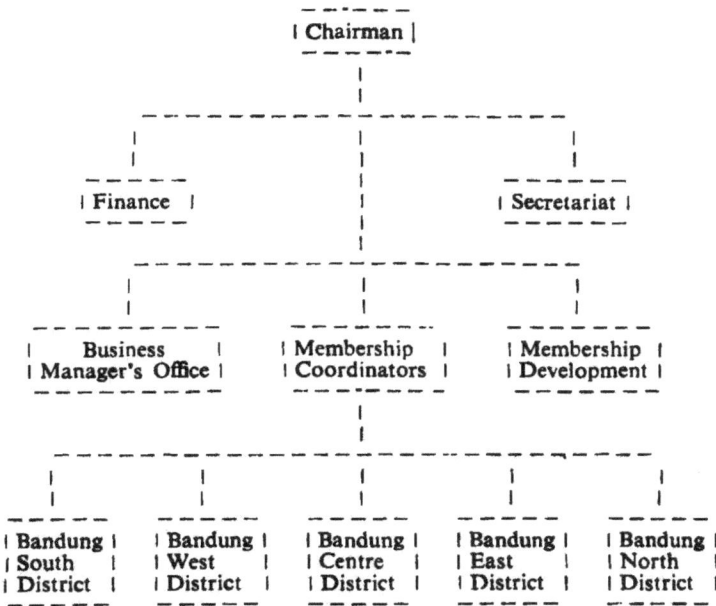

Figure 12.3: Organisational structure of Bina Karya.

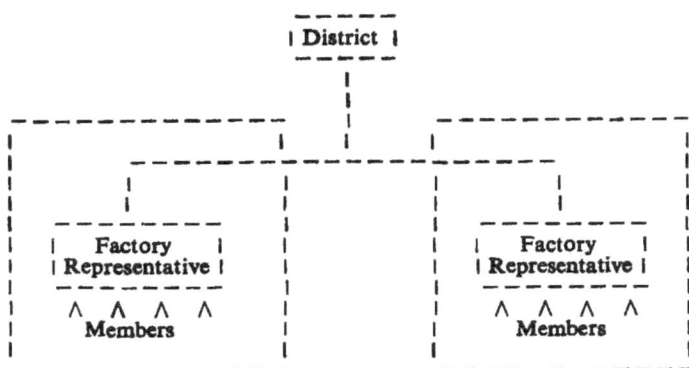

Figure 12.4: Membership representation.

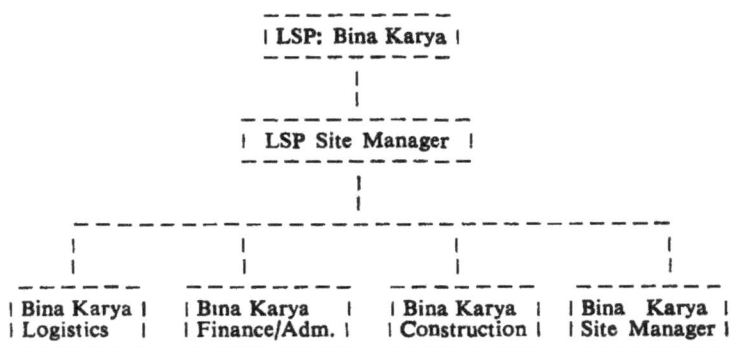

Figure 12.5: Settlement development team.

Members or heads of households at the cooperative are between 25 and 35 years of age. Their educational backgrounds
vary: by age 35 most have had the equivalent of junior, if not
senior, high school education; about 20 per cent never finished
elementary school, and 3 per cent are college educated.

Bina Karya members usually work at two jobs; permanent employment includes employment in the private sector, e.g., as
labourers at textile factories; as employees of an aircraft manu-
facturer; or employees in the public sector, e.g., as government
employees, university personnel, public school teacher. Part-time
work is required to supplement their incomes. Members work as

small businessmen in the informal sector, where they are involved in service and manufacturing industries: electronics servicing, tool manufacturing, spindle production, small grocery store, tailoring, etc. In many families, the wife and children work to augment the salary of the head of the household.

About 80 per cent of Bina Karya's members work as labourers or occupy equivalent wage positions in other jobs; 15 per cent of members are shift bosses, and the remaining 5 per cent are divisional bosses. The lowest wage per person per month was Rp 40,000 in 1984-85; the highest wage/person/month was Rp 110,000. The family income spread per month was Rp 60,000 to Rp 110,000, with an average of Rp 80,000 per month. (US1 $\approx$ Rp 1,136).

Monthly living expenses for the average family are between Rp 55,000 to Rp 60,000, which leaves only Rp 20,000 to Rp 25,000 per month as a savings. Fully 90 per cent of the members do not own housing, and until moving to the Bina Karya site, had had to live in unsanitary and expensive rental housing in Bandung. (Monthly rentals in a *kampung*—densely built-up, inner-city community—vary between Rp 17,000 and Rp 36,000, but rental contracts must be paid in a lump sum on an annual basis, posing a serious financial problem for many families).

THE PROGRAMME

Bina Karya's activities have embraced the design and construction of 120 housing units, training of the group's leader in book-keeping and administrative practices for cooperatives, skills training for members, and on-going social programmes. The housing units have just been completed (September 1985) at an average cost of Rp 1.8 million per unit; the unserviced land cost in 1980 was Rp 150,000 per unit; and monthly installment costs per unit Rp 25,000. Density at the site is about 60 units per ha or 300 people per ha.

The preceding activities were identification of the community's potential. The study inventoried the individual member's skills as well as his economic status. Individual patterns of income expenditure were examined to assess each family's savings potential: this varied according to the number of dependents. (including members of the extended family), and the gross income of the

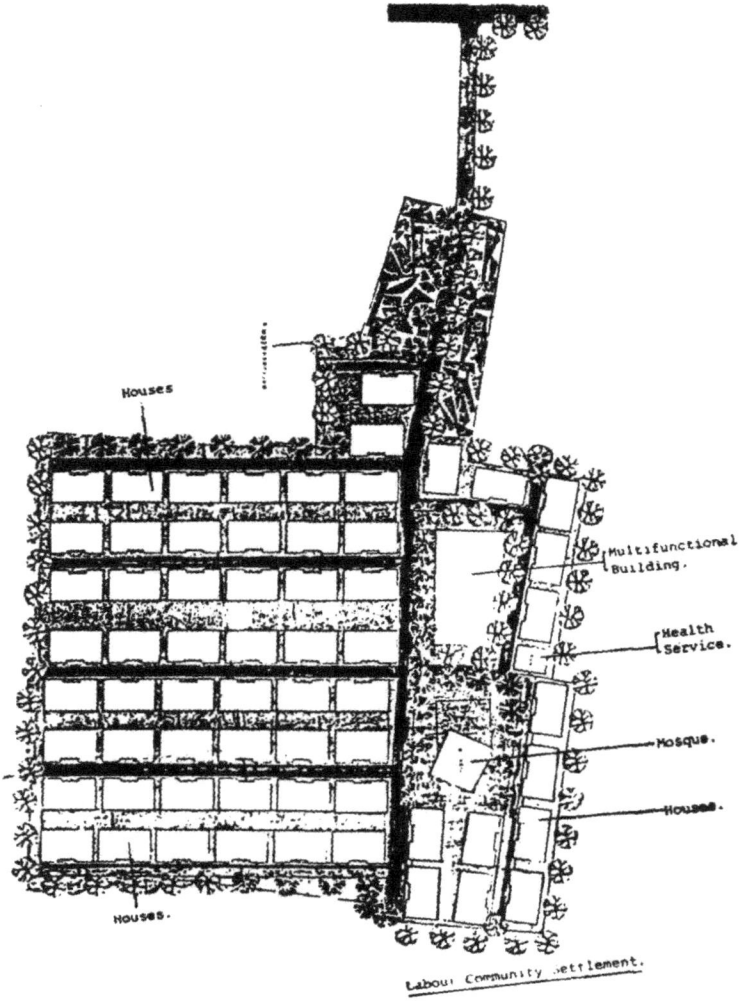

Houses

Multifunctional
Building.

Health
Service.

Mosque.

Houses.

Houses

Houses.

Labour Community Settlement.

family. This type of research, called PAR (see Figure 12.6), enabled LSP field workers to identify with individual members how his or the family's skill levels could be developed in order to increase gross income derived from secondary jobs. This latter increase enabled many more families to participate in the housing programme.

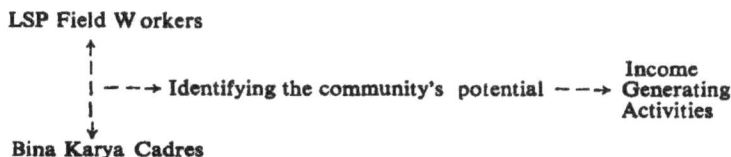

LSP Field Workers
↑
│ ─ ─→ Identifying the community's potential ─ ─→ Income Generating Activities
↓
Bina Karya Cadres

Figure 12.6: Par methodology on Bina Karya Movement.

Social preparation, beyond the problem identification stage, consisted of two parts: *firstly*, a process of education, information, and interactive decision making; *secondly*, skills training. The former was conducted informally, often in people's homes and was designed to make members more aware of their problems and of ways of solving them. Members were encouraged to identify their problems (information process) and to work towards solutions with LSP field workers and other members of the cooperative (interactive decision making). The education component was carried out simultaneously, often with assistance from religious leaders in the community, who encouraged members to exert more effort on their own behalf rather than waiting passively for help from external sources.

Other types of social preparation have been designed to reinforce solidarity between members; these include holding regular meetings for the membership, and organizing self-help building activities which bring members together.

CONCLUSIONS

It is noteworthy that cooperatives serve four major groups in Indonesia: there are cooperatives for government employees, institutional cooperatives for employees of large institutions (hospitals, universities, etc.), village unit cooperatives for rural residents, and finally, cooperatives for all other groups in Indonesian society. Bina Karya Housing Cooperative is an example of the last type, its membership being drawn primarily from labourers in private industry.

Housing cooperatives for government and institutional employees would normally seek financial assistance from the National Savings Bank, or a similar government institution. Bina Karya, however, has received no government support as a result of former government policies which effectively excluded poor people like its members from qualifying for government financial support.

Its private status and independence have enabled Bina Karya Housing Cooperative to develop a singular philosophy and approach. The cooperative's coordinator and members work very closely together to find long-term solutions to the social, vocational, and housing problems of the group, using a participatory process to achieve these goals. Members have participated fully in decisions with regard to goal setting, site selection, unit design, construction process, and savings campaigns.

Another noteworthy feature of Bina Karya is the element of self-help. The first houses were entirely built by member recipients, and site supervision, book-keeping, and administration were managed by the cooperative's coordinators.

The government of Indonesia is, of course, building low-income housing units but these are generally targeted at government employees who can afford to make a down payment, about Rp 300,000 in 1985, who already have savings accounts established in government savings institutions, and who earn more than Rp 40,000. Poor people in Indonesia earn much less than this a month and daily necessities consume a large proportion of this, making it almost impossible for a low income family to participate in a government housing scheme.

It is evident that cooperativism has many advantages. Bina Karya's membership has worked together to improve the standard of living of workers, through skills training; to improve living conditions of member families, by providing each with an individually owned residence in a good quality environment; and to raise morale among members, through social programmes and participation.

While self-help is not an essential ingredient for successful cooperative housing development, Bina Karya demonstrates that it has been a contributing factor to the strong solidarity which exists between members. Genuine participation is perhaps a more powerful factor in the cooperative's successful pursuit of its goals. Assisted by a local technical advisory group and with financing from a funding agency, the members of Bina Karya have achieved a high standard of accommodation and new job prospects through a cooperative approach which provides a very convincing example of how Indonesia might begin to solve the housing problems of its poor.

Final Note

The Bina Karya's labour community has shown that there is a possibility to stimulate the formation of groups which can promote socio-economic change in communities and enhance the expression of their rights without arousing government opposition. Surely, there is a need to promote socio-economic institutions operating at the grass-roots level which can meet and satisfy the needs of underprivileged groups and serve as a basis for the establishment of community-based institutions. These institutions would endeavour to respond to a community's socio-economic interests and to provide training for people in how to participate in a democratic institution, thereby strengthening the foundation for national development, they could take the form of cooperatives or pre-cooperatives for the urban poor, small and landless farmers, factory workers, women working in the informal sector, fishermen, and others.

CHAPTER 13

Sugar Production and Rural Development: A Case Study of Fiji

A slump in sugar prices is likely to be a continuing feature of the world sugar trade in the next two or three years. . . . In attempting to control costs, we should also keep up our enthusiasm and sustain sugar cane production to compensate for the low prices. . . . There is bound to be a favourable turn of events in the future and we must continue to maintain and preferably increase production to reap the benefits when prices do improve.[1]

While the contribution by Fiji to the annual world production is negligible (0.36 per cent), it remains significant in terms of the Dominion's economy (see Figure 13.1).

The two charts given in Figure 13.1 further accentuate the significance of sugar as an export crop and a large contributor to the country's Gross Domestic Product. The Fiji economy is heavily dependent on sugar—its quality, quantity, and hence prices.

FIJI

Fiji is an Archipelago of over 300 Islands of varying sizes in the South Pacific. Of these, only about 100 are permanently inhabited, and over 90 per cent of the land area of the country is occupied by the two largest islands—Viti Levu (4,113 sq miles) and Vanua

DOMESTIC EXPORTS 1979 - $1638 m.

(Excludes Re-Exports)

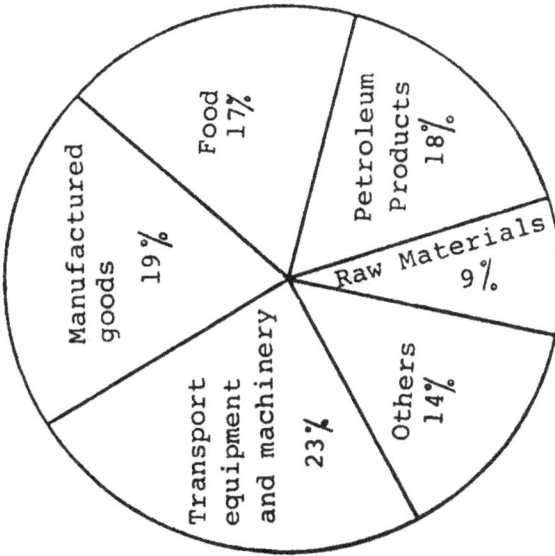

Sugar
70%

Food
15%

4% 4% 7%

Coconut

Gold

Others

IMPORTS 1979...$393 m.

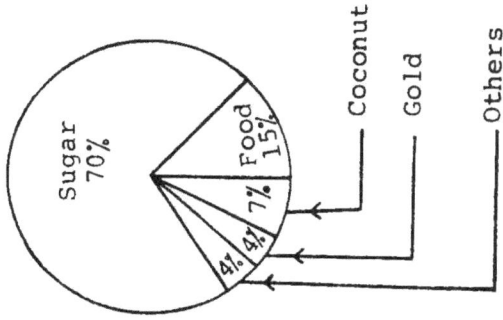

Manufactured
goods
19%

Food
17%

Transport
equipment
and machinery
23%

Petroleum
Products
18%

Raw Materials
9%

Others
14%

Source: Fijis Dev. plan 8(1981-1985), Vol.1.Central Planning Office

Fig. 13.1

Levu 2,993 sq miles). The capital city of the country, Suva, is on the east coast of Viti Levu and hosts about 11 per cent of Fiji's total population. Vanua Levu hosts about 18 per cent of the population and its main town is Labosa. The islands have a tropical climate with an average annual rainfall on the windward side of about 120 inches and a temperature ranging from 20°C to about 30°C.

Fiji became a Dominion in the British Commonwealth on 10 October 1970, having been a British Colony since 1874.

Population and Employment

The population of Fiji (according to the census of 1976) was 588,068. Because of the high growth rates in recent years the population is predominantly youthful, with over 41 per cent under 15 years of age.

The growth rate of the population, which rose from 1.6 to 3.3 per cent in the inter-censal period from 1936 to 1966, was estimated to have fallen to 2.1 per cent in 1976, due mainly to a Family Planning Programme.

The total labour force in 1976 was 163,544, which represented an average annual growth rate of 3.5 per cent from 1966.

Approximately 63 per cent of the population live in rural areas.

Table 13.1: Employment of Labour by Sectors

	No.	%	No.	%
Agriculture, Forestry & Fishing	68,122	56.5	71,597	43.8
Mining & Quarrying	1,903	1.6	1,548	1.0
Manufacturing	8,845	7.3	12,142	7.4
Construction	7,302	6.1	10,416	6.4
Electricity, Gas & Water	896	0.7	1,516	0.9
Commerce	10,031	8.3	16,177	9.9
Transport, Storage & Communication	6,460	5.4	8,407	5.2
Business Services	960	0.8	3,274	2.0
Social & Personal Services	16,055	13.3	38,457	23.4
Total	120,574	100.0	1,63,534	100.0

Source: Nationwide Unemployment Survey 1973, Bureau of Statistics.

In Fiji, one would expect the level of recorded unemployment to be higher in the urban (formal) sector than in the rural (informal) sector. The subsistence sector has a far greater capacity to absorb surplus labour than the formal sector. However, it must not be concluded that unemployment is only a problem in urban areas. There may be a relatively high level of hidden unemployment and under-employment in rural areas. It is relatively difficult to establish accurate data on unemployment in the latter case. Table 13.2 presents data on recorded unemployment in urban areas.

Table 13.2: Urban Unemployment (1976)

	Male	Female	Total	Unemployment rate	% of national unemployment	% of national population
Total Urban	5,489	2,370	7,859	11.0%	66.4%	37.1%

Source: Fiji's Eighth Dev. Plan (1981-85), Vol. 1. CP. O. Suva.

Agricultural Sector

Sugar is the only industry that utilises land intensively and absorbs a large production of the total work force (about 45 per cent of the total labour force). Within the agricultural sector, sugar cane accounts for nearly half of the output while subsistence production accounts for 37 per cent.

About 21,000 growers (average family size 4 to 5) grow sugar cane on average farm size of 4.05 hectares. On such a small-scale farming operation, a large number of factors influence sugar production. These include physical factors such as soils, climate, topography, agronomic practices, land tenure,[1] the last but not the least—the price of cane.

[1] In Fiji 84 per cent of the land is owned by native owners i.e., the indigenous inhabitants. Land is initially leased for a period of 30 years, after which the lessee is entitled to 10 years extension, depending on satisfactory fulfilment of lease conditions. Native Land Trust Board (N.L.T.B) administers the leasing arrangement and distributes rents from lessees to the respective owners and their beneficiaries.

Agriculture is expected to provide the major thrust in the over-all development of Fiji in the next planned phase. Government's agricultural efforts are to concentrate on a number of commodities with significant potential for export development, notably cocoa, ginger, coconut, citrus and other tropical fruits, such as passion-fruit, mangoes, and pineapple.

Government is also trying to consolidate development in capital intensive schemes and facilitate drainage, irrigation and land-scaping works to bring self-sufficiency in rice production to the rural areas.

Rice is a staple food for more than half of Fiji's population.

Other domestic food crops, such as *cassava, dalo kumala,* yams, chilis, tumeric, peanuts, tea and vegetables are produced by both the cane growers and 'organised growers' (those who grow only these crops for cash). A large portion of the cane grower's domestic food crop would be for his own use. This, he plants on portions of land left fallow in crop rotation.

Sugar Cane Plantation (Phases)

Sugar cane started on the basis of a 'plantation system'. The system, however, required large amounts of labour. Towards the 1900s, the Colonial Government recruited labourers from India.

At the time the indenture system ended, the Colonial Sugar Refining Company (C.S.R.) had almost full control of the sugar industry, and thus the majority of indentured labourers came under its control. With the end of the system, the C.S.R. Company was faced with the problem of lack of labour, and so had to change its land policy. The Company divided its land into farms of about 4.0 hectares to be rented out to tenant farmers. Thus the basis of the present-day system was laid, whereby a farmer rents his land and sells his cane to the mills.

In 1962, the South Pacific Sugar Mills Company was founded by the C.S.R. Company to look after its sugar interests in Fiji. It continued the C.S.R. policy of helping the smaller growers by providing services such as pest control, developing new breeds of cane, and general advice to the independent farmer (grower). This, along with assistance in harvesting and cartage costs, has kept the small farmer in business.

Following a dispute between the C.S.R. and growers in 1969 an inquiry headed by Lord Denning recommended changes which the C.S.R. Company said made it impossible to continue to mill sugar commercially in Fiji. The recommendations stated that after the growers and the millers had paid their own costs, the profits were to be divided on the basis of 65 per cent for the growers, 35 per cent for the millers with a guaranteed $75 per tonne for the growers' cane, consequently, the C.S.R. Company decided to end its operations in Fiji at the end of the 1972 season.

As a result of this decision, the Fiji Government decided to buy the sugar company. This, then, gave birth to the present Fiji Sugar Corporation Ltd,[2] one of the statutory bodies of the Government.

The Sugar Industry and Its Targets

The Fiji sugar industry has set a target of 600,000 tonnes of sugar in the planned period 1982-85. This, it hopes to achieve through the adoption of improved varieties, i.e., introduction of high-yielding varieties, improving farm management practices, hence farm budgeting, using better rates of farm inputs and by encouraging more intensive care to areas that require it.

The major negative factor, of course, is the poor price for sugar sold in the open market. Only around 40 per cent of the country's sugar exports are bought by the EEC at a guaranteed price under the LOME Agreement.

Despite this, the trend has shown a continuing increase in sugar production. One may pause to wonder—why? The simple answer is—Why not? (after all, 70 per cent of the country's exports rely on sugar, and hence its importance for nation building. Table 13.3 shows the continuing trend in increase of sugar production.

Table 13.3: Sugar Cane Production Statistics

	Unit	1976	1977	1978	1979	1980	1981	1982
Sugar cane	'000 tonnes	2,283	2,674	2,849	4,058	3,360	3,931	4,075
Sugar	'000 tonnes	296	362	347	473	396	470	487
Exports (f.o.b)	F Mn	67.70	93.58	83.27	116.96	174.18	131.56	139.08*

* estimated

By 1985/1986 the industry hopes to achieve an average yield of 66 tonnes/hectare from the same 76,000 hectares of cane land to obtain a crop of 5,000,000 tonnes. This will be equivalent to about 600,000 tonnes of sugar annually.

The Corporation has prepared a plan—commonly known as the '3-year plan of activities'—which amongst other strategies and objectives emphasises the need to:

1. Develop new areas already contracted (those included in the 3-year phase) in stages that will allow 80 per cent of the total sugar cane contract area to be under cane by 1985/1986.
2. Improve the utilisation of land on existing cane farms by placing under crop 80 per cent of the total contract area, through identifying the constraints and promulgating corrective action (more on this later).
3. Increase yield per hectare on existing cane farms by improving the farm, i.e., crop planning, farm budgets, agronomic practices, and utilising optimum levels of fertilisers and other inputs.

However, a number of constraints may inhibit the achievement of these planned targets, namely: land topography, climate. Economic/political, policies/developments, and inflation. The gravity of the problem, insofar as land topography is concerned, is evident from the data given in Table 13.4, which also reflects the trend in sugar-producing areas.

Table 13.4: Per cent of Sugar Production Areas in Fiji under Various Topographical Classes

	up to 1950s	1950s	1960s
Flat	40.2	7.5	1.6
Rolling	23.1	17.6	7.6
Steep	5.4	33.5	17.8
Very Steep	—	23.9	31.4
Mixed	31.3	17.5	41.6

Source: [1]Modified table—D.C. Prasad, *Reviews*, Vol. 3, July 1982.
[1]These figures have been modified by P.C. Prasad on information through an agronomist—F.S.C. Ltd, 1978. The plausibility of data is questionable as it has been extrapolated by the author.

Inflation

Due to increases in the price of imports, mainly petrol, transport equipment and machinery (and implements), the rate of inflation has been rising since 1974. In 1978 the inflation rate was 6.1 per cent. The rates are higher for 1980 and 1981, at 13.5 per cent and 14.5 per cent respectively.

Table 13.5: Cost Increases (1974-1981)

Growers' costs	% Increase 1974-1981
Fertiliser: Sulphate of ammonia	25
muriate of potash	47
Harvesting costs per tonne (Cane)	160
Farm implements	176
Other costs (Miller's)	
Fuel	236
Lubricants	125
Materials & spare gear	292
Wages	179
Average sugar price in 1974—243/tonne	
Average sugar price in 1981—282/tonne	
Per cent increase in prices—16%	

Source: Fiji Sugar Journal, Vol. 7, Dec. 1982, Suva—Fiji.

Income Distribution

The price of cane is the main factor that determines the level of affluence in the rural sector. At the current price of 25 per tonne of cane, a grower with an average 4.0 hectare farm can only draw an income of approximately 4,000. The net disposable income will vary, but range from 3,000 to 3,500. Of course, growers with smaller holdings than the average will receive concomitantly lower incomes. This category of growers will work on others' farms as labourers and/or seek employment in sugar factories and elsewhere (if available).

Most of the incomes derived by growers are spent on consumer goods. Those who can save (especially the larger farm-holders) will invest their savings in farm improvements. The level of savings is greater for those who also grow subsistence crops, e.g., rice, *cassava*, *dalo*, yams and vegetables.

Incentives to Cane Farmers by Government

The incentives provided by the Government to encourage farmers to maintain their levels of income, create self-sufficiency,
and also to maintain and/or increase their levels of production
include the following:

   a. Cheap loans to farmers by the Fiji Development Bank for
      farm improvements, purchase of implements, tractors, and so
      forth. (An analysis of FDB loans is given in Appendix G.)
   b. A 25 per cent tax rebate on normal income, as a measure to
      cushion the shock of a drop in sugar price.
   c. Reduction of export duty on sugar cane and molasses from
      4 to 2 per cent.
   d. Raising the minimum income liable to tax from F 1,000 to
      F1200 per annum.

Other agencies such as banks, shopkeepers, moneylenders, the
Agricultural Loan and Credit Society, and Housing Authority
also give loans to growers.

Spread Effect of Income Generated by Sugar

The spread effects of sugar cane income benefit many people. To
start with, the grower's entire livelihood is, by and large, dependent
on this income. Shopkeepers, banks, market vendors, transport
operators also benefit, and substantial Government revenue is
accumulated via direct and indirect taxes.

While some of the Government revenue is re-directed to the rural
sector, simultaneously, since sugar is a 70 per cent export earner,
some portion of the Government earned revenue also goes for
investment in the urban sector. Roads or highways, bridges,
government buildings and wharves are also Government investments largely financed by sugar earnings.

A comparison of the urban and rural average household weekly
real income is given in Table 13.6.

The data in Table 15.6 are most useful in defining and relating
orders of magnitude of income and expenditure.

Table 13.6: Average Household Weekly Real Income

		Income 1977	Index
Urban:	Suva	87.5	1.00
	Nadi, Lautoka	88.8	1.02
	Labasa	91.7	1.05
	Others	81.2	0.93
Rural:	Central Division		
	Western Division*	100.4	1.15
	Northern Division*	87.9	1.00

*Sugar producing divisions.

CONCLUSION

Because of the small size of the domestic market, Fiji's relative geographic isolation, and the structure of international freight tariffs, the potential for industrialisation is limited. Processing of locally produced primary inputs for either domestic consumption or export is now an area that is actively pursued.

Agriculture is expected to provide the major thrust in the overall development of Fiji.

Sugar, therefore, must remain a large export earner for meeting imports and improving the ratio of rural/urban income.

The absence of a sugar income would create a gross disparity between the formal (urban) and informal sector. Sugar is the backbone of the country and will probably remain the main source of 'bread and butter' for many more decades to come.

Tourism, which is doing unexpectedly well, will help to offset deficits in Government spending.

Under a very precarious marketing condition and with constant fluctuations in the price of sugar, diversification within the sugar industry ought to be actively pursued.

The Fiji sugar industry has already made a start in this direction and has a South Pacific Distillery producing several commodities, such as gin, vodka, rum, and industrial spirits. Cane-rind board will shortly be manufactured locally. Feasibility studies on ethanol do not look very prospective at the moment.

A shift from monoculture-crop practices is gradually taking effect, wherein cane growers are encouraged to plant root crops, vegetables, cereals and tropical fruits. It is hoped that this will augment the incomes of both the urban and the rural people.

NOTES

1. Rasheed A. Ali (Managing Director, Fiji Sugar Corporation Ltd.), 1982, 'Survival in recessionary times,' *Fiji Sugar Journal.*
2. Fiji Sugar Corporation Ltd. is owned by the Government with 90% (approx.) shareholding. The corporation is headed by the Managing Director, who is assisted by a highly qualified and experienced team (Executive Management Group). The corporation has an eminently qualified Board of Directors, representing business, farming, planning and administrative aspects.

APPENDIX A

Agricultural Extension

Field Extension—An Alternative Approach
(Fiji Sugar Industry)

Because of its utmost importance to the economy of Fiji, sugar must remain (at least for the next two decades) the main contributor to the nation's economy. To achieve the targets set by the industry, a considered decision has been made: (a) to increase farm efficiency, (b) to cut down costs, and (c) to increase productivity, personnel and farms.

The extension approach explained below is designed to revamp efforts in field extension.

Undoubtedly, this will give rise to useful discussions on both its shortcomings and methodology.

First, a model of the integrated approach to agricultural extension is given as follows:

IDENTIFYING AREAS THAT NEED ADVICE

1. Those that need general farm advice.
2. Those that need intensive care.
3. Those considered 'No lapses.'*

See Figure on page 249.

Activities required by extension works and farmers are:

Extension Works	Growers (Farmers)
Target setting	Cultivation practices
Demonstration, i.e. field days, extension meetings, etc.	Planting, land preparation and replanting
Farm management courses	Soil conservation/trash conservation
Follow-up on operations, rainfall control	Varietal control

*'No lapses'—those whose problems and constraints are beyond the grower's and the extension worker's control.

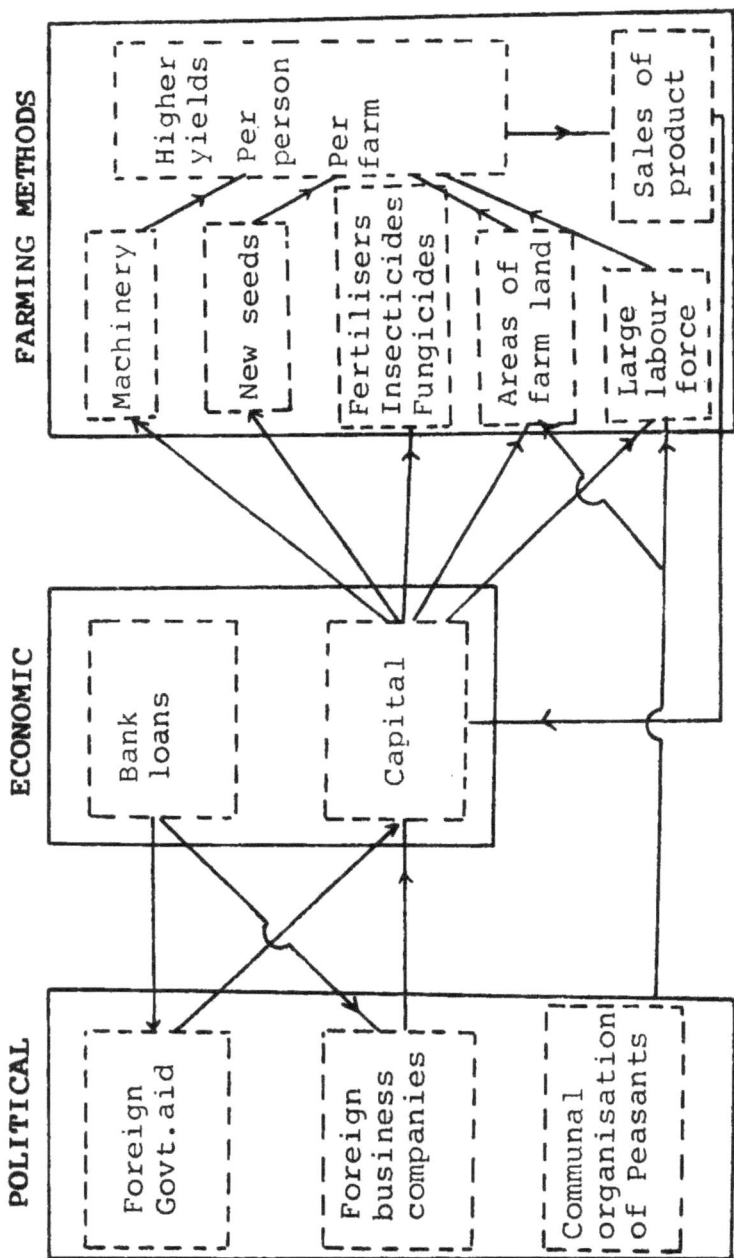

TEACHING METHODS

Group contacts
Mass media
Result demonstration
Extension meetings

Individual contacts
(T.V.) on the spot
advice

General
farm advice

Intensive scheme
care

No lapses

Growers whose TPCHA
≤ 37.5

Growers whose TPCHA
below 37.5

LOW TPCHA

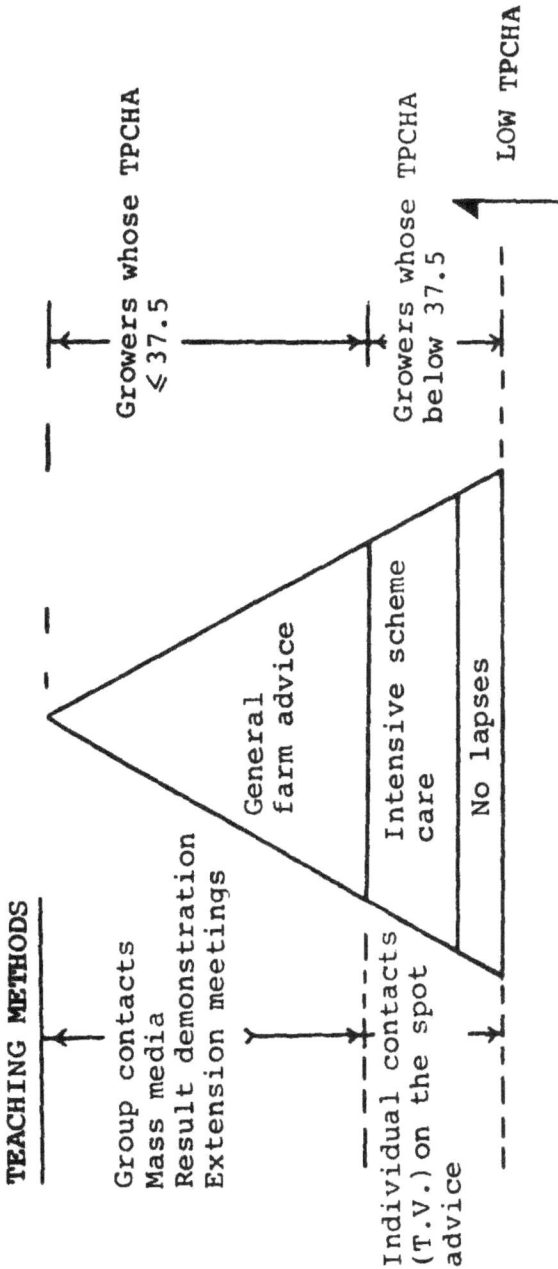

Note: TPCHA—tonnes per contract hectare—is derived by dividing the total tonnes produced annually
by the contract hectare.

Crop planning and laying down farm production plans	Application of inputs (recommended levels)
Farm budgets	Farm budgets (on expenses)
Establishment of accurate areas under cane, i.e., disposition of cane land	Drainage improvements Disease and pest control
Reporting evaluation	Evaluation (cost/benefit analysis)

General Farm Advice

Growers falling in this category receive attention in groups. Firstly, problems are identified under different headings, viz., cultivation methods, soil conservation, varietal control, drainage, crop planning, and so on.

The extension worker groups growers (in localities) and gives advice and assistance on problems common to all.

1. Organising extension meetings/field days and demonstration.
2. On the spot discussions with organised gangs/groups, i.e., harvesting gangs, drainage gangs, etc.
3. Group meetings of sirdars* to impart knowledge, deliver commodities, etc.
4. Using Farm Advisor Information Services to narrate success stories, radio interviews and discussions.

Intensive Farm Advice

This category of growers receives intensive care, viz., individual contracts. Generally these growers will be the ones with constraints beyond their means. They would require an extension officer's assistance.

---

*Sirdars are elected representatives of a gang of growers (a gang normally comprises 15-50 growers from one locality—a well-defined geographical area). The Sirdar, who is a paid member of the gang, supervises the daily harvest transport and administration of the gang. About 100 gangs make a sector (500-600 growers), 3-7 sectors make a district, and 2-3 districts serve a mill. There are 4 sugar mills in Fiji—3 on Viti Levu and 1 on Vanua Levu.

APPENDIX B: POPULATION

POPULATION OF TOWNS AND URBAN AREAS BY ETHNIC ORIGIN, SEX AND NUMBER OF HOUSEHOLDS AS OF 13TH SEPTEMBER 1979

		Suva City	Suva Peri-urban	Lautoka City	Lautoka Peri-urban	BA Town	BA Peri-urban	Labasa Town	Labasa Peri-urban	Levuka Town	Levuka Peri-urban	Nadi Town	Nadi Peri-urban	Savusavu Town	Savusavu Peri-urban	Sigatoka Town	Sigatoka Peri-urban	Nausori Town	Nausori Peri-urban	Unincorporated Townships Koro vou	Navua	Raki Raki	Tavua	Vanu koula	Total Urban Population
Part-Chinese	M	1,074	380	216	6	86	6	47	38	12	11	68	28	53	24	47	13	16	4	7	10	17	10	17	2,113
	F	1,009	280	186	2	88	2	35	12	39	2	65	19	30	21	35	8	7	1			10	15	10	1,868
	T	2,083	610	402	8	174	8	82	24	77	13	133	47	83	45	82	21	23	5			27	15	27	3,981
Europeans	M	1,256	341	149	3	16		47		17	2	63	17	3		3	2	19	9	2	5	5	6	70	2,103
	F	1,160	362	146	2	19	1	35		57		81	51	7		17	3	16	2	2	4	3	3	61	1,974
	T	2,415	703	295	5	35	2	82		76	127	120	132	10	2	36	3	25	9	3	9	11	3	131	4,077
Fijians	M	11,281	12,591	2,866	1,146	654	138	520	418	292	462	842	228	212	218	195	836	760	664	50	387	431	453	2,200	39,215
	F	11,750	12,681	2,975	1,064	706	138	574	403	333	460	964	295	218	199	295	784	856	607	78	310	415	468	2,137	40,090
	T	23,031	25,272	5,841	2,210	1,360	276	1,094	821	645	922	1,806	523	430	212	394	1,620	1,616	1,271	128	597	846	921	4,337	79,314
Indians	M	14,965	11,723	7,304	1,944	1,360	276	1,919	3,846	91	112	2,314	1,241	524	29	653	83	1,662	3,057	67	1,024	1,168	584	477	57,824
	F	14,793	11,715	7,466	1,883	1,481	276	1,309	3,871	89	155	2,332	1,180	657	32	657	92	1,592	3,113	60	920	1,400	580	470	57,808
	T	29,758	23,438	14,770	3,827	1,919	1,482	3,846	7,717	180	314	4,646	2,421	1,310	61	1,310	175	3,254	6,170	127	1,944	2,768	1,164	947	115,632
Part-European	M	1,276	855	464	49	168	1	168	80	14	5	82	21	46	14	23	6	67	17	1	7	51	5	222	3,683
	F	1,402	748	430	40	146		146	75	67	2	10	12	18	13	9	5	18	35	1	7	41	2	203	3,574
	T	2,678	1,603	894	89	301	6	314	155	60	127	43	4	86	27	47	11	137	35	14	14	92	7	425	7,257
Rotumans	M	953	404	165		11	1	31	314	155	112	99	66	86	11	6		23	14	2		11	7	271	2,005
	F	976	401	168		6		25	32	38	2	39	9	6		3		26	8			11		268	2,019
	T	1,929	805	333		17		56	38	2	43	82	12	86	20	9		49	22		2	51	11	539	4,024
Other Pacific Islanders	M	584	845	57	14	1	1	12	5	14	67	5	10	2	1	2	2	8	5	1	7	2	2	8	1,656
	F	625	818	48	18		6	18	3	60	15	10	4	18	2	6	6	12	8		6	6		8	1,670
	T	1,209	1,663	105	32	2		23	7	29	127	21	4	33	3	1	8	22	13	1	13		1	18	3,326
All Others	M	297	48	15	1	2	1	7	3	3	3	18	6			1	8	32	13	1	2	11	11	268	509
	F	227	57	17	1	2	1	2	18	76	18	6	6					34			6	18	2	1	375
	T	524	105	32	2	3	2	3	21	18	6	6	6					66	2		4	18		1	884
Total	M	31,686	27,137	11,236	3,164	2,839	1,628	2,141	4,315	702	701	3,400	3,093	892	267	905	929	2,622	3,779	139	1,324	1,871	1,072	3,266	109,108
	F	31,942	27,062	11,436	3,011	3,078	1,628	2,187	4,313	695	666	3,538	2,964	862	274	911	890	2,640	3,780	151	1,244	1,884	1,072	3,159	109,387
	T	63,628	54,199	22,672	6,175	5,917	3,256	4,328	8,628	1,397	1,367	6,938	6,057	1,754	541	1,816	1,819	5,262	7,559	290	2,568	3,755	2,144	6,425	218,495
Number of Private Households		11,561	8,897	4,138	1,039	1,081	559	818	1,521	244	242	1,356	1,061	314	94	346	316	725	1,143	57	431	664	369	1,098	38,074
Number of Collective Households		84	23	8	2	3		11		9	1	1	1	1	1	2	1	16	1	2				1	167

Source: Report on the Census of the Population 1976.

FLOW CHART - INTENSIVE FARM ADVICE

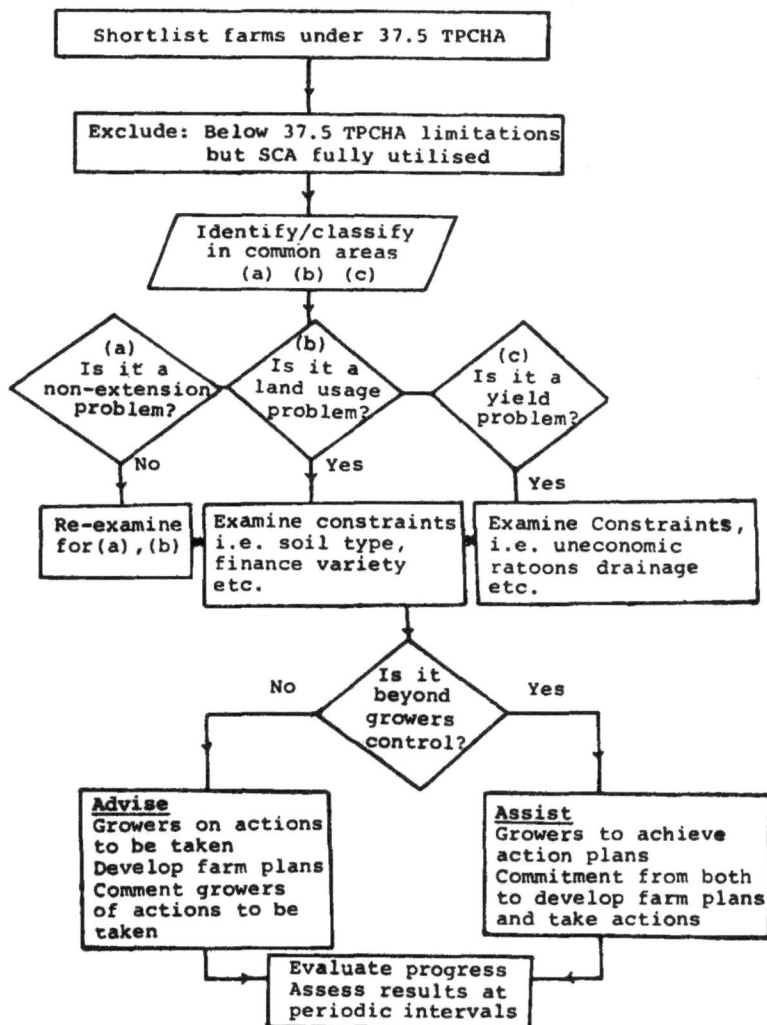

```
┌─────────────────────────────────────────┐
│  Shortlist farms under 37.5 TPCHA        │
└─────────────────────────────────────────┘
                    │
                    ▼
┌─────────────────────────────────────────┐
│  Exclude: Below 37.5 TPCHA limitations   │
│  but SCA fully utilised                  │
└─────────────────────────────────────────┘
                    │
                    ▼
         ╱───────────────────╲
        ╱  Identify/classify   ╲
        ╲  in common areas      ╱
         ╲  (a) (b) (c)        ╱
          ╲───────────────────╱
```

```
   ◇ (a)            ◇ (b)            ◇ (c)
   Is it a          Is it a          Is it a
 non-extension     land usage        yield
   problem?         problem?         problem?

      │ No             │ Yes            │ Yes
      ▼                ▼                ▼
```

| Re-examine for(a),(b) | Examine constraints i.e. soil type, finance variety etc. | Examine Constraints, i.e. uneconomic ratoons drainage etc. |

```
              ◇ Is it
                beyond
     No         growers        Yes
               control?
      ┌──────────┘ └──────────┐
      ▼                        ▼
```

Advise
Growers on actions to be taken
Develop farm plans
Comment growers of actions to be taken

Assist
Growers to achieve action plans
Commitment from both to develop farm plans and take actions

Evaluate progress
Assess results at periodic intervals

SCA—Sugar cane area.

APPENDIX C: Employment and Wages (A)

PAID EMPLOYMENT, ESTIMATED NUMBERS OF WAGE AND SALARY EARNERS BY INDUSTRY AS AT END OF JUNE

	1971	1972	1973	1974	1975	1976	1977	1978	1979	1980
1	2	3	4	5	6	7	8	9	10	11
Agriculture, Forestry and Fishing										
Wages	2,936	2,362	2,528	2,226	2,198	2,110	2,139	2,369	1,958	2,298
Salaries	956	418	915	664	647	489	302	418	345	329
Total	3,892	2,780	3,443	2,890*	2,845*	2,599*	2,441*	2,787*	2,303*	2,627*
Mining and Quarrying										
Wages	1,695	1,547	1,569	1,783	1,642	1,349	1,566	597	500	788
Salaries	158	198	179	180	255	201	275	212	224	267
Total	1,853	1,745	1,748	1,963	1,897	1,550	1,841	809	724	1,055
Manufacturing										
Wages	8,681	8,413	8,598	10,118	11,364	10,162	9,800	11,833	12,274	13,469
Salaries	1,439	1,415	1,518	1,722	1,820	1,282	1,453	1,651	1,674	1,944
Total	10,120	9,828	10,116	11,840	13,184	11,444	11,253	13,484	13,948	15,413
Electricity, Gas and Water										
Wages	1,087	1,251	1,525	1,467	1,348	1,501	1,563	1,596	2,009	1,812
Salaries	144	190	202	192	184	264	316	238	327	473
Total	1,231	1,441	1,727	1,659	1,532	1,765	1,879	1,834	2,336	2,285

Construction										
Wages	7,834	7,961	9,111	7,979	8,044	7,171	7,575	8,245	9,313	8,531
Salaries	454	278	343	312	405	501	554	650	490	504
Total	8,288	8,239	9,454	8,291	8,449	7,672	8,129	8,895	9,803	9,035
Wholesale and Retail Trades and Restaurants and Hotels										
Wages	6,852	7,300	7,005	7,236	7,707	8,564	8,780	9,315	9,693	10,059
Salaries	2,638	2,588	2,663	2,778	2,612	3,137	3,337	3,463	3,406	3,319
Total	9,490	9,888	9,668	10,014	10,319	11,701	12,117	12,778	13,099	13,378
Transport, Storage and Communication										
Wages	2,697	2,979	2,928	3,815	4,059	4,081	3,974	4,090	3,812	4,553
Salaries	2,033	2,246	1,981	2,365	2,364	2,693	3,222	3,212	4,299	3,569
Total	4,730	5,225	4,909	6,180	6,423	6,774	7,196	7,303	8,111	8,122
Finance, Insurance, Real Estate and Business Services										
Wages	477	620	1,092	1,233	1,206	1,223	1,353	1,191	1,315	1,308
Salaries	1,250	1,406	1,509	2,108	2,286	2,474	2,816	2,995	3,067	3,128
Total	1,727	2,026	2,601	3,341	3,492	3,697	4,169	4,186	4,382	4,436

(Contd.)

Appendix C (*Contd.*)

	1	2	3	4	5	6	7	8	9	10	11
Community, Social and Personal											
Wages		5,423	5,641	5,556	6,777	7,294	7,153	6,780	7,052	6,673	6,574
Salaries		10,234	11,586	12,254	14,043	14,541	15,819	16,578	17,456	17,160	17,559
Total		15,657	17,227	17,810	20,820	21,835	22,972	23,358	24,508	23,833	24,133
Total											
Wages		37,682	38,074	39,912	42,634	44,862	43,314	43,530	45,935	47,547	49,392
Salaries		19,306	20,325	21,564	24,364	25,114	26,860	28,853	30,649	30,992	31,092
Total		56,988	58,399	61,476	66,998	69,976	70,174	72,383	76,584	78,539	86,484

*Reduction in number employed due to change in classification to ISIC 3: Manufacturing and ISIC 9: Community, Social and Personal from 1974 and onwards.

APPENDIX D: EMPLOYMENT AND WAGES

NUMBERS IN WAGE EMPLOYMENT, WAGE RATES AND F.N.P.F. CONTRIBUTORS

Year at end of June	Number of wage earn- ers employ- ed	Changes in wage em- ployment base year 1970=100	Mean hourly wage rates (cents)	Changes in wage rates base year 1970=100	FIJI NATIONAL PROVI- DENT FUND		Total number of salaried personal employed
					Number of contributors to F.N.P.F. in May of each year	Total Contri- butions receiv- ed during year ending 30th June $ 000	
1	2	3	4	5	6	7	8
1970	33,867	100	30.91	100	48,125	3,717	17,723
1971	37,682	111	34.05	110	53,897	4,308	19,306
1972	38,074	112	38.55	125	57,390	5,414	20,325
1973	39,912	118	49.69	161	62,701	7,325	21,564
1974	42,634	126	61.22	198	66,647	9,121	24,364
1975	44,862	132	74.62	241	63,792	12,444	25,114
1976	43,314	128	83.48	270	64,254	16,719	26,860
1977	43,530	128	88.90	288	65,575	19,592	28,853

(*Contd.*)

Appendix D (*Contd.*)

1	2	3	4	5	6	7	8
1978	45,935	136	98.65	319	66,141	22,272	30,649
1979	47,547	140	106.00	343	70,945	26,610	30,992
1980	49,392	146	116.00	375	72,856	33,208	31,092

Source: Annual employment censuses of the Bureau of Statistics and Annual Reports of the Fiji National Provident Fund.

Notes: Wage earner figures relate solely to manual workers in regular wage-earning employment in June each year. Self-employed persons such as farmers and fishermen or seasonal workers such as cane cutters, are not included in these figures. Domestic servants are also excluded.

Totals are based on 100% coverage of establishments and cover both private and public sectors regardless of their size.

APPENDIX E: NATIONAL INCOME

GROSS DOMESTIC PRODUCT OF FIJI 1950-1981

	Current Prices						Constant Prices		
Year	Gross domestic product at current factor cost ($ million)	Annual growth rate of GDP (%)	Estimated mid-year population (000)	GDP per head of population ($)	Annual growth rate of GDP per head (%)	Gross domestic product at constant factor cost ($ million)	Annual growth rate of GDP (%)	GDP per head of population ($)	Annual growth rate of GDP per head (%)
1	2	3	4	5	6	7	8	9	10
1950	36.0	—	288	125	—				
1953	50.8	12.2	318	160	8.6				
1957	61.1	4.7	354	173	2.0				
1962	90.2	8.1	421	214	4.3				
1963	93.9	4.1	435	216	0.1				
1964	99.6	6.1	449	222	2.8				
1965	104.7	5.1	462	227	2.3				
1966	108.8	3.9	474	230	1.3				
1967	117.3	7.8	485	342	5.2				

(Contd.)

Appendix E (*Contd.*)

1	2	3	4	5	6	7	8	9	10
						Constant Prices (1968 Prices)			
1968	129.6	10.5	495	262	8.3				
1969	140.5	8.4	506	282	7.6				
1970	168.9	20.2	521	324	14.9	148.7	—	285.4	—
1971	184.7	9.3	533	347	7.1	157.6	6.0	295.7	3.6
1972	230.5	24.8	544	424	22.2	170.0	7.9	312.5	5.7
1973	300.6	30.4	556	541	27.6	191.6	12.7	344.6	10.3
1974	410.5	36.6	565	727	34.3	191.6	2.6	348.0	1.0
1975	515.4	25.5	576	895	23.1	196.8	0.1	341.7	−1.8
1976	570.6	10.7	585	975	8.9	202.1	2.7	345.5	1.1
						Constant Prices (1977 Prices)			
1977**	605.7	—	596	1,016	—	605.7r	—	1,016r	—
1978**	642.9	6.1	607	1,059	4.2	616.6r	1.8	1,016r	1.8
1979	779.4	21.2	621r	1,255r	18.5r	690.9r	12.0r	1,113r	9.6r
1980p	917.1r	17.7r	634r	1,447r	15.3r	668.5r	−3.2	1,054r	−5.3r
1981p	1084.5r	18.2r	647r	1,676r	16.0r	710.9r	+6.3r	1,099r	+4.3r

**The Bureau of Statistics has recently completed and revised new series of GDP estimates based on benchmark data of 1977. It has not been possible, however, to revise earlier estimates at this point in time. Consequently, annual growth rate of GDP and annual growth rate of GDP per head have not been given for 1977.

p Provisional
r Revised

APPENDIX F

SUGAR INDUSTRY PRODUCTION AND PRICES

Year Season	Number of contracts	Area harvested (kilo hectares)	Production (tonnes '000)	Average production per hectare (tonnes/hectares)	Prices paid to growers ($/tonne)	Input of cane per tonne of sugar (tonnes)	Sugar production (tonnes '000)	Molasses production (tonnes '000)	Exports of Sugar[a]		
									Quantity (tonnes '000)	Value (f.o.b.) ($'000)	Unit value ($/tonne)
1	2	3	4	5	6	7	8	9	10	11	12
1966	15,579	43	2,227	51.8	6.39	7.2	309		242	21,096	87
1967	15,609	45	2,197	49.9	6.23	7.4	297		323	23,780	74
1968	15,596	46	2,871	62.4	6.40	7.2	399	95	346	24,856	72
1969	15,596	47	2,376	51.6	6.62	7.8	305	108	322	28,134	87
1970	15,542	46	2,886	62.7	7.62	8.0	361	107	334	31,820	95
1971	15,548	47	2,545	54.1	7.95	7.9	323	85	340	32,851	97
1972	15,612	44	2,238	52.0	9.90	7.4	303	77	279	34,423	123
1973	16,533	46	2,496	55.4	9.76	8.3	301	95	271	34,280	126
1974	16,546	45	2,151	48.8	20.57	7.9	272	71	258	66,952	260
1975	17,264	45	2,160	49.0	31.60	7.9	273	76	250	94,717	379
1976	17,667	47	2,283	48.6	24.18	7.7	296	81	250	67,704	271
1977	18,395	52	2,674	50.1	26.74	7.4	362	105	324	93,576	289

(Contd.)

Appendix F (Contd.)

1	2	3	4	5	6	7	8	9	10	11	12
1978	18,456	54	2,849	52.8	24.99	8.2	347	106	294	83,273	283
1979	19,152	62	4,058	65.5	23.50	8.6	473	163	428	116,962	273
1980	19,700	67	3,360	50.2	35.19	8.5	396	129	441	174,175	395
1981	21,000	66	3,931	59.6	25.00^p	8.4	470	152	408	131,561	322

*The sugar export price closely approximates the actual realised average prices for production because local consumption accounts for a small percentage of total production. The price paid to the growers for the 1970 season and after is based on the formula laid down under the Denning Award.

bRelates to seasons.

pProvisional.

Remarks: The downward trend experienced in the tonnage of cane and sugar produced from the year 1972 has now been reversed. There was a remarkable increase in 1977's production due to a bout of exceptionally dry weather. Production in 1979 totalled 473,000 tonnes—a record despite a fall in the sugar content of cane.

Source: Fiji Sugar Corporation and Trade Reports.

APPENDIX G: MONEY AND BANKING

FIJI DEVELOPMENT BANK LOANS ($ '000)

At end of period	Approvals[a]					Outstanding[b]			
	Commercial to Fijian	Industrial (General)	Agricultural (General)	Seaqaqa loan scheme	Total	Commercial to Fijian	Industrial (General)	Agricultural (General)	Total
1	2	3	4	5	6	7	8	9	10
1971	—	954	214	—	1,168	—	1,840	1,035	2,875
1972	—	391	529	—	920	—	1,826	925	2,751
1973	—	1,132	934	—	2,066	—	1,911	1,230	3,141
1974	—	1,518	1,963	—	3,481	—	2,870	2,261	5,131
1975	NA	1,551	2,907	NA	4,458	NA	3,369	3,571	6,940
1976	1,409	2,285	3,251	4,899	11,844	NA	7,407	5,045	12,452
1977	1,836	4,171	4,717	2,591	13,315	2,443	4,673	11,380	18,496
1978	2,489	7,573	5,022	1,496	16,580	3,633	7,973	14,964	26,570
1979	2,539	5,523	4,863	618	13,543	4,896	12,555	17,478	34,929
1980	2,581	7,461	6,685	1,138	17,865	5,389	17,690	20,853	43,932
1981	1,436	7,074	6,577	1,003	16,090	5,257	18,920	24,581	48,758
1977 Qtr 1	321	1,129	587	1,415	3,452	1,529	3,822	8,260	13,611
Qtr 2	366	364	1,599	580	2,909	1,576	4,295	9,468	15,339
Qtr 3	561	1,599	1,430	502	4,092	2,182	4,295	10,466	16,907
Qtr 4	588	1,080	1,101	93	2,862	2,443	4,673	11,380	18,496

(Contd.)

Appendix G (Contd.)

1		2	3	4	5	6	7	8	9	10
1978	Qtr 1	598	1,380	852	290	3,120	2,751	5,118	12,262	20,131
	Qtr 2	418	1,502	1,764	489	4,173	3,030	5,780	12,957	21,767
	Qtr 3	692	2,015	1,018	92	3,817	3,296	6,550	14,474	24,320
	Qtr 4	790	2,667	1,390	625	5,472	3,633	7,973	14,964	26,570
1979	Qtr 1	691	1,209	1,340	252	3,492	4,096	9,369	15,411	28,876
	Qtr 2	589	1,139	1,160	159	3,047	4,269	10,843	15,967	31,079
	Qtr 3	470	1,278	868	64	2,680	4,399	11,626	16,929	32,954
	Qtr 4	789	1,897	1,495	143	4,324	4,896	12,555	17,478	34,929
1980	Qtr 1	612	1,448	1,081	167	3,308	4,966	13,724	18,174	36,864
	Qtr 2	763	2,412	1,627	422	5,224	5,067	14,570	18,163	37,800
	Qtr 3	590	1,889	1,582	260	4,321	5,280	16,303	19,452	41,035
	Qtr 4	616	1,712	2,395	289	5,012	5,389	17,690	20,853	43,932
1981	Qtr 1	365	1,263	997	165	2,790	5,327	17,809	21,600	44,736
	Qtr 2	347	2,165	1,689	541	4,742	4,954	18,025	22,002	44,981
	Qtr 3	286	2,444	2,486	76	5,292	4,966	18,151	23,790	46,907
	Qtr 4	438	1,202	1,405	221	3,266	5,257	18,920	24,581	48,758
1982	Qtr 1	307	1,234	1,983	237	3,761	5,076	19,247	25,650	49,973

ᵃ Refers to Net Approvals

ᵇ Outstanding represents cumulative disbursements of approved loans not yet repaid.

Remarks: The increase in approvals after 1975 was due to the Bank's decision to participate in the Seaqaqa Scheme and reflects the implementations of an amendment to the Fiji Development Bank Act requiring the Bank to 'give special consideration and priority to the economic development of the rural and agricultural sectors of the economy of Fiji'. Additionally, in May 1975 the Bank introduced commercial and industrial loans to the Fijian Scheme to assist Fijians entering the commercial sector—which also raised approvals.

Source: Fiji Development Bank.

APPENDIX H: NATIONAL INCOME

GDP BY ACTIVITY AT CURRENT PRICES, AT FACTOR COST ($ '000)

Activity	1977	1978	1979	1980ᵖ
1. Agriculture, Forestry and Fishing	141,298	141,073	167,974	211.522
2. Mining and Quarrying	682	618	1,373	2,540
3. Manufacturing	69,407	70,803	98,509	117,593
4. Electricity, Gas and Water	6,054	7,195	10,833	14,986
5. Building and Construction	49,209	47,492	57,241	63,260
6. Wholesale and Retail Trade; Hotels, Restaurants and Cafes	104,649	112,928	143,876	162,942
7. Transport and Communication	54,634	61,149	67,416	81,650
8. Finance, Real Estate and Other Business Services	77,294	86,525	100,646	114,166
9. Other Services	117,166	131,569	148,682	174,204
10. All Activities not classified elsewhere	1,183	599	3,253	3,253
11. Less Imputed Bank Service Charges	−15,850	−17,002	−20,400	−29,037
Total: All Activities	605,726	642,949	779,403	917,079
% Change over previous year		+6.13	+21.22	+17.66
Per Capita Income ($)	1016.49	1059.22	1255.08ʳ	1446.50

ᵖ Provisional

ʳ Revised

Education and Land Tenure: The Colonisation Process in Northern Mato Grosso, Brazil

BRAZIL THE REPUBLIC; MATO GROSSO, THE STATE

In Brazil, also called Bolivia, there are about 120,000,000 people. The Federative Republic of Brazil has an area of 8,511.965 kms. Its capital is Brasilia, a planned city in the central part of the country. Rio de Janeiro is no longer the capital, but is still a very important political, economic and cultural centre.

The Brazilians are very proud of their country for many reasons. It is the largest country in Latin America, in extension and population. In fact, the capitalist world, especially the core-industrialised countries, is also very proud of Brazil. Among other things, it is the largest country in the world in terms of an external debt of 88 million dollars, plus a short-term debt of 11 million dollars, yielding a total debt of 99 million (American) dollars. The closest competitors are also from Latin America: Mexico, Venezuela and Argentina. The 'international banks' are preoccupied with these debts. The economic recession is going to be intensified and unemployment is going to increase.

Brazil is a large country and hence it would be difficult to cover all aspects of it in a short paper. Thus only some aspects of just one of its 23 federal states—the state of Mato Grosso—are presented here.

Mato Grosso occupies 10.35% (881,001 km²) of the country. Its population, estimated at 1,142,000 inhabitants in 1980, has been growing very fast, as well as the population of Cuiaba, the state capital (Table 14.1).

Table 14.1: Resident Population

	1970	1980	% Annual Increase
Brazil	93,139.000	119.099.000	2.49
Mato Grosso	599.000	1.142.000	6.66
Cuiaba	100.865	213.151	7.77

In fact, the state is only now being occupied. Since the 1950's different colonisation policies have been tried, which generally failed. But the scene has been changing, especially during the last decade.

This demographic occupation is due not to the colonisation policies of expansion of the agricultural frontier, but more to the process of concentration of land tenure in the south and southeast of the country.

As land tenure becomes more concentrated due the exportation model adopted by Brazilian agriculture, thousands of families are literally being expelled from their small family properties. These are the 'colonists' who occupy the state of Mato Grosso and a significant part of the Central, Western and Amazonic regions. Expropriated from their properties by multi-national agricultural export companies, they migrated to Mato Grosso.

Land Tenure

Nevertheless, although Brazil is a large country, with only 14 inhabitants/km², still its problems are enormous: there is not 'enough' land for those who work it. In Mato Grosso, with only 1.3 inhabitants/ km², land tenure is one of the most crucial problems.

Although most people now live in urban areas (68%) in Brazil, (58% in Mato Grosso), land tenure is still the most important problem in the state. In 1980, about 60% of the total landowners, most of them landlords, were outsiders, and most of them residents of Sao Paulo state. In Mato Grosso, where the basic infrastructure for agricultural production is just being built, owning large properties is merely a speculative affair.

In the last decade about 50 new colonisation projects were approved by the Federal Government. Although that represents an important migratory flow towards the state of Mato Grosso, it is still insignificant in terms of land tenure structure: speculative nonproductive landlords still predominate (Table 14.2).

Table 14.2: Land Tenure in Mato Grosso (1980)

Extension/ha	Establishments	%	Area/ha	%
1—10	23.960	37.7	108.102	0.3
10—100	21.642	34.1	792.669	2.2
100—1000	13.234	20.8	4,031.465	11.3
1000—10000	3.884	6.1	11,742.902	32.9
10000 or more	650	1.0	19,008.750	53.2
unknown	70	0.1	—	—
Total	63.440	100.0	35,683.888	100.0

Producer/Condition

Proprietary	34,853	54.9	32,019.001	90.1
Renter	10,301	16.2	666.635	1.9
Partner	4,113	6.4	606.561	1.6
Occupant	13,963	22.1	1,754.434	4.7
Unknown	210	0.3	637.257	1.7
Total	63,440	100.0	35,683.888	100.0

Education

It is easy to imagine what the most general problems are when a population is rapidly expanding in an area just occupied, viz., health care, sanitation, production storing and draining, transportation infrastructure and, of course, education. The Brazilian Constitution states that school is obligatory and guaranteed by the state for all children from 7 to 14 years of age. But the reality, especially in the rural areas, is still far removed from the constitutional ruling.

True, the percentage of the school-age population (7-14) attending school is steadily rising, but nonetheless the absolute number of children outside school is likewise increasing rapidly (Table 14.3).

Table 14.3: School Attendance in Mato Grosso (1976-1980)

Year	Population/7—14			% attendance
	Total	In school	Outside school	
1976	187.944	125.425	62.519	66.7
1977	204.867	137.306	67.561	67.0
1978	221.790	152.647	69.143	68.8
1979	238.714	161.141	77.573	67.5
1980	254.586	174.483	80.103	68.5

Regarding the schools in the state of Mato Grosso, most are public municipal schools, located in rural areas. But the great majority are one-classroom/one-teacher schools. In addition, most of the rural teachers are lay teachers with just about four years of schooling, who work for ridiculous salaries.

As can be seen from Table 14.4, the number of rural teachers (1,215) is just barely superior to the number of rural classrooms (1,159) which, in turn, as just slightly higher than the number of rural schools (964). This shows that rural schools, most of them under the responsibility of the municipalities, are one-classroom/ one-teacher schools.

Table 14.4: First Grade Schools in Mato Grosso—1980

	Schools		Classrooms		Teachers	
	Municipal	Total	Municipal	Total	Municipal	Total
Urban	65	336	237	2,518	599	7.506
Rural	964	1.219	1.159	1,503	1,215	1.625
Total	1,029	1,555	1.396	4.021	1.814	9.131

COMMENTS

The colonisation policy of expansion of the agricultural frontier in the Amazonic region of Brazil hides the reality of some very important contradictions. The Brazilian Government refers to colonisation as its land reform—a legal land reform based on the Land Statute of the Military Government of 1964. Nevertheless, although the Land Statute allows for a general and even radical land reform, it has been implemented only under very special circumstances.

In fact, the Amazonic 'colonists,' most of them expropriated from their small family properties in the south, are currently being expelled towards the north by large enterprises, mostly multinational ones. Family enterprises in the south tend to disappear as these enterprises expropriate and expel rural workers, concentrate land property, and increase economic efficiency and agricultural productivity through intensive culture, mainly for the purpose of exportation.

Under these circumstances, when 'social tension' is generated, the Land Statute applied is a means of re-settling southern peasants in northern Mato Grosso. In this way, use of the Land Statute is subordinated to the process of capital realisation by large enterprises. The Statute is an instrument for controlling social tension and conflicts generated by the process of expropriation and concentration of property and capital. In fact, it is the fulcrum of government strategy for the countryside, and either alone or together with other measures serves to control conflicts, claims and social fights.

What are the perspectives of the colonisation projects spread all over the Amazonic region? The agrarian policy of the Brazilian government and some of the oldest projects exhibit certain tendencies.

Generally, the 'colonists' are left on their own, almost entirely, to 'colonize' the Amazonic region. They have only a very incipient knowledge about land quality, rain station, and what cultures are the most appropriate. They have very limited credit, a very precarious transportation infrastructure, and almost no facilities to store their production. If they survive four or five years under these conditions, they generally succeed. But most simply cannot afford to survive that length of time under such adverse circumstances. And the same process tends to repeat itself. They sell their property and move further north to Para, Rondonia and Acre, or simply quit and install themselves along the fringes of the nearest urban centre. Many enterprises are now developing large cattle-breeding projects in the Amazonic region, using the infrastructure originally planned to serve the colonisation projects, as well as the cheap labour force already settled there.

It is difficult to say what the tendency will be—whether the process will or will not remain the same throughout the Amazonic region. But we are absolutely sure that the present agrarian policy of the Brazilian government has as one of its basic priorities to concentrate land property, as well as capital reproduction. We are also absolutely certain that things happen because men want them to happen. And something is going to happen before the Amazonic region becomes a vast multi-national pasture.

CHAPTER 15

Relative Prices of Farm and Non-Farm Sectors in Tanzania, 1965-1985

INTRODUCTION

Agriculture is the mainstay of the Tanzanian economy, providing a livelihood for about 85 per cent of the population, while another 5 per cent are engaged in agro-businesses or servicing the agricultural sector. During the period 1964/65-1980/81 agriculture contributed an average of 40 per cent of the country's GDP, over half of which was accounted for by peasant agriculture.

Agriculture presently accounts for over 80 per cent of the total export earnings, which are greatly needed so that the nation can acquire capital and consumer goods from abroad. Agriculture also provides food for the growing population. Agriculture is an important source of income and employment for the majority of Tanzanians. Tanzanian agriculture also provides resources for the other sectors of the economy and provides a market and raw materials for the expanding agro-based industries.

Although agriculture is the mainstay of the Tanzanian economy, its productivity is relatively low. During the Second Five-Year Plan (1969-74) agriculture's contribution to the GDP increased at the rate of 2.2 per cent per annum, which means it did not keep pace with the population growth of 2.7 per cent per year during the same plan period.[1] Equally disquieting is the record of negative physical export growth of about 2 per cent per annum for the period 1966-80. Declining trends in agricultural production have manifested themselves even during the period 1981-85. Particularly severe declines have been shown by the traditional cash crops such as sisal, cashew nuts and pyrethrum (Table 15.1). Since agriculture provides the bulk of export earnings—the initial foreign exchange—which in turn make it possible for the country to import capital goods for industrial and agricultural development, its slow rate of growth (or worse still its decline) inhibits the national economy and hinders the realisation of its policy of self-reliance.

It is significant that the non-agricultural sectors have grown at a much higher rate than the whole economy—7.5 per cent versus 5.0 per cent from year to year.[2] Although for the period 1976-79 remarkable increases in food production occurred these were outstripped by the nation's food requirements. Thus the country was forced to import food grains from overseas, which cost about 10 per cent of its total foreign exchange earnings. Had food aid, in the form of grants and concessional aid, not been available, the nation would have spent up to 20 per cent of its foreign exchange earnings on importing food. In a nutshell, therefore, Tanzanian agriculture has performed badly during the past fifteen years. Several causes, have been advanced to explain this state of Tanzanian agriculture, but dependence on the vagaries of the weather is perhaps the most dominant factor.

PRICES AND PRICING POLICIES IN TANZANIA

Guided by its socialist policies, in the early 1970s Tanzania introduced price-control system and established the Price Commission. This commission was charged with the function of Price-setting and control of most goods, including textiles, steel and metal products, foodstuffs, radiosets, batteries, edible oils, beer and various kinds of liquour. A crucial component in the price-control system in Tanzania has been the *pan-territorial pricing mechanism*; all goods handled by the state institutions are to be sold or purchased at prices which are uniform in all parts of the country. The rationale behind this policy is the need to achieve *egalitarianism* and reduce regional disparities among the people. People who live in the remote and generally lagging areas, should not have to pay more for the goods they buy or receive less for the goods they sell than their fellow citizens who are favourably placed. The state institutions (parastatals) handling such goods were required by the Government to bear the full transport costs of the goods they handled. These costs were eventually met by the Government through subsidies and budgetary allocations.

The problems, which faced the pan-territorial pricing mechanism were several. Firstly, the escalation of transport costs necessitated the diversion of scarce resources including foreign exchange into transport. Secondly, goods were often not delivered to or purchased from the remote areas because there was no incentive for the agencies and institutions and even private transporters concerned with purchasing and/or distribution, to move their vehicles into the remote parts of the country, when their goods could be disposed of or acquired in the urban centres or near the main roads and railheads. Scarcities of essential goods became very acute in the rural and remote areas; although scarcities were felt in the urban centres as well, the extent and frequency of such were definitely much less.

The problem of scarcities was exacerbated by the over-expanding parallel market popularly known as 'magendo'. In some areas the parallel market was the only outlet through which agricultural producers, could sell their produce and thus realise cash incomes to meet their other needs. Naturally, the prevalence of the parallel market and its sustenance is anathema to the Government since it erodes the tax base and weakens governmental control of the movement of commodities.

In 1981 regional retail price differentials for certain essential goods, including food crops, were introduced in order to ensure that these goods did reach those areas for which they were destined. For food crops this measure was envisioned to take advantage also of agro-ecological specifities. For example, in dry areas sorghum and millet growers received a premium price, while those growing maize in these areas received a floor price. The objective of this measure was to encourage the growing of sorghum and millet in these dry areas and to simultaneously discourage maize production. The rationale for the measure was to encourage people to consume what they produce and thus minimise the need for the

Table 15.1: Production of Major Agricultural Commodities in Tanzania, 1965-1985 ('000 tonnes)

Commodity	1965	1966	1967	1968	1969	1970	1971	1972	1973	1974	1975	1976	1977	1978	1979	1980	1981	1982	1983	1984	1985
Coffee	34.2	51.9	40.2	51.5	46.1	49.7	52.4	47.0	50.1	53.5	44.9	54.9	54.8	52.5	49.6	50.0	66.4	54.8	53.8	48.0	53.4
Sisal	214.2	221.5	220.1	196.9	209.3	202.2	157.0	155.4	128.0	118.0	116.0	104.7	91.9	81.4	81.4	88.0	73.7	46.2	37.5	32.3	32.3
Cotton	56.2	86.2	60.8	62.9	56.8	60.7	54.8	64.5	60.0	57.0	55.6	40.4	47.0	60.5	58.4	53.8	44.2	44.2	43.9	52.0	31.5
Cashewnuts	63.7	71.1	76.5	117.0	114.6	111.0	125.2	145.1	97.8	83.4	68.0	56.4	40.5	41.5	60.0	44.2	60.0	32.5	32.5	30.2	17.2
Tobacco	5.1	5.1	7.8	7.3	11.7	11.0	10.8	15.3	11.9	18.4	19.1	18.4	17.1	16.7	16.7	15.9	13.6	13.6	13.5	13.4	12.6
Tea	3.7	6.8	7.2	7.9	8.8	8.5	10.6	12.8	13.9	14.5	13.9	15.3	16.7	17.3	16.3	15.5	13.6	15.5	15.9	15.9	17.6
Pyrethrum	3.7	4.4	6.7	4.8	3.8	2.7	9.1	4.3	4.0	3.8	3.3	3.1	2.9	1.6	1.6	2.0	2.0	1.7	1.7	1.4	1.2
Sugar	67.4	71.0	71.8	82.4	92.0	87.3	88.5	92.3	106.4	114.4	95.7	114.5	104.7	123.0	105.7	114.1	124.3	102.0	131.5	108.1	108.1
Sub-total	450.2	518.0	490.5	530.7	543.1	533.1	497.2	507.3	514.9	459.3	441.5	416.3	407.8	391.6	393.9	372.6	416.5	371.3	311.2	329.9	273.9
Maize	82.7	123.3	108.4	126.8	52.5	193.2	186.4	143.0	106.4	73.8	23.9	91.1	124.0	213.1	222.3	161.5	104.6	90.0	85.3	69.1	178.5
Paddy/Rice	21.9	42.2	33.7	45.0	78.6	102.2	60.8	44.6	59.7	24.6	11.7	16.0	24.6	26.9	29.7	29.9	20.0	18.9	12.1	15.9	
Wheat	30.2	32.9	29.1	23.8	19.9	40.0	47.1	56.9	51.3	28.0	14.0	11.0	35.0	27.4	28.9	26.6	27.9	23.6	30.7	33.2	50.3
Sorghum	12.8	12.5							2.0	2.0	3.0	46.0	44.0	59.0	20.4	18.9	10.7	4.5	2.4	14.7
Beans	17.2	22.8					6.1			7.3	10.2	31.7	28.3	35.2	16.2	12.3	11.3	3.7	14.7	5.7
Cassava								14.3		19.9	17.8	17.4	19.9	36.9	63.8	44.0	7.5	9.9	18.6	19.8	12.9
Sub-total	164.8	233.7	171.2	195.6	151.0	335.4	250.6	245.1	182.4	82.3	141.7	251.1	337.7	429.2	317.4	204.0	166.5	169.3	140.3	278.0	
Groundnuts	—	—	—	—	—	3.5	3.1	3.3	3.5	1.4	0.5	0.5	0.4	1.5	2.6	5.5	1.7	0.3	0.2	0.9	0.6
Sesame	—	—	—	—	—	7.5	5.4	7.7	7.3	6.6	5.3	7.5	7.5	6.6	6.6	3.9	7.5	4.2	4.2	6.2	3.2
Sunflower	—	—	—	—	—	5.8	7.8	6.5	8.9	6.6	6.9	5.9	4.7	7.2	12.1	15.6	10.8	9.4	9.5	4.4	7.7
Soyabeans	—	—	—	—	—	0.2	0.3	0.9	0.8	0.4	0.3	0.9	0.6	1.1	1.0	1.1	0.2	0.2	0.3	0.6	
Castor	—	—	—	—	—	6.0	14.4	12.9	10.3	5.6	3.3	2.2	2.4	2.2	1.7	1.3	0.6	0.7	0.6	0.2	0.6
Sub-total	—	—	—	—	—	23.0	31.0	31.3	30.8	20.6	16.3	20.2	15.9	18.1	24.1	27.3	21.7	14.8	14.9	12.0	12.7
Total	615.9	751.7	661.7	726.3	694.1	891.5	822.5	789.2	790.8	662.3	578.2	674.8	787.4	847.2	717.3	642.2	552.6	495.4	482.2	564.6	

Sources: Annual Economic Surveys (for the relevant years), Ministry of Finance, Economic Affairs and Planning,
Dar es Salaam.
Annual reports and Bulletin of Crop Statistics, Marketing Development Bureau of the Ministry of Agriculture,
Dar es Salaam.
Sub-total and total figures are author's computations.

state to transport at high cost the so-called preferred grains (maize, rice and wheat).

Producer Prices

Producer prices have been deemed as important incentives in inducing increased agricultural production as well as in determining agricultural output mix.[3] However, this fact seems to have received a rather late recognition, if one looks at the generally stagnant producer prices between the mid-sixties and mid-seventies. Since the mid-seventies the Government has exercised an active use of prices to spur increased production, especially of food crops (see Tables 15.2 and 15.3). The 1972-74 drought and the subsequent large food imports (Table 15.4) definitely influenced government thinking on the subject. Based on trends of producer prices during the period 1971/72-1984/85, the following observations are pertinent:

i) Producer prices for export crops were lower in real terms during the early 1980s than they were in the early and mid-1970s. In fact the weighted average export crop price was the lowest in the whole period of 1971/72-1981/82. The highest weighted average export crop price was reached in 1976/77 at the time of the coffee price boom and has declined in real terms by 60% since then.

ii) For food crops the 1980s' prices are above the pre-1974/75 levels in real terms. However, there has been a continuous decline since 1977/78 due to a higher inflation rate. In Tanzania the inflation rate jumped from 12% in 1978/79 to above 30% during the early 1980s and has persisted at that level into the late 1980s.

iii) The relative average prices of export crops to food crops have declined, especially since 1976/77, they plummeted from a ratio of 5.6 to 3.2 in 1981/82 (Table 15.5). This ratio is perhaps an understatement of the decline since the parallel market effect was not included (see below).

iv) Of the food crops, the non-traditional marketed crops such as sorghum, millets, pulses and cassava, experienced a rather fast increase in producer prices in the mid-seventies. These crops are sometimes referred to in Tanzanian literature as 'new crops,' since they have only recently received official recognition and are, therefore, procured by the National Milling Corporation (NMC)

Table 15.2: Announced Producer Prices for Selected Export Crops 1971/72-1984/85 (cents/kg—current prices)

Crops	1971/72	1972/73	1973/74	1974/75	1975/76	1976/77	1977/78	1978/79	1979/80	1980/81	1981/82	1982/83	1983/84	1984/85
Coffee														
Mild														
Arabica	450	415	440	385	800	1,500	1,089	907	1,142	1,236	1,490	1,509	1,680	2,350
Robusta														
Dry														
Cherry	400	365	375	315	600	885	527	464	555	450	553	894	880	1,200
Cotton-														
AR	110	113	113	150	200	200	230	240	300	320	370	470	600	840
-BR	55	60	60	65	100	100	115	120	130	150	170	250	320	450
Tobacco-														
flue	580	585	585	585	700	740	740	740	800	1,050	1,260	1,800	1,800	2,520
-fire	210	213	240	255	300	450	520	520	625	625	770	1,150	1,150	1,610
-burley	—	—	—	—	—	480	480	480	650	650	680	1,000	1,100	1,000
Cashew														
nuts-SG	95	95	95	105	105	110	115	170	180	300	500	500	700	980
-UG	75	75	75	95	95	95	100	140	150	200	350	350	490	690
Tea (green														
leaf)	73	71	74	74	80	90	150	150	150	150	150	200	280	410
Pyre-														
thrum	285	275	275	421	400	400	400	400	600	750	1,000	1,000	1,400	1,960

			1,700	1,800	1,200	1,500	2,500	4,500	4,500	4,500	4,500	4,500	4,500	8,000
Carda-mom	—	—	55	70	75	75	100	100	100	120	170	170	200	350
Castor	49	53												

Sources: Marketing Development Bureau, Price Policy Recommendations for 1984/85 Price Review. Annual reports for 1983/84 and 1984/85, Ministry of Agriculture, Dar es Salaam.

Note: Currency equivalents: Tanzanian shilling (Tsh) = 100 Tanzanian cents.
US $1 = Tshs 8.2 until March 1982 US $1 = Tshs 12.2 since June 1983;
US $1 = Tshs 18 since June 1984; US $1 = Tshs 40 since June 1985.

Table 15.3: Announced Producer Prices for Selected Food Crops 1971/72-1984/85 (cents/kg-current prices)

Crops	1971/72	1972/73	1973/74	1974/75	1975/76	1976/77	1977/78	1978/79	1979/80	1980/81	1981/82	1982/83	1983/84	1984/85
Preferred staples														
Maize	24	26	33	50	75/80	80	85	85	100	100	150	175	220	400
Paddy	52	56	57	65	100	100	120	120	150	175	230	380	400	600
Wheat	57	57	57	77	100	120	125	125	135	165	220	250	300	450
Drought staples														
Sorghum	—	30	50	55	75	90	100	100	100	100	100	160	200	300
Bulrush millet	—	30	50	55	75	90	100	100	100	100	100	160	200	300
Finger millet	—	—	50	55	80/85	95	200	200	200	150	150	150	n.a.	n.a.
Cassava-														
Gr I	—	—	31	36	40	50	60	65	65	65	70	90	120	200
Gr II	—	—	29	34	38	40	50	50	50	50	50	70	90	90
Oilseeds														
Sunflower (Jupiter)	43	57	55	75	100	110	150	150	150	160	180	260	350	525
Sesame	113	120	160	200	200	250	300	330	350	400	450	570	700	1,050

Ground nuts	100	103	115	150	200	250	400	400	400	420	480	580	800	1,200
Copra	—	—	—	—	135-220	210-230	220-250	230	230	250	300	420	600	900
Others														
Grapes	—	250	250	250	250	350	350	350	400	400	500	600	900	1,000
Beans Gr I	—	—	—	—	—	200	200/350	350	350	350	350	350	500	800
Gr II	—	—	—	—	—	175	175/275	275	275	275	275	275	275	350

Source: Marketing Development Bureau, Price Policy Recommendations for the 1984-85 Price Review.

Table 15.4: Cereal Imports in Tanzania (1971/72-1983/84 ('000 tonnes)

Cereal	1971/72	1972/73	1973/74	1974/75	1975/76	1976/77	1977/78	1978/79	1979/80	1980/81	1981/82	1982/83	1983/84
Maize	92.3	78.9	291.1	225.4	107.0	41.6	34.3	–	32.5	174.6	234.6	122.7	228.6
Rice	16.0	8.0	72.6	64.3	29.0	40.0	49.0	54.0	54.7	65.2	70.2	45.2	58.8
Wheat	21.0	8.2	60.0	121.0	60.2	34.0	41.0	45.1	33.0	48.7	83.1	11.4	41.2
Total	129.3	95.1	423.7	410.7	196.2	115.6	124.3	99.1	120.2	388.9	387.9	179.3	328.6
Value* in Tshs mil.	85.0	24.0	775.0	732.0	256.9	194.0	201.5	297.0	552.0	831.2	862.2	549.5	807.9

Sources: Ministry of Agriculture, Dar es Salaam, 1985.

    The Economic Journal, Bank of Tanzania, Dar es Salaam, 1979 edition.

*Prices of cereals in 1981/82 (World Bank) were:

    Maize—US $ 190 per ton,

    Rice—US $ 500 per ton and

    Wheat—US $ 240 per ton.

Note: For currency equivalent see note on Table 15.2.

—the parastatal organisation charged with procurement and distribution of food crops in the country.

v) For both export and food crops producer prices during the years 1980-85 have increased relatively fast for some but have remained unchanged or changed only slowly for others (see Tables 15.2 and 15.3).

From the foregoing observations it is possible to discern a generally declining trend in real producer prices since 1976/77, which acts as a disincentive to increased agricultural production and makes non-agricultural activities relatively more attractive. Table 15.6 gives a clear picture of the impacts of the above trends.[4] Export crop performance was the hardest hit, facing an absolute decline in physical outputs from 611,654 tonnes in 1973/74 to 469,057 tonnes in 1978/79, a decrease of 23.3%. Staple food cereals during the same period increased in marketed output by 81.5%. The change in relative prices of food crops in favour of food crops accounts for this better performance of the staple cereals. However, production of food crops declined thereafter, reaching an output of 278,000 tonnes in 1985, a decrease of 35.2% of the 1979 output of 429,200 tonnes.

A detailed analysis of performance of various crops during the period 1965-85 has been presented in Table 15.1 above. The picture is quite dismal for export crops, especially for sisal and cashew nuts, of which Tanzania was the leading producer in the world in the 1960s and early 1970s. The most dramatic impact of the price trends is seen in the 'new crops,' Purchases of sorghum, millets, cassava and pulses rocketed from 23,107 tons in 1973/74 to 216,371 tons in 1978/79, a phenomenal increase of 836.4% over the period. The highest increase was achieved, however, by sorghum/millets when they reached 2,308.9%. However, the situation is somewhat different after 1980, as Table 15.1 clearly demonstrates. Part of the cause of this situation is the stagnation of producer prices of these 'new crops' since 1977/78 as exemplified by Table 15.3. During this period the NMC had large stocks of these crops which it could not easily and quickly dispose of. The NMC procures food grains mainly for urban consumers, who prefer maize, rice and wheat (the so-called *preferred staples*) to the 'new crops'. The demand for the 'new crops' is highest when the *preferred staples* are scarce or not available due to drought, as was

Table 15.5: Average Producer Prices for Food Crops and Export Products 1971/72-1981/82 (cents/kg-constant prices)[a]

Year	Food Crops Weighted Average Price[b]	Export Products Weighted Average Price[b]	Ratio of Export/Food Crop Price
1971/72	n.a.	1,045	n.a.
1972/73	171	919	5.4
1973/74	157	873	5.6
1974/75	163	698	4.3
1975/76	200	955	4.8
1976/77	237	1,331	5.6
1977/78	289	880	3.0
1978/79	260	839	3.2
1979/80	223	779	3.5
1980/81	177	695	3.9
1981/82	170	640	3.2

Source: Marketing Development Bureau, Price Policy Recommendations for the 1982/83 Agricultural Price Review: Summary.
[a]Deflation using the Nation Consumer Price Index.
[b]Weights used are values of official purchases.

the case in the years 1972-74.

For export crops, f.o.b. prices, determined by international markets, have stagnated and the share in unit price going to the peasant producer has declined. Increases in unit overhead costs brought about by increased inefficiency and mismanagement of the crop authorities—the state organisations charged with the responsibilities to procure, transport, store and of procurement, transportation, and distribution/disposal storage, of agricultural produce—and reduction in volume of crops handled, are the main reasons behind the decline in shares going to the agricultural producers. Between 1971/72 and 1978/79 the share in total price going to the peasant producer fell from 70% to 35% for cashew, 70% to 45% for cotton, 61% to 48% for tobacco, and 80% to 45% for coffee.[5] The decline in shares hindered potential higher increases in the production of export crops. However, these trends were reversed in 1981, when the producer share of export value was raised to 56%. The figures for 1982 and 1983 were even better, 70% and 75% respectively. The 1984 figure of 62% represents

**Table 15.6: Trends in Total Marketed Crop Production in Tanzania
1973/74-1978/79 (Metric tonnes)**

Crop category		1973/74	1978/79	Increase/decrease in percentage
Traditional (Export crops	crops)	611,654	469,057	−23.3
	(Staple grains)	166,097	301,388	+82.5
	(Oilseeds)	19,875	22,787	+4.7
Subtotal		799,626	793,232	−0.7
New Crops (Sorghum/ millets)		4,089	98,500	+2.308.9
	(Cassava)	19,018	63,767	+235.3
	(Pulses)	n.a.	54,104	n.a.
Subtotal		23,107	216,371	+836.4
Total		820,733	1,009,603	+23.0

Source: F. Ellis, *Agricultural Pricing and Marketing Policy in Tanzania* in
the 1970s as quoted by Msambichaka and Noulu, 1982, 'A review of
impact of agricultural incentives: Prices and credits, in University of
Dar es Salaam, 1982, Evaluation of the Iringa Resolution: 'Siasa ni
Kilimo' 1972-1982, Dar es Salaam, Table 2, p. 48 (mimeographed).

a drop in the producer share of export value, with the decline
continuing into 1985.

During the early 1980s prospects for increasing producer prices
of food crops were dim since efforts to raise them had to take
into account consumer prices, especially in the urban centres, and
the Government's ability to subsidise them in order to keep them
low. Under the conditions of galloping inflation and a dearth of
consumer goods, pressure on the Government to maintain low
consumer prices was enormous and indeed imperative. However,
governmental efforts to maintain low consumer prices were detrimental to increased agricultural production since they held down
the producer prices. In mid-1984 the Government lifted subsidies
on maize flour. One can anticipate that the Government was
caught in a dilemma, with simultaneous efforts directed toward

increasing producer prices and keeping consumer prices low through subsidies. The dilemma was further compounded by the ever-expanding parallel market where food commodities were available at greatly higher prices than in the official market.

Perhaps, the Tanzanian Government yielded to the pressure exerted on it by the declining agricultural production and from the IMF, with which it has had prolonged and sometimes acrimonious negotiations about adjustment policies for the country.[6] This year also saw increases in producer prices of export crops for the crop year 1984/85 in line with domestic inflation, which was then running at about 33.3%.

Before closing this section we would like to briefly discuss the issue of crop price relativities; firstly, whether the relative levels appear correct and secondly, whether relative price levels are being changed in the most desirable fashion. These are important questions since it has been observed that peasants switch from one crop to another (others) depending upon which one is currently fetching a better price. Examples of this occurrence commonly mentioned in Tanzanian literature are taken from Kigoma region[7] where peasant producers have been switching from cotton to maize and beans despite immense bureaucratic exhortation to grow the former, primarily to enable the nation to earn foreign exchange, and Lindi and Mtwara regions in the case of cashew and pigeon peas.[8] Tables 15.2 and 15.3 clearly illustrate this point, especially in the late 1970s. For example, in 1977/78 the producer prices for cotton and beans were 230 cents and 350 cents respectively, whereas in the previous year (1976/77) both these crops fetched a producer price of 200 cents/kg. In the same year the prices of cashew and pigeon peas were 11.5 cents/kg and 350 cents/kg respectively. It is obvious that this price-setting ignores economic rationality, since cotton and cashew are by far more costly in terms of effort (labour) and gestation period; a producer has to wait quite sometime before he/she can reap the fruits of his/her labour. It is little wonder that peasants in Kigoma switched from cotton to maize and bean production, while their brethren in Lindi and Mtwara regions changed from cashew nuts to pigeon peas, leading to a consequent decline in production of the export crops in those regions. In this respect the situation was somewhat better in the 1980s than in the 1970s. Price-setting, which ignores peasant production costs and ecological specificities, is bound to encounter the difficulties discussed above.

Another point is the rapidity with which some price ratios have been changed. For example, the official producer price of beans was 250% of the price offered for maize in 1976/77, but was 412% by the purchasing year of 1977/78 (see Table 15.3). In addition to the effects they have on the producers (see above), such sudden changes in crop relativities cause problems to the marketing parastatals in the sphere of crop finance, transport and warehousing facilities, manpower and logistics, not to mention that the situation yields considerable scope for the parallel market to thrive. The Marketing Development Bureau, an institution under the Ministry of Agriculture charged with the responsibility of crop-marketing intelligence in the country, estimates that as much as 70% of the marketed production of maize and beans passes through unofficial markets.[9] However, in the early 1980s there were relatively few rapid changes in producer price ratios, except for the 1984/85 season (see Tables 15.2 and 15.3). Nevertheless, the price-setting mechanism (which holds prices of certain crops at constant levels in money terms for several years and then suddenly raises them in one big jump) leaves a lot to be desired. Frequent and smaller price changes are undoubtedly more effective and certainly to be preferred over sudden ones.

There is a need for a concerted effort to popularise the consumption of the 'new crops' since it appears that large stocks of these crops have made little difference to the importation of staple grains. The NMC has sustained large expenditures in the purchase, storage and disposal of 'new crops'; between 1976/77 and 1981/82 the NMC accumulated an overdraft of Tshs 2 billion with the National Bank of Commerce. Needless to say, this overdraft became a debt of the NMC to the Bank and thus had to be repaid from normal budgetary allocations from the Treasury. Naturally, one feels bound to urge the authorities to promote increased commercial consumption of the 'new crops', which should be matched with the promotion of their increased production in order for the nation to reduce its dependence on food imports. In the present situation of foreign exchange shortage and a hostile international economic order, continued dependence on food imports, and especially on food aid, is dangerous to national independence and is bound to compromise the nation's commitment to its policy of socialism and self-reliance.

It is appropriate in concluding this section to point out that there has been a general deterioration in incomes among the peasants in the rural areas. Part of this problem has been undoubtedly caused by the decline in real terms of producer prices for peasant crops, which are the main, if not the only, source of their cash income. Even the prevalence of the parallel market may not have benefited a substantial section of the peasantry due to the dearth of transport and communication facilities and equipment.

Consumer Prices

In this section we shall look at the consumer prices of both farm and non-farm commodities. In 1982/83 'sembe' (maize flour) retailed at 250 cents/kg, unmilled maize at 335 cents/kg, rice 535 cents/kg and wheat flour 565 cents/kg. These prices were last reviewed in June 1981 when the retail price of 'sembe' was doubled and in January 1980 when the prices of rice and wheat flour had a 53% and 51% rise respectively over the 1979 prices (see Table 15.7). It is evident from the data presented in this Table that the real price of 'sembe' reached its lowest level in 1983 for the entire period 1973-85, while both rice and wheat flour reached their lowest levels in 1982, that is, a year earlier than the former. However, the data for these latter commodities in 1985 show a decline in real prices compared to the 1984 data. Given this situation of 'sembe,' one understands why the Government subsidised the price of 'sembe' until 1984, when it stopped because of the circumstances already discussed above. Rice and wheat received no subsidy and, therefore, their prices took full costs into consideration. From 1984 'sembe' was priced at full cost also.

Although the official prices have declined in real terms, a less satisfactory scenario emerges when one takes into consideration the fact that the purchasing power of the *minimum urban wage* earners has been declining since 1975, as illustrated in Table 15.8. For example, in 1983 the minimum wage of Tshs 600 per month was sufficient to buy 8 kg of 'sembe' per day, which, though a little above the lowest level prevailing from 1976-79, was much less than its purchasing power in the early to mid-1970s and also

Table 15.7: Official Retail Prices of Major Staples in Tanzania (in cents/kg) (in July of each year)

	1973	1974	1975	1976	1977	1978	1979	1980	1981	1982	1983	1984	1985
Current Prices													
Sembe	80	125	125	175	175	175	175	125	250	250	250	800	1,375
Maize grain	—	—	—	—	—	—	—	—	—	335	439	540	760
Rice	165	200	400	400	350	350	350	535	535	535	720	1,340	1,450
Wheat flour	165	240	375	375	375	375	375	565	565	565	800	1,450	1,715
Constant Prices (1983/84) (a)													
Sembe	488	640	506	643	594	530	469	257	410	318	250	563	762
Maize grain	—	—	—	—	—	—	—	—	—	426	439	380	421
Rice	1,007	1,025	1,620	1,516	1,189	1,059	938	1,101	876	680	720	944	804
Wheat flour	1,007	1,230	1,519	1,422	1,274	1,135	1,005	1,163	926	718	800	1,070	554

Source: Marketing Development Bureau, Price Policy Recommendations for the 1984/85 Agricultural Price Review.

[a]Using Tanzania Consumer Price Index as a deflator.

Table 15.8: Minimum Urban Wage Levels and Their Purchasing Power in Terms of Sembe, Rice and Wheat Flour

	1973	1974	1975	1976	1977	1978	1979	1980	1981	1982	1983	1984	1985
Minimum urban wage (Tshs/month)													
Nominal terms	240	340	380	380	380	380	380	480	600	600	600	810	810
Constant 1984 terms	1,985	2,360	2,085	1,951	1,748	1,558	1,380	1,338	1,331	1,032	813	810	632
Purchasing power of minimum urban wage (kg/staple grain/day's wage) (in Dar es Salaam)													
Sembe	10.0	9.1	10.1	7.2	7.2	7.2	7.2	12.8	8.0	8.0	8.0	3.4	2.0
Maize grain	—	—	—	—	—	—	—	—	—	6.0	4.6	5.0	3.6
Rice	4.8	5.7	3.2	3.2	3.6	3.6	3.6	3.0	3.7	3.7	2.8	2.0	1.9
Wheat flour	4.8	4.7	3.4	3.4	3.4	3.4	3.4	2.8	3.5	3.5	2.5	1.9	1.6

Sources: Marketing Development Bureau.
        Bureau of Statistics.

in 1980. A similar pattern is discernible in the case of rice and wheat flour. Obviously, it would take only small increases in consumer prices of these agricultural commodities for the purchasing power of the minimum wage to fall to its lowest level for at least a decade. Under these circumstances, it is little wonder that considerable pressure was exerted, especially from the trade union, to raise the minimum wage in 1983.

However, in the rural areas and most urban centres outside Dar es Salaam, negligible quantities of food staples are available at official prices. The prices of food grains sold in the parallel market are considerably higher than the official prices. There are substantial seasonal price fluctuations and variations of commodities and places according to the rules of supply and demand. An indication of the magnitude of consumer price differences between official and parallel markets, between months and different locations can be traced in Table 15.9.

Table 15.9: Parallel Market Prices for Rice in Selected Urban Centres (Tshs/kg)

	September 1981	March 1982
Dar es Salaam	5.35 (official price)	n.a.
Morogoro	10.30	17.40
Moshi	12.60	25.00

Source: Bureau of Statistics (input for the National Consumer Price Index).

There was a deliberate government policy to subsidise the consumer price of 'sembe' but no subsidy existed for unmilled (grain) maize sold by the NMC. Consequently, the official retail price of milled grain (sembe) was about one-third higher than that of maize flour. The explicit 'sembe' subsidy was largely derived from the Treasury, although about one-quarter originated from the one shilling per kilo cross-subsidy included in the retail price of sugar. As noted, these subsidies were removed in 1984, at which time also the minimum wage was raised from Tshs 600 per month to Tshs 810 per month. According to the data presented in Table 15.8 it is evident that the increase in minimum wage has had little compensatory effect on the incomes of urban dwellers, who actually need it most.

Government policy for rice and wheat flour was that full-cost retail prices should apply. However, for three years (1980-82) there was no revision in their retail prices. Given the fact that Tanzania's consumer price index (CPI) had increased by some 85% during that time, both these products were implicitly heavily subsidised at their prevailing shiling retail prices (rice at Tshs 5.35/ kg and wheat flour at Tshs 5.65/kg) and the cost of that subsidy was borne by the NMC or, to be more precise, by the NMC's overdraft with the National Bank of Commerce.[10] Little wonder, therefore, that the NMC's indebtedness to this financial institution was enormous. amounting to over Tshs 2.8 billion in 1980, not to mention financial losses emanatlng from spoilage (lost, strayed, stolen, deteriorated, rotten, exported to avert further losses, or turned into poultry feed after deterioration) of maize, sorghum, millets and cassava over 1977-79 totalling 500,000 tonnes worth Tshs 2.5 billion. This problem was caused to some extent by government policy determined to provide urban dwellers, particularly Dar es Salaam inhabitants, with cheap food.

As can be seen from Table 15.10 there has been a general rise in prices and cost of living over the past decade. There was a gradual price rise in the late 1960s and early 1970s, but since 1974 sharp rises in consumer prices have been a common phenomenon. The price index of goods and services consumed by town dwellers in Tanzania rose by 12% in 1974 and 1977, but only by 7.2% in 1976. Taking 1977 as the base year, retail prices had risen over 5.5 times for all consumer items, while those of foodstuffs had gone up over 5.0 times by 1985. Obviously, there were sharper increases in consumer prices on a year-to-year basis, especially during the period 1981-85. The reasons contributing to the price rise included higher prices of petroleum products, charcoal, foodstuffs (vegetables, fruits, fats, spices, beans), textiles, footwear and transpott. For example, the price index for textiles and footwear, transport, fuel and lighting, and utensils had risen by 2.5 to 4.5 times in the period 1975-81. As noted earlier, a rise in consumer prices affects one way or another the material conditions of the people, both in urban and rural areas. Due to the paucity of relevant data it is not possible to gauge precisely the effect of the price rises on the low-income earners, both in urban and rural areas. Nonetheless, it is possible to conclude from the evidence

Table 15.10: Index of Retail Prices of Goods Consumed by Minimum
Wage Earners in Dar es Salaam (1977=100)

Year	All items	Food
1966	30.0	29.5
1967	30.8	30.0
1968	31.9	30.4
1969	32.3	29.9
1970	33.4	31.0
1971	34.6	32.5
1972	38.2	36.0
1973	41.7	40.5
1974	54.5	53.1
1975	80.1	79.7
1976	98.9	98.4
1977	100.0	100.0
1978	135.0	138.9
1979	141.0	141.9
1980	165.2	168.0
1981	215.9	215.7
1982	262.9	266.5
1983	325.0	318.3
1984	381.8	348.4
1985	559.7	508.0

Source: Hali ya Uchumi wa Taifa, 1986 *Economic Survey* p. 51.

available that there has been a general deterioration in the material conditions of the majority of the Tanzanians during the past ten to fifteen years. Despite government subsidies (up to the middle of 1984) on consumer prices, which have gone up by over 5.0 times during the period 1977-85, incomes of urban workers have only doubled, thus making the life of the ordinary people more difficult than in the early 1970s.

CONCLUDING REMARKS

This paper has attempted to discuss the prices of farm and non-farm commodities in Tanzania with a view to underpinning their effect on the urban-rural economy in general and on the incomes of the majority of the people, who fall in the low-income category, in particular. State intervention in the area of pricing policies has been problematic as it has failed to resolve the conflicts of interest between the peasant producers and the urban dwellers. Attempts to keep consumer prices low through subsidies have tended to hold the lid down on producer prices. Conversely, increased consumer prices have led to pressures to raise wages, especially the minimum wage, and to the need for increased subsidies, which the government had almost maximised by the early 1980s. Thus the removal of these subsidies and an increment in the minimum wage in mid-1984 were a logical outcome of these conflicts of interest. Nonetheless, the need to rationalise the pricing policies is indicated, especially from the point of view of creating the necessary incentives for peasant producers.

It has been demonstrated that there has been a general deterioration in the material conditions of the majority of Tanzanians, i.e., those who are the low-income earners. However, the rural people have been worse off than their brethren in the urban centres, either because of public policies which worked against them or their disadvantageous geographical position. Even the pan-territorial pricing mechanism could not mitigate these negative effects on the rural people. In a nutshell these measures have exacerbated the imbalance of the terms of trade between the urban and rural sectors, with the latter coming off worse than the former.

NOTES

1. Government of Tanzania, 1976, *Third Five-Year Plan for Economic and Social Development 1976-81*, Government Printer, Dar es Salaam, p. 14.
2. *Ibid.*
3. Tanganyika African National Union, 1972, *Siasa ni Kilimo* (Politics Is Agriculture), TANU Publicity Section, Dar es Salaam, p 18. This document of Party policy strongly asserted for the first time the use of producer prices to spur increased agricultural production in the country.
4. Many commentators on Tanzanian agricultural development mention a host of factors which, in one way or another, have hindered its progress. Some of the factors mentioned include lack of a coherent national agricultural policy (however, such a policy was adopted in 1983, but the impact of its implementation has still to be seen), ineffective supportive services

(extension and research), inefficient and ineffective marketing institutions, poor or inadequate transport and communication facilities, lack or inadequacy of rural credit, inadequate manpower, scarcities of consumer goods in the rural areas, etc. For details, see J. De Vries, 1977, 'Ujamaa villages and problems of institutional change with emphasis on agricultural extension and development, 'Rural Economy Paper No. 3, University of Dar es Salaam, Morogoro; H. Hansel, J. De Vries and P.C. Ndedys (eds.), 1975, *Agricultural Extension in Ujamaa Village Development*, Faculty of Agriculture and Forestry, Morogoro; J. Ngasongwa, 1980, A Study of Agricultural Development in Morogoro Region: A Historical Perspective, M.A. Dissertation of the University of Dar es Salaam; J. Ngasongwa, 1981, 'The Political Economy of Food Production in Tanzania,' Paper presented at the Annual Conference of the Agricultural Economics Society of Tanzania, held at Morogoro on 29-30 November 1981. Also see A. Coulson, 1977, 'Agricultural policies in mainland Tanzania,' *Review of African Political Economy*, no 10 pp 74-96; and M. Lofchie, 1978, 'Agrarian crisis and economic liberation in Tanzania,' *Journal of Modern African Studies*, no 16 (3) pp 451-79.

5. For a detailed analysis, see F. Ellis, 1982, 'Agricultural pricing policy in Tanzania, *World Development*, vol 10 no 4, Permagon Press, London, pp 263-83.

6. Tanzania's economic difficulties began to take their toll on the national economy in 1979 and soon thereafter the Government approached the IMF which, as it is wont to do, issued a number of conditions, most of which were unacceptable to the Tanzanian authorities.

7. J. Ngasongwa, 1980, A Study of Agricultural Development in Morogoro Region: A Historical Perspective, M A. Dissertation of the University of Dar es Salaam, Dar es Salaam, pp 45-7.

8. See F. Ellis, 1980, 'Agricultural pricing policy in Tanzania 1970-79 implications for agricultural output, rural incomes and agricultural marketing costs,' ERB Paper 80.3, University Dar es Salaam, Dar es Salaam.

9. Marketing Development Bureau, 1984, *Price Policy Recom-mendations for 1984/85*: *Agricultural Price Review* MDB, Dar es Salaam.

10. Marketing Development Bureau, 1982, *Price Policy Recom-mendations for July 1982: Agricultural Price Review*, MDB, Dar es Salaam, p. 41.

CHAPTER 16

Rural Transformation Through River Basin Development: A Case Study of the Upper Benue River Basin Development Projects (UBRBDP) Nigeria

INTRODUCTION

Up to the early 1970s, Nigeria depended almost entirely on the export of agricultural products for her foreign exchange earnings. This situation changed with the appearance of oil (petroleum) which became dominant as a foreign exchange earner and relegated agriculture to the background. This structural change in the export-earning sector of the economy quickly filtered through the socio-economic fabric of the agricultural-producing sectors, leading to a massive rural-urban migration of actual and potential farm workers in search of the 'good things of life' oil would provide. And coincidental with the structural changes during this period was the government's neglect of agriculture, which resulted in the gradual decline in food production. The short-run natural antidote to the food-shortage problem therefore was to import foodstuffs.

Apparently, the importation of foodstuffs did not prove to be the answer to the nation's food problem and the rural-urban migration because of the inherent foreign exchange impact on the nation's economy. The value of food imports, for example, was N509.76 million in 1964; by 1980 the figure had risen to the staggering sum of about N9,658.10 million.[1] By 1976 the need to increase food production became pressing, and the idea of irrigated agriculture via river basin developments was conceived. In that year eleven river basin development authorities were established, one of which is the Upper Benue River Basin Development Authority (UBRBDA) (Table 16.1). The areas of jurisdiction of the River Basin Development Authorities were clearly demarcated and vary from about 17.407 million hectares in the Niger River Basin Development Authority to about 1.614 million hectares in the Niger Delta Basin (Fig. 16.1).[2] In the current

Table 16.1. River Basin Development Authorities in Nigeria

River basin development	Area (million hectares)	Mean annual rainfall (mm)
1. Sokoto-Rima River Basin Development Authority	13.370	500-1250
2. Hadejia-Jama'are River Basin Development Authority	7.822	500-2000
3. Chad Basin Development Authority	12.342	500-2000
4. Upper Benue River Basin Development	13.849	750-2000
5. Lower Benue River Basin Development Authority	10.106	1000-2000
6. Cross River Basin Development Authority.	3.078	1500-2000+
7. Anambra-Imo River Basin Development Authority	2.932	1500-2000+
8. Niger River Basin Development Authority	17.407	750-2000
9. Ogun-Oshun River Basin Development Authority	5.771	1000-2000
10. Benin-Owena River Basin Development Authority	5.870	1250-2000+
11. Niger Delta River Basin Development Authority	1.614	2000+

Source: Adeniji, F.A., 1982, Paper presented to the Fourth Afro-Asian International Conference on Irrigation and Drainage, (unpublished).

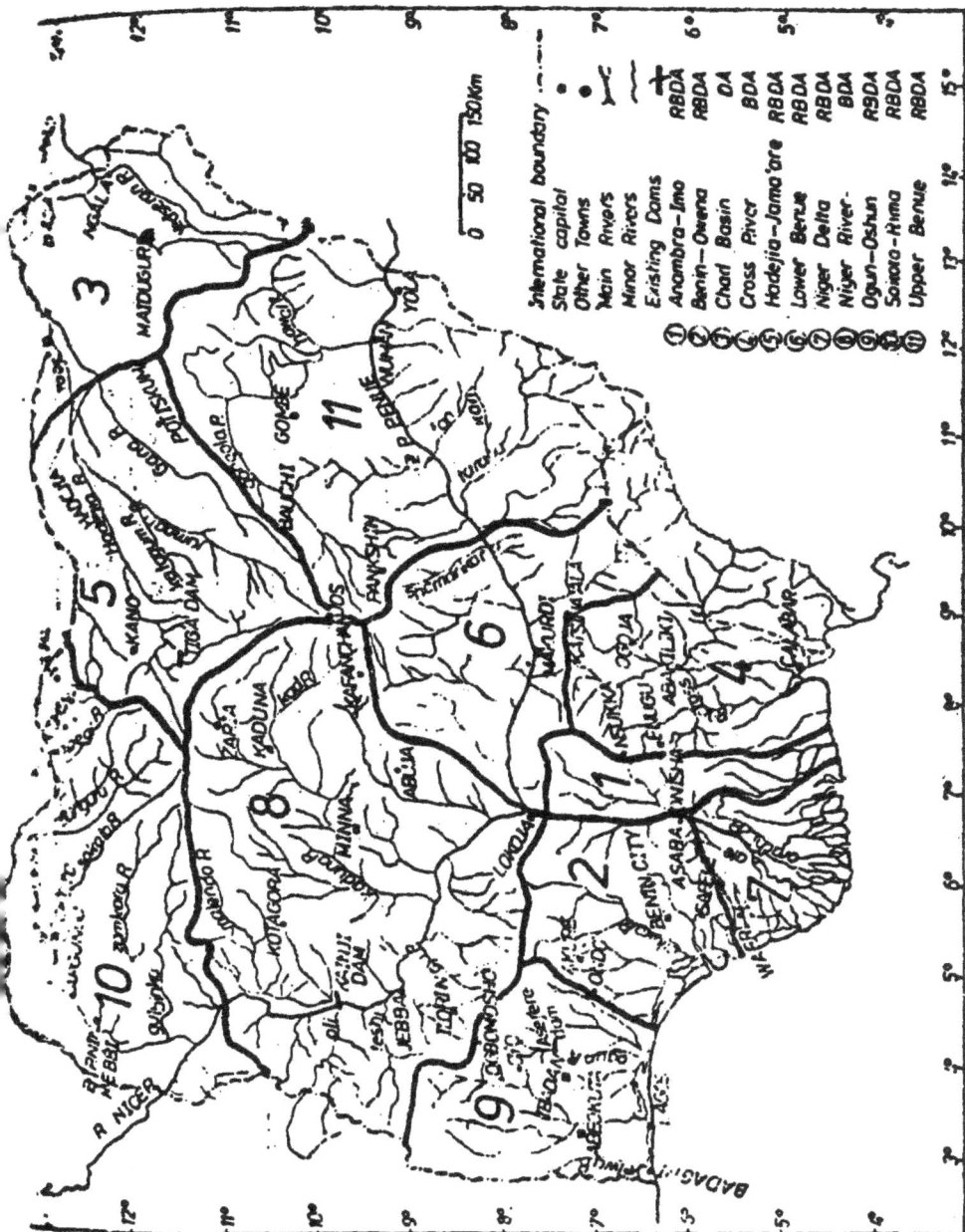

Fig. 16.1. Surface water sources and River Basin Development Authorities (R.B.D.A.) of Nigeria

Fourth National Development Plan (1980-85), a total of N5.620 billion was allocated to crops, N2.266 billion to irrigation and water resources development, and N0.675 billion to forestry.[3]

Objectives

The UBRBDA's function is to develop surface and underground water resources for agricultural, industrial and domestic purposes, and for rural development. This study seeks mainly to examine the extent to which the UBRBDA has harnessed the water resources of the Upper Benue River basin to increase crop production. In achieving this end, the study looks at the impact of the Authorities' agricultural programmes on rural employment, the local farmer's participation in the river basin projects, and their response to mechanised farming techniques. Table 16.2 shows the estimated development possibilities and benefits derivable from the UBRBDA projects. The overall contribution to national development through agriculture by 1985 was anticipated at about N160 million per year by the proposed budgets.

Methodology

The study covers the various projects that have been started in the Upper Benue River basin since the inception of the scheme in 1979. Some 20 farms were randomly selected from the operational area for primary data. Secondary data were obtained from the officials of the River Basin Authority and the Water Resources Ministry.

ESTABLISHMENT OF PILOT FARMS

Crop production ranked first in the Authorities' list of objectives with regard to the utilisation of the river basin land area. The mechanism adopted to achieve this objective was to establish pilot farms (11 of them in 1979) in various locations within the operational areas. The pilot farms were used in part by the Authority as demonstration plots to educate farmers in the use of modern equipment in crop production, and were leased in part to them for private individual cultivation. Essentially rice and maize were to be produced, and 98 per cent of the total cultivated land areas under rainfed and irrigated conditions was used for the

Table 16.2. Estimated Development Possibilities and Benefits Derivable from the Various Basins and Projects

Basin	Project	Area Proposed to be Developed by Envisaged Schemes (hectares)	Ultimate Annual Yield (tonnes)
1. Benue	Dasin Hausa	150,000	to be assesed
	Yola Reclamation	1,200	29,850
	Mayo-Ine	6,000 (30,000 ultimate)	104,520
	Kilange	17,000	to be assesed
2. Gongola	Dadinkowa	44,000	496,800
	Dagel	5,685	156,000
	Tallum	400	6,968
3. Donga	Donga Scheme	14,896	307,650
	Donga small scale Irrigation project	3,800	77,938
	Suntai	8,000	70;000
4. Taraba	Gassol irrigation (Lower Taraba)	35,000	300,000
	Upper Taraba (Shina-Jigawal)	8,000	40,000
5. Mambilla Plateau	Shina-Jigawal (development)	155,000	144,770*
6. Minor irrigation schemes	In Gongola and Bauchi States under Smaller catchments/pumped irrigation Scheme	Being estimated	

*Includes tea, coffee, and kola nuts to a considerable degree.
Source: Upper Benue River Basin Development Authority, Performance report for the period October 1979-August 1981.

production of these two crops. Table 16.3 shows the total land area brought under cultivation of rice and maize in the various pilot farms during the 1981 cropping season.

In the 1981 cropping season a total of 3,352 hectares (950 for maize, and 2,402 for rice) were cultivated. This represents a proportional share of 28% and 72% respectively of the total cultivated land area.

Table 16.3: Cultivated Hectarage in UBRBDA Pilot Farms, 1981

Pilot Farm	Authority's		Farmer's		Total	
	Maize	Rice	Maize	Rice	Maize	Rice
	(hectares)		(hectares)		(hectares)	
1. Bagel	5	5	39	105	44	110
2. Dadinkowa	1	6	82	33	83	39
3. Tallum	4	3	260	19	264	22
4. Gurin	—	25	—	10	—	35
5. Lau	—	50	—	20	—	70
6. Gassol	32	124	54	114	86	238
7. Donga	13	8	70	40	83	48
8. Bamtaji	—	100	—	150	—	250
9. Kura	70	—	70	—	140	—
10. Mayo-Ine	250	—	—	—	250	—
11. Traditional areas through tractor hiring units	—	—	—	1,590	—	1,590
Total	375	321	575	2081	950	2402

Source: Upper Benue River Basin Development Authority, *Annual Report* Yola, 1981.

Crop Production and Yields

Since the establishment of the pilot farms in 1979, yearly productivity increase has been recorded. In the 1979 cropping season, a total of 64.9 tonnes of rice was obtained in all the pilot farms. This figure rose to 182.3 tonnes in the 1980 cropping season, representing a 181% increase over the previous year. In the 1981 cropping season, 5,419 tonnes of rice were recorded as yield. This represents an increase of 2,872% over the previous year (Table 16.4).

Increases in maize yields were similarly recorded during the period: 97.7 tonnes in 1979, 158.8 tonnes in 1980—an increase of 62.5%, and 1,711 tonnes in 1981—an increase of 977% over 1980. Although there are no supporting statistics, all the farmers interviewed indicated that they had experienced increases in yields over those obtained on their own private farms before cultivating on the UBRBD plots.

Table 16.4: Crop Production by Participating Farmers and the Authority (in tonnes)

Pilot farm	1979		1980		1981	
	Maize	Rice	Maize	Rice	Maize	Rice
	(tonnes)		(tonnes)		(tonnes)	
1. Bagel	—	11.7	—	10.5	85	388
2. Gassol	11.0	13.3	53.6	84.6	174	144
3. Gurin	—	23.2	—	11.8	—	5
4. Lau	—	—	—	—	—	10
5. Dadinkowa	7.2	4.4	69.7	39.6	164	155
6. Bamtaji	—	—	—	—	—	575
7. Kura	—	—	—	—	140	—
8. Donga	3.5	12.3	1,5	34.8	166	110
9. Tallum	76.0	—	34.0	1.0	482	150
10. Mayo-Ine	—	—	—	—	500	—
11. Traditional areas under tractor hiring units	—	—	—	—	—	3,650
Total	97.7	64.9	158.8	182.3	1,711	5,187

Source: Upper Benue River Basin Development Authority, *Performance Report*, (October 1979 – August 1981).

Extension Programmes and On-the-Job Training

To achieve the objectives of the River Basin Authority it was deemed necessary to enlist the local farmer's interests and participation at different stages of the scheme, such as project selection, execution, and implementation. To this end several field days and demonstration classes were organised to train farmers in—

a) proper land preparation;

b) use of high yielding varieties resistant to pests and diseases;

c) correct levels of fertiliser application, types of fertilisers and times of application;

d) plant diseases and times of planting; and

e) crop protection methods against pests, diseases and handling of chemicals and equipment.

Farmers' Participation

Local people, farm and non-farm, usually under-employed or unemployed, showed considerable interest in the programme and the participation rate among them has increased since the scheme began in 1979. Table 16.5 shows the number of participating farmers in the scheme from 1979 to 1981.

The total number of farmers that participated on all the pilot farms in the 1979 cropping season was 171. This number rose to 451 in the 1980 cropping season representing an increase about 164% over the previous year. In the 1981 cropping season a total of 1,194 farmers participated on all the pilot farms. This represents an increase of 165% over the number of participants in the previous year (1980).

Almost all the participating farmers on the projects engaged in maize and rice cultivation.

The farmer participation programmes were strongly supported by extending the following services free or at subsidised rates:

a) land preparation, including ploughing and harrowing and (services given free of charge);

b) seed, fertiliser and agro-chemicals (given at subsidised rates);

c) water charges for irrigation (given at subsidised rates);

Table 16.5: Number of Farmers Participating on the Various Pilot Farms

Sl. No.	Pilot farm	1979	1980	1981
		(Number of farmers participating)		
1.	Bagel	30	79	388
2.	Dadin Kowa	41	153	175
3.	Tallum	30	71	150
4.	Gurin	—	—	5
5.	Lau	---	—	10
6.	Gassol	40	63	144
7.	Donga	20	45	140
8.	Bamtaji	—	—	30
9.	Kura	—	—	60
10.	Mayo-Inc	—	- -	31
11.	Lake Geriyo	10	40	61
	Total	171	451	1,194

Source: Upper Benue River Basin Development Authority *Performance Report*, (October 1979—August 1981).

d) tractor hiring through tractor units established at strategic locations in the project areas (at subsidised rates); and

e) technical services and supervision of operations (rendered free of charge).

Modern Production Techniques

The extension programmes were coupled with the provision of good quality seeds and planting materials, and 'on-the-job training' in the cultivation of selected crops, mostly maize and rice. The use of tractors and other farm machinery and implements and fertilisers were actively practised. Tables 16.6 and 16.7 show the production methods used by the farmers before and after the introduction of the Upper Benue River Basin Development Projects.

Only 25% of the farmers in the Lake Geriyo Vegetable Garden, 30% of those in Mayo-Ine pilot farms, 15% of those in Gassol pilot farm, 25% of those in Tallum pilot farm and 15% of those in Donga pilot farm indicated that they had used fertilisers on their own farm plots before the introduction of the projects. But they also added that fertilisers were not always available and when they were, the quantities were small and not available at the right time.

Table 16.6: Proportion of Respondents on the Pilot Farms Using Modern Farming Techniques before the Scheme

| Modern Farming Techniques | Pilot farms | | | | |
	Lake Geriyo	Mayo-Ine	Gassol	Tallum	Donga
1. New and improved planting materials (seeds/seedlings)	—	—	—	—	—
2. Fertilisers	25%	30%	15%	25%	15%
3. Irrigation facilities	—	—	—	—	—
4. Modern farming implements (tractors, combines and other farm machinery)	—	—	—	—	—

Source: Derived from questionnaire developed for this study.

Table 16.7: Proportion of Respondents Using Modern Farming
Techniques after Introduction of the Scheme

	Pilot Farms				
Modern Farming Techniques	Lake Geriyo	Mayo-Ine	Gassol	Tallum	Donga
1. New and improved planting materials (seeds/seedlings)	100%	100%	100%	100%	100%
2. Fertilisers	100%	100%	100%	100%	100%
3. Irrigation facilities	100%	—	100%	—	100%
4. Modern farming implements (tractors, combines and other farm machinery)	100%	100%	100%	100%	100%

Source: Derived from questionnaire developed for this study.

Farmers were interviewed as to whether they used modern farming techniques on the irrigation projects. All of them in the various pilot farms, except those in Tallum and Mayo-Ine (who use the rainfed system of cultivation), indicated that they used new and improved planting materials, fertilisers and modern farming implements, such as tractors, combines and other farm machinery.

Size of Farm Holdings

The farmers' farms before the introduction of the UBRBD projects were very fragmented and scattered although the average farm size was larger than the one allocated to each farmer on the various projects.

Tables 16.8 and 16.9 show the average farm size of the local farmers both before and after the introduction of the UBRBD projects.

Before the introduction of the Upper Benue River Basin Development Projects, the land in most of the areas was sub-divided and fragmented, with labour organisation being a simple family affair. The techniques of production were also traditional.

Of the eleven pilot farms of the Upper Benue River Basin Development Authority, only Gassol and Lake Geriyo pilot farms had non-farm rural employees before the introduction of the scheme. Therefore it was only the farmers on these pilot farms who indicated an increased average farm size. These groups of farmers were landless before the introduction of the projects.

The farmers in the lake Geriyo Vegetable Garden (pilot farm) were mostly petty traders before the introduction of the projects. This group of farmers had no access to any land area. The other group of farmers in the Gassol pilot farms were mostly fishermen before the introduction of the project and were persuaded to farm plots of land with the introduction of the projects.

From an analysis of Tables 16.8 and 16.9, it can be seen that 95% of the farmers in Lake Geriyo Vegetable Garden, 55% in Mayo-Ine pilot farm, 10% in Donga pilot farm, 20% in Gassol and 10% in

Table 16.8: Average Farm Size of Project Farmers on Their Former Non-irrigated Farms

Average Farm Size (hectares)	Pilot Farms				
	Lake Geriyo	Mayo-Ine	Gassol	Tallum	Donga
	(Per cent of farmers responding)				
0-5	95%	55%	20%	10%	10%
6-10	5%	35%	—	40%	75%
Above 10	—	10%	—	50%	15%

Source: Derived from questionnaire developed for this study.

Table 16.9: Average Farm Size of Project Farmers in Pilot Farms

Average Farm Size (hectares)	Pilot Farms				
	Lake Geriyo	Mayo-Ine	Gassol	Tallum	Donga
	(Per cent of farmers responding)				
1-2	100%	65%	25%	25%	10%
3-4	—	20%	55%	65%	75%
5 and above	—	15%	20%	10%	15%

Source: Derived from questionnaire developed for this study.

Tallum, indicated that they had a scattered farm ranging in size from about 0 to 5 hectares before the introduction of the projects. Thirty-five per cent of the farmers in Mayo-Ine, 40% in Tallum and 75% in Donga pilot farms reported farms ranging in size from 6 to 10 hectares before the introduction of the projects. Similarly, 50% of the farmers in the Tallum pilot farm said they had farm plots ranging from 10 hectares and above. It is therefore evident that the pilot farms are smaller in size than those earlier owned by the farmers.

CONCLUSIONS AND POLICY IMPLICATIONS

This study has dealt with the impact of the Upper Benue River Basin projects on agriculture or, to be more specific on maize and rice production. The study shows that given the proper guidance and inputs the local farmer can be much more productive under an intensive irrigation system than he could be under an extensive rainfed system of cultivation. Essentially, this means that economic progress in agriculture can be made under small farm-size conditions. The low level of technology in the less developed countries compared to that in the developed often gives rise to questions about the desirability of increasing the size of farms.[4] But this study has shown that the relevant variables in transforming traditional agriculture in most less developed countries, such as new varieties, increased use of fertiliser, and improved water and crop practices, involve no direct economies of scale and could be suitable for use on small farms.

Secondly, this study has shown that the current early stage of industrialisation in Nigeria, associated with rapid rural-urban migration, can also lead to the transformation of the rural sector. This rural transformation through river basin developments can be used to reverse out-migration from rural to urban. The policy can be used to check the serious unemployment and underemployment in urban areas, and minimalise the drain on public revenue since authorities try to maintain minimal levels of urban services for rapidly expanding populations.[5]

Thirdly, the high rate of growth of participating farmers in the projects within the first three years of the River Basin's operations and the ease with which the participants are able to adopt the new technologies in crop production reveals a rich but unutilised stock of indigenous knowledge which could be put to profitable use. Given, therefore, the high level of under-employment in the non-farm sectors of the rural areas, it might be possible to restructure the rural income distribution pattern, and solve some of the nation's food problems by employing in agriculture the hordes of under-employed in the rural areas.

NOTES

1. 'Towards self-sufficiency in food production,' *Nigeria Illustrated*, Special Issue, October 1982, p 11, Jeromelaiho and Associates, Ikeja, Nigeria.
2. For a detailed analysis of the area, topography and objectives of the River Basin Developments, see 'The river basin developments,' *Federal Military Government Decree 1976*, Federal Ministry of Information, Lagos, 1976.
3. B.N. Okigbo, 1981, 'Technical and environmental problems of irrigation and mechanisation, and possible solutions in Nigeria's Green Revolution Programme,' Paper presented at the First National Seminar on the Green Revolution in Nigeria, Ahmadu Bello University, Zaria, Nigeria.
4. K.L. Bachman *et al.*, 1967, 'Economies of farm size' in Southworth and Johnston (eds.), *Agricultural Development and Economic Growth*, Cornell, ch 7.
5. Lyn Squire, 1981, *Employment Policy in Developing Countries —A Survey of Issues and Evidence*, Oxford, ch 7.

REFERENCES

Bachman, K.L. *et al.*, 1967, 'Economies of farm size' in Southworth and Johnston (eds.), *Agricultural Development and Economic Growth*, Cornell.

Berry, R.A. and N.R. Cline, 1979, *Agrarian Structure and Productivity in Developing Countries*, John Hopkins University, Baltimore, Maryland.

Chambers, R. and M. Howes, 'The use of indigenous technical knowledge in development,' *IDS Bulletin*, vol 10 no 2.

Etuk, E.G. and G.O.I. Abalu, 1981, 'River Basin Development Northern Nigeria: A Case Study of the Bakolori Project'.

Federal Ministry of Information, Lagos, 1976, 'The river basin developments, *'Federal Military Government Decree 1976*, Lagos, Nigeria.

Federal Ministry of Agriculture and Natural Resources, 1974, *Agricultural Development in Nigeria, 1973-1985*, Joint Planning Committee, Lagos, Nigeria.

Nigeria Illustrated, October 1982, 'Towards self-sufficiency in food production,' Ikeja, Nigeria.

Okigbo, B.N. 1981. Technical and environmental problems of irrigation and mechanisation, and possible solutions in Nigeria's Green Revolution Programme. Paper presented at the First National Seminar on the Green Revolution in Nigeria, Ahmadu Bello University, Zaria, Nigeria.

Squire, Lyn, 1981. *Employment Policy in Developing Countries—A Survey of Issues and Evidence*, Oxford.

Upper Benue River Basin Development Authority, 1981, *Performance Report for the Period October 1979-August 1981*, Yola, Nigeria.

Upper Benue River Basin Development Authority, 1981, *Annual Report*, Yola, Nigeria.

Wallace, Tina, 1978, Rural Development through Irrigation: Studies in a Town on the Kano River Project. Centre for Social and Economic Research, Ahmadu Bello University, Zaria, Nigeria (mimeographed).

CHAPTER 17

Implications of the New Educational Policy for Rural Development in Nigeria

In October 1982, a new educational policy came into operation in Nigeria. The main aim of this policy, known as 6-3-3-4, is total reorientation of attitudes towards education as a whole in the country.

Current Conception of Education

At present, education is regarded as an elitist good, a channel through which you graduate from using your hands to using your pen. In other words, the moment the educatee receives the education, he is not likely to take a job that will involve him in serious physical exertions. This is because he automatically assumes (or the system makes him assume) that his place of work is an office and, that too, an office in the urban area. Of course, this does not mean that no educatee will become involved in vocational or technical occupations, but the fact remains that those who enter such occupations are regarded as less intelligent than those who do not. The natural consequence of this attitude is a reduction in skilled manpower, especially at the lower and middle levels. At the same time, the system over-produces unskilled educatees with high expectations in life, who feel they are too well qualified to work in rural areas. As a result, development programmes suffer because the essential skilled personnel—technicians, nurses, teachers, etc.—are always in short supply and the few available frown at the prospect of working in rural areas. The effect of the educational system, therefore, is not only to deprive rural areas of the educated people they might produce, but also to discourage other educated people from living and working in these areas. The total effect is to leave the rural areas further deprived of even such basic necessities as water, medical facilities, schools, and decent housing. To obtain some idea of the extent of this deprivation, let us look at the distribution of educational resources in one of the states of the Federation, Kano State.

EDUCATIONAL RESOURCES IN KANO STATE

Population Distribution

According to the 1963 census, Kano State had a population of about 5.7 million people. Of this number, 367,657 or 6.5% live in urban areas. The rest, 93.5%, live in rural areas.

Educational Resource Allocation

According to the 1970/71 budget, the total recurrent expenditure was £14,822,947 (approx N 30 mm). Education received the largest allocation of funds—£1,625,468 or 11% of the total. In terms of capital expenditure for the same year, £2,664,240 were allocated to the entire social sector, out of which education again received the largest share—£1,044,285 or 40% of the total sectoral allocation: Table 17.1 gives a more detailed picture of the situation. Looking at the figures presented in Tables 17.1 and 17.2, it is obvious that high priority was attached to educational development in the state. Let us now see how the financial resources were used to provide the requisite educational facilities.

The most interesting aspect of Tables 17.3 and 17.4 is the striking urban bias in the allocation and distribution of educational resources. If you take primary schools, for example, Kano metropolis with a population of only 6.5% (less than 10%) of the total population had 49 schools out of 285 or 17% of the total. Now, the total number of school aged children (5-9 year olds) in the state at that time was 853,065. Of this number 48,165 lived

Table 17.1: Actual Recurrent Expenditure by Ministry (1970/71)

Total expenditure	£14,822,947
Governor's office	371,757
Judiciary	196,488
Public Service Commission	24,025
Agriculture and related resources	547,196
Education	1,625,468
Establishment	52,600
Finance	136,343
Health and Social Welfare	1,073,483
Trade and Industry	34,132
Works and Survey	1,257,132

Source: *Kano State Statistical Yearbook*, 1970, p. 52.

Table 17.2: Actual Capital Expenditure by Sector (1970)

Social Sector	£2,664,240
Education	
Buildings	602,919
Capital loans and grants payment	441,366
Urban and Rural Water Supply	862,835
Health	
Buildings	514,401
Hospital equipment	74,594
Development Sector	£4,752,821
Agriculture	
Buildings	40,985
Credit and other services	750,889
Fisheries & livestock	118,071
Irrigation	651,547
Forestry	89,399
Others	69,379
Road Development	1,049,451

Source: *Kano State Statistical Yearbook*, 1970, p. 53.

**Table 17.3: Distribution of Educational Facilities
in the State (1970/71)**

No. of Schools in the State (1970)

All types	310
Primary	285
Secondary	16
Teacher training	7
Technical	1

Distribution of Primary Schools by Administrative Area (1970)

Administrative Area	Population	No. of Primary Schools
Kano Metropolitan	365,000	49
Gwarzo	1,110,400	38
Danbatta	1,299,100	38
Birnin Kudu	1,437,500	39
Rano	1,239,900	39
Gumel	657,000	22
Hadejia	251,200	35
Kazaure	313,500	15

Source: *Kano State Statistical Yearbook*, 1970, p. 97.

**Table 17.4: Distribution of Post-Primary Institutions
by Administrative Areas (1970)**

Administrative Area	No. of Post-Primary Schools
All administrative areas	25
Kano Metropolis	14
Danbatta	1
Gwarzo	2
Birnin Kudu	2
Rano	3
Gumel	1
Hadejia	1
Kazaure	1

Source: *Kano State Statistical Yearbook*, 1970, p. 105.

in the urban area while the rest—804,900—lived in the rural area. With 49 schools and 48,165 children, the chances of an urban child obtaining admission was 1983. On the other hand, the chance of a rural child gaining admission in a rural school was 1:3500 (i.e., 236 schools for 804,900 school-aged children). In other words, the urban child's chances of going to school were 3.5 times greater than the rural child's.

As for the post-primary institutions, there were altogether 25 such institutions in the state in 1970. However, 14 of them or 56% of the total, were situated in Kano metropolis alone. The urban bias here is too obvious to merit further analysis.

Distribution of Teachers

In 1970, there was a total of 1,923 primary school teachers in the state. However, 564 of these or 30% of the total, taught in the urban area. In other words, the urban area with a population of far less than 10% of the total population of the state had 17% of all the primary schools in the state, 56% of the post-primary institutions, and 30% of the teachers.

Teacher Quality

Let us now examine the quality of the teachers themselves. Teachers in Nigeria were graded 1 to 4 in descending order of qualifications and experience. A grade-1 teacher was one who had spent 8 years in a post-primary institution (5 years in a Teacher Training College and 3 years in Advanced Teacher Training College). A grade-2 teacher had spent 5 years in a teacher training college, while a grade-3 teacher had spent 3 years and passed an examination at the end of those three years. A grade-4 teacher, on the other hand, had not passed the examination at the end of his 3-year course at the teacher training college. An ungraded teacher was one who had not attended a teacher training college, and was often a primary school leaver who could not gain admission into a higher institution. Let us now examine Table 17.5.

The most obvious fact that emerges from this table is that the higher the teacher's qualifications and experience, the less likely that he would be teaching in a rural school. In other words, the less qualified a teacher, the more likely he would be teaching in

Table 17.5: Distribution of Primary School Teachers
by Qualifications (1970)

Administrative Area	All Qualifications	Better than Grade II	Grade II	Grade III	Grade IV	Other
Metropolis	564	5	334	61	4	151
Gwarzo	257	—	138	24	1	94
Danbatta	234	—	112	24	1	97
Birnin Kudu	261	—	88	41	2	130
Rano	168	—	50	18	2	98
Gumel	121	—	53	17	—	51
Hadejia	235	—	111	19	3	102
Kazaure	83	—	36	11	2	33
All Areas	1,923	5	922	215	15	756

Source: *Kano State Statistical Yearbook*, 1970, p. 105.

a rural school. This is clearly shown by the fact that all the five better-than-grade two teachers were teaching in the urban area— not one of them was teaching in a rural area. On the other hand, 73% of the grade-four teachers and 80% of the ungraded, untrained teachers were teaching in rural schools.

Equity and Efficiency Implications

The foregoing observations have serious equity and efficiency implications. In terms of equity, even though the urban centre had far less than 10% of the population of the state, it claimed a disproportionate share of the available educational resources. Furthermore, as just seen above, the best qualified teachers were also found in the urban schools. The urban child thus not only had better chances of going to school (almost 4.0 times greater than the rural child's), but he also had better chances of doing well and proceeding to the next level because his school was better equipped than the rural school. Thus the urban child was better placed to move socially up in life than the rural child.

In terms of allocative efficiency, scarce resources are not efficiently utilised when most are concentrated in one place instead of where they are most needed and more apt to be utilised more effectively. We have already seen that the government paid particular attention to educational development by providing 11% of the recurrent expenditure and 40% of the sectoral capital expenditure. But we have also just seen that most of this was concentrated on only 6.5% of the total population, thereby depriving 93.5% of adequate educational resources. Apart from the equity aspect, this is certainly not the most efficient way of allocating scarce resources.

Developmental Implications

In addition to the equity and efficiency implications, the developmental implication of this lopsided resource allocation policy deserves attention. Because the bias was in favour of the urban area, the rural area was neglected in the provision of basic amenities, the main function of which is not only to improve the standard of living of the people of a given area, but also to attract others to come and live and work in the area. A paradox seems to have developed however; firstly, few skilled people are willing to work in rural areas due to the absence of these facilities. But secondly, now that the government wants to provide these facilities to the rural areas, the skilled people required to install and maintain them are reluctant to go because the facilities they want do not exist. For example, the government wants to equip the rural schools with better qualified teachers but such teachers will not go because the rural schools are not good or because health facilities are poor. More qualified health personnel may not want to go because there are no good schools available for their children. In other words, the people who are supposed to go and develop the rural areas are reluctant to do so because these areas are undeveloped!

THE NEW EDUCATIONAL POLICY

What the N.E.P. aims at, as mentioned earlier, is a change in total attitude towards education. In other words, the aim is to increase the supply of skilled manpower with the right mental attitude towards work and the developmental needs of the country. The policy hopes to achieve this goal through the following measures: The old system of primary, secondary and university levels still remains. Under this system a child spends seven years in primary school, five years in secondary school and three to five years in the University. Those who failed to gain admission to a secondary school could still secure admission to a teacher training or vocational college in that order. In other words, the main aim of every primary school leaver was first to secure admission to a secondary school because it was through the secondary school that one could more easily continue on to university. Furthermore, secondary education could, if nothing else, secure one a job in an office in the government or the modern sector. The system of rewards, incentives, and recognition was one which favoured the secondary school, liberal arts route.

Under the new system a child spends six years in primary school, after which he proceeds to a junior secondary school where he spends three years. From a junior secondary school he proceeds to a senior secondary school where he spends another three years. Thereafter he proceeds to university and spends four years. The distinguishing feature of the new policy is that every child in the junior secondary school level must take a combination of courses that reflect the developmental needs of the country. The courses are categorised into liberal arts, commercial, technical, and science, and each student is compelled to take courses from each of these categories. Unlike the old system where a student used to be given arts or science courses only, now every student must take a bit of each. The idea is that by the end of the three years, a student should have fully ascertained where his aptitude lies and will consequently proceed to the senior secondary school of his aptitude. Unlike the junior secondary school, the senior secondary schools specialise in different fields— science, technical, commercial, and so forth. For example, if a student discovers that his aptitude lies in the technical field he will proceed to one of the technical secondary schools and (probably) later to one of the universities of technology. If, on the other hand, his interest lies in knowing what happened, say, during the colonial period, he is likely to proceed to one of the liberal arts senior secondary schools.

You may ask what happens to a primary school leaver who cannot secure admission to a junior secondary school. In this case he may go to one of the vocational or teacher training colleges.

If, however, a secondary school student cannot proceed to the next level, he may secure admission in a technical college or polytechnic or find employment, perhaps, with the Rural Electricity Board, or wherever his skill may be required. The important point is that he has acquired a more readily utilisable skill.

Implication of N.E.P. for Rural Development

The question now is, how can the New Educational Policy help in promoting rural development? An immediate consequence of the new policy is expansion of educational facilities at all levels. For example, the Kano State Government only recently opened 126 new junior secondary schools in the State, most of them in the rural area. Furthermore, the admission policy to these schools is such that each school has a catchment area from which to draw the bulk of its students. In addition, a school must not be more than a certain kilometer radius from a child's home.

What this means for the rural area is that increased educational provisions will increase the rural child's chances of going to school (by reducing the present ratio of 3.5:1), thereby ultimately reducing inequality in the distribution of income in the country. In other words, the new system is not only likely to reduce the present inequality in the distribution of educational resources between urban and rural areas, it is also likely to ensure that scarce resources are more efficiently allocated by investing them in areas where they can be more effectively utilised. Thus, in terms of equity and efficiency, the new policy is likely to benefit the rural sector. Furthermore, the fact that a child will now attend school at home or nearer home, increases his chances of staying in his home village rather than going to the urban centre in search of employment or a better life. This, in turn, should reduce rural brain drain, thereby increasing not only the quantity but also the quality of the skilled people working in rural areas. This, in turn, should make it possible for development programmes to be more successfully executed in rural areas. Consequently, rural areas should become more attractive to live and work in, thereby helping to solve the paradox mentioned earlier.

Of course, all these possibilities can only be hypothesised at the moment, because the policy has just come into effect. On the surface at least, the rural area stands to benefit from N.E.P. It must, at the same time, be emphasised that the degree to which this will happen depends on the continued willingness of the government to pursue rural development programmes vigorously. In other words, unless the prospect of securing a job in an area is bright, the educatees will ultimately flock to the cities. On the other hand, unless the skilled people are available and willing to work in rural areas, rural development programmes are not likely to succeed. The N.E.P. is only likely to take care of one aspect of the problem—increased availability of skilled manpower.

CHAPTER 18

Cocoa Rehabilitation Programme in Nigeria, 1972-1981

An Export to Check Rural-Urban Drift and to Reduce Poverty Among Peasant Cocoa Farmers

Until the advent of the oil boom, the main source of income for millions of farmers in the southern forest zones of Nigeria, namely, Ondo, Oyo, Ogun and Bendel states was cocoa. Other producing areas included Cross River, Imo, Kwara, Lagos, Anambra, Gongola and Benue, listed in order of production. Cocoa was also Nigeria's greatest foreign exchange earner. Nigeria accounted for about 21% of the world's total production and, for a long time, was second only to Ghana. Between 1958 and 1965 Nigeria's cocoa production increased steadily from 88,645 tonnes to 310,176 tonnes annually. The steady increase was the result of large-scale plantings in the 1950s because of the good prevailing producer prices and effective Government subsidised pest and disease control programmes.

However, the period 1961-1969 witnessed lower world markets and producer prices, which compelled many farmers to abandon their plantations as far as maintenance practices were concerned, and to reject all propaganda with respect to new plantings or replanting. This situation caused cocoa farmers untold hardships and led to a very serious downward trend, so much so that between 1974

Table 18.1: Comparative Production Statistics of Cocoa Beans by the Countries of the Production Alliance 1969/70
1978/79 Seasons (all figures in metric tonnes)

Producing Countries	1969/70	1970/71	1971/72	1972/73	1973/74	1974/75	1975/76	1976/77	1977/78	1978/79
Ghana	414,300	406,000	470,000	415,700	343,000	381,600	396,000	324,000	276,000	265,000
Nigeria	223,000	307,900	256,600	241,300	214,900	214,500	217,500	166,400	204,400	133,400
Brazil	200,600	182,400	164,300	158,700	242,400	265,500	251,100	226,200	279,300	306,000
Ivory Coast	180,700	179,600	225,800	185,400	210,000	241,000	227,300	230,000	303,600	312,000
Cameroons	108,300	112,000	123,000	106,900	110,000	118,000	96,000	82,000	106,000	108,000
Ecuador	55,000	71,600	64,900	54,000	71,300	75,300	60,000	72,300	78,000	78,000
Togo	23,600	27,900	29,000	18,600	16,500	15,000	17,800	15,500	16,700	13,000
Sao Tome & Principe	9,700	10,400	10,400	11,300	10,400	7,900	7,000	5,500	7,000	7,000
Gabon	4,700	5,000	5,300	5,000	5,000	5,000	4,000	3,500	3,600	4,000
Trinidad & Tobago	5,400	4,100	4,500	4,800	3,400	4,700	3,000	400	4,000	3,000
Total	1,225,300	1,306,900	1,353,800	1,206,700	1,226,900	1,328,500	1,279,700	1,129,400	1,278,600	1,229,400

Note : All figures are approximated to the nearest hundred.
Source: Nigerian Cocoa Board, *Statistical Bulletin*, October 1980, p. 36.

and 1978, Nigeria had fallen to fourth position with Ghana, Brazil and the Ivory Coast leading. The purported reasons for Nigeria's drastic reduction in cocoa production and the consequent decline in cash returns to farmers were:

a) Ageing cocoa trees among the early plantings.

b) Ageing cocoa farmers themselves, because at that time most of their children went to school or took up appointments in urban centres.

c) Poor maintenance practices.

d) Negative attitude of young men to investment in cocoa farming.

e) Increasing incidence of cocoa pests and diseases.

f) Lack of credit facilities from the Government or financial institutions.

g) Scarcity and increasing cost of labourers.

h) Unfavourable weather conditions.

i) Opportunities in urban centres brought about by the oil boom.

The serious downward trend of this important foreign exchange earner and the plight of the affected peasant farmers caused the Federal Military Government of Nigeria much concern. It decided that something must be done quickly to restore the cocoa industry to the pre-eminence which it had hitherto enjoyed. This decision was also prompted by the inherent danger in total dependence on oil, which was booming at that time as the country's main foreign exchange earner and was also luring rural people to urban centres. The movement decided therefore to embark on a massive rehabilitation programme for Nigeria's main agricultural products, especially cocoa, to provide employment and cash for the cocoa farmers, check drift to urban centres and, above all to improve the traditional sources of foreign exchange earnings.

With respect to cocoa, the number one cash crop, the FMG sought and obtained the assistance of the World Bank to enable it to embark on widespread cocoa development projects in the main cocoa-producing states of Ondo Oyo, and Ogun states. This programme was christened Cocoa Phase I and started in October 1971 with a World Bank loan of N 4.75 millions for replanting and planting an estimated 17,600 hectares.

Table 18.2: Cocoa Development Programme: World Bank Appraisal Targets (ha)

State	1972	1973	1974	1975	1976	1977	1978	1979	1980	1981	Total
Oyo	980	1817	3527	5344	7126	6700	6700	—	—	—	32,194
Ogun	356	661	1285	1943	2591	2186	2470	—	—	—	11,492
Ondo	891	1652	3207	4848	6478	8000	8000	—	—	—	33,086
Bendel	—	—	—	600	1100	1100	1200	—	—	—	4,000

Source: FDA, 'Cocoa and oil palm dev. programme in Nigeria,' 1972-1979, p. 4.

In consideration of the recommendations of the World Bank Reconnaisance Mission in November 1972, it was decided to increase the scope of the programme by another 25,300 hectares and to include the number four producing state, Bendel. To achieve this, the government entered into negotiations for another World Bank loan of 13.20 million Nigerian Pound in June 1974. With this loan, the second phase (Cocoa Phase II) of the Cocoa Development Programme commenced in 1975 with Bendel state participating together with Ondo, Oyo and Ogun states.

Table 18.3: Assistance Arrangements for Cocoa Small Holders (ha)

Year	0	1	2	3	4	5	Total
Cash Loan							
Grants N Pound	68	32	100	52	12	10	274
Seedlings	900		900				1800
Fertilisers (kg)	50		50				100
Insecticides							
(litres)	2	2	2	2	2	2	12

Source: FDA, 'Cocoa and oil palm dev. programme in Nigeria,' 1972-1979, p. 9.

The two phases of the development programme were planned to meet the needs of cocoa farmers with small holdings varying from 0.8 to 1.6 ha. with credit components never before enjoyed by them. However, to ensure easy loan recovery, it was mandatory for participating farmers to be members of registered cooperative societies. The loans were expected to be granted by the state governments along with subsidised inputs such as improved planting materials, fertilisers, pesticides and, importantly too, supervision. In total, the FMG's objective was to encourage farmers to resume modern husbandry techniques in their plantations, replant declining plantations and engage in newer plantings with improved and early maturing strains of cocoa to substantially increase exportable cocoa. In keeping with this objective, it contributed 25% to the total development costs.

Considering the magnitude of the programme and to ensure its success, the Federal Department of Agriculture set up a Monitoring and Evaluation Unit (MEU). It was charged with these responsibilities:

a) Ensure high crop husbandry by participating farmers.
b) Ensure proper procurement and disbursement procedures.
c) Collect data to determine project performance.
d) Evolve the basis for a stable progress reporting system.
e) Assist in the identification and performance of new projects.

An evaluation carried out in 1976 rendered the following progress report:

Ondo State   —115% of the planned target
Oyo State   —110% of the planned target
Ogun State   —108% of the planned target
Bendel State — 55% of the planned target

In the case of Bendel State, the low performance was due to its late start by one year. It therefore had to carry forward its remaining 1,800 ha for 1979 planting. By 1978, a total of 70,001 ha of the 79,770 ha targeted had been planted.

The erstwhile Nigerian Produce Marketing Board and its subsequent successor, the Nigerian Cocoa Board, one of the new commodity Boards established by Decree No. 29 of 1977 were not left out in the bid to revitalise the cocoa industry. In particular, the Nigerian Cocoa Board was charged with the marketing, export sales and shipment of Nigerian cocoa, coffee and tea, such as would ensure encouraging prices to the producers and allowances to the licenced buying agents. The NCB was also mandated to make spraying pumps and chemicals available to farmers at highly subsidised rates, to combat the devastating incidence of pests and diseases in cocoa farms. The quantity of cocoa spraying chemicals distributed by the NCB and the subsidy given for them during the period 1968/69—1977/78 were most encouraging (see Table 18.4).

The Nigerian Cocoa Research Institute of Nigeria (CRIN) was also involved in this effort to make the cocoa industry regain its preeminence. As the research institute was charged with the responsibility of cocoa research, it was mandated to intensify research efforts to produce better and early yielding cocoa strains for new plantings and engage in massive farmer and extension staff training courses to ensure the success of the development programme. The institute lived and continues to live up to expectations. For

Table 18.4: Seasonal Quality of Cocoa Spraying Chemicals Distributed by the Western Nigeria Marketing Board Nigeria Cocoa Board (1969/70–1978/79) Seasons

Chemicals	1969/70	1970/71	1971/72	1972/73	1973/74	1974/75	1975/76	1976/77	1977/78	1978/79
1	2	3	4	5	6	7	8	9	10	11
1. Ganunalin (in litre tins)	1,459,119	1,470,808	671,448	1,610,716	489,398	274,935	1,156,823	408,873	897,415	524,944
2. Perenox (in 3 kg tins)	111,216	113,778	13,194	79,843	20,370	77,874	138,424	6,581	79,928	52,138
3. Caocobere (in 3 kg tins)	183,343	136,760	65,355	34,151	42,558	26,346	58,146	—	151,172	N.A.
4. Copper Sulphate (in 1 kg)	6,083,280	7,808,836	44,352	7,991,961	3,399,507	5,535,540	93,056	1,078,433	2,930,175	1,519,125
5. Kokotin (in 1 lirre tins)	579,521	384,621	233,776	86,877	290,936	34,745	127,760	—	48,392	N.A.
6. Bestan (in 0.91 kg tins)	4,338	16,910	9,064	7,521	8,772	290	680	—	13,095	N.A.

(Contd.)

Table 18.4 (*Contd.*)

1	2	3	4	5	6	7	8	9	10	11
7. Nordox	—	—	2,226	662	3,423	441	36	—	—	N.A.
8. Kocide (in 0.91 kg tins)	—	—	—	—	12,220	—	—	—	11,200	—
9. Inden × 100 kg	—	—	—	—	—	—	1,412	240	—	—
10. Elecron Soup (in 1 kg tins)	—	—	—	—	—	—	—	13,663	—	24,142
11. Unden 20 (in 1 litre tins)	—	—	—	—	—	—	—	4,730	8,430	1,760
12. Unden Difflotan (in litre tins)	—	—	—	—	—	—	—	49	666	375
13. Othobux	—	—	—	—	—	—	—	—	200	—

Note: N.A. means NOT AVAILABLE.
Source: Nigerian Cocoa Board *Statistical Bulletin*, April 1979, p. 37 and October 1980, p. 42.

Table 18.5: Amount Spent on Chemical Subsidy by the Western Nigeria Marketing Board Nigerian Cocoa Board (1969/70-1978/79 Seasons)

Year	Amount in Nigerian Pound
1969/70	1,928,206.00
1970/71	2,074,916.00
1971/72	1,611,318.00
1972/73	1,703,895.00
1973/74	1,236,300.13
1974/75	2,149,602.50
1975/76	3,167,833.48
1976/77	3,669,377.50
1977/78	2,628,682.02
1978/79	2,053,549.28

Source: Nigerian Cocoa Board, *Statistical Bulletin*, October 1980, p. 39.

instance, it designed and installed many modern central fermentation and drying sheds for farmers to reduce processing drudgery and ensure quality c ocoa beans.

The third phase could not take off as planned due to technical hitches over the unacceptable agreement requirements of the World Bank. However, encouraged by the achievements of the first two phases, the FMG decided to extend the programme to all producing areas on its own. Consequently, it commissioned a study of the following:

a) Review of the cocoa sector in Nigeria.

b) Replanting uneconomic farms.

c) Replanting areas of mass infection with swollen shoot disease.

d) New plantings, particularly in areas where cocoa had not been planted previously.

e) Rehabilitation of mature cocoa.

f) Maintenance of areas replanted or newly planted under phases I & II of the Cocoa Development Programme.

g) Development and maintenance of feeder roads.

h) Establishing or expansion of project entities.

i) Research.

j) Training.

k) Technical assistance.

Table 18.6: Cocoa Development Projects — Target and Achievements 1972-1981

Year	Oyo State CDU		Ondo State CDU		Ogun State CDU		Bendel State TCU		Total	
	Target	Achievements	Target	Achievements	Target	Achievements	Target	Achievements	Target	Achievements
1972	980	894	1,891	1,016	356	250			2,227	2,160
1973	1,817	1,677	1,652	2,139	661	374			4,130	4,190
1974	3,527	3,263	3,207	3,578	1,285	919			8,019	7,760
1975	5,830	5,407	5,407	4,261	1,840	2,336			13,677	12,186
1976	5,830	20,577	6,478	18,812	2,720	7,321	600	182	16,128	21,209
1977	5,830	5,545	8,000	4,747	2,160	946	1,100	613	17,090	11,866
1978	5,556	4,567	*	4,619	2,469	1,018	1,100	628	9,225	11,003
1979	*	2,136	*	4,100	1,864	1,609	1,200	2,222	*	9,683
1980	*	4,360	*	2,074	*	917	*	1,838	*	7,351
1981	5,000	3,827	*	2,798	2,000	1,654	100	104	*	8,383
Total	34,370	41,012	25,635	37,150	15,355	13,465	4,100	4,164		95,791

*Since 1978 some states fixed no targets, but planted to the extent of funds available.

Source: FDA, 'Report on joint tree crops rehabilitation meeting', March 1982, Appendix 1A.

The report of the commission paved the way for the inclusion of all the other cocoa-producing states, i.e., Cross River, Imo, Kwara, Rivers, Lagos, Anambra, Gongola and Benue. Financial grants were given to the states to assist them in the execution of the programme on the basis of the purchase figures provided by each state. For instance, between 1980 and 1981, a total sum of N_2 1,119,000 was released to the NCB for disbursement to the cocoa-producing states strictly for input purchases.

By 1981, a further evaluation of the programme showed that the four leading producing states had planted on their own 15,734 ha in 1980 and 1981, bringing the total for the period 1972-1981 to 95,791 ha. The small producing states together had also planted several thousands of hectares by 1981. Although statistical data are not available for inclusion in this paper, the magnitude of the plantings can be imagined from the fact that Kwara state alone, whose programme the writer supervised and which accounts for less than 0.5% of Nigeria's total production, planted 505.5 ha. during the three-year period, 1979-1981. According to reliable information, Cross River state, which produces about 2.5% of the national total, planted 7,518.8 ha between 1978 and 1980.

Also, by 1981, development of farm roads, one of the integral components of the programme, had recorded a measure of success as shown in Table 18.7.

Table 18.7: Development of Farm Roads by CDU/TC

State	Roads Cleared (km)	Roads graded (km)	Culverts Constructed (no.)	Drainage and Retaining walls (m³)
CDU Oyo	238.0	313.5	388	15.144
CDU Ondo	—	113.6	172	—
CDU Ogun	41.2	13.0	54	—
TCU Bendel	3.0	3.0	2	—
Total	282.2	443.1	616	15.144

Note: No record of farm road developments was kept by the other producing states.

Source: FDA, 'Report on joint tree crops rehabilitation meeting, March 1982, Appendix 1B.

The story so far is that of a programme designed by planners exclusively to improve the conditions of rural cocoa farmers in Nigeria. The programme has been well embraced by the farmers in view of the encouraging incentives given them and the fact that Nigeria, compared to other members of the Cocoa Producers' Alliance in West Africa, has paid the highest producer prices for Grade-I cocoa since the 1969/70 season, as shown in Table 18.8.

Table 18.8: Comparative Producer Price Statistics of Cocoa by Countries of the Cocoa Producer's Alliance in West Africa (1969/70-1978/79)[a]

(in Nigerian £)

Season	Ghana	Nigeria	Ivory cost	Cameroons	Togo
1969/70	209.26	292.00	210.12	224.31	232.29
1970/71	213.32	302.00	224.31	224.31	250.64
1971/72	154.82	302.00	225.74	238.90	260.25
1972/73	194.82	302.00	249.29	263.95	272.75
1973/74	257.86	450.00	347.50	315.91	300.12
1974/75	309.46	660.00	166.42	319.83	306.50
1975/76	418.86	660.00	195.88	341.62	315.35
1976/77	576.61	660.00	185.49	404.58	350.64
1977/78	616.44	030.00	743.12	553.95	409.37
1978/79	601.00	1,030.00	760.00	790.00	608.00

[a]Price expressed in Nigerian currency the official exchange rates for the currencies of these countries for the appropriate seasons were used.

Source: Nigerian Cocoa Board, *Statistical Bulletin*, October 1980, page 38.

Because of the interest and increasing demands of the farmers, proposals were made to expand the programme and even extend it to other agricultural cash crops such as oil palm, rubber, ground nuts and coffee. In a nutshell, the programme has yielded the desired results in the following ways:

a) Improved crop husbandry practices;

b) Increased production;

c) Provided better incentives to farmers and licenced buying agents.

d) Improved infrastructural development (roads);

e) Checked rural-urban drifts; and

f) Increased revenue to Government.

However, it was not possible to obtain the latest statistical data from the Nigerian Cocoa Board and hence the resultant yield increases to data could not be ascertained. Even if the purchase figures were available, these would be incomplete in view of the increasing domestic consumption of cocoa by the local manufacturing industries which have sprung up throughout Nigeria in recent years. Also the activities of smugglers who buy cocoa cheaply from rural farmers for resale on the black markets in neighbouring countries at higher prices have been difficult to check. It must be realised, that cocoa, like most tree crops, takes up to eight years from time of planting to economic bearing. Thus, only the first two or three years' plantings could be expected to have started giving economic yields in 1981.

Whether or not spectacular yield increases have accrued, the fact remains the programme has succeeded to some extent in reversing rural-urban drifts among peasant cocoa farmers and improved their cash earnings as well. The heavy funding by the Government and the zeal of the farmers are both commendable efforts that have led to the continuance of the programme to the present day.

CHAPTER 19

Coping with the Unemployment Problem in Kenya: A Case Study of the Village Polytechnic Movement

Unemployment in Kenya is rising at a very alarming rate and is causing great concern to the government. The youth, comprising over 60% of the country's population, are hit hardest. Many school leavers often find themselves either in the streets or just at home jobless. Unemployment is even more than a tragedy for the individual concerned; it is often a traumatic experience for whole families, many of whom have made years of sacrifice to educate their child. An effort by a para-church organisation, The National Christian Council of Kenya (NCCK), to solve this problem in 1966 gave birth to what is now commonly known as 'Village Polytechnics'.

Objectives

The purpose of the village polytechnic programme has been to offer training to school leavers for rural self-employment. The method of attaining this objective now seems rather clearly to be through locally financed and operated, low-cost rural vocational training centres. In other words, the programme aims to tackle effectively the problem of training youths who have no other opportunities.

The NCCK was only able to create a few youth centres (as they were called initially) and began teaching youths simple skills. By 1970, the government had began to realise the utilitarian value of what this organisation was doing and offered assistance to some of these centres. Those assisted were also upgraded to become Village Polytechnics. By 1975, there were 150 centres, of which 100 were government-assisted. They comprised about 6,000 trainees, the majority of whom were C.P.E. holders. Village Polytechnics are therefore low-cost post-primary training centres in rural areas. They are part of the response to two familiar and pervasive features of the Kenya scene. First, the fact that approxima tely 200,000 pupils leave primary school each year with no prospect of regular wage employment in the modern sector of the economy, and second, the frequent assertion that community self-help can ameliorate this situation. Thus the Village Polytechnics are seen as a means of alleviating unemployment.

Managerial Framework

Village Polytechnics are normally established on a *harambee* basis since they are largely financed locally, but centrally supervised and directed. Each village polytechnic is run by a manager and locally elected management committee. Instructors are rquired to man the courses offered. Government assistance takes the form of:

a) ideas, supervision and direction;
b) training village polytechnic instructors and managers;
c) grants towards equipment; and
d) grants towards salaries for instructors and managers.

The students have to pay a certain fee, which varies from project to project. Over 35 courses are offered, including carpentry, masonry, tailoring and dressmaking, motor mechanics, sign writing, agriculture, metal work, plumbing, business education, and home economics, course offerings vary from place to place depending on local needs. Some village polytechnics teach trainees skills required by the local communities, e.g., beekeeping, pottery, basket weaving, brick-making, bread-making, etc. Traditional skills have generally been neglected, an aspect that needs to be recaptured. The Ministry of Culture and Social Services is responsible for the entire village polytechnic programme, and its responsibility facilitated by the existence of a Youth Division.

Distribution of Village Polytechnics in Kenya

Presently, there are about 300 government-assisted village polytechnics spread unevenly throughout the country. Table 19.1 compares the area in square kilometres of each province, the population, and the number of village polytechnic projects established between 1977 and 1981.

Table 19.1: Distribution of Village Polytechnics

Province	Population	Area (sq. km)	No. of Projects		
			1979	1980	1981
Central	2,345,833	13,188	43	49	52
Nyanza	2,643,956	12,526	39	45	46
Eastern	2,719,851	154,540	34	39	39
Coast	1,342,794	83,041	35	37	37
Western	1,832,663	8,223	31	55	35
Rift Valley	3,240,402	170,146	30	30	35
N/Eastern	373,787	126,902	7	7	7
Nairobi	627,775	684	2	2	2
Total	15,127,061	569,250	221	264	253

Source: Central Bureau of Statistics and Centre for Research and Training, Karen.

It is readily seen from Table 19.1 that the North eastern, the third largest province has only seven village polytechnics, while the Central Province, which is the second smallest, has the highest number, i.e., 52 (this includes Nairobi which is an urban area). From the population statistics of North eastern, it is clear that this is due to the scanty population in the region. It is also a very dry place without cash crops. The present distribution of projects is therefore due to certain factors, namely:

a) High potential areas are usually well off in all aspects of their infrastructure. They have cash crops like tea and coffee, which yield high incomes for the people. Thus the *harambee* contributions in these areas are very high. The highest amount of cash collected in a single *harambee* meeting was Kshs. 33 million (in 1982) in Muranga District of Central Province. This explains why Central Province, though fairly small compared to the other provinces, has the highest number of village polytechnic projects.

b) Population is another very crucial factor. Areas which are fertile, with good rainfall, tend to have the highest populations as well. The number of school leavers in such places is therefore also higher, creating the need for more village polytechnics. One of the most populated areas in Kenya (and in all of Africa as well) is Kakamega District in the Western province. It has an area of 3,495 sq km, a population of 1,030,887, and 19 village polytechnics—the highest number of projects in a single district.

c) Political factors also contribute. Strictly speaking, village polytechnics are established when the local people think they need one to absorb their children. They then organise themselves and start collecting contributions to put up a polytechnic. When politics interfere, a politician may suggest that he will use his influence to get the village polytechnic started. Areas with very strong political figures are thus enabled to establish more projects than areas in which such leaders are weak.

d) Community behavioural attitudes also play an important role. Nomadic tribes in the Northeastern province are resistive to permanent institutions since the next season may find them in a different place. Certain communities have outgrown their traditional attitudes faster than others and have identified the current problem of unemployment. They cooperate more readily in establishing a project to offset the problem.

Enrolment

Enrolment in village polytechnics has been rising quite steadily in recent years. The majority of those who attend village polytechnics are Standard-seven leavers but some Form-four leavers are also being admitted since job opportunities are just as slim for them.

Table 19.2 presents data on the number of Standard-seven leavers between 1975 and 1981, those who got places in Form I, those whose whereabouts are unknown, and those who got places in village polytechnics.

One outstanding fact from Table 19.2 is that the village poly-

Table 19.2: Standard-seven Leavers/Village Polytechnic Enrolment%

Year	Std-7 Leavers	Possibly Absorbed in Form I	% of In-take	Not Known Where-abouts	Possibly Absorbed in V.P.S.	% of intake
1975	227,439	45,488	20	181,951	9,000	5
1976	243,366	48,671	20	194,695	9,300	4.5
1977	237,218	59,304	25	177,914	9,650	5
1978	258,505	64,626	25	193,879	9,875	5
1979	281,689	70,422	25	211,267	10,501	5.4
1980	351,407	105,422	30	245,985	14,997	5
1981	371,525	130,034	35	241,491	15,497	7%

Source: Ministry of Basic Education.

technic programme absorbs a very small proportion of Standard-seven leavers—5%. Consequently, every year over 200,000 pupils join the ranks of the unemployed. The situation is no better for Form-four leavers, although understandably the numbers are much lower. It may be worth noting from the Table that the increment in percentage of intake in Form I is due to an increase of *harambee* and private secondary schools, which are not government financed.

The very small contribution made by village polytechnics in the fight against unemployment probably explains the conclusion drawn by D. Court regarding them.

Village Polytechnics, far from being obvious panaceas for large-scale rural development, are unproven instruments of anything beyond the ability to occupy a handful of primary-school leavers for a period of time. Yet. . . as village polytechnics may represent the first sign of demand for fundamentally new, rurally based. . . training, their experience may provide important lessons which can be generalised to the widespread and long-term problems of combating under-employment.[2]

Success and Failures of the Village Polytechnic Programme

To a large extent. the village polytechnic programme is still new and has suffered from time to time through transference from one Ministry to another, making proper record-keeping a difficult task. Without proper records, measuring the extent to which the programme has been a success or a failure is problematical. According to the original objectives of the programme, a village polytechnic was supposed to be a *low-cost training centre* in a rural area aimed at giving *primary school leavers* from *that area skills, understanding and values,* which would enable them to look for money-making opportunities *where they live,* and to contribute to rural development by building up the economic strength of their own community. Presently, many village polytechnics are offering what can no longer be called low-cost training because of the type of equipment required and the fees the trainees have to pay. The majority of the village polytechnics in which the standard of training is high charge fees up to Kshs. 2,000 for two years. The question of boarding facilities has also come about because of a common belief that the best education is found where boarding facilities are available. This has encouraged the recruitment of trainees from far places and resulted in higher fees, because 'richer' outsiders are preferred to the relatively poorer locals. This indicates that the village polytechnic is no longer catering to the local needs as was originally intended. It is worth noting that although the majority of of the trainees are primary leavers, KJSE leavers and O-level graduates are also competing for places.

The village polytechnic programme was also supposed to eliminate rural-urban migration by keeping the graduates practicing in the rural areas. However, most of them still have the mentality that big money is found in big towns and often prefer to either look for jobs in cities or to establish their small business. Many still see self-employment as a stepping stone to permanent employment in some company or in the government.

The most important objective of the programme however, was to try and train youths to enable to obtain some kind of productive employment. There has certainly been success as far as training is concerned, but the issue of finding employment has continued to be a problem. (This is because the village polytechnic programme only trains but it is not involved in the placement of the graduates for employment.) A few projects have had a loan scheme for leavers to help them purchase the most important tools, but it has been difficult to operate such a scheme because the number of trainees turned out is high while the funds are few. Motor mechanics, for example, is a very popular course among boys and yet the equipment involved in setting up a garage is very expensive. Some have feared that we may be training professional thieves by failing to look for a solution to employment placement. Again, those from well-to-do families stand better chances than those from poor families, showing that we have successfully dealt with the issue of poverty.

The reports received from project managers, however, often indicate that many graduates manage to obtain temporary employment. The picture is not so bleak. According to the reports received in 1980, over 60% of both male and female graduates were in some form of self-employment while 10% formed work groups (see Table 19.3).

Table 19.3: 1980 Leavers

Sex	Total	Self Employ-ment%	Working in Groups%	Not Known
Male	5,220	86.6	9.6	3.8
Female	2,331	65.3	13.1	21.6

Source: Centre for Research & Training, Karen.

The commendable aspect of the village polytechnic programme is that it has been able to utilise resources which would otherwise lie idle. It has become a channel for using funds raised locally and encourages initiative from local people, local staff and local leadership qualities. This further encourages the spirit of self-reliance.

SUGGESTIONS AND CONCLUSION

Considerable ambiguity regarding the objectives of polytechnic training is inevitably mired in dilemmas concerning organisation of the training. Practically all village polytechnics commence with three conventional courses: carpentry, masonry and tailoring. The trend is to copy what other village polytechnics offer, regardless of whether such courses are relevant in a village polytechnic. This has led to duplication of trades/courses from polytechnic to polytechnic without much thought given to the local needs of a particular area. One wonders whether we shall not soon saturate the market. However, for success of the programme and particularly the ability of the village polytechnic graduates to continue being engaged in productive employment, there is a need for a survey of what the local needs are for each village polytechnic and to train students accordingly. It is important to realise that training alone does not create jobs; the problem is that of identifying or creating the demand at which to direct instruction. Training should not only aim at the provision of skills and values, which in addition to fitting people for recognised money-earning roles, motivates trainees to seek out new latent opportunities, but also to perform tasks of community and family improvement which may have no immediate monetary returns.

Most village polytechnics in the process of training enrollees make a considerable number of salable items. Of late, the emphasis on big money from contracts has been so great that some village polytechnics have been known to make up to Kshs. 50,000 a year. This is really more like contract-labour, which does little to train the student in the marketing skills and initiative needed for local self-employment. It is an aspect which needs to be looked into and appropriate steps taken.

The idea of government assistance to village polytechnics has been misunderstood by some communities. They have taken it to mean full government support or control which then excuses them from giving the village polytechnic any support. This stifling of local initiative and self-help is unhealthy and probably more education will be needed in such communities. For even greater success, more commitment on the part of top government officials is essential to streamline the entire programme. Issues such as the system of purchasing the tools required, the quality bought, and more serious supervision, are all crucial questions which, if handled better, could lead to even greater success of the programme.

Finally, it is important to realise that the problem of youth employment does not so much lie in the number of primary-school leavers. It lies much more in the whole philosophy of education, which mentally prepares the pupils for formal, non-rural employment in the context of an economy that has failed to generate sufficient employment opportunities of this sort. In the foreseeable future this deficiency will continue unless fundamental changes both inside and outside the school are forthcoming. The village polytechnic programme is making its own contribution in fighting unemployment. The experience being gained can be utilised designing other useful programmes. It is clear that the question of unemployment needs efforts from a wider scope.

NOTES

1. *Harambee* is a Swahili word meaning 'pull together' therefore people pool their contributions for the specified project.
2. D. Court, 1974, *Dilemmas of Development: The Village Polytechnic Movement as a Shadow System of Education in Kenya,* Oxford University Press, Oxford.

CHAPTER 20

Development of Agricultural Infrastructure as a Strategy for Agricultural Development

A Case Study of the Small-Farm Sector in Malawi

Malawi is one of the smallest countries (92,989 sq km) in the Central African Federation, and gained Independence in 1964. Having no substantial mineral resources and less scope for the flow of foreign capital into the country, Malawi must contend with subsistence agriculture and the export of a few primary products. The economy mainly depends upon the export of primary estate crops, i.e., tobacco, tea, cotton, and others, which are partly produced in large estates,[1] and partly in small holder African farms. Indeed, the agrarian structure of the economy constitutes 84 per cent of small-farm subsistence agriculture and the balance by large estates (Table 20.1). The highest priority of the country after Independence has been to achieve self-sufficiency in food production, in addition to exporting cash crops to earn substantial foreign exchange to pay for imports. The cash crops compete with food crops both for labour and land.

The population of Malawi was estimated at six million in 1981, with a density of 59% per square kilometre of land area and a population growth rate of 2.9%. The per capita GDP was US$ in 1982. The high rate of population growth resulted in increased pressure on quality land with the desire to grow more

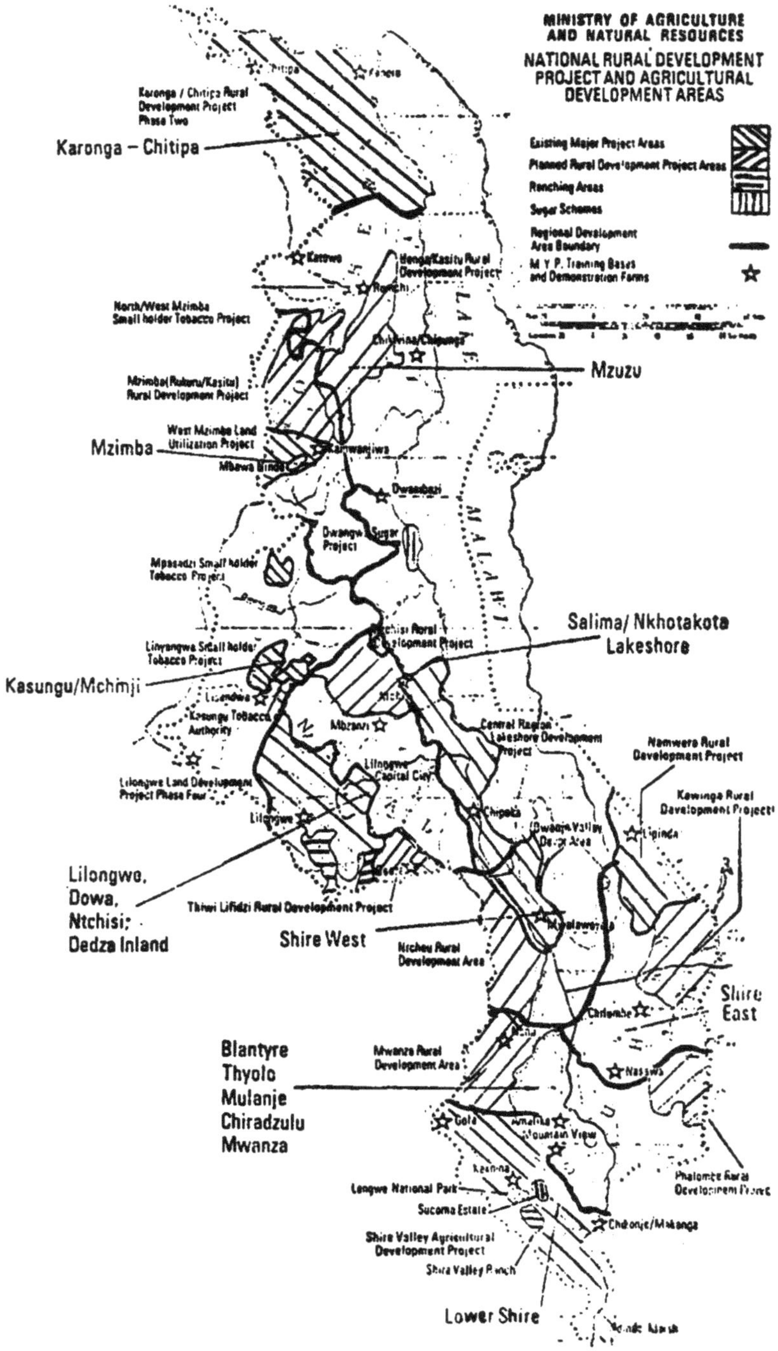

Fig. 20.1. Republic of Malawi.

Table 20.1: Farm Size Distribution and Fragmentation, 1968/69

Size of Holdings (Acres)

	1.9 and under	2.0 to 3.9	4.0 to 5.9	6.0 to 11.9	12.0 and over	Total All Holdings	
						%	'000
A. Percentage of holdings							
Northern region	31.9	34.6	17.6	14.4	1.5	100.0	117.1
Central region	17.8	30.4	22.3	25.4	4.1	100.0	316.9
Southern region	35.6	36.5	15.9	11.2	0.9	100.0	451.0
All Malawi	28.7	34.1	18.4	16.7	2.1	100.0	885.0
B. Average number of acres per holding							
Northern region	1.0	2.8	4.8	8.0	14.1		3.5
Central region	1.2	2.9	4.8	7.6	15.3		4.7
Southern region	1.1	2.8	4.8	7.6	14.1		3.2
All Malawi	1.2	2.9	4.8	7.8	14.9		3.8
C. Average number of fields per holding							
Northern region	3.2	4.2	4.3	5.0	5.9		4.0
Central region	1.9	2.1	2.6	3.1	3.9		2.5
Southern region	2.3	3.3	4.4	4.7	4.4		3.3
All Malawi	2.4	3.0	3.6	3.9	4.2		3.1

Source: National Statistical Office, Malawi. National Sample Survey of Agriculture 1968/69.

food and additional cash crops to earn more income. Malawi's small-holder agriculture went from a slow and steady transformation of subsistence agriculture to the stage of an inevitable process of structural diversification of the farm sector.

The total land available for cultivation is around 13,114,000 acres; and the average size of holdings is 2 hectares. The small holders constitute 84% of the cultivators. The Government of Malawi after Independence favoured promotion of the agricultural sector and 85% of the total agricultural produce is derived from small-holder agriculture to meet the country's food needs and to provide raw materials for domestic industries. Half of the export surpluses of Malawi's total merchandise exported was from the small-holder sector whereas the large estate sector dominated by foreign-owned tea and tobacco plantations accounted for only one-third of the merchandise exports and one-fourth of waged employment.[2] Moderately fertile soils and favourable climate make the country suitable for the production of a variety of food and cash crops.[3] As a natural consequence of the existing agrarian structure, the small-farm sector has become predominant and widespread throughout the country.

With Malawi's poor industrial base and greater dependence on agriculture, the country is clearly in urgent need of a breakthrough in per-acre productivity through substantial investment in the agricultural sector (Table 20.2), as a necessary prerequisite for a diversified modern agriculture. Consequent to this, the main drive must be to build an infrastructural base (Growth Promotional Institutions) as a strategy to realise the national objectives. Such a strategy would include:

a) Strengthening the Government administration machinery by formulation of an Agricultural Development Agency (ADA), under the National Rural Development Programme (NRDP).

b) Establishment of agricultural research stations.

c) Strengthening Agricultural Extension Services and Training Institutes for innovation and diffusion of new agricultural technology in the country.

d) Establishment of an Institutional Marketing System (AD-MARC) for orderly marketing of agricultural produce (both domestic and export) to achieve a steady and self-sustained growth in the agricultural economy.

Table 20.2: Malawi: Functional Analysis of Total Revenue and Development Account Expenditure, 1967-1981/82

(Kwac ha millions)

	1967	1968	1969/70 (15 months)	1970/71	1971/72	1972/73	1973/74	1974/75	1975/76	1976/77	1977/78	1978/79	1979/80	1980/81 (budget)	1980/81 (prelim)	1981/82 (budget)
	1	2	3	4	5	6	7	8	9	10	11	12	13	14	15	16
Economic Services & Investment	*16.5*	*19.1*	*26.4*	*33.7*	*33.3*	*30.8*	*31.2*	*40.9*	*69.3*	*61.6*	*84.8*	*112.2*	*109.0*	*145.0*	*152.0*	*149.8*
Agriculture	5.4	6.7	10.1	9.9	12.5	12.2	14.5	18.6	20.4	20.0	25.1	26.0	34.6	47.7	46.4	59.6
Transport	3.5	5.6	8.2	18.9	7.8	7.6	7.5	13.2	36.4	24.5	43.7	63.6	47.0	65.9	75.9	54.5
Power	0.6	0.1	—	0.7	3.2	2.6	0.6	1.1	2.3	5.5	3.9	6.9	7.6	11.8	11.2	5.6
Water	0.4	0.4	0.5	0.3	0.7	0.6	0.4	0.7	0.8	0.7	1.4	5.0	6.1	9.3	8.1	12.5
Posts & Tele-communication	2.0	2.1	1.7	1.8	1.8	2.5	2.7	2.9	4.6	4.4	5.0	4.8	5.1	3.9	4.6	5.9
Finance, Commerce & Ind.[a]	4.6	4.2	5.9	7.1	7.3	5.3	5.5	4.4	4.8	6.5	5.7	6.6	8.6	6.4	6.7	11.7
Social Services & Investment	*11.3*	*13.2*	*16.6*	*15.7*	*16.1*	*17.4*	*19.8*	*22.9*	*25.2*	*26.7*	*31.3*	*41.8*	*46.3*	*55.1*	*55.5*	*73.7*
Education	7.2	7.9	11.9	10.9	10.3	10.9	11.4	12.5	13.0	14.1	18.2	24.9	25.5	31.4	30.6	47.5
Health	2.9	3.0	3.9	3.2	3.6	3.9	5.5	7.0	8.2	8.8	8.7	11.3	14.8	17.4	15.9	17.9
Housing	0.6	0.7	0.6	0.3	0.6	0.6	0.7	0.4	1.4	1.1	1.5	1.1	1.6	1.7	3.3	2.0
Community Development	0.6	1.6	0.2	1.3	1.6	2.0	2.2	3.0	2.6	2.7	2.9	4.5	4.4	4.6	5.7	6.3

(Contd.)

Table 20.2 (Contd.)

	1	2	3	4	5	6	7	8	9	10	11	12	13	14	15	16
Administrative Services Inv.	*13.3*	*14.2*	*20.8*	*17.9*	*21.1*	*22.7*	*26.9*	*32.2*	*42.3*	*42.6*	*48.8*	*76.0*	*104.8*	*99.3*	*107.2*	*92.5*
Administration & Buildings[b]	8.2	8.9	14.5	12.4	15.2	16.5	17.8	22.9	26.7	26.5	26.5	35.1	69.5	66.3	67.6	53.0
Defence[c]	1.2	1.2	1.4	1.3	1.5	1.5	4.3	4.6	9.3	8.1	13.8	28.8	19.0	18.2	21.0	22.0
Justice	3.9	4.1	4.9	4.2	4.4	4.7	4.8	5.7	6.3	8.0	8.5	12.1	16.3	14.8	18.6	17.5
Debt Service[d]	*4.0*	*4.0*	*6.1*	*6.8*	*8.1*	*9.9*	*10.5*	*13.9*	*14.5*	*15.7*	*17.3*	*20.3*	*36.6*	*44.8*	*58.8*	*71.5*
Pensions	3.9	3.8	3.8	3.0	3.0	2.9	3.6	3.7	3.1	2.9	2.7	2.9	4.1	4.1	4.6	4.8
Total	49.0	54.3	73.7	82.1	81.6	83.8	92.0	114.6	154.4	149.5	184.9	253.9	300.9	348.2	378.6	392.1
Notes																
Total Expenditure in Constant 1973 Kwacha	69.4	72.0	95.5	97.7	90.1	91.5	92.0	100.3	120.8	107.6	123.8	163.0	165.3	162.0	176.1	n.a.
GDP Deflator (1973 = 100)	70.6	75.4	77.2	84.0	90.6	91.5	100.0	114.3	127.8	138.9	150.1	155.7	182.0	215.0	215.0	n.a.

Notes

[a]Includes capital transfers and other economic services from revenue account and Government buildings organisation from development account.

[b]Comprises general administration from revenue account and Government buildings excluding army buildings (see c). new capital and miscellaneous services from development. account.

[c]Includes army buildings listed under 'Government Buildings' In development account.

[d]Includes amortisation.

Source: World Bank, 1982, *Malawi: growth and structural change—A Basic Economic Report*, Table 7.04 and 7.06.

Favoured with potential resource endowments, and the limited size of its domestic market, the economy is dependent upon external markets to earn foreign exchange. Further, by adopting a dual structure in agriculture of both a small-holder sector and an estate sector, the former received more weightage under the NRDP to achieve higher productivity rate of subsistence crops to meet the country's increasing demand for food and to grow cash crops to obtain additional income. To realise this objective a substantial investment was made during the period 1967 to 1981.

The promotion of an agricultural infrastructure may lie in the fields of organisation of agricultural research and machinery for the diffusion of such knowledge through extension and training programmes, organisation of farmers to strengthen their bargaining power to acquire input supplies, marketing of farm output at favourable (price) conditions through marketing institutions, and formulation and adoption of a pragmatic agricultural policy.

Malawi's drive for infrastructure building began to be discernible as a broad-based strategy from the beginning of the mid-sixties, i.e., agricultural research was organised by the Agricultural Research Department (ARD), Ministry of Agriculture and Natural Resources (MANR), Agricultural Faculty of the University of Malawi (Banda College), and the Tea Research Foundation. ARD organised research through research stations established in many parts of the country with sub-stations in varying ecological zones and a large number of district trail sites for all crops and livestocks. Since Malawian farmers by tradition do inter-cropping, there is need for developing new genetic material for better yield and for general agronomic performance under a mixed-cropping system, in terms of individual hybrid varieties to meet the farmers' tastes and pest-resistance qualities. Furthermore, improvement in soil conservation and integration of research and extension services through adoptive trail sites have to be strengthened by training and visit systems throughout the countryside. At the inception of NRDP in 1977, the Extension Services were being conducted in two ways: the major Integrated Rural Development Project Areas had their own efficient Services while the 85 per cent of the cultivators kept outside the project areas were served under the National Extension Services, which proved weak and inadequate to meet the situation. The NRDP recognised the importance of strengthening extension and training services in the country and therefore adopted a policy based on geographical units—called Ecological Planning Areas, and organised training services to farmers at various centres.

The novel feature of the Agricultural Extension and Training Services in Malawi is the group approach, particularly the organisation of small farmers into groups called 'Farmers Clubs' for every large village or a cluster of small villages. 'Farmers Clubs' receive all types of modern input supplies and also institutional credit, distributed on an equal basis, which work as a safety valve against exploitation by large farmers or middlemen. There is sufficient evidence that the farmers used the inputs then received very economically and productively. At the same time, the recovery of loans was rather easy because linking of credit with marketing was a well-established policy and the newly established Agricultural Development and Marketing Corporation (ADMARC) was the sole agency for the distribution of inputs and marketing of agricultural produce. Hence recovering the loans advanced to farmers did not prove problematical.

The extension workers gave advice to farmers and taught recommended practices largely through demonstrations to the entire group. The group demonstration was followed by visits to as many individual farms as possible, at least once in 15 days, to ensure that the farmers followed the recommended practices. When necessary, further advice was provided. The ratio of extension workers to farm households varies from project to project and non-project areas. In project areas it is as low as 1:200 to 500; outside the project area, the ratio is 1:1400:2400.[4] The high ratio of farm households to extension workers in non-project areas is a critical problem that the extension workers have failed to meet.

A large number of farmers in the small-holder sector have suffered consequently. Apart from this prevailing socio-economic system, exploitation by large farmer-politicians in the process of availing of institutional aid and its misappropriation has also been noticed. By and large, however, the small-farm sector is well organised and, consequently, the chances of exploitation of the small farmer by the large farmer are slender. The strategy of the Agricultural Extension Services is similar in most Asian countries, such as India and Thailand. The major difference is the greater discipline among the extension staff and farmers in Malawi, and particularly the high degree of female participation (in the small-farm sector) in the extension and training programmes. Indeed, a high degree of active participation by women over the last 15 years (Table 20.3) has been one of the most successful features in both project and non-project areas. Research extension and training has been integrated in the Domasi Irrigation project.[5] In this project the Chinese Agricultural Research Mission, Farmers Club, and the Research Extension Services have exhibited a novel group approach to realising the objectives set by national policy programmes.

Training farmers has been an integral part of the extension services; courses are held throughout the year in all training centres. The curriculum includes a wide range of subjects, such as crop and animal husbandry, special courses on tobacco diseases, curing and grading, dairy health, nutrition, and local leadership. To provide more intensive training to farmers, two types of training centres have been established throughout the country. Day-training centres consisting of a classroom attached to an EPA field office offer one-day sessions for groups of 25 to 40 farmers on current topics, either suggested by the field staff or requested by the village farmers' clubs. Residential Training Centres offer one-week and two-weeks courses on subjects largely determined by the project staff. The day centres recorded about 70,000 student days and the residential centres 85,000 student days per year in 1980[6] (see Table 20.3).

Marketing agricultural produce is considered the most critical aspect of the production and stability of a small-farm economy. The organisation of efficient institutional marketing systems is considered the essential condition for protecting farmer interests and accelerating the processes of agricultural diversification and modernisation.

The Ministry of Agriculture and Natural Resources has established the Agricultural Development and Marketing Corporation (ADMARC) to exercise total control over the trade in commercial crops and to exercise regulatory functions in the marketing of food crops. ADMARC operates through a network of buying stations in each district in Malawi and also a number of sub-centres and produce depots (for storage and warehousing; later these also

Table 20.3: Farmer Training Summary

	1970	1971	1972	1973	1974
Farm Institutes					
No. of centres active	2	2	2	2	2
No. of men attending courses	1,296	1,468	1,568	1,252	1,435
No. of women attending courses	645	716	959	759	876
Total student days	18,245	19,428	24,085	22,410	22,884
Divisional Training Centres					
No. of centres active	13	14	14	13	13
No. of men attending courses	6,621	8,065	6,967	6,714	6,077
No. of women attending courses	3,539	4,427	5,509	4,385	3,361
Total student days	44,132	46,272	45,617	48,412	44,149
Rural Training Centres					
No. of centres active	50	44	44	48	46
No. of men attending courses	33,088	31,573	33,541	31,554	24,198
No. of women attending courses	16,822	20,524	30,112	36,519	33,352
Total student days	49,910	52,097	63,540	68,241	57,516
All Centres					
No. of men attending courses	41,005	41,104	42,076	39,520	31,710
No. of women attending courses	21,006	25,712	36,980	41,664	37,589
Total student days	112,288	118,279	133,242	139,063	124,549

Source: MANR (Ministry of Agriculture and Natural Resources).

serve as distribution points). The commodities are purchased at a guaranteed price, which remains constant during the marketing season throughout the country. The narrow shape of the country and its broken topography make transportation difficult and expensive. ADMARC's purchases through its network of buying stations has certainly reduced the burden of transport costs for farmers. In addition to marketing principal commodities, such as maize, tobacco, cotton, ground nut, rice, pulses, and cassava, ADMARC is also entrusted with the distribution of agricultural inputs to farmers working on traditional land. Finally, ADMARC also reduces marketing risks and uncertainities in many areas, such as transportation, handling, processing and packaging, and storage and warehousing.

The price policy of ADMARC, formulated by MANR, announces the producer's price for all commodities handled by the corporation every year, before the commencement of the cropping season. This measure helps the farmer to forecast the expected (price) earnings for the crops he grows and enables him to change crop plans and allocate farm resources more productively to maximise his farm income. But, as a matter of fact, the chances of the second line of action being adopted are rare, since the farmers by tradition grow a certain set of crops under a given farm's conditions.

The prices fixed for such important commodities as tobacco, cotton and ground nut are considered less attractive because they remain almost constant over a period of time. Nevertheless, ADMARC has made a substantial profit percentage, ranging between 28 to 29 per cent in both domestic and export markets[7] (Table 20.4). The other important feature of ADMARC purchases of agricultural produce is the cross subsidisation between crops and geographical areas. Its activities in marketing of rice and maize usually run at a loss, which is compensated by the profits earned from the marketing of tobacco, cotton, ground nuts, and so on. ADMARC's uniform buying prices have consistently remained below the unit prices realised on export crops, suggesting that its tradelink activities generally look profitable. However, ADMARC's monopoly trading and its high-cost operations, including transport cost and subsidies for food crops, have become too great a financial burden for efficient operation. Consequently, the less attractive prices offered for cotton, ground nuts and tobacco—the cash-crop component of the small-farmer sector—have lost takers in the last decade. The small-holder sector is very responsive to prices and thus there has been a fall in the production of cash crops.

The other significant feature in the development of Malawi's agriculture during the last 10 to 15 years is its dualistic tendencies, i.e., modern estate sector and traditional small-farm sector. The farmer who is more dynamic and market oriented grows such crops as tobacco, tea, and sugar; adopts modern techniques and machinery; and uses the package of new inputs including irrigation. The output has increased by 15% per annum and exports have risen from 35 to 70%. The concurrent share in employment generation has been over 50% of the new jobs available. Although the small-farm sector still continues some elements of traditional practices, especially tools and implements, it is slowly moving towards a fundamental transformation in the process of farming— from traditional practices to a dynamic market-oriented agriculture. The signs of transformation from subsistence or self-sufficient farming to market-oriented farming are slowly but steadily increasing within the socio-economic framework of the small-farm holder.

The principal crops grown in customary land are maize, tobacco, cotton, rice, pulses and cassava. Under rainfall conditions and also in the new irrigated projects, farming methods are extremely labour-intensive; the majority of small farmers (75 to 85%) cultivate land with single hand tools such as hoes, knives or axes. Bullocks and bullock carts or modern machinery are still quite rare in spite of the fact that the farmer is very responsive to new technology (inputs like H.Y.V. seeds) since its adoption works out economically in small-farm conditions. Indeed, the breakthrough in productivity rate in the small-farm sector has been quite substantial with the use of new input combinations, as evidenced by the increase in per acre yield for major crops under various farm conditions.

Table 20.4: ADMARC Crop Trading—Accounts, 1969/70-1980/81

	1969/70		1970/71		1971/72		1972/73		1973/74		1974/75		1975/76		1976/77		1977/78		1978/79		1979/80		1980/81	
	MK '000	%	MK '000	%	MK '000	%	MK '000	%	MK '000	%	MK '000	%	MK '000	%	MK'000	%	MK '000	%	MK '000	%	MK '000	%	MK '000	%
Purchase of crops	10074	50	23538	65	13959	51	16477	58	14343	48	17157	47	20459	51	23042	39	27857	38	30522	59	28228	55	29900	53
Buying and direct expenses	3110	13	3727	18	3992	15	4943	17	6036	20	7114	19	7780	19	10267	18	12244	17	12916	25	17707	35	20114	36
Administrative expenditure	878	15	908	4	911	3	857	3	1448	5	1281	4	1859	5	2527	4	3427	5	4106	8	4821	9	5874	10
Net profit on crop trading	3977	22	2559	13	8714	31	6327	22	8112	27	11148	30	9977	25	22685	39	30040	40	4180	8	70	1	327	1
Net sales value of crops purchased	18039	100	20832	100	27576	100	28604	100	29939	100	36700	100	40075	100	58520	100	73568	100	51724	100	50836	100	56215	100
Sales of crops	19175		21084		27612		29226		33479		38042		41446		56833		78048		47331		56335		63271	
Selling expenses	847		926		901		1652		2271		2176		1847		2338		3120		3189		3528		3584	
Sales less selling expenses	18328		20158		26711		27574		31208		35866		39599		54495		74928		44142		52807		59687	
Movement of stock— increase/ (decreases)	(289)		(674)		865		1030		(1269)		834		478		4025		(1360)		7582		(1971)		(3472)	
Net sale value of crops purchased	18039		20832		27576		28604		29939		36700		40075		58520		73568		51724		50836		56215	

Source: ADMARC, 1970, 1980, Annual Reports, Malawi.

Average Yield of Maize in 1977/78[8]

a) Local maize without fertiliser	900 1b/acre
Composite maize without fertiliser	1,000 1b/acre
Hybrid maize without fertiliser	1,400 1b/acre
b) Local maize with fertiliser	2,000 1b/acre
Composite maize with fertiliser	2,200 1b/acre
Hybrid maize with fertiliser	2,881 1b/acre

The above table clearly illustrates the higher farm output when a compact technology mix is adopted, especially in the small-farm sector.

Indices of moving average prices over a 15-year period for five principal crops sold to ADMARC (Table 20.5)[9] suggest that the output marketed by them increased at about 3.6% per annum between 1967 to 1979 (tobacco—4.7% maize—3.9%, cotton—3.6% rice—14.6% and ground nut—minus 3.9%). Indeed, the performance of the small farmer fell from the average growth of 5.0% p.a. to 3.2% per annum versus the constant rise of the estate sector by 15% per annum.[10] Several reasons for the fall in growth rates of the small-holder sector were:

1) lack of price incentives as a result of appropriation of large profits by ADMARC;

2) risks and uncertainties in using hybrid varieties both at the time of production and marketing;

3) inadequate supplies of inputs including credit;

4) prevalence of tendency cultivation in some parts of the estate sector;

5) conservative attitudes in replacing traditional practices with new production techniques (tools and equipment);

6) rapid expansion of estates through alienation of customary land; and

7) constant migration of rural folk from one part of the country to other parts as a consequence of inadequate supply of basic human needs (water) in rural areas.

However, in spite of some of the setbacks in the processes of agricultural development (small-farm sector) in Malawi, one may conclude that the small-holder sector is highly responsive to prices. It responds positively in favour of price incentives obtained for the production of rice and tobacco, and negatively towards cotton

Table 20.5. ADMARC Producer Prices 1966-80

(Tavbala per pound)

	1966	1967	1968	1969	1970	1971	1972	1973	1974	1975	1976	1977	1978	1979	1980
1	2	3	4	5	6	7	8	9	10	11	12	13	14	15	16
Cotton															
Grade A	6.0	5.0	5.0	5.0	5.5	5.5	6.0	7.0	8.0	8.5	9.3	10.5	10.5	10.5	10.5
Grade B	2.0	3.0	3.0	3.0	4.0	4.0	4.5	4.5	5.5	6.0	6.5	8.0	8.0	8.0	8.0
Grade C		2.0	2.0	2.0	2.0	2.0	2.5	2.5	3.5	3.5	4.5	6.0	6.0	6.0	6.0
Groundnuts															
Chalimbana															
Grade A tunda/ Kalisere	5.0	5.0	5.0	5.0	6.0	6.0	6.5	7.5	8.0	8.5	9.0	10.0	10.0	15.0	15.0
Grade B —Splita and Shrivela	4.0	4.0	4.0	4.0	4.0	4.0	4.5	5.5	6.0	6.5	7.0	8.0	8.0	12.0	12.0
Grade X	2.0	2.0	2.0	2.0	2.5	2.5	2.5	2.5	3.0	3.5	3.5	4.0	4.0	4.0	4.0
—Manipintar and Malimba (shelled)	—	—	—	—	4.0	4.0	5.0	6.0	6.5	7.0	7.0	—	8.0	9.0	9.0
—Manipintar and Malimba (unshelled)	—	—	—	2.5	2.5	2.5	3.3	4.0	4.5	4.5	4.5	5.0	5.0	6.0	6.0

Rice															
Grade I	2.0	2.0	2.0	3.0	3.3	3.3	3.3	3.3	4.0	4.5	4.5	4.5	4.5	4.5	4.5
Grade II	—	—	—	2.0	2.5	2.5	2.5	2.5	3.0	3.5	3.5	3.5	3.5	3.5	3.5
Grade III	—	—	—	—	1.7	1.7	1.7	1.7	2.0	2.5	2.5	2.5	2.5	2.5	2.5
Maize															
Grower	0.9	1.0	1.1	1.1	1.3	1.3	1.3	1.3	1.8	2.3	2.3	2.3	2.3	2.3	3.0
Trader	—	—	—	1.7	1.7	1.7	1.7	1.7	2.8	2.8	2.8	2.8	2.8	2.8	—
Tobacco															
Grade C1	na	11.0	12.0	15.0	15.0	15.0	15.0	15.0	18.0	20.0	20.0	27.0	27.0	27.0	:
C2	na	9.0	12.0	14.0	14.0	14.0	14.0	14.0	17.0	19.0	19.0	26.0	26.0	26.0	:
(Chikopa) K	na	—	—	13.0	13.0	13.0	13.0	13.0	16.0	18.0	—	—	—	—	:
G1	na	8.0	8.0	10.0	10.0	10.0	9.0	10.0	12.0	14.0	18.0	24.0	24.0	24.0	:
F	na	8.0	9.0	8.0	8.0	9.0	9.0	9.0	11.0	13.0	13.0	18.0	18.0	18.0	:
X1	na	2.0	2.0	9.0	9.0	9.0	9.0	9.0	11.0	12.0	16.0	21.0	21.0	21.0	:
G2	na	3.0	4.0	8.0	8.0	8.0	8.0	8.0	9.0	11.0	15.0	20.0	20.0	20.0	:
X2	na	—	—	2.0	2.0	3.0	3.0	3.0	4.0	5.0	5.0	6.0	6.0	6.0	:
L	na	—	—	na	na	10.0	9.0	10.0	12.0	12.0	12.0	16.0	16.0	16.0	:
H	na	—	—	—	10.0	10.0	10.0	10.0	12.0	12.0	12.0	16.0	16.0	16.0	:
Oriental															
Grade A1	na	25.0	25.0	25.0	25.0	25.0	25.0	25.0	25.0	27.0	27.0	27.0	27.0	27.0	:
A2	na	21.0	21.0	21.0	21.0	21.0	21.0	21.0	21.0	23.0	23.0	23.0	23.0	23.0	:
B1	na	17.0	17.0	17.0	17.0	17.0	17.0	17.0	17.0	19.0	19.0	19.0	19.0	19.0	:
B2	na	12.0	12.0	12.0	12.0	14.0	14.0	14.0	14.0	15.0	15.0	15.0	15.0	15.0	:
Kappa	na	10.0	10.0	8.0	8.0	8.0	8.0	8.0	8.0	9.0	9.0	9.0	9.0	9.0	:

(Contd.)

1	2	3	4	5	6	7	8	9	10	11	12	13	14	15	16
Southern															
Division S1	—	—	—	—	—	—	—	—	—	—	20.0	27.0	27.0	27.0	··
Fire															
Curved G2	—	—	—	—	—	—	—	—	—	—	17.0	26.0	26.0	26.0	··
T1	—	—	—	—	—	—	—	—	—	—	16.0	24.0	24.0	24.0	··
T2	—	—	—	—	—	—	—	—	—	—	12.0	18.0	18.0	18.0	··
X	—	—	—	—	—	—	—	—	—	—	5.0	6.0	6.0	6.0	··
L	—	—	—	—	—	—	—	—	—	—	12.0	16.0	16.0	16.0	··
Coffee															
Cherry															
Grade I	na	na	3.33	3.33	3.33	3.33	3.75	4.0	4.0	4.0	4.5	6.0	6.0	6.0	··
Cherry															
Grade II	na	na	2.1	2.1	2.25	2.25	2.25	2.5	2.5	2.5	3.0	4.0	4.0	4.0	··
Mouri	na	na	2.5	2.5	2.5	2.5	2.5	2.5	2.5	2.5	3.0	4.0	4.0	4.0	··
Village Processed															
Parchment															
Grade I	na	na	15.0	15.0	15.0	15.0	17.0	17.0	17.0	17.0	20.0	27.0	27.0	27.0	··
Grade II	na	na	10.0	10.0	10.0	10.0	10.0	10.0	10.0	10.0	13.0	18.0	18.0	18.0	··
Grade III	na	na	na	na	2.5	2.5	2.50	2.50	2.25	2.25	3.0	4.0	4.0	4.0	··

Source: ADMARC various years, *Annual Report*, Ministry of Agriculture and National Resources, and official sources.

and ground nuts.[11] Although ADMARC's main objective was to safeguard the interests of the farmer by offering fair prices for agricultural produce and to reduce the risks and exploitation from private traders, it failed in its objectives with the formulation and adoption of a rigid agricultural price policy. While the estate sector remained the main segment in earning foreign exchange and generating employment, its expansion has significantly slowed down during the past 15 years, due mainly to the fact that the terms of trade and balance of payments in the international market remained unfavourable to Malawi. Besides the unfavourable balance of trade and payments, tight credit conditions, shortage of trained manpower, shortage of fuelwood for curing tobacco, and the constant and rigid price policy of ADMARC also resulted in the slow growth of the estate sector.

However, promotion of the small-farm sector is the key element in the development strategy of Malawi. Its consistent growth and and increasing surpluses are considered essential conditions for diversification of the agrarian economy in Malawi. The growth rate of at least 5% per annum has to be maintained and adequate price incentives and marketing services made readily accessible. Hence the agricultural price policy has to be more pragmatic and viable to achieve self-sufficiency in food production and the export surpluses necessary to boost the rural income. To achieve this type of development strategy, there should be a steady and secular growth of the small-holder sector and a higher rate of gross national investment in agriculture must be ensured. Thus, the development of an agricultural infrastructure, adoption of intensive cultivation to increase productivity per unit of land and labour, adequate supplies of modern inputs, better crop planning and resource allocation, development of irrigation, soil conservation, integration of research and training programmes, organisation of a viable institutional marketing system, and the adoption of a progressive price policy—all these are indispensable factors in the strategy for the development of the small-farm sector.

NOTES

1. Estates mainly under the management of foreign landlords and very few under natives.

2. World Bank, 1982, *Malawi: Growth and Structural Change—A Basic Economic Report.*
3. Ministry of Agriculture and Natural Resources, Malawi, 1975, 'Marketing of small-holder agricultural produce in Malawi,' *Reports*, vol I, no 16.
4. World Bank, 1982, *ibid.*
5. The author was a member of the team evaluating the progress of the Domasi Irrigation Project in 1982.
6. Malawi Government, Malawi, 1981, *Economic Report.*
7. Agricultural Development and Marketing Corporation, Malawi, 1975, *Ten Years of Progress.*
8. World Bank, 1982, *ibid.*
9. *Ibid.*
10. *Ibid.*
11. Malawi Government, Malawi, 1981, *ibid.*

REFERENCES

Agricultural Development and Marketing Corporation, 1975, 1981, *Ten Years of Progress*, Malawi.

Agricultural Extension and Training Department, 1974, Annual *Report*, Malawi.

Brown, Peter and Anthony Young, 'The physical environment of central Malawi.'

Malawi Government, 1971, 1972, 1981, 1982, *Economic Report.*

Malawi Government, 1977, *Census Report*, Vols. I and II, Malawi.

Malawi Government, 1982, Preliminary Draft: Integrated Rural Development Plan to Zomba and Machinga District in Malawi.

Malawi Government, *Youth in Malawi*, Malawi.

Ministry of Agriculture and Natural Resources, 1975, *Marketing of Small-Holder Agricultural Produce in Malawi*, Vols. I and II, Malawi.

Stevens, Robert D., *Tradition and Dynamics in Small Farm Agriculture.*

World Bank, 1981, 1982, *Annual Reports.*

World Bank, 1982, *Malawi: Growth and Structural Change—A Basic Economic Report.*

——*An Outline of Agrarian Problems and Policy in Nyasaland.*

——*Report: Shire Valley Development.*

——*Investment Background in Malawi.*

CHAPTER 21

Rwanda's Profile of Development

DEMOGRAPHY

The population of Rwanda is estimated at 5,450,000 inh (1982). This figure is based on the first general census of the population in August 1978 and the official estimate of the growth rate at 3.1%/year. The birth rate has remained at about 50%, while the death rate of 19% is tending towards a slight decline. This means a population growth of more than 160,000 per annum. Life expectancy is still low at 45 years and child mortality still high at 127% (probably underestimated) but has been worse (200% in 1940).

A quick flashback will help us to see in this rapid population growth one of the reasons for the destruction of the traditional ecological balance.

1936: 1,762,564 inh.
1950: 1,897,750
1960: 2,750,000
1970: 3,756,600

A division of the population based on age is also significant: Children under five years of age comprise 20% and under fifteen years 48% of the population. This leads us to think that the population will double in 22 years.

Table 21.1: Rwanda — Social Indicators Data Sheet

Land area (thousand sq. km.)

Total	26.3		
Agricultural	14.6		

	Rwanda			Reference Groups (Weighted Averages Most Recent Estimate)[a]	
	1960[b]	1970[b]	Most Recent Estimate[b]	Low Income Africa South of Sahara	Middle Income Africa South of Sahara
GNP per capita (US $)	70.0	100.0	200.0	238.3	794.2
Energy consumption per capita (Kilograms of coal equivalent)	..	15.8	29.5	70.5	707.5
Population and vital statistics					
Population, mid-year (thousands)	2916.0	3847.0	4947.0		
Urban population (per cent of total)	2.4	3.2	4.2	17.5	27.7
Population projections					
Population in year 2000 (millions)			9.5		
Stationary population (millions)			29.0		
Year stationary population is reached			2110		
Population density					
Per sq. km.	110.9	146.3	188.1	27.7	55.0
Per sq. km. agricultural land	193.1	253.1	328.8	73.7	130.7
Population age structure (per cent)					
0-14 yrs.	44.3	45.7	46.6	44.8	46.0
15-64 yrs.	53.0	51.6	50.7	52.4	51.2
65 yrs. and above	2.7	2.7	2.7	2.9	2.8

Population growth rate (per cent)					
Total	2.8	2.8	2.8ᵈ	2.6	2.8
Urban	5.6	5.6	5.8	6.5	5.1
Crude birth rate (per thousand)	51.1	49.8	49.6	46.9	46.9
Crude death rate (per thousand)	26.9	22.1	18.7	19.3	15.8
Gross reproduction rate	3.4ᵉ	3.4	3.4	3.1	3.2
Family planning					
Acceptors, annual (thousands)	..	..	..	..	..
Users (per cent of married women)	..	..	..	..	..
Food and nutrition					
Index of food production per capita (1969-71=100)	81.0	102.0	107.0	89.5	89.9
Per capita supply of calories (per cent of requirements)	80.0	96.0	98.0	90.2	92.3
Proteins (Grams per day)	49.0	61.0	51.3	52.7	52.8
of which animal and pulse	25.0	34.0	..	17.8	16.1
Child (ages 1-4) mortality rate	41.0	32.2	25.4	27.3	20.2
Health					
Life expectancy at birth (years)	37.2	42.4	46.7	45.8	50.8
Infant mortality rate (per thousand)	..	127.0	..	..	..
Access to safe water (per cent of population)					
Total	..	..	35.0	23.9	27.4
Urban	..	..	41.0	55.0	74.3
Rural	..	..	35.0	18.5	12.6

—*(Contd.)*

	Rwanda			Reference Groups (weighted average most recent estimate)[a]	
	1960[b]	1970[b]	Most Recent Estimate[b]	Low Income Africa South of Sahara	Middle Income Africa South of Sahara
Land area (thousand sq. km.)					
Total	26.3				
Agricultural	14.6				
Access to excreta disposal (per cent of population)					
Total	..	53.0	57.0	26.2	..
Urban	..	83.0	87.0	63.5	..
Rural	..	52.0	56.0	20.3	..
Population per physician	138095.0[e]	62048.4	38916.7	31911.8	13844.1
Population per nursing person	11197.0[e]	9181.4	10494.4	3674.9	2898.6
Population per hospital bed					
Total	..	822.9	652.1	1238.8	1028.4
Urban	..	47.8	45.4	272.8	423.0
Rural	..	3224.4	1604.8	1745.2	3543.2
Admissions per hospital bed	..	21.2	21.3	..	..
Housing					
Average size of household					
Total	..	..	..	..	..
Urban	..	..	..	..	..
Rural	..	..	4.5	..	..

Average number of persons per room					
Total	..	..	..	..	..
Urban	..	..	..	..	..
Rural	..	..	..	..	..
Access to electricity (per cent of dwellings)					
Total	..	..	..	..	..
Urban	..	..	..	..	..
Rural	..	..	..	..	..
Education					
Adjusted enrolment ratios					
Primary: Total	49.0	73.0	64.0	56.4	73.7
Male	68.0	83.0	68.0	70.7	96.8
Female	30.0	64.0	59.0	50.1	79.0
Secondary: Total	2.0	2.0	2.0	10.0	16.2
Male	2.0	3.0	3.0	13.6	25.3
Female	1.0	1.0	1.0	6.6	14.8
Vocational enrol. (% of secondary)	40.0	12.0	17.0	8.0	5.3
Pupil-teacher ratio					
Primary	39.0	60.0	53.0	46.5	36.2
Secondary	14.0	13.0	15.0	25.5	23.6
Adult literacy rate (per cent)	16.4[c]	23.0[e]	..	25.5	..
Consumption					
Passenger cars per thousand Population	0.4	0.9	1.6	2.9	32.3
Radio receivers per thousand Population	..	7.8	17.1	32.8	69.0

—(Contd.)

| | Rwanda | | | Reference Groups (weighted averages most recent estimate[a]) | |
	1960[b]	1970[b]	Most Recent Estimate[b]	Low income Africa South of Sahara	Middle Income Africa South of Sahara
Land area (thousand sq. km.)					
Total	26.3				
Agricultural	14.6				
TV receivers per thousand Population			..	1.9	8.0
Newspaper ('daily general interest')					
Circulation per thousand population			0.04	2.8	20.2
Cinema annual attendance per capita			14.6	1.2	0.7
Labour force					
Total labour force (thousands)	1650.6	2089.7	2582.3		
Female (per cent)	49.1	48.6	48.1	34.1	36.7
Agriculture (per cent)	95.4	93.2	91.2	80.0	56.6
Industry (per cent)	1.1	1.6	2.0	8.6	17.5
Participation rate (per cent)					
Total	56.6	54.3	52.2	41.7	37.2
Male	58.9	56.9	55.0	54.3	47.1
Female	54.4	51.9	49.5	29.2	27.5
Economic dependency ratio	0.8	0.9	0.9	1.2	1.3
Income distribution					
Per cent of private income Received by					
Highest 5 per cent of households	..	..	..	..	..
Highest 20 per cent of households	..	..	..	..	..

Lowest 20 per cent of households	..	..			
Lowest 40 per cent of households	..	..			
Poverty Target Groups					
Estimated absolute poverty income Level (US $ per capita)					
Urban	..	..	148.0	136.0	381.2
Rural	..	..	85.0	84.5	156.2
Estimated relative poverty income Level (US $ per capita)					
Urban	..	..	..	99.1	334.3
Rural	..	..	43.0	61.2	137.6
Estimated population below absolute poverty income level (per cent)					
Urban	..	..	30.0	39.7	..
Rural	..	..	90.0	68.8	..

.. Not available.
. Not applicable.

ªThe group averages for each indicator are population-weighted arithmetic means. Coverage of countries among the indicators depends on availability of data and is not uniform.

ᵇUnless otherwise noted, data *for 1960* refer to any year between 1959 and 1961; *for 1970,* between 1969 and 1971; and for *Most Recent Estimate,* between 1976 and 1979.

ᶜ1962.

ᵈRecent estimated growth rate is 3.2%.

ᵉ1973.

We must also not forget the three million Rwandese living in adjacent countries (Uganda and Zaire); their existence is a further threat to the country, as was seen in the latest expulsion of Rwandese from Uganda.

This population growth, already significant in itself, has to be related to spatial repartition. The density in relation to the total surface area of the country is already 207 inh/km^2, the highest in Africa (except for the Island of Mauritius). But if the surfaces that cannot be cultivated are omitted (lakes, natural parks, rivers etc.), the density is 306; with regional differences, depending on soil and climate—380 inh/km^2 in Ruhengeri and 135 inh/km^2 in Kibungo (1978).

We must also take into account the 'urban' population: Rwanda is one of the three lowest urbanised countries in the world, with only 5.2% of the population considered urban. This rate is probably overestimated due to a very broad definition of urban areas. The 1978 census boasted 12 cities, which could more appropriately be labeled 'villages'. There are only four centres with more than 10,000 people: Kigali, the capital (160,000), Butare (21,000), Ruhengeri (16,000), and Gisenyi (12,500).

It is important to understand that rural housing is spread over the hills, with each family living on its own hill. There is no village tradition, as such, in Rwanda.

Schools, dispensaries, communal administrative centres and parishes are also spread over the hills, with no grouping of these various infrastructures. Commercial centres are merely a cluster of small shops open during the day; shopkeepers return to their hills in the evening. But a significant trend is evident in that shopkeepers have begun to build their houses behind their shops. Also, officials traditionally must build a house in their birthplace; more and more are building near a commercial centre because water and electricity, impossible to introduce in the hills, are available infrastructures in these centres. The traditional spreading out of housing is often cited as the primary reason for the high costs of these infrastructures which, in turn, prohibit bringing such necessary services to the people. This statement has yet to be proved against the following refutations:

1) Low cost of the basic infrastructure: tapping of water resources and building new roads and classrooms would be done by

the population itself.

2) A greater density of population implies a density of infra-structures.

3) Although the population has grown, it remains confined within the country, except for those who have already migrated to neighbouring countries.

Speaking of migration, this phenomenon ceased twenty years ago for political reasons. However, in spite of the absence of indus-tries in Kigali city a rural exodus has begun, raising the city's population from less than 10,000 inhabitants in 1962 (date of In-dependence) to 160,000 in 1982. Before Independence the entire administration and colonial infrastructures were concentrated in Bujumbura (now capital of Burundi) and nothing existed in Kigali. If the population continues to grow at the current rate of 8% per annum, Kigali will become a city of more than 500,000 inh before the year 2,000. The fact that the population of Kigali doubles every eight years gives rise to many problems, among them the very high costs of infrastructures (increased by the relief).

AGRICULTURE

Two elements—a rapid demographic growth and a very low urbani-sation of an almost exclusively rural population—help us to under-stand the dramatic land problem of Rwanda, with a non-extend-able surface that is already almost totally occupied.

Leaving the 5.3% urban rate aside (which, as shall be seen later, is not a correct estimate) and dividing the population by the average number of persons in a family (4.7 after the census), one obtains the number of rural families, i.e., 1,099,277 (1982).

The surface available for agriculture in the country has been estimated as 51% of the total surface (the rest is occupied by lakes, forests, natural parks, research centres, roads etc.). Should the whole available surface be cultivated (which is hardly the case), the average area per family would be 1.2 ha. As a matter of fact, more than 60% of the population probably have less than one hectare, as indicated by the following data collected in 1976:

surfaces (in ha)	−0.5	0.5—0.99	1.0—1.49	1.5—3.49	3.5—4.99	+5.0
% of total in farms	36.3	27	20	12.2	4	0.5

At present, the inequalities are not so large, but they are growing. Many tradesmen and officials are seeking to invest their savings, to ensure the future of their children, in one of the safest values— land. The government has issued a decree forbidding all trade in land (despite the fact that in Rwanda land is considered private property, and not communal as in other African countries). But this law is seldom respected.

It should also be emphasised that an estimated number of 40,000 new peasant families seek settlement every year. This situation has disastrous effects in various sectors:

1) Nutrition: more extensive culture of sweet potato, worsening of child nutrition, and growth of kwashiorkor.

2) Employment: rapid rise in under-employment in the hills and alcoholic consumption (banana beer).

3) Ecology: traditional agricultural techniques, perfectly adapted for a sparse population, are having a drastic effect now. Vertical slopes, traditionally preserved, are now being cultivated. Fields are no longer allowed to lie fallow and soil exhaustion is not compensated by the use of fertiliser, natural or chemical. One might also mention the diminution of livestock, but this has never been tied into agriculture.

In analysing the production and surface data available for the last ten years (1967-77), the following trends are evident:

a) total food production has increased about 4.48% per annum; and

b) the surface brought under cultivation has increased 3.85% per annum.

The following conclusions can be inferred from the foregoing trends:

1). The increase in food production proceeds essentially from extension of the cultivated surface.

2) The increase due to intensification is less than 1% per annum (0.63% on the average), which makes one question the common methods used in agriculture (see below).

3) The increase in cultivated surface is of about the same order as the increase in population. Disregarding the banana plantations (their surface area increases about 6% per annum), the rest of the food-producing area has increased in rhythm with the population increment. Since there are no more 'new lands' available, it is imperative that some other means, rather than extension of agricultural lands, be found to maintain the balance between population and production.

How can a policy of more intensive agriculture be implemented?

First of all the national authorities must be convinced of its absolute necessity. Words do not suffice. The Five-Year Plan (77-81) called for a priority in food agriculture, but the proposed rate of growth was only 3% versus 12% for export agriculture. Considerable foreign aid was extended to tea plantations during these years—certainly an excellent avenue for obtaining foreign exchange. But because tea plantations tend to occupy the valleys, their development takes place at the expense of traditional farming, for which the valleys are quite essential in the dry season.

A recent nutritional survey in a region of tea plantations revealed that 57% of the families not involved in the cultivation of tea had sufficient calories in their food, but only 5% of the families devoted to the cultivation of tea.

Once the priority of intensive agriculture has been defined (although the agriculture budget does not exceed 5% of the ordinary budget of the state—95% of the population), it is necessary to develop a model for popularisation of suitable methods. For years, typically all the projects in Rwanda have been based on the model evolved by the national research centre for an intensive micro-farm of one hectare. But this theoretical model, developed in a laboratory, does not take into account these facts: most of the peasants have less than one hectare and often their land is divided into many plots spread over the hills.

The national research centre retains various European techniques in its technical package: a) separation of different cultivations; and b) sowing of selected seeds—which under local conditions would further deteriorate production-versus the traditional technique of mixing cultures to provide a permanent soil cover and thus better protection against erosion. Sowing different varieties of bean seeds is a guarantee of production in a country where phytosanitaire products are still absolutely impossible to obtain (if one variety is attacked, the others continue to produce).

Seed selection and experimental cultivations are generally done in a laboratory where European conditions are reproduced inso-far as possible. Vulgarisation is not the research centre's responsi-bility, but the government's. Such projects are totally ineffective because the experts in agricultural problems, the agronomists (for theory) are cut off from the peasants (for practice). Only tests done in a mutual joint effort between the two partners can be successful.

Large integrated regional development projects are rapidly in-creasing under the momentum of aid from large international organisations. But several considerations are involved. First, the preliminary study. Foreign experts come to Kigali for two or three weeks to define the project and to propose growth rates for pro-duction (which ensures repayment of loans). But these growth rates are based on *foreign agricultural techniques*, which are total-ly unsuitable (see above) because the foreign experts have no time for regional planning based on advice from the peasants. The proposed objectives are agreed to by the national authorities, if advantages to the local managerial staff are forthcoming (see below) and external financing sufficient.

How are these large regional development projects implement-ed? They commence with the construction of houses *for the foreign experts* and, later, for the local staff. *Service cars* are given to the local staff (since cars are considered necessary for setting up com-merce) as well as gratuities over and above the official salaries paid them by the government. All too often the greater part of external aid is spent in this manner. Are these projects therefore a policy of development of the rural masses or merely the 'pur-chase' of a favoured class constituency linked to foreign investors who depend on them? Is it possible to imagine any useful and trustful relationship being established between such technicians and the peasants?

How does one form and inform the peasant? Generally grass-root technicians are given an accelerated training programme (two or three months, without basic agronomic education) and made responsible for the 'pilot' plots assigned the peasants. We have already studied the bad results of this policy, based on the contention that the peasant needs someone to look after him.

Very few studies have been done on the dynamics of rural areas, on existing or potential cooperatives—traditionally discarded in an African society where differences are great.

People also seldom think about the future of a project, i.e., what will become of the monitors once the project is over?

A foreign director of the largest school for agronomy in Rwanda once said to me: 'To listen and to work with the peasants is not possible. The agronomists must give them precise instructions and penalise them when these instructions are not followed.' If this is the kind of authority and contempt agronomists feel is necessary to maintain relations with the peasants, I greatly fear the results will be negative.

Let me conclude the foregoing remarks with an example of a very large integrated development project in the region of Gisenyi. The aim of this project was the re-afforestation of 10,000 hectares with pine, after the destruction of one of the last natural forests in the country. It is significant that after elaborating their plan, the foreign experts in charge of the project met with the local mayors. The mayors raised important objections to the project, pertaining mainly to the protection of springs and the erosion that would result from the work of re-afforestation. Since the foreigners considered the project highly profitable, the mayors' objections were brushed aside.

Six thousand workers were engaged for the work of afforestation, and received a salary for three or four years.

In spite of requests from the communes and alternate proposals, such as cooperative afforestation (which would have been much more economical), the project centered on a state forest, which held no interest for the peasants.

The salaries received by the 6,000 unskilled workers were so low that no savings or small investment, other than drinking beer, was possible during the three or four years they worked.

What were the results of this project?

a) erosion and exhaustion of the springs;

b) afforestation with no guarantee for the future (what will a population without land and wood for its own use do?); and

c) proletarianisation of an entire population, with no education toward self-organisation and self-reliance given to the peasants.

EMPLOYMENT

The employment problem is very difficult indeed. A survey made
in 1976 and confirmed in the 1978 census (active population aged
15 to 64 or 2,650,000 inh.) proposed the following repartition
of the work force (in per cent):

—traditional farming	89.1
—paid workers on traditional farms	2.3
—private and parastatal sectors	2.7
—public sector	1.2
—informal sector	2.8
—domestic service	0.8
—other	1.1

A few cogent observations can be drawn from the foregoing
data:

1) Nine-tenths of the population work on their farms which
are already too small. The peasants allocate more than one-third
of a day's work to agricultural tasks. It is admitted that the labour
force is 30% under-employed because of disguised under-employment for 930,000 persons in 1982, or to put it another way, according to our estimate of 1976, more than 150 million days of work
were not utilised. Differences between regions and between seasons should also be noted.

2) Paid work in traditional farming is important, but more
often than not, only part time.

3) The 'modern' sector of production (private and parastatal)
occupies only a small minority of the population. The specific
policy operating in this sector is significant: 51% of the enterprises employing 20 or more workers are located in the capital,
and these 'large firms' absorb 60% of the permanent paid works.
Small enterprises, employing fewer than 20 workers have already
spread out, with only 26% located in Kigali.

4) It is significant that the informal sector constitutes a group
more important than the 'modern' sector of production, although
there has been no policy working in this direction.

Since the active population has risen from 2.2 million in 1976
to 2.5 million in 1981, it is necessary to create 75,000 new posts
every year, just to keep pace with the actual rate of under-employ-

ment. (The Plan of 1977-81 proposed the creation of 25,000 new posts but did not fulfill this objective.)

Supposing a slow-down in the growth of self-employment in traditional farming (reduced to 1.2% instead of 3.1% of the annual growth), 45,000 jobs per year would have to be found for the people forced to leave their farms (1.9%). Let us also not forget the natural growth of the non-agricultural sector (11% of the population), requiring another 9,300 jobs per year.

Finally, 54,300 jobs would have to be created per year, outside the traditional farm requirements, to avoid a further deterioration in under-employment. Yet in the modern sector of the economy, no more than 2,000 jobs were created per annum according to the 1976 survey (the number has risen since then).

Faced with this situation, what kind of employment policy does the government intend to implement? This problem is still presented as a first priority, but often ignored by foreign plan advisers, who are interested first and foremost in foreign exchange and then in industrial production to ensure a growth of GNP. Such a policy[1] is not based on an analysis of the problems that beset Rwanda, but on the European model, which is particularly desirous of selling modern technology. The implementation of such a foreign-based policy would engender even greater problems for Rwanda:

1) Massive rural exodus of people unemployed at the regional level, who would find no jobs in Kigali. Modern industries cost a great deal of money in order to create jobs. According to an actual investment programme, an investment of 5 million FRW was projected for one employment; in other words, a minimum programme of 10,000 jobs per year would cost 50 million!

2) Massive inequalities between a few people well paid in a modern industry and the masses, and also between the regions and the capital.

3) Heavy foreign dependency—technology, spare parts, special raw material importation, etc. But Rwanda is very isolated. The choice is between 1,200 km from Mombasa on a non-secure road through Uganda or air transportation, which is expensive. In fact, one-third of the cost of imported products is imputed to transport. Yet one cannot ignore that the imports are also the first revenue source for the state; 60% of the revenue provided

in the national budget is derived from taxes on imports and the export of coffee. Thus one can understand the contradiction between the desire to limit imports, especially of luxury items, but an interest in paying official salaries.

Having surveyed the harmful effects of a foreign-oriented policy, and given our regional experience, I would like to propose six steps toward the implementation of an intermediate technology policy in Rwanda (a country with no traditional crafts other than basketry):

1) Identify local needs, as well as regional and national (the local market is too limited due to small revenue returns).

2) Identify all local raw materials which could be transformed into marketable products through cottage industries.

3) Search for needed intermediate technologies, i.e., those requiring more than simple manual work, in which productivity is low, but not requiring sophisticated foreign technology.

4) Search for old craftsmen in Rwanda or abroad who could teach new techniques to people in the region, and popularise the the products among the youth.

5) Help young people organise themselves in autonomous productive groups (cooperatives—*not* technical schools) and instruct them in management and accountancy systems that are easy to understand.

6) Help the local cooperatives by providing assistance in the marketing of their products, sending in special tools and raw materials that are not available locally, and establishing a credit system.

INCOME

In 1976, the average annual income of the rural population (95% of the total population) was estimated at 9,890 FRW per capita, of which 3,980 FRW is in currency. The income of the non-rural population was estimated at 24,190 FRW. Important differences between the rural and urban populations are readily apparent. An analysis of the scales of the different sectors revealed the following relations:

1) Between peasants and officials: the average gross wage of an official (142,500 F in 1976) established a relation of 1:14 (without taking into account the *extra* revenue of officials).

2) Between officials (clerk to Secretary-General): 1:20.

3) In the private sector, between unskilled labourers and managerial staff: 1:20.

4) Between Rwandese and foreigners: According to the local newspaper, the 32 members of the expatriated managerial staff of SOMIRWA (Society of Miners of Rwanda) together earned more than the 9,500 Rwandese workers and staff involved in this enterprise.

Income in terms of currency is very low for the peasant. Generally he sells a basket of sweet potatoes on the market to buy a piece of soap or some salt.

A high percentage of the income in currency (a little less than half) originates from coffee and reaches about 50% of the peasant families in the country. Actually, the peasants receive one-third of the price of coffee arriving in Mombasa; governmental taxes and the price of transport absorb the other two-thirds.

It was possible to make some surveys regarding monetary income in the rural sphere, in the commune of Kanama (10 cells were approached on five different occasions; a cell is the basic political unit and comprises 500 people). These surveys were undertaken between 1978 (Rumbati), 1979 (Rumbati, Nyagasozi, Kagera, Ruraji, kasonga, Giseyo) and 1981 (Nyabishongo, Kagera and Nyamugali). Because of the short time lapse between surveys, it was difficult to reckon a change in income, even though a distinct difference was apparent between 1978 and 1981.

The commune of Kanama is a good example of the rural environment in Rwanda. Tea, not coffee, is grown here and the area can be divided into two geographical regions. The first has a median altitude (1,850 m), with good lava soil, and a very high population density (more than 500 inh/km²)—Rumbati, Nyagasozi, and Nyamugali, and is located near an important commercial centre, a bishopric, and a tarmac road. The second region is at an altitude of 2,000 m, has a lower population density (300-400 inh/km²), with poorer soil, and more isolated—farther than 10 km from the centre and without an access road because of the hills.

These surveys revealed that the average family income in terms of currency is about 2,074 FRW per month (average of 10 cells). Wages occupy first place, constituting more than the monetary income of the families (56%) and originate mainly (more than half) from a tea plantation. But only 37% of the families earn wages, which are far more important to the cells neighbouring the centre than to cells farther removed.

In the survey of five cells made in 1979, the average wage income per family was more than 1,000 F in the two cells nearest the centre (1,105 in Nyagasozi and 1,070 in Rumbati), but under 600 F in the others (593, 535, and 266 F).

A comparative survey in Nyamugali and Kagera revealed a significant difference in the average wages (1,220 to 5,065 F); Nyamugali, the cell nearest the commercial centre, revealed other significant differences. Half the families have a paid job, mainly in tea plantations, and possess two thirds of the cell's monetary income. A few families in this cell were without land for the first time.

In order of importance, the second source of monetary income is banana beer (15% of the total currency income). This income is more evenly distributed, since about 66% of the families enjoy it. But in this respect also the cells of Kagera and Nyamugali are interesting: all the families in Kagera earn a monetary income from beer, but only 63% in Nyamugali (because the other families have no land). The contribution of banana beer to monetary income is much more important to an isolated cell like Kagera (33% of the monetary income) and less significant (relatively speaking) in Nyamugali (8%).

The monthly monetary income of a family converted into a per capita monetary income per year (divided by an average family of 4.7 members and multiplied by twelve) is 5,295 FRW for the ten cells, but only 3,673 FRW if the cell of Nyamugali with its much higher income is left out.

The absence of coffee is certainly one of the reasons for these much lower incomes (3,980 FRW at the national level in 1976).

The monetary income is concentrated: 50% of the families of Nyabishongo receive 13% of the monetary income, while 50% of the monetary income belongs to 15% of the families who have the highest incomes. Differences are more significant between the regions of this commune, namely, a ratio of 1:10 between the cell of Gisayo located near the border of the forest at a higher altitude (2,200 m) with a lower income and no banana trees, and the cell of Nyamugali located near the market.

A survey of Nyabishongo made it possible to establish the redistribution of the monetary income:

—food and beverages: 42 to 56% (beverages alone accounted for 16.6%, which is quite a sizable sum;
—clothes: 17 to 31%
—housing and equipment: 14 to 16%
—taxes and leisure activities (tobacco): 5 to 8%
—school and health: 2%
—various (workers, transport etc.): 2 to 4%.

The other surveys confirmed the progress of rural housing parallel to a better monetary income: 100% pisé masonry houses with 85% leafed roofs in Gisayo near the forest (monetary income: 769), 61% pisé masonry houses with 69% leafed roof in Kagera (monetary income: 2,839), and 37% pisé masonry houses with 49% leafed roofs in Nyamugali (monetary income: 7,793). The remaining families are building houses of bricks and tuiles (iron roof).

It was very difficult to estimate the non-monetary income, and could only be done in Nyabishongo after spending an entire year surveying all the daily food consumed. The non-monetary income was calculated from the entire food prepared by the family, at the market price; and the wood used in cooking (not the leaves). The non-monetary income was thus established at 5,491 FRW or 55% of the total income of Nyabishongo in 1980 (9,983 FRW).

SCHOOLS

The primary school attendance rate is already 56.8%. Generally speaking, people say that two-thirds, of the children begin primary school and one-third finish (six years). Of this one-third, 10% are admitted to secondary schools (six years) on the basis of a national examination, seriously administered but highly affected by various balance principles (ethnic, regional, religious, and so on).

In a recent and famous interview (November 1982), the Minister of National Education, accused of favouring only his place of birth, indirectly recognised the accusation by arguing the intellectual retardation of the region. He also explained that it is equitable to give a place in the secondary school to children of high officials, even when they fail the national examination, because of the service rendered to the country by their parents.

The number of places in secondary schools is very limited due to the obligation of boarding schools (see below); thus other, qualified children must be excluded.

If the access to the ruling class was very open until now because of the eradication of the Tutsi feudalist elite in 1959 and because of independence in 1962, this kind of practice intends to close the door to the ruling class.

Primary schools are spread over the hills. The absence of cities involved a similar distribution for the secondary schools, built without a national plan, which are located more often near one or the other parish. For this reason, all secondary schools are boarding schools. Because each school is specialised, the children are named by the Ministry of Education for a given school and thus are sent all over the country. This involves some major costs (transportation, boarding expenses) but is certainly an important factor in achieving national unity.

The secondary schools are modeled along the classical European lines and have virtually no ties with the rural society in a particular region, other than commodities from the market.

Access to the National University (+ 1,000 students) or obtaining a scholarship to study abroad, follow the same principles outlined for admission to a secondary school.

A very important reform came in 1979 for the purpose of bringing the schools closer to rural society. The general outlines of this reform are given below:

—scholastic study of the national language (*kinyarwanda*);
—suppression of re-doubling in class to avoid delays in scholastic education;
—extension of formal education for another two years with an accent on practical application—agriculture, carpentry, building, cooking, and so forth; and
—after the eighth year of formal education, 10% of the children succeeding in the national examination would go on to studies in a specialised secondary school and the remaining 90% would attend a rural post-primary school for three years (ERAI, i e., *Ecoles Rurales et Artisanales Intégrées*).

But this reform was highly theoretical and engendered a series of new problems:

```
 ┌ ─ ─ ─ ─ ─ ─ ─ ─ ─ ─ ─ ─ ─ ┐
 │ CONSCIENTISATION PROCESS │
 └ ─ ─ ─ ─ ─ ─ ─ ─ ─ ─ ─ ─ ─ ┘
```

BANKING (DOMESTICATING)   LIBERATING EDUCATION
        EDUCATION

```
                              ┌ ─ ─ ─ ─ ─ ─ ┐
                              │  ACTORS  │
                              └ ─ ─ ─ ─ ─ ─ ┘
```

            Teacher   Teacher — Student
         ↓   ↓   ↓   ↓
Student   given reality which   interaction
             man must accept, and to
             which he must adjust   transform reality as a problem
                                         to be worked and solved

```
                         ┌ ─ ─ ─ ─ ─ ─ ─ ┐
                         │  METHODS  │
                         └ ─ ─ ─ ─ ─ ─ ─ ┘
```

Transference of knowledge and slogans   Reflection and action together
                                           reflection only = verbalism
                                           action only   = actionism

Teacher	*Students*	*Teacher-Student*
teaches	are taught	exchange
knows everything	know nothing	research
thinks	are thought about	mutual education
talks	listen meekly	creative subjects
acts	have the illusion	
	of acting through	
	the action of the	
	teacher	
disciplines	are disciplined	
subject of the		
learning process	objects	

```
                         ┌ ─ ─ ─ ─ ─ ─ ─ ┐
                         │  OBJECT  │
                         └ ─ ─ ─ ─ ─ ─ ─ ┘
```

Alienation   Liberation
                                           (critical consciousness)

Men become *objects*, convinced of   Men become *subjects* of their history,
their radical incapacity to control   conscious of their radical capacity
reality and their destiny   to liberate themselves mutually
(fatalism)   and to create new reality, as a
                                         new common destiny

'Nobody can save himself, nobody can save the others, people save
themselves together' (Paulo Freire).

'One tree can't be a forest.'   'One stake does not build a house.
                                              (proverbs from Rwanda)

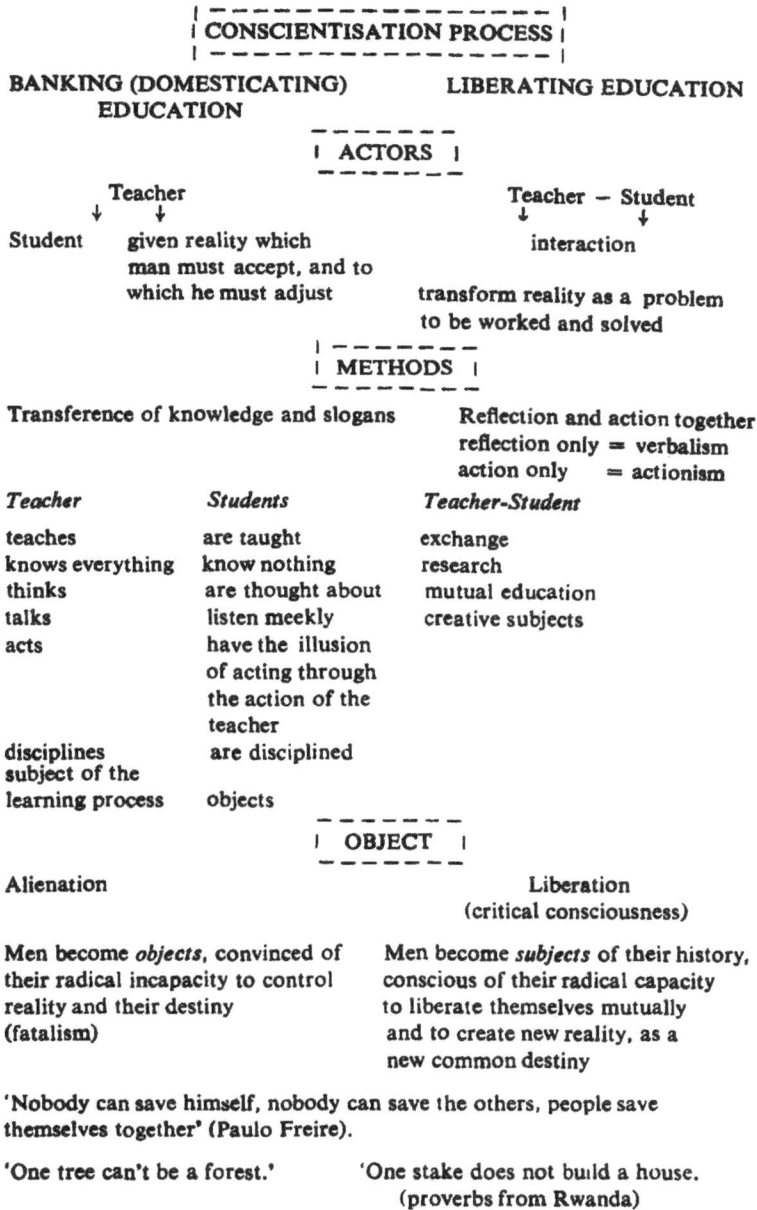

Figure 21.2: Conscientisation process.

1) Enormous investments and very high costs in new salaries (the national education budget already constitutes the most important in the entire budget at 21%). Requiring a host of new teachers would mean employing many who are not educated, and result in a school of poor quality (as would the suppression of re-doubling).

2) Practical education requires land (there is no more), production material (with night watchmen to safeguard against thievery), and qualified teachers (with just a special three-month study course in all these crafts, no teacher could be a good instructor).

3) The ERAI is rural oriented and thus rejected by the official class in Kigali. This class sends their children to European schools and has also built a private school with a traditional scholastic programme taught in French (because convinced that there would be no intellectual future for their children otherwise).

4) This reform practically speaking, is a deception. Will children after 11 years of schooling (8 + 3) agree to return to the hills? It is more likely that they will seek a job, confident in a skill they really don't possess, and find no jobs available. Subsequently, they will become embittered and prepare for a revolution, that will never take place because they have never learned self-organisation.

THE DEVELOPMENT PLAN

The government has initiated, in principle, a very interesting policy of local autonomy for development. The country has been divided into 143 communes of ± 30,000 inh, with a *mayor nominated by the central government* (but hailing from his commune) and *elected communal advisors*. Each commune, considered a basic cell for development, has financial autonomy, i.e., its own revenue and budget. Each pays its employees and can negotiate directly with foreign non-governmental agencies for aid to realise its development programme.

This important concept is exposed to dangers through an increase in expenses not met by an increase in revenue in the communes, mismanagement of the communes and lack of competence of the mayors and their aides (generally teachers of primary schools) to initiate a global development. Nevertheless, the country can still be considered at the communal level a 'laboratory of developmental experiences' (cooperatives, health centres, crafts, and so forth).

At the country level it appears that the authorities are finding it difficult to implement a genuine global national development policy. The MRND (*Movement Revolutionaire National pour le Dèveloppement*), the unique party of the country, is not an effective mobilising power and various international organisations and foreign countries generally impose their own concepts on proposed projects. The Five-Year Plans remain mainly as an exercise in modernity for foreign experts, wherein each ministry can pursue its own policies. What seems essential is the realisation of foreign financing for as many projects as possible. It is significant that 85% of the development budget is financed by foreign aid, and the major expenses in the national budget (45%) are the salaries of the officials.

CONCLUSIONS

No conclusions are offered, because this is merely a 'discussion paper'.

NOTES

1. A UNIDO expert in Kigali once explained to me the economic necessity of Rwanda adopting a profitable industrial policy through the investment of capital and the importation of foreign technology to ensure good productivity. When I asked him what could be done at the regional level, the expert replied that it could be studied later, benefiting perhaps through a conversion of raw materials.

CHAPTER 22

The Popular Revolutionary Republic of Guinea: Effective Discrimination Against Small Farmers in a Socialist Economy

Even the most elementary data in Guinea are extremely scarce, often contradictory, and generally very unreliable. Some basic 'country profile data' (World Bank compilation) are presented in Appendix A. The stagnation of the agricultural sector in Guinea may be of interest in that the problems considered (State intervention in farming and marketing, disincentive effects of price structures and an over-valued local currency) are those faced by a number of other developing countries, though generally less acutely.

THE AGRICULTURAL SECTOR—IMPORTANCE AND EVOLUTION

In the absence of any proper demographic data, an educated guess would place the population resident in rural areas at 80-85%, the labour force primarily engaged in agricultural activities at about 80%, and the present share of agricultural and related activities at about 44% GDP.

The recent evolution of *output* from the main economic sectors (using an index based on constant prices) is presented in Table 22.1. The changing *shares* of these sectors in GDP for these same years are presented in Table 22.2. Leaving aside the problem of pricing,[1] and data reliability, the following points emerge from the data presented in these two tables.

1. Agricultural output has steadily declined in absolute terms — by 15.2% from 1976 to 1980, or about 3.8% p.a.—during a period of slow overall GDP growth. So if we assume a rate of population growth of about 3.0% p.a., this decline means a decline in agricultural output per head of about 6.8% p.a.

2. The relative share of agricultural output in GDP has also steadily declined over the same period, from 53% to 44% of GDP.

Table 22.1: Indices of Contribution of Principal Sectors
to GDP, at Constant (1973) Prices

	1976	1977	1978	1979	1980
a) Agriculture, livestock, fishing etc.	100	94.4	94.8	88.9	84.8
b) Industry and mining	100	101.3	109.7	108.4	114.2
c) Services, etc.	100	98.4	115.1	125.1	129.2
Total GDP	100	96.7	103.2	102.1	103.0

Table 22.2: Shares of Principal Sectors in GDP,
at Constant (1973) Prices (percentages)

	1976	1977	1978	1979	1980
a) Agriculture, livestock, fishing, etc.	53	52	49	47	44
Agriculture	38	36	33	31	28
Livestock	4	4	4	4	4
Fishing	1	1	1	1	1
Forestry	10	11	11	11	11
b) Industry and mining	17	17	17	18	19
c) Services, etc.	30	31	34	35	37
Total	100	100	100	100	100

Poverty and Rural Development

This stagnation of agricultural production is also, and not surprisingly, reflected in official import-export statistics. The dramatic decline in exports since 1957 (pre-Independence) is very evident. modified only by a pick-up in palm kernel exports since 1977.

Colonial Guinea was, in fact, geared to the export of such commodities as bananas, coffee, pineapples and palm kernels, which were grown on small, highly subsidised, foreign-owned plantations, and sold on the protected French market. By compensation, one might expect to see a switch in resources to food crops for local consumption and an increase in national food self-sufficiency.

Table 22.3: Merchandise Exports of Selected Agricultural Commodities

('000 tonnes)

	1957	1964/65	1972/73	1974/75	1976	1977	1978	1979
Bananas	91	42	9	1	—	—	—	—
Coffee	10	5	4	2	1	2	1	2
Pineapples	2	5	8	8	3	2	2	2
Palm Kernels	22	25	16	9	7	10	13	15

Instead, food imports have increased rather steadily. Cereal imports, only 7,000 tonnes in 1958, have now reached about 80—100,000 tonnes p.a.

Another consequence of the decline in agricultural production has been the very low capacity utilisation of agro-industrial plants,[2] built after Independence in the late 1960s and early 1970s, and the resultant high unit costs (though lack of agricultural inputs has not been the *only* constraint).

This disappointing performance contrasts with Guinea's very considerable potential: variety of eco-regions, generous endowment of water resources, fair rainfalls (1,200 mm p.a. in the *driest* areas), large livestock herd (estimated at over 2 million head of N'dama trypanosomiasis-resistant cattle), and general lack of population pressure. Such potentials should enable the country to be a net exporter of agricultural produce.

Government Agricultural Policy

The very poor performance of the agricultural sector is especially alarming in view of the fact that since the early 1970s it has been consistently accorded the 'priority of priorities' in official policy pronouncements.

Let us examine the different components of government policy to see what has gone wrong.

a) GOVERNMENT INVESTMENT EXPENDITURE—LEVEL AND
   DIRECTION

The most obvious category of government resource transfer to agriculture is the extent of public investment expenditure in this sector.

The total investment expenditure levels and sectoral shares over the first three Plan periods, and projected expenditures for the current fourth Plan are presented in Table 22.4.

Both the relative share and the absolute level of investment expenditure devoted to Rural Development increased considerably in the 1973-78 Plan—with the projected share and level are higher still for the current Plan.

Though no disaggregated data are available regarding the composition of this expenditure, it appears to have been almost exclusively devoted to the collective/state farming sector, to the virtual exclusion of the small-farmer sector.

Table 22.4: Government Investment Expenditure Levels and
Sectoral Shares (Based on Current Prices)

	Actual 1960-63	Actual 1964-71	Actual 1973-78	Projected 1981-85
Total capital expenditure (millions of sylis) of which:	3,725.5	8,760.0	9,865.8	31,920.0
Rural development	13%	7%	27%	31%
Industry & energy	17%	48%	40%	32%
Public works & transport	34%	33%	15%	18%
Other sectors	36%	12%	18%	19%
Total	100%	100%	100%	100%

The Third Plan period does indeed coincide with the inaugura-
tion of the Mechanised Production Brigade strategy, in which
some 4,300 collective farms were established across the country
(see Appendix B for a note on the various collective experiments
in agriculture). It is estimated that in 1975 and 1976 some 4,000
tractors were imported from Eastern Europe and the USSR to
equip these farms, which alone must have accounted for a very
considerable share of the investment in Rural Development in the
Third Plan Period. Aside from equipping these Brigades, another
large segment of investment expenditure was undoubtedly given to
the various State agro-industrial ventures set up in this period.

The composition of planned investment flows to agriculture
under the current (1981-85) Plan is similar: 24% has been allotted
to the development of the latest variant in collective farming, the
Provincial Agro-Pastoral Farms or FAPAs (see appendix B); and
40% to large-scale agricultural or agro-industrial joint venture
enterprises (in association with foreign capital). This leaves only
26% *at most* of the agricultural investment expenditure for the
small-farm sector—but, of course, there are other competing
claims (administration buildings and equipment), and indications
of *actual* costs of setting up the FAPAs suggest that they will
overrun their allotted share of resources.

To put this investment pattern into perspective, it is worth
noting that even on *official* estimates, the area cultivated by the
Mechanised Farming Brigades was about 100,000 ha in 1976,
declining to 25,000 ha in 1979, while the total area cultivated by
small-holders was of the order of 1 million hectares for both years
(though slightly less in 1979 than in 1976).

This '*uneven* distribution' of investment resources does not
necessarily imply 'inequitable' allocation. After all, the MFBs
are collective farms in which the entire local community is supposed to participate and gain revenue thereby. In practice, however, the several reasons noted in Appendix B, participation has
been limited and the capital equipment has actually profited *no
one* very much (apart, perhaps, from its occasional re-sale or use
for private transport by LRP officials).

The inefficiency of this continuing pattern is very evident:
physical yields per hectare are very low (often less than half those
of small farms), and financial costs per unit output very high

(1.5 to 3.0 times higher than on small farms—and this even with imported inputs bought with 'artificially cheap' foreign exchange!).

b) PRICES AND MARKETING SYSTEM

But the simple exclusion of small farmers en masse from public investment hardly explains the *decline* in agricultural production noted above. A much more important factor seems to be the price structure and marketing system in Guinea.

After Independence, in conformity with official socialist ideology, the State took control of the formal industrial and trading sectors, leaving only petty market trade in private hands. During the 1970s, however, an attempt was made to extend State intervention right across the retail spectrum, banning all petty market trade. This extremely unpopular measure had to be relaxed in 1977 (though it was never absolutely enforceable), and the 'economic policy' were disbanded after a massive and violent demonstration of housewives and petty traders (mainly women) in Conakry. The necessity for a private retail market is now acknowledged, where all but certain priority goods (fuel, cement, drugs, etc.) can be brought; these same goods are still sold, in much more limited quantities, in LRP stores at much lower official prices.

The retail prices for several key goods are given in Table 22.5.

Until 1981, the small farmer was also faced with the State as the sole legal purchaser of his produce. Procurement quotas were established and had to be delivered for sale at the LRP stores (and still do for livestock) at the official price. These official produce prices have remained mostly unchanged since the early 1970s, and are indeed well below production costs. Since 1981 private traders have been legally allowed to purchase directly from the farmers, legalising an exciting, but previously clandestine and obviously more limited activity.

The relation between small farmers' production costs, and official and private producer prices for a few key crops has already been shown in Table 22.5.

Given such a price structure, farmers have, whenever possible, either sold to private traders or smuggled their crops across the border (particularly crops like coffee or tea), or simply retreated into subsistence farming, under-stated their production and/or bribed local inspectors in order to avoid procurement quotas.

Table 22.5: Price Structure for Some Key Items—1981 (in *sylis*)

| | Estimated Small-holder Produc-tion Cost[1] | Producer Price | | Retail Price | | C.I.F. Price |
		Official	Private	Official	Private[2]	
Rice (kg)	30	15	50	20	64	7.4
Maize (kg)	27	7	35	18	46	3.2
Ground nuts (kg)	31	9	45	18	74	11.4
Coffee (kg)	62	45	95	—	—	64.5
Beef (kg)	—	15	50/60	50/75	150/250	36.0
Sugar (kg)	—	—		40	210	18.1
Cement	—	—		175	1,000	78.0
Diesel fuel (litre)	—	—		19	30/60	5.2

[1]Small-holder production cost estimates are based on the use of 'tradi-tional' production techniques with *no* improved inputs. Imputed labour cost per day is 135 sylis, reflecting *actual* rural wage rates (and not official 'norms' which are much lower).

[2]Prices are private market prices in Conakry (and vary, of course, in other parts of the country).

Estimates of the per cent of the total production of major crops sold through official channels in 1980 are given in Table 22.6.

This confusing array of producer and consumer prices makes any analysis of agricultural-industrial 'terms of trade' movements very difficult. Indeed, since it proved difficult to find many con-sumer goods of agricultural inputs in the rural areas (the State being sole official but inefficient supplier), a 'terms of trade' analysis would hardly make any sense.

Table 22.6: Crops Sold through Official Channels in 1980 (Estimated, Per cent)

Rice (paddy)	2%
Digitaria	5%
Maize	8%
Ground nut	1%
Cassava	1%
Coffee	23%*

*Assumably, three-fourths of the coffee crop was smuggled to the Ivary Coast and Sierra Leone.

The data in Table 22.5 also indicate wide differentials between the c.i.f. cost of imported goods, and their *official* retail price; the latter are 2.0 to 3.0 times higher. This differential goes into State trading company profits, which contribute a large share of government revenue.

This brings us to a consideration of the exchange rate, which is intimately linked to the problem of the internal price structure.

c) EXCHANGE RATE MANAGEMENT

The *syli* is a non-convertible currency whose value in terms of other currencies is determined by its 'special drawing right linkage. For a number of years the dollar parity has been about $1 = 20 *sylis* (1 *syli* = 5 U.S. cents).

There are good reasons for concluding that this exchange rate substantially under-values the real scarcity of foreign exchange to the economy, i.e. that the *syli* is substantially over-valued:

a) A very obvious symptom of over-valuation is the existence of a black market for currency, in which the *syli* is exchanged at 1/7 or 1/8 its official value.

b) More fundamentally, comparative purchasing power studies (relating the value of a typical 'basket' in *sylis* in Conakry to the value of the same 'basket' in C.F.A. Francs of Leons, bought in Dakar. Bamako or Freetown) indicate that the 'real value' of the *syli* is nearer to 40-60 *sylis* to the dollar (indicating an over-valuatic of 2.0 to 3.0 times). Of course the currencies in neighbouring countries might be under-valued! Confirmation of over-valuation of the *syli* is given by calculation of the 'standard conversion coefficient', based on the actual rate of conversion of the frontier prices of traded consumer goods into prices on the local market, which indicates that the 'real value' may be only around 1/7 the official value of the *syli*. Both methods have their limitations, but seem to very strongly support the contention that the *syli* is over-valued and, perhaps, by several times.

An over-valued exchange rate means that, in terms of the local currency, imports are bought cheaper and exports are sold cheaper —which encourages the demand for the former and discourages the supply of the latter. What are the implications for the agricultural sector?

Exports

Guinea is, of course, a 'small country-price taker' for all her agricultural exports, and thus faces export prices fixed in dollar terms. The consequently low value in *sylis* received by the official exporting agency means that only very low prices can be paid to the local producers (quite apart from the separate consideration of trading margins accruing between the field and the port)—so low, indeed, that they are below the production costs of the export crops grown by small-holders (using virtually no artificially cheap imported inputs by way of compensation). Therefore, a very large part of the local coffee (75%) and tea production, which, as it happens, is cultivated near the borders, is exported illegally into the Ivory Coast and Liberia. It is estimated that such unofficial receipts of foreign exchange may be equivalent to as much as 10% of the total official export receipts, *including* mineral exports.

Imports

The overvalued *syli* has reduced the apparent cost to the government—until recently sole official importer—of imported goods. Final consumer demand for these goods is, of course, somewhat dampened, inasmuch as the government trading margins exacted before sale are 200 to 300%.

But despite such trading margins, the official retail prices for food imports still considerably undercut local small-farmer production costs. These costs, of course, consist mainly of imputed costs for labour, which must be measured by actual rural wage rates, which, in turn, reflect actual wage-good prices in local markets (cheap official goods being virtually unavailable in the rural areas).

Any partial 'compensation' to agriculture through the possibility of access to cheap imported inputs is however foregone by the government's policy of directing these inputs to technically disastrous collective farms.

CONCLUSIONS

Having noted the deleterious effects on agriculture of government policy, one must ask why these policies are still pursued (though admittedly monopoly control of marketing is being relaxed somewhat).

a) The continuing emphasis on, and investment of resources in, collectivist agriculture is, of course, explicable in part by the ideological commitment of the government to a socialist society, however vaguely defined. There is also a feeling, sometimes expressed in official circles, that in the 1960s and early 1970s huge resources were made 'available' to small farmers via the collectives—and their failure to take advantage of these resources obliged the government to switch to the FAPAs, which are less collectivist and more like State farms. Peasant farmers are presumably not interested in development.

After all, the FAPAS do provide employment for the several thousand graduating from agricultural institutes every year, and lengthen the arm of the State into the countryside, otherwise an exclusively private domain. And who knows, however inefficient they may now be, due simply perhaps to lack of experience and teething problems, in the long run they might just prove their worth!

b) Although the government is undoubtedly aware of the implications of the marketing-price structure-exchange rate set of problems, and has indeed partially instituted some reforms, it is not easy to see how to change direction.

In the first place the government is highly dependent on the State trading companies' profits (which are possible thanks to the over-valued exchange rate) for revenue. In 1979 these profits constituted almost one-fourth of the total current revenue.

This same exchange rate also permits the supply of relatively cheap food to the towns, and particularly to the employees of the State who, of course, benefit most by the rationing system. It must be remembered that the wage/salary structure in the State sector has not changed for over 10 years, and indeed reflects the official exchange parity of the *syli*. Thus while a devaluation, with accompanying measures, might help to boost agricultural production and marketable surplus, this would only be in the medium run. In the short run, what will the urban inhabitants eat?

State employees of various kinds, the most vocal and immediate interest group exerting pressure on policy, have learned over the years how to 'get by' on their devalued salaries. Partly through their preferential access to officially priced goods for their own consumption, and partly through the infinite number of possibilities for 'deviating' official goods, equipment, spare parts, etc., to the private market, public employees at all levels have learned to come to terms with the peculiar situation prevailing in Guinea. Any change would only mean risk for them, at least in the short run, and as a group they will oppose it (however much the more technocratically minded may, in private, deplore the situation).

NOTES

1. All outputs are valued at official prices. However, there is a very considerable private 'parallel' market where prices for the same goods are several times higher. To the extent that agricultural output is relatively more interested in this private trading than the output of other sectors, the real GDP share of agriculture will increase, but not necessarily the variations in this share.

2. Data for 1979 reveal the following percentages of plant utilisation: fruit juice plant—9%; preserved fruit plant—13%; ground nut oil mill—25%; and sugar/alcohol plant—13%.

APPENDIX A: COUNTRY DATA—GUINEA

Area	*Population*	*Density* (1978)
245,900 sq km	5.1 million (mid-1978)	20.9 per square km
	Rate of Growth: 2.9% (1970-78)	

Population Characteristics[1]		*Health*[1]	
Crude birth rate (per 1,000)	46.0	Population per physician	16,629
Crude death rate (per 1,000)	21.0	Population per hospital bed	616

Income Distribution		*Distribution of Land Ownership*	
% of national income, highest quintile	n.a.	% Owned by top 10% of owners	n.a.
lowest quintile	n.a.	% Owned by smallest 10% of owners	n.a.

Access to Piped Water (1978)		*Access to Electricity* (1978)	
Occupied dwellings without		% of population — total	5.0
piped water (%)	88.0	— rural	2.6
—urban	56.0		
—rural	97.5		

Nutrition[1]		*Education* (1978)	
Calorie intake as % of requirements	84.0	Adult literacy rate %	20.0[a]
Per capita protein intake (grams/day)	42.7	Primary school enrolment %	34.0

Gross National Product in 1978

GNP per capita in 1978: US $262.1

	US$ Mln.	%	Annual Rate of Growth (%, 1973 prices)	
			1973-79	1979
GNP at market prices	1,373	100.0	3.5	0.4
Gross domestic investment	190	13.9	0.9	8.4
Gross national savings	114	8.3	207.1	6.9
Current account balance	—76	—5.5	.	.
Exports of goods, NFS	328	23.9	15.6[a]	—7.1[a]
Imports of goods, NFS	350	25.5	—2.0	—8.0

Output, Employment and Productivity in 1978

	Value Added		Labour Force		V.A. Per Worker	
	US $ Mln.	%	Thousands[3]	%	US $	%
Agriculture	635	43.5	1,875	82.0	339	53.1
Industry	370	25.3	252	11.0	1,468	230.1
Services	454	31.2	160	7.0	2,838	444.8
Total	1,459	100.0	2,287	100.0	638	100.0

Government Finance

	General Government			Central Government		
	(US $ Mln.)	% of GDP		(US $ Mln.)	% of GDP	
	1978	1975/76	1978	1978	1975/76	1978
Current receipts	437.5	29.0	30.0	417.6	26.7	28.6
Current expenditure	261.7	16.7	17.9	239.6	15.1	16.4
Current surplus	175.8	12.3	12.0	178.0	11.6	12.2
Capital expenditure	89.9	15.8	6.2	84.4	15.4	5.8

Money, credit and prices	Sept. 1974	1975	1976	1977	1978	Prelim. 1979
	(Million US $ outstanding and period)					
Money supply	515.1	528.8	492.6	481.9	480.1	532.9
Bank credit to private sector[5]	497.6	553.6	592.1	595.7	619.8	866.6
Bank credit to private sector	49.9	51.1	44.8	53.4	56.7	36.9
	(Percentage or Index Numbers)					
Money as % of GDP	50.3	48.6	39.4	36.7	31.6	33.9
General price index (1973 = 100)[4]	104.2	109.2	115.8	119.9	122.4	125.2
Annual percentage changes in:						
General price index[4]	4.2	4.8	6.0	3.5	2.1	2.3
Bank credit to public sector[5]	—	11.3	7.0	0.6	4.0	39.8
Bank credit to private sector	—	2.4	-12.3	19.2	6.2	-34.9

Balance of Payments

	1976	1977	1978
		(Mln. US $)	
Exports of goods, NFS	252.6	293.2	327.9
Imports of goods, NFS	287.3	261.9	350.1
Resource gap (deficit = —)	-34.7	31.3	-22.2
Interest payments (net)*	-40.0	-38.9	-43.8
Other factor payments (net)	-13.1	-34.4	-42.8
Net transfers	7.9	15.7	32.8
Balance on current account	-79.9	-26.3	-76.0
Direct private foreign investment	n.a.	n.a.	n.a.
Net MLT borrowing			
Disbursements†	70.0	56.1	113.1
Amortization††	91.0	122.3	119.2
Subtotal	-21.0	-66.2	-6.1
Other capital (net) and capital n.e.i.	-0.1	1.7	-3.8
Increase in reserves (+)	11.0	-2.7	-21.3
Gross reserves (end year)	53.2	50.5	29.2
Petroleum imports§	n.a.	n.a.	48.9
Petroleum exports	—	—	—

Merchandise Exports *(Average 1976-78)*

	US $ Mln.	%
Bauxite	204.3	7.2
Alumina	77.5	26.9
Other commodities	9.4	3.2
Total	291.2	100.0

External debt, December 31, 1979

	US $ Mln.
Public debt, incl guaranteed	990
Non-guaranteed private debt	208
Total outstanding & disbursed	1,198

Net debt service ratio for 1978

	%
Public debt incl. guaranteed	37.5
Non-guaranteed private debt	14.0
Total outstanding & disbursed	49.7

Rate of Exchange

	Annual Averages					End Period
	1975	1976	1977	1978	1979	1979
US $ 1.00 = GS	20.3	21.4	21.1	19.7	19.1	18.7
GS 1.00 US = $	0.049	0.047	0.047	0.051	0.052	0.053

IBRD/IDA Lending (March 31, 1980)

(Million US $:)

	IBRD	IDA
Outstanding & disbursed	58.3	24.3
Undisbursed	—	41.7
Outstanding incl. Undisbursed	58.3	66.0

[1]Most recent estimates (1974-78).

[2]Adjusted for change in terms of trade.

[3]Applying 1980 data for labour force share in total population.

[4]GDP implicit deflator.

[5]Net of Government deposits.

[6]Scheduled payments.

[7]Of which private US$5.4 mln. 1977 and US$8.0 mln. 1978.

[8]Of which private US$25.3 mln. 1976, US$24.5 mln. 1977, and US$24.7 mln. 1978.

[9]Including direct imports of parapublic mining enterprises.

[10]Education sector memorandum (Sept, 1980) provisional estimate.

APPENDIX B: SOCIALIST AGRICULTURAL
EXPERIMENTS IN GUINEA

In line with an official socialist ideology, and consistent with a takeover by the State of the formal industrial and commercial sectors of the economy, the Guinean government has been pursuing various attempts at a socialist transformation of agriculture since achieving national independence.

In the early 1960s a number of State farms and State-imposed cooperatives were set up. The latter were quickly abandoned due to lack of interest on the part of the peasants. Subsequently, in 1966, Centres of Revolutionary Education were set up in provincial towns to educate the rural youth in modern agricultural methods and in 'socialist attitudes', who would then be technically and politically prepared to set up cooperatives in their villages. Indeed, in the same period it was decreed that all secondary and higher educational establishments devote one-third of the school day to cultivation of a school plot, to upgrading work on the land and, by sale of produce, contributing to school finances.

In the early 1970s, the collectivisation strategy was given a new thrust—after the acknowledged failure of the earlier attempts—by the creation of collective Mechanised Production Brigades across the country—one in each of the 4,300 local Revolution Power sections (the lowest level administrative unit). About half of these were equipped with tractors, and the rest with animal-drawn implements. Some 50/100 ha were allotted to each, to be farmed on a collective basis by local peasants under the supervision of the LRP committee, with the produce requisitioned by the State Marketing office (and part of the proceeds set aside to repay equipment loans). In practice, for lack of spare parts, inadequate tractor maintenance, lack of fuel, and above all the diffidence of the peasants, the areas cultivated have been limited and declining, and yields generally less than half that realised on the peasants' own plots.

The latest thrust of the collectivisation strategy, conceived in 1979—indeed the spearhead of the government's present rural development strategy—is the creation of a network of Provincial Agro-Pastoral Farms (FAPAs). These FAPAs—one in each of the 330 provinces—serve a dual purpose: they themselves are production units (agro-pastoral, but also processing) for supplying official distribution channels, but they also contribute to a network of agricultural extension centres to promote the modernisation of surrounding peasant agriculture and to supply modern inputs. In the long run, indeed, official statements vaguely imply that FAPAs and LRP collectives somehow coalesce with peasant farms, forming one great cooperative organisation for rural production, thereby revolutionising rural social relations.

Each FAPA has been assigned 100 to 200 hectares and is equipped with tractor and implements. The farm is managed by a staff nucleus of agriculturalists, who train and are supported by 25 to 50· fresh agricultural graduates, who cultivate their own land and act as extension workers. Government provides the equipment and initial inputs, and pays salaries for the first three years, after which each FAPA is supposed to be financially self-supporting. Evidence on this latest experiment is hardly encouraging.

　a) *As production units* they seem to be highly inefficient. On the one hand, the areas cultivated and their yields are limited due to tractor breakdowns, etc., at crucial moments, and due to staff lacking both expertise or incentives (since they are on *fixed* salaries and the salaries are *low*, frequently their own fuel, spare parts, seeds, etc., are resold on the private market). On the other hand, expensive imported equipment and farm buildings push up overhead costs to exorbitant levels. It is thus estimated that FAPA costs per unit of output may range from 1.5 to 3.0 times those of the peasant farm (and this *even* with immense subsidisation of imported inputs because of an overvalued exchange rate).

　b) *As extension centres* they are likely to be even less successful. Themselves using resources and techniques inaccessible to the neighbouring peasant, offering no local research programmes, and comprising an ill-prepared and unmotivated staff—they have nothing to teach or offer the local farmers. And the local farmers, already hostile in some cases because some of the best local land has been assigned to the FAPA, or possibly conscripted for the construction of farm buildings, or for land clearance, are hardly likely to be convinced of the need to 'modernise' after a glimpse of the very poorly maintained fields and unimpressive crop stands on the FAPAs.

The foregoing is further exacerbated by the conflict between the two objectives of the FAPAs—to attain financial autonomy *and* to perform an extension role. With the authorities' increasing insistence on the former and their three years' grace period soon to expire, one suspects that the FAPA staff will be too preoccupied with legitimate or illegitimate revenue-raising activities to afford time for other tasks.

To offset the enormous cost of these farms, which is likely to exceed considerably the one-fifth of the Rural Development investment allocation under the current Plan, it has been calculated that their marketable surplus of grain will only be around 20,000 tonnes p.a., equivalent to only 25 to 30% of the present imports (and infinitesimal compared to estimates of the total national cereal production of 400,000 tonnes rice, 350,000 tonnes maize, and 100,000 tonnes other cereals.)

CHAPTER 23

Planning for Poverty Alleviation Through Rural Development in India

Nearly 50 per cent of the citizens in India live in poverty. The majority of the rural poor consist almost exclusively of landless labourers and small and marginal farmers and any programme which aims at benefiting the rural poor must focus on these people. It is estimated that there are 800 million people in the world who are in absolute poverty and hence poverty is a global problem. In India, as per the latest estimates, 48.13 per cent of the population or 305.2 million persons belong to this class.

Towards the achievement of 'Growth with Social Justice' a number of measures have been initiated for creating permanent productive assets and also providing employment opportunities. The programmes were continued from Plan to Plan and integrated rural development was thought of in the year 1975. In Indian conditions the problems are low national income and its unequal distribution, slow pace of development, and inequitable distribution of the small gains of development. The incidence of poverty is much more common among the agricultural labour households than among the rural households. In spite of planned development for over three decades, the dimensions of the problem have grown and the number of persons living below the poverty line has not diminished. Therefore, the programmes to reduce poverty in the rural sector are likely to achieve the intended results only when these programmes become inter-related and focus on a specific area. A massive poverty alleviation programme is necessary in a society where deprivation is both widespread and enormous. The process of economic growth, including its income redistribution bias, involves a number of inter-connected and mutually complimentary activities and a sound development strategy should recognise not merely the overall goal, but also the wide range of apparently diverse but mutually reinforcing activities.

The major thrust of the seventh Five-Year Plan is to strengthen the socio-economic infrastructure of development in the rural areas and to alleviate rural poverty. Alleviation of rural poverty is the prime objective of the Seventh Plan. Therefore, the main stress is to identify the rural poor and provide them an appropriate package of programmes. The main strategy is to increase production and productivity in agriculture and allied sectors, to take up programmes which help to raise the income level of the rural poor, skill formation, provision of adequate credit to support these programmes, promotion of marketing facilities, provision of additional employment opportunities to the rural poor, provision of essential minimum needs, and preparation of a series of projects for the scientific utilisation of the local resources.

Three broad categories of programmes have been identified for accelerated rural development. These relate to resource and income development programmes for the rural poor such as the integrated rural development programme, special area development programmes such as the drought-prone area programme and desert-development programme, and works programme for the creation of supplementary employment opportunities. The Sixth Plan has given an important place to rural reconstruction.

Integrated Rural Development Programme

The integrated rural development programme is a major poverty alleviation programme, which was taken up in 2,000 blocks during the year 1978-79 and also in taluks covered by special programmes such as the SFDA and DPAP. On 2nd October 1980, the programme was extended to 300 blocks annually. The target during the plan period is to assist 15 million families now below the poverty line to achieve a level of income well above the poverty line. The objective is to assist at least 600 families in a block. Each taluk receives Rs. 35.00 lakhs during the plan period. The allocation for the first year of the plan was Rs. 5.00 lakhs per block. It was Rs. 6.00 lakhs per block for the second year.

The outlay for the next three years of the plan period was Rs. 8.00 lakhs for each block for each year. The programme is funded equally by the State and Central Governments.

In the implementation of the programme, the identification of the beneficiaries is the important task as the main stress is to identify the poorest among the poor. For this, household surveys were initiated. In the State, with respect to 31 blocks, the studies were entrusted to research institutions, universities and the management consultants In the remaining 144 blocks, the studies were initiated by the District Rural Development Societies. The block plans seek to ensure optimum utilisation of local resources, integration of various on-going programmes and formulation of development plan with the aim of providing economically viable activities to the rural poor. A household rather than individual approach is followed, implying that the economic uplift of the household is sought through a package of activities involving all working members with particular attention to economic programmes for women, scheduled castes and scheduled tribes. The families selected are provided with multiple benefits through a package of programmes that enable them to cross the poverty line.

The programmes for a particular family are selected considering the aptitude, preference, economic viability and feasibility, available potentials and infrastructural support, facilities for training and so forth. The scheme of programme suggested for each family is based on the level of per capita income of the family below the poverty line.

Block level planning for the rural poor has to be much wider and more comprehensive in scope and content than administrative coordination. The emphasis of the plan should be such as to cover specific programmes for rural poor families, development schemes for developing economic activities in the area based on local resources with special emphasis on those relating to the upliftment of rural poor, and programmes of infrastructural development.

Decentralisation of the planning process was considered an effective way of preparing local level plans. Operational strategy also involves devising a suitable mechanism not only for plan formulation, but also for the implementation of the plan in an integrated and coordinated manner. This requires evolving a system design for the effective and meaningful collaboration of all sectoral departments at the district and block level for the formulation and implementation of district and block plans in a complementary manner. Financing institutions should also be associated with the preparation of the local plans so that the development schemes are viable and the credit plans are realistic. The district credit plans should be prepared taking into account the overall require-ments of the local level plans prepared by the local authorities, and adequate provision should be made for the flow of credit matching the requirements of the subsidies available for the rural poor under the integrated rural development plans. Institutional arrangements for the transfer of technology to the rural poor will have to form an integral part of the efforts to develop skill and status. The success of the programme mainly depends upon the mobilisation of institutional resources as most of the programmes are linked with credit.

Such a type of approach to planning at the block level requires strengthening of the planning machinery and the planning process at the grass-root level.

District Rural Development Societies have been set up in all the districts of the country. The main object of setting up of these so-cieties is speedier and effective implementation of the programme, avoidance of lapse of grants at the end of the financial year, and also maintenance of the tempo of progress during the beginning of the year even if there is delay in sanctioning the plans.

For carrying out household surveys to assess the potential of the region, the cluster approach is desirable. The first step is the identification of the available resources, natural and otherwise, the extent of development already attained and the scope for further development in the clusters selected. It is necessary to involve voluntary organisations and other institutions including industrial enterprises who could be involved in the process of rural develop-ment. The voluntary organisations should take up the work re-lating to health, nutrition, and development of scientific agricul-ture. They should also take up the work relating to the establish-ment of cooperatives which would assist the people in taking up subsidiary occupations.

The first task of the voluntary organisation is to undertake a socio-economic survey of the region so that the potential for development can be assessed. These agencies should bring about the necessary coordination among the various village institutions in order to strengthen the infrastructure base. Based on the report of the economic survey, such programmes as the construction of approach roads, sanitation, health, development of village industries, education and agricultural development programmes could be taken up. They should also make efforts to allow for the supply of inputs, availability of credit and marketing. Necessary guidance has to be provided for the establishment of village and cottage industries. Voluntary organisations could take up this task and stop the exploitation of the villagers. There is a need for strengthening these agencies as the involvement of such organisations is the focal point for development.

Training of Rural Youth for Self-Employment

This programme was initiated on 15th August 1979 with the principal objective of removal of unemployment among youth. The main thrust of the scheme is on equipping rural youth between ages 18-35 with the skills and technology necessary to enable them to take up vocations of self-employment. The selection of beneficiaries is based on income criteria. Training of rural women is also being taken up under this programme. The objective is to train a minimum of 40 youths in each block. The scheme envisages organisational and operational linkages with other institutions so that supporting services such as credit, marketing, supply of raw materials, and design development are also provided to the trainees well in time.

Drought-Prone Area Programme

The Drought-Prone Area Programme was initiated in the states during 1970-71 and the main objective was to provide employment opportunities to the rural people affected by drought. The areas were identified on the basis of objective criteria such as incidence of rainfall, declaration of scarcity in the past, extent and periodicity of failure of crops, percentage of cropped area under irrigation, and existence of schemes of long-term development of the area. The programme was taken up in 557 blocks in 74 districts in 13 states. Creation of durable assets and providing employment opportunities was the main objective. Initially, it was started as a rural works programme, with the major stress on development of irrigation, soil conservation, afforestation and roads. During the Fifth Plan, with experience in implementation, the strategy which until then was *asset formation* and *employment creation*, was shifted to a more comprehensive and diversified approach to development. Other sectors, such as forestry, animal husbandry, fisheries, agriculture and horticulture were brought in. During this Plan, another dimension was added to the strategy by the introduction of a *watershed approach* to this area development programme. The optimum utilisation of land and water resources became the accepted policy. In planning for watershed development, the socio-economic factors—landholding structures, cropping pattern, economic status of the local people, their livestock holdings—will have to be comprehensively looked into. The identified watersheds in the block will have to be resource-inventoried. The ultimate objective of such planning is specialisation in production and restoration of the ecological balance; involvement of the local community in such a planning process is very vital. The major elements of the strategy are the development and management of irrigation resources, soil and moisture conservation and afforestation, restructuring of cropping pattern and pasture development, changes in agronomic practices, livestock development and development of small and marginal farmers and agricultural labourers. The long-term approach of crediting the necessary infrastructure for a viable economic base in the region and providing productive employment in these backward areas, especially for the weaker segments of the population, and enhancement of their employment and income potential through the development of long-term stable enterprises for these communities, are inter-linked objectives that run concurrently in the Drought-Prone Area Programme. The plans prepared on a watershed basis are aggregated to form a coherent and integrated block plan.

Since the introduction of D.P.A.P. in India and up to 1981, an investment of the order of Rs 480 crores has been made and there have been substantial noticeable benefits. The allocation in the Sixth Plan (1980-85) was Rs 175 crores, to be shared equally by the Centre and the states. The major drawback in the programme was that large areas, which are frequently prone to droughts, were outside the programme areas. This was because the identification of the area was done keeping the district as a unit and blocks/ taluks outside these districts were omitted. The Government of India, therefore, constituted a *task force* in June 1980 to review the coverage of the programme, and also the strategy of development. The report was available by the end of 1981 and the recommendations came into force from 1st April 1982. The area is now extended to 113 more blocks, bringing the total number of blocks covered to 670. In Karnataka, the number of blocks have increased from 46 to 70. With the introduction of IRD throughout the entire country, which is basically a beneficiary-oriented programme, the infrastructure support will flow from DPAP.

Desert Development Programme

The Desert Development Programme was started in the year 1977-78. It covers both the hot and cold regions of the country. The hot regions cover 11 districts in Rajasthan, 4 districts in Haryana, and three districts in Gujarat; the cold regions cover two districts in Jammu and Kashmir and one district in Himachal Pradesh. The main objective of the programme is integrated development of desert areas by increasing the fertility, income levels, and employment opportunities of the inhabitants through optimum utilisation of physical, human, livestock and other biological resources. The major activities envisaged under the programme area:

a) afforestation and grassland development;
b) groundwater development and utilisation;
c) construction of water harvesting structures;
d) rural electrification for energising pump-sets; and
e) development of agriculture/horticulture/animal husbandry.

The areas covered under this programme are primarily those which were recommended by the National Commission on Agriculture in its report on desert development. During the Fifth Plan an expenditure of Rs. 23.13 crores was incurred and the allocation during the Sixth Plan was raised to Rs 50 crores.

National Rural Employment Programme (NREP)

The programmes discussed so far aim at resource endowments in individual family units or area basis. As for the object of providing supplementary employment opportunities, a beginning was made in that direction through the Food-for-Work programme. The problem of employment in rural areas is mainly seasonal in character and largely under-employment. Fuller employment opportunities for the rural workforce will in the main have to be found within the agricultural and allied sectors themselves, through intensification and diversification of agriculture based on expansion of irrigation and improved technology. The very dimensions of the problem call for a multi-pronged strategy aimed on the one hand at resource development of the vulnerable sections of the population, and on the other at provision of supplementary employment opportunities to the rural poor, particularly during the lean periods, in a manner which will at the same time contribute directly to the creation of durable assets for the community. NREP, conceived against this background, aims to take care of the rural poor. Under this programme, development projects and target group-oriented employment generation projects will be closely intertwined.

The programme will operate on a 50:50 basis between the centre and the states. A provision of Rs. 360 crores was made for 1981-82 alone in the Plan. A quick evaluation of the Food-for-Work programme conducted by the Programme Evaluation Organisation of the Planning Commission in August-October 1979 clearly stated that 'the beneficiaries of the programme reached the poorest sections of the rural society. Of the total beneficiaries, 42% were Scheduled Castes and 13% Scheduled Tribes. Of the persons engaged in the programme, 20% were females. Again, of the total beneficiaries, 50.6% were agricultural labourers and 19.7% non-agricultural labourers.' It has further stated that 'the programme stabilised the food grain prices in the rural areas. It also left a favourable impact on the life and living conditions of the village community, in terms of employment as well as income.'

COMPREHENSIVE RURAL DEVELOPMENT

Comprehensive rural development should take care of development of the rural areas as a conscious effort to link infrastructural activities with beneficiary-oriented programmes. The programmes of IRD, DPAP, DDP, NREP and others should not function as isolated ones and should ensure proper linkages among them.

Table 23.1: Selected Statistics and Indicators of Rural and Urban India

S.No.	Item	Year	Unit	Rural	Urban	All India
1	2	3	4	5	6	7
1.	Population					
	(a) Total	1981ᵃ	Million	502	156	658
	(b) Percentage	1981ᵃ	%	76.3	23.7	100
2.	Density	1981ᵃ	Per sq. km.	161	2,743	221
3.	Decennial growth	1961-71	%	21.9	38.2	24.8
		1971-81ᵃ	%	19.0	46.0	24.4
4.	Literacy rate	1971	%	23.7	52.4	29.4
	(including 0-4 age group)	1981ᵃ	%	29.6	54.4	36.2
5.	Sex-ratio	1971	Females per 1000 males	949	858	930
		1981ᵃ	do	953	896	935
6.	Age dependency ratio	1971	%	96.0	78.6	92.2
7.	(a) Percentage of scheduled caste population to total	1971	%	16.1	8.8	14.6
	(b) Estimated scheduled caste population	1980	Million	83.6	12.6	96.2
8.	(a) Percentage of scheduled tribe population to total	1971	%	8.4	1.2	6.9
	(b) Estimated scheduled tribe population	1980	Million	43.6	1.7	45.3
9.	(a) Percentage of workers to total population	1971	%	33.8	29.3	32.9
	(b) Workforce	1980	Million	175.4	41.9	217.3
10.	Average household size	1971	Persons	5.5	5.2	5.5

(*Contd.*)

Table 23.1 *(Contd.)*

1	2	3	4	5	6	7
11.	Crude birth rate	1978	Per 1000 population	34.7	27.8	33.3
12.	Crude death rate	1978	do	15.3	9.4	14.2
13.	Infant mortality rate	1979	Per 1000 live births	136	70	125
14.	Average age at marriage for females	1971	Years	16.7	19.2	17.2
15.	Consumer expenditure per person per month	1977–78	Rs.	75.6	108.7	—
16.	People below poverty line[b]					
	a) Number	1979–80	Million	259.5	57.3	316.8
	b) Percentage	1979–80	%	50.7	40.3	48.4
17.	Unemployment	1980	Million	17.1	4.4	21.5
18.	Labour force	1980	Million	215.9	52.1	268.0
19.	Percentage unemployed in labour force	1980	%	7.9	8.4	8.0
20.	Net domestic product	1970–71	%	68.2	31.8	100.0

[a]Excluding Jammu & Kashmir and Assam.
[b]The poverty line is defined as the level corresponding to a consumer expenditure of Rs. 76 per capita per month in rural areas and Rs. 88 in urban areas.

Sources:
1. Census of India. 1981; Paper I of 1981, Provisional Population Tables.
2. Census of India, 1971; Series I-India, General Population Tables.
3. Sample Registration Bulletin, Vol. XIV, No. 1, June 1980.
4. Sixth Five-Year Plan, 1980-85.
5. Draft Five-Year Plan, 1978-83.

Planning at the block level for such a task is stupendous. India has made a modest beginning in that direction with a view to introduce:

a) deliberate measures for the removal of disabilities from which the poorer segments of the community suffer; and

b) measures by which employment and income opportunities for the poor and the productive capabilities of economically weak producers can be significantly increased.

In such a task numerous problems in planning and implementation occur. Poverty cannot be eradicated in a short period and requires a long horizon. The problems should be discussed in this context. In the Seventh Plan, with a much sharper focus poverty is likely to be reduced to a substantial extent. However, the effort has to be much more pronounced during the Eighth Plan.

Table 23.2. Distribution of Villages According to Population (1971) – All India

Population of the Village	Number of Villages	Percentage to Total Number of Villages	Percentage of Population to Total Rural Population
Less than 200	1,50,072	26,1	3.5
200–499	1,68,561	29.3	12.9
500–999	1,32,990	23.1	21.5
1,000–1,999	81,973	14.2	25.8
2,000 and above	42,337	7.3	36.3
Total	5,75,933	100.0	100.0

*Excludes three villages of Manipur, tne details of which are not available.
Source: Census of India, 1971.

Table 23.3: **Number of Administrative Units and Panchayati Raj Bodies (1979-80)**

S.No.	Item	Unit	All-India
1.	Districts	No.	404
2.	Zilla parishads	No.	252
3.	DPAP districts	No.	74[a]
4.	Panchayat samitis	No.	4,481
5.	CD blocks (also IRD blocks)	No.	5,011
6.	Gram panchayats	Thousands	212.2
7.	Population covered by gram panchayats	Millions	4,454
8.	Villages and hamlets covered by gram panchayats	Thousands	595
9.	Average no. of villages per gram panchayat	No.	2.80
10.	Average population per gram panchayat	No.	2,098
11.	Average no. of panchayat samitis per zilla parishad	No.	17.8
12.	Average no. of gram panchayats per zilla parishad	No.	842
13.	Percentage of rural population covered by gram panchayats	%	99.1
14.	Percentage of blocks covered by gram panchayat samitis	%	89.2[b]
15.	Percentage of villages covered by gram panchayats	%	97.9
16.	Average no of gram panchayats per panchayat samiti	No.	47.4
17.	Percentage of districts covered by zilla parishads	%	99.1[b]

[a]Relates to the year 1978.
[b]Relates to the year 1979.

Source: *Panchayati Raj at a Glance* 1979-80.

Table 23.4: Rural Development¹ – Outlay in the Sixth Plan (1980-85)

(Rs. in crores)

S.No.	Item	Outlay
1.	Integrated Rural Development and related Programmes	3,486.64
2.	National Rural Employment Programme	
3.	Cooperation	914.24
4.	Special Employment Programmes	610.65
5.	Community Development and Panchayati Raj Institutions	352.20
	Total	5,363.73

¹Relates to programmes of the Ministry of Rural Development and the concerned Departments of the State Governments. Excludes Rural Health, Education, etc.

Source: Sixth Five-Year Plan, 1980-85.

Table 23.5: Special Programmes of Rural Development Outlays
(1980-81 and 1981-82)

(Rs. in crores)

S.N.	Item	Outlay	
		1980-81	1981-82
1.	Integrated Rural Development Programme	92.0	145.0
2.	Drought-Prone Area Programme	40.0	40.0
3.	Subsidy for Minor Irrigation		
	(i) Outside the Special Programme Area	4.0	—
	(ii) For 2-4 hectare farmers	3.0	—
4.	Special Livestock Production Programme	6.0	(a)
5.	Training of Rural Youth for Self-Employment (TRYSEM)	3.0	1.5
6.	Construction of Rural Godowns (National Grid of Rural Godowns)	2.0	3.0
7.	Desert Development Programme	8.0	8.0
8.	National Rural Employment Programme (NREP)	340.0	180.0
	Total	498.0	377.5

*To be funded out of IRD funds.

Source: Ministry of Rural Development.

Table 23.6. Selected Programmes of Rural Development Outlay (1980-85) State-wise

(Rs. in crores)

S. No.	States	Special Programmes of RD (including NREP)	C.D. and Panchayati Raj	Cooperation	Total
1.	Andhra Pradesh	87.25	59.50	29.60	176.25
2.	Assam	42.25	8.00	25.60	75.85
3.	Bihar	190.00	22.35	27.25	239.60
4.	Gujarat	144.00	6.30	32.00	182.30
5.	Haryana	28.93	16.50[a]	26.80	72.23
6.	Himachal Pradesh	16.90	3.00	6.75	26.65
7.	Jammu & Kashmir	24.10	6.00	5.00	35.10
8.	Karnataka	49.15	2.50	50.00	101.65
9.	Kerala	25.10	41.40	22.00	88.50
10.	Madhya Pradesh	155.00	15.00	47.90	217.90
11.	Maharashtra	81.00	0.51	57.44	138.95
12.	Manipur	7.00	2.00	1.80	10.80
13.	Meghalaya	3.00	2.40	3.28	8.68
14.	Nagaland	6.50	7.00	1.50	15.00
15.	Orissa	105.00	5.25	30.00	140 25
16.	Punjab	36.00	18.15	41.50	95.65
17.	Rajasthan	105.75	0.33	24.38	130.46
18.	Sikkim	—	0.25	1.60	1.85
19.	Tamil Nadu	120.00	78.00	25.33	223.33
20.	Tripura	6.55	4.48	5.00	16.03
21.	Uttar Pradesh	147.96	18.37	55.36	221.69
22.	West Bengal	126.00	18.00	46.00	190.00
	Total States	1,507.44	335.29	566.00	2.408.72
	Union Territories	1.78	9.61	18.08	29.47
	All India	1,509.29	344.90	584.08	2,438.19

[a]Includes Rs. 10 crores for NREP.

Source: Sixth Five-Year Plan, 1980-85, Planning Commission, Government of India p. 185.

Table 23.7. Population below Poverty Line for Selected Years—Rural India

Year	Percentage of Population below Poverty Line	Number of Persons below Poverty Line (millions)
1972-73	54.09	—
1977-78	50.82	251.7
1979-80	50.70	259.6
1984-85	40.47	224.0

Source: Sixth Five-Year Plan, 1980-85.

Table 23.8. Population below Poverty Line in Rural India—State-wise

S. No.	State/Union	% of Rural Population below Poverty Line in 1977-78	Rural Population below Poverty Line in 1981[a] (in millions)
1.	Andhra Pradesh	43.9	18.0
2.	Assam	52.6	—
3.	Bihar		36.0
4.	Gujarat	43.2	10.1
5.	Haryana		2.3
6.	Himachal Pradesh	28.1	1.1
7.	Jammu & Kashmir	32.7	13.1
8.	Karnataka	49.9	10.2
9.	Kerala	46.0	9.4
10.	Madhya Pradesh		24.8
11.	Maharashtra		22.4
12.	Manipur	30.5	0.3
13.	Meghalaya	53.9	0.6
14.	Nagaland	—	—
15.	Orissa		16.0
16.	Punjab		1.5
17.	Rajasthan	33.7	3.0
18.	Tamil Nadu	55.7	18.0
19.	Tripura		1.2
20.	Uttar Pradesh	50.2	45.6
21.	West Bengal		23.5
22.	All Union Territories	34.3	—
	All-India	50.8[b]	254.7

Note: The above estimates of the Planning Commission based on the all-India poverty line of Rs. 65/- per capita per month in 1977-78 prices corresponding to minimum daily calorie requirements of 2,400 per person in rural areas, and the poverty line of Rs. 75 per capita per month corresponding to daily calorie requirement of 2,100 in urban areas.

ªThe percentages of incidence of rural poverty in 1977-78 are applied to the 1981 census population figures on the assumption that there is no change in the former during 1977-81. This was done in the absence of latest data relating to the former.
ᵇWeighted.

Source: Sixth Five-Year Plan, 1980-85.

Table 23.9: Estimates of Rural Poverty in India

S. No.	Year	Organisation/ Researcher	Est. Number of Poor (millions)	% of Rural Population below Poverty Line
1.	1960-61	Dandekar & Rath	135.0	40.0
		Ahluwalia	152.0	42.0
		Vaidyanathan	213.5	59.5
		Ojha	184.2	51.8
2.	1961-62	Ahluwalia	157.0	42.3
3.	1962-63	NIRD	166.0	44.9
4.	1963-64	DeCosta	161.8	34.6
		Minhas	221.0	57.8
		Ahluwalia	189.0	49.1
5.	1964-65	Vaidyanathan	235.7	60.0
		Bardhan	174.4	51.6
		Ahluwalia	198.0	50.4
6.	1965-66	Ahluwalia	205.0	51.1
7.	1966-67	Ahluwalia	235.0	57.4
8.	1967-68	Ahluwalia	241.0	57.9
		Dandekar & Rath	166.4	40.0
		Vaidyanathan	—	67.8
		Minhas	210.0	50.6
		Ojha	289.0	70.0
9.	1968-69	Ahluwalia	227.0	53.5
10.		NIRD	196.0	46.2
11.	1970-71	Ahluwalia	217.0	49.1
		IIPO[1]	198.9	45.0
12.	1971-72	NIRD	183.0	41.5

(*Contd.*)

13.	1972-73	NIRD	212.3	47.5
		Planning		
		Commission[2] (Draft		
		Five-Year Plan)	200.0	35.6
14.	1973-74	Ahluwalia	221.0	47.6
		IIPO	208.0	44.8
15.	1974-75	NIRD	232.0	50.1
16.	1975-76	NIRD	225.0	47.7
17.	1976-77	NIRD	216.0	45.2
18.	1977-78	Planning		
		Commission	251.7	50.8
		IIPO	246.4	50.8
19.	1979-80	Planning		
		Commission	259.6	50.7

Note: [1]Refers to 1971;   [2]Refers to 1973

Sources and Definitions of Poverty Line

Ahluwalia, M.S., 1978, 'Rural poverty and agricultural performance in India,' *Journal of Development Studies*, vol 14 no 3, April 1978. (Rs. 180, p.c., c.e., p.a., at 1960-61 prices).

Balakrishna, S., 1980, 'Incidence of rural poverty in recent years,' *Behavioural Sciences and Rural Development*, vol 3 no 1. (The regression equation between NDP from agriculture and Ahluwalia's time-series estimates of incidence of poverty.)

————— and P.K. Ghosh, 1980, 'Poverty-line—redefined and confirmed,' *Behavioural Sciences and Rural Development*, vol 3 no 1, January. (The regression equation between NDP from agriculture and Ahluwalia's time-series estimates of incidence of poverty.)

Bardhan, P.K., 1974, 'On the incidence of poverty in rural India in the sixties,' *Sankhya*, vol 36 ser C pts 2 and 4. (Rs. 180, p.c., c.e., p.a., at 1960-61 prices.)

Dandekar, V.M. and N. Rath, 1971, *Poverty in India*, Indian School of Political Economy, Poona. (Rs. 180, p.c., c.e., p.a., at 1960-61, prices, yielding a minimum of 2,250 calories per day.)

Government of India, Planning Commission, 1981, *Sixth Five-Year Plan, 1980-85*, New Delhi. ([1] for 1972-73 Rs. 480, p.c., c.e., p.a., at 1972-73 prices; [2] for 1977-78 Rs. 741.60, p.c., c.e., p.a. [2,400 calories per day].)

Indian Institute of Public Opinion, 1978-9, 'The measurement of deprivation by degrees of destitution in Indian States 1973-74,' *Quarterly Economic Report*, vol XXIV no 1 October 1978/ January 1979. ([1] for 1970-71 Rs. 336, p.c., c.e., p.a.; [2] for 1973-74 Rs. 516, p.c., c.e., p.a.; [3] for 1977-78 Rs. 780, p.c., c.e., p.a. [2,400 calories p.e. per day].)

Minhas, B.S., 1974, 'Rural poverty, land redistribution and development strategy: Facts,' *Sankhya*, vol 36 ser C pts 2 and 4. ([1] for 1963-64, two alternative levels of Rs. 240 and Rs. 200 per capita annual consumption expenditure at 1960-61 prices: [2] for 1967-69 Rs. 240, p.c., c.e., p.a.)

Ojha, P.D., 1970, 'A configuration of Indian poverty: Incidence and levels of living,' *Reserve Bank of India Bulletin*, vol 24. ([1] for 1960-61 Rs. 216, p.c., c.e., p.a., at 1960-61 prices; [2] for 1967-68 estimates of minimum desirable income, i.e., Rs. 216 to Rs. 480 per annum.)

Vaidyanathan, A., 1974, 'Some aspects of inequalities in living standards in rural areas,' *Sankhya*, vol 36 ser C pts 2 and 4. (Rs. 240 p.c., c.e., p.a., at 1960-61 prices.)

Table 23.10. Distribution of Household Income (1977-78)—Rural India

S. No.	Percentage of Households	Average Annual Income per Household	% Share in Total Income
1.	Bottom 5	797	1.0
2.	5-10	1,153	1.5
3.	10-20	1,486	3.8
4.	20-30	1,871	4.8
5.	30-40	2,267	5.8
6.	40-50	2,694	8.1
7.	50-60	3,150	8.1
8.	60-70	3,749	9.6
9.	70-80	4,591	11.8
10.	80-90	5,903	15.1
11.	90-95	8,327	10.7
12.	Top 5	10,495 to 28,200[a]	20.9

[a]For top 5 per cent, the range of the average household incomes computed for each 1 per cent group in same level is given.

Source : *Household Income and its Disposition*, National Council of Applied Economic Research, 1980.

Table 23.11-A: Integrated Rural Development Programme: Cumulative and Financial Position (March, 1981)

(Rs. in million)

S. No.	Item	Total
1.	Loans disbursed:	
	(a) Through Cooperatives:	
	(i) Short term	4,034
	(ii) Medium term	1,723
	(iii) Long term	1,883
	Total:	7,640
	(b) Through Commercial Banks	3,769
2.	Funds released	4,239
3.	Expenditure incurred	4,606

Source: Ministry of Rural Development.

Table 23.11-B: Integrated Rural Development Programme: Cumulative Physical Progress (March, 1981—Scheme-wise)

S. No.	Scheme	Families (in thousands)		Percentage of SC/ST to Total
		Total	SC/ST	
1.	Agriculture	8,870.2	1,543.9	17.4
2.	Irrigation	1,286.2	251.9	19.6
3.	Forestry & pasture dev.	35.7	11.2	31.4
4.	Animal husbandry	1,599.5	393.2	24.6
5.	Fishery	34.5	8.8	25.5
6.	Sericulture	19.9	9.3	46.7
7.	Bee-keeping	2.1	0.6	28.6
8.	Village industries	91.7	23.4	25.5
9.	Tertiary sector	165.2	56.3	34.1
10.	Others	110.2	28.2	25.6
	Total	12,215.2	2,326.8	19.0

Source: Ministry of Rural Development.

Table 23.12: Integrated Rural Development Programme: Physical Progress
and Expenditure (1980-81)—State-wise

S. No.	State	No. of Families Identified ('000)	No. of Families Benefited ('000)	Total Expenditure (Rs. in lakhs)
1.	Andhra Pradesh	203.5	148.0	1,333
2.	Assam	1.3	5.6	67
3.	Bihar	230.7	139.0	921
4.	Gujarat	177.3	74.3	569
5.	Haryana	41.1	52.7	356
6.	Himachal Pradesh	31.3	48.1	107
7.	Jammu & Kashmir	3.5	9.4	37
8.	Karnataka	102.9	63.9	389
9.	Kerala	14.6	33.5	207
10.	Madhya Pradesh	96 0	135.6	798
11.	Maharashtra	27.1	85.4	907
12.	Orissa	150.6	101.8	541
13.	Punjab	49.2	102.7	731
14.	Rajasthan	123.2	155.2	1,045
15.	Tamil Nadu	472.4	219.7	1,287
16.	Uttar Pradesh	594.2	1,310.7	2,824
18.	WestBengal	43.1	37.4	244
	All-India	2,647.3	8,775.6	12,740

Source: Rural Development Statistics, National Institute of Rural Development, Hyderabad, 1982, pp. 110-111.

Table 23.13: Drought-Prone Area Programme (1980-81): Physical Progress

S. No.	Item	Unit	Progress
1.	Soil and moisture conservation	Thousand Ha.	139.7
2.	Creation of irrigation potential	,,	44.6
3.	Forestry and pasture development	,,	82.2
4.	Distribution of milk animals	Nos.	10,184
5.	Organisation of milk producers co-ops.	Nos.	538
6.	Organisation of sheep co-op. Societies	Nos.	49
7.	Number of beneficiaries:	Lakhs	9.9
	a) Scheduled caste	Lakhs	2.2
	b) Scheduled tribe	Lakhs	0.8
8.	Employment generated	Lakh mandays	469.5

Source: Ministry of Rural Development.

Table 23.14: National Rural Employment Programme: Physical Progress (1980-81) and Cumulative

S. No.	Item	Unit	Progress 1980-81	Cumulative
1.	Foodgrains allocated	Lakh tonnes	20.88	48.92
2.	Foodgrains released	,,	20.48	50.81
3.	Foodgrains utilised	,,	13.33	37.07
4.	Physical Assets created under Food-for Work-Programme:			
	a) Area covered under soil conservation and afforesation	Lakh ha.	1.01	9.62
	b) Area brought under irrigation through minor/major irrigation	,,	2.47	11.38
	c) Area made cultivable through flood protection	,,	0.58	4.22
	d) Area covered under plantation	,,	2.00	4.61
	e) School buildings constructed/repaired	Thousand	14.6	113.1
	f) Panchyat ghars constructed:	No.	885	3,347
	g) Road work:			
	(i) Maintained/improved/repaired	Lakh km.	1.87	4.68
	ii) New roads constructed	,,	0.18	2.21
	h) Construction of intermediate main drains, field channels and land levelling, etc.	Thousand ha.	2.8	160.1
	i) Other works		210.0	374.9
5.	Employment generated	Lakh mandays	3,265	13,059

Source: Ministry of Rural Development.

Table 23.15: Percentage of Population below the Poverty Line in 1977-78

	State	Rural	Urban	Combined
1.	Andhra Pradesh	43.89	35.68	42.18
2.	Assam	52.65	37.37	51.10
3.	Bihar	58.91	46.07	57.49
4.	Gujarat	43.20	29.82	39.04
5.	Haryana	23.25	31.74	24.84
6.	Jammu & Kashmir	32.75	39.33	34.06
7.	Karnataka	49.68	43.97	48.34
8.	Kerala	46.00	51.44	46.95
9.	Madhya Pradesh	59.82	48.09	47.71
10.	Maharashtra	55.85	31.62	57.73
11.	Orissa	68.97	42.19	66.40
12.	Punjab	11.87	24.66	15.13
13.	Rajasthan	33.75	33.80	33.76
14.	Tamil Nadu	55.68	44.79	52.12
15.	Uttar Pradesh	50.23	49.24	50.09
16.	West Bengal	38.94	34.71	32.54
	All India	50.82	38.19	48.13

Note: Estimates made by the Planning Commission.

Source: *P.T.I. Economic Service*, February 1, 1981.

www.ingramcontent.com/pod-product-compliance
Lightning Source LLC
Chambersburg PA
CBHW041219030426
42336CB00024B/3392